1985

EXILES AT HOME

A Story of Literature in Nineteenth Century America

Daniel Marder

UNIVERSITY
PRESS OF
AMERICA

LANHAM • NEW YORK • LONDON

Copyright © 1984 by

University Press of America,™ Inc.

4720 Boston Way
Lanham, MD 20706

3 Henrietta Street
London WC2E 8LU England

Printed in the United States of America

ISBN (Perfect): 0-8191-4285-9
ISBN   (Cloth): 0-8191-4284-0

All University Press of America books are produced on acid-free paper which exceeds the minimum standards set by the National Historical Publications and Records Commission.

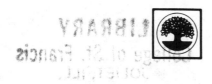

iii

Dedicated

to

Samantha, Mary and Danya

Acknowledgements

This work developed from an article contributed to a special issue of *Mosaic* (Spring 1975) devoted to "The Literature of Exile." I am indebted to its editors, R. G. Collins and John Wortley for the beginnings. Parts of Chapter 3 appeared in *College Literature* (Spring 1981). Personnel of the libraries at the University of Cambridge and the British Museum, where a good deal of the research was conducted, have provided inestimable aid. Students in a graduate seminar were especially helpful in defining the dimensions of the work and testing the insights. I am grateful for the research assistance of Michael Warner, Charlotte Thompson, and Heleno de Godoi Sousa. Benjamin Franklin Whitehill's careful reading prevented more than a few embarrassing errors. I am indebted to Elise Grant for aid in manuscript preparations. My greatest debt is owed to Professor Richard Sullivan of Rutgers University who provided criticism as well as research during the years of his graduate residency at the University of Tulsa. He will recognize more than one of his ideas merged with mine in this text. Dr. Charles Swan of the University of Keele in England where I completed the Melville chapter will be surprised at my acknowledgement of his testy commentary. It too contributed.

Contents

Preface

Two Anglo-Saxon poems render opposing views of the exile. In *Beowulf* the exile is Grendel, a destroyer of the harmonious community. Persecution of this monster exile is a sign of righteousness and nobility. This view accords with the Roman's. Cicero called exile the severest of penalties. Essentially, this view is anti-poetic, the destroyer rather than the maker or celebrator.

Against this view is the spiritual exile, *Guthlac*. He banishes himself and lives among devils banished from heaven because of their pride. This view also accords with the Roman's, and the Greek's as well. The spiritual exile is the moral and righteous conscience of Plutarch and Seneca who try to use the dubious consolation of Socrates that no virtuous man is an exile because his true home is within himself. Guthlac cannot join the devils because they do not share his innocent spirit. He is twice exiled, first physically, and then spiritually. Spiritual exile is the longing for the warmth and love of community and the utter inability to accept what belonging the devils can accommodate.

Here is the condition of the American exile who sees that he can do nothing to change his homeland, cannot abide it, yet yearns for the comforts of belonging to it. He is an exile at home.

Common views of nineteenth century America emphasize not the lost home in Europe, but the enthusiasm for the fresh culture aborning, the American spirit of progress, achievement of human destiny, and transcendental connections, although notes of doubt occur frequently, even in the positive elevations of Emerson and the celebrations of Whitman. The enthusiasm serves the disillusionment which is then found to follow in the next century. But the ambience of this enthusiasm contributed in itself to a sense of exile in the writers of the nineteenth century. It was then — between the severences of the political revolution at the beginning and the scientific revolution at the end — that American writers freshly and most painfully suffered the sense of exile at home.

This study interprets six writers who wished to belong but could not. Ironically, these exiles at home produced much of the major work we identify with the burgeoning period of our national literature.

The chapters render the story of exiling as a continuation of an old world habit of vision. Nostalgia for the European past is seen as a retreat to a familiar image. Deceiving, the image provides an alleviating interlude in the continuous search for the metaphysical idealization of mankind, once perceived as Eden.

Underlying the method of this study is the obvious premise that literature reflects its author in spirit if not overt experience. The spirit of exiling is traced through the authors' lives and works. For Cooper, Dickinson, Melville and Twain, this premise should not trouble even the most critical reader. But Poe's emphasis on craftsmanship and Hawthorne's on ambiguities perhaps suggest distinctions between author and work. Both qualities, however, are innate in all the other writers, although not so deliberately announced. Even in that twentieth century literature where the author tries to hide or eliminate the self, the writing surely reflects the writer. Because the theme of exiles at home applies to author and character alike, they are treated here as aspects of one another.

The story of exiling requires the span of the authors' lives and works, though not necessarily in chronological order. This study, therefore, should serve as a fuller source of interpretation for these six authors than one usually found in thematic interpretation. The interpretation of any one work depends upon the author's development at the time of its writing as well as the author's other works.

Daniel Marder

Chapter 1
Exile and American Tradition

. . . the Wanderer, weary of exile,
* * *
Homeless and hapless, since the days of old,
When the dark earth covered my dear lord's face,
And I sailed away with sorrowful heart,
Over wintry seas, seeking a gold-lord,
If far or near lived one to befriend me . . . [1]

If the old English *Wanderer* should ever find a "gold lord" to befriend and comfort him, he will be less an exile than refugee. There may remain the nostalgia, the memory, distorted through years of dreaming and idealizing. But those who have regained home values—comfort, acceptance, belonging, love—are no longer exiles. In the exodus from Egypt the Jews were a moving society seeking a refuge where they could replant the culture they carried with them. The pilgrims of Plymouth readily compared themselves with the Hebrews. Both had a far greater sense of gain than loss. It was not the outcast condition that pained them, as with the exile, but the present suffering of migration and settlement in strange places; their temporary pains were soothed with great hopes for the future.

In *Exile's Return,* Malcolm Cowley recognizes the distinction between refugee and exile:

—a whole world of people with and without talent but sharing the same ideals happily deserted the homeland. Each year some of them returned while others crowded into their places: the migration continued at a swifter rate. But after the middle of the decade the motives behind it underwent an impeccable but real change in emphasis. The earlier exiles had been driven abroad by a hatred of American dullness and puritanism, yet primarily they had traveled *in search* of something—leisure, freedom, knowledge, some quality that was offered by the old culture. Their successors felt the same desires, but felt them less strongly. Instead of being drawn ahead, they were propelled from behind, pushed eastward by the need of *getting away from* something. They are not so much exiles as refugees.[2]

But Cowley has reversed the roles as we ordinarily understand them. Being driven out, all are exiles, but the first group, like the old English wanderer and Bradford's pilgrims, still hope and seek refuge, while the second are beyond hope, not seeking, and so are condemned to remain in the state of exile. The earlier group included Stein, Josephson, Cummings, Pound, Eliot, Hemingway, Fitzgerald, Hart Crane, all seeking and to various extent, finding cultural refuge. "With a greater frequency than ever," wrote Matthew Josephson, "our illiminati buy tickets for a more possible world, for a more breathable air."[3] These Americans were exiles, not in Europe, but in America. *Exile's Return* should have applied not to the American homecoming from abroad, but to the European return, to the search for a lost culture.

We are accustomed to envision the European return as a movement occurring mainly in the early twentieth century. It was then, Hugh Kenner notes in *A Home Made World,* that the "threat and fascination of Europe hung over cautious minds like a menacing cloud."[4] American vastness in itself contributed to the individual's sense of isolation from the main stream of human community. These American minds conceived of European society as the homeland, while the actual home seemed a place of futility and anarchy. In abandoning the American wasteland for the refuge of European cosmopolitanism, the exile of the twentieth century was actually following American literary tradition.

Nostalgia for the European home had been a strain in the American literature from its inception. Puritan poetry was written with one eye, perhaps both, on England. Anne Bradstreet was referred to as *The Tenth Muse Lately Sprung Up In America* (1650). During the Revolution, the nostalgia curled into the form of protest, the movement for American literary independence. In the Preface to the *United States Magazine* (1779), Hugh Henry Brackenridge boasted:

> The British officers . . . have been forced to acknowledge, not without chagrin, that the rebels, as they are pleased to call us, had some damn'd good writers on their side of the question, and that we had fought them no less successfully with the pen than the sword. We hope to convince them yet more fully that we are able to cultivate the belles letters, even disconnected with Great Britain.[5]

But the sources of his *topoi,* as with other European colonials, were rooted still in the civilization born on the Mediterranean shores, Greek, Roman, Jewish.

In the nineteenth century, one by one, American authors returned — Irving, Cooper, Emerson, Hawthorne, James, Howells, Twain, Crane. By the time of Gertrude Stein's lost generation, the European sojourn had been established as something of a ritualistic requirement for men and women of American letters. Those who found the old country to be their "gold-lord" stayed on, no longer exiles. To Henry Adams, Europe was rotten to the core, England crassly materialistic and France hopelessly corrupt, yet he stayed. Gertrude Stein was fond of saying that America was her country but Paris was her hometown. The old world provided an acceptable milieu, a refuge of artistic commonality. In Europe the American artist could join others in the Byronic tradition of rejecting a handed-down society and of questing for individual enlightenment and expression. There was a community for the artist who preferred the life of the inner self to externalities, who distrusted official modes of social organization and who needed to create a system of his own to avoid enslavement. Within an artistic community, the writer could feel a unity between moral and social structure; individual conceptions of virtue were not separate from social roles.

Even the European developments in science and philosophy at the turn of the century served, not to distinguish the American exiles of the twentieth century from those of the nineteenth, but rather to buttress their traditional insistence on the life of the inner self. Theories of relativity and indeterminancy, the notion that matter itself was not always matter but process, reinforced the idea of reality as a matter of individual perception. These new developments, however, provided a refuge for the early twentieth century exile which was not available to the nineteenth century counterpart. Along with the Bloomsbury group—fostering post-impressionism, literary interiority and circumstantial morality—were the imagists with Ezra Pound in their midst, eschewing literary statements and insisting upon image clusters alone to evoke experience. For Pound, experience was a radiant cluster of ideas rushing into, through and out of a stable shape of movement, a vortex of a culture and a tradition.[6]

Such a vortex was the cultural refuge the American exile at home envisioned in the nineteenth century. For him there were no moveable feasts. He was not "one of us." He could not share in the feeling, "however ill-grounded," as Cowley put it, that "made them regard other members of their own age group, whether artists are athletes or businessmen, as belonging to a sort of secret order . . . leagued in rebellion against the stuffy people who were misruling the world."[7] Exiles at home in nineteenth century America could not share morality or sensitivity to art and its theories, nor could they share in the ritual of escape, the orgies of bizarre behavior that followed rather established patterns.

It was when the party broke up, when the refuge dissipated, that the lost generation really got lost, and exile began for the twentieth century American abroad. Robert McAlmon's *Being Geniuses Together* (1938) was no longer possible. Hart Crane jumped off the stern of a steamer returning him from Mexico. He was only one more contemporary who "had begun to disappear into the dark maw of violence," as Scott Fitzgerald observed.[8] Crane had won a prize with *The Bridge* (1930), seen as a hopeful Whitmanesque response to Eliot's abandonment of modern society in *The Waste Land* (1922). Apparently Crane found that the currents flowing beneath *The Bridge* led not to social cohesion (the history he cites is "tortured") but to an eternal return for the exile: "No embrace opens but the stinging seas."[9] Eliot, of course, found another means of return in the rituals of monarchy and religion. After McAlmon died bitter and lonely in an El Paso hotel, a condition he always managed to escape in the elan of impeccably bad behavior, William Carlos Williams recalled that his magazine, *Contact,* implied all the young man had most on his mind. By then the European sense of being absurd together had alleviated the exile's sensitivity.

The notion that a sense of exile is man's modern feeling, results apparently from our persistent focus on only one or two aspects of the condition—isolation or alienation.[10] Loss, the most essential characteristic, is mostly ignored in our tendency to equate the state of exile with isolation or alienation and to attribute the condition to the intellectual and industrial changes that began after the Civil War. The isolated individual is outside of society while the alienated is hostile as well as outside. Jamesian devotion to living in art rather than life can account for the isolated, and disillusionment with American promise can account for the alienated, but neither are sufficient to account for the exile, who has lost what was once possessed. He has abandoned home because he could not abide it or it could not abide him, yet he yearns to belong as a divorced person might yearn for binding.

In time the pain of loss attenuates. The American sense of cultural loss was most acute after the political severing of the Revolution at the end of the eighteenth century. At the beginning of that century there appears to be little sense of divorce from England. William Byrd, for example, was educated in England as custom dictated and then divided his mature years between Virginia and England as if they were one culture. In spite of Benjamin Franklin's image as typical American, he considered himself thoroughly English until the Revolution. New world literary effort customarily followed British styles and fashions. It was after the Revolution that the American writer became aware of the cultural losses and conscientiously attempted literary independence by focusing on American scene and character. From Brackenridge onward, however, they displayed a common aversion to American licentiousness as contrasted with the disciplined manners and learning of the lost culture. The essential feature that distinguished Cooper's American village culture from Britain's was the threat of self-aggrandizement at the expense of the community. It is the absence of European cultural constraints that drives Leatherstocking from his place, first on the edge of the settlement and finally from the plains of the West.

When Leatherstocking's story is echoed in the twentieth century by William Faulkner's Ike McCaslin, the licentiousness and greed have come to dominate American society and the remnants of English cultural values are seen almost as relics. The balance between nature and human civilization, disturbed in Cooper's first Leatherstocking tale, *The Pioneers* (1823), can be envisioned later only as an imagined past, one that is pristinely American, not a memory of another culture.

It was during the nineteenth century, between the severences of the political revolution at the beginning and the scientific revolution at the end, that American writers freshly and most painfully suffered the sense of exile at home.

I

The condition of exile in America results from excessive individuality, another American tradition. It is more encompassing than the familiar "rugged individualism," a term usually confined to economic exploitation and acquisition. American literature follows this American tradition. Without a shared body of inherited habits, attitudes, and institutions to mediate between the individual and the state, Tocqueville observed, "Each man is forever thrown back on himself alone, and there is great danger that he may be shut up in the solitude of his own heart."[11] To Emerson and Thoreau, the private vision that solitude yields was sacrosanct; joining the common denominators of society was yielding individuality. But society, for Emerson at least, did not comprise a conspiracy, as Tony Tanner sees it in today's American literature, "plotting to shape individual consciousness to suit its own ends."[12] Yet the threat of depersonalization to Chief Broom in *One Flew Over The Cuckoo's Nest,* where community is a combine that controls all the cogs through a gigantic machine, is much the same as the threat to Hawthorne's "Wakefield," who found stepping aside, outside the system, is stepping into a void.

The void in our current literature is sometimes seen as a prelinguistic consciousness while society is an entity composed of linguistic structures. Without societal imposition of language there is no identifiable self, only an amoeba-like immediacy in the flow of existence. But with this imposition, this enculturing, there is behavioral control. The essential paradox, nevertheless, is the same one we find in Hawthorne and Melville, that identity depends upon societal recognition but societal recognition tends to erase the individuality of the identified. Those who accept this situation become performers, fabricating a variety of identities for a variety of occasions, like Melville's confidence man and Hawthorne's masks. The self is thus an accumulation of identities as perceived by others, concerned basically with convincing postures rather than integral truths or morals.[13] Within however, twentieth century individuals seek mediation, not between self and culture or community as in the previous century, but only between the world of things identified in language and the internal self. Tony Tanner envisions such struggles taking place in his *City of Words* and in Richard Poirier's *A World Elsewhere*. These are places of refuge from the threats of pure autonomy on the one hand and total enslavement on the other, that is, of disappearance into the self or diffusion into the world's uses.

Although the exile at home in the nineteenth century also perceived this struggle—Melville continuously fought the impress of written forms and his Ahab tragically confused the language with the referent, while Hawthorne's Hester could not escape the identity imprinted on her by the scarlet 'A'—they were more centrally absorbed with an external elsewhere, upon the face of the earth or beyond it. They were still close in time to the European culture and could look upon it as the potential refuge, just as their European forebearers had looked upon America. They could either submit to the patterns of Europe, however displaced and transfigured in the American environment, or forego identity. Even if the exile posed as an Emersonian scholar who would think his own thoughts, the pose itself was patterned by a European language. American culture was a displaced culture. Freedom from that culture was shapelessness, licentiousness, myriad private realities without agreements or communications. Even those who thought positively of the American spirit surrendered to the spiritual comfort of the old world: "I find myself in my element in European life," Margaret Fuller wrote home in 1846, "Encumberances are cleared away that used to weary me in America."[14]

Common views of nineteenth century America emphasize not the lost home but the enthusiasms for the fresh culture aborning, the American spirit of progress, achievement of human destiny, and transcendental connections, although notes of doubt occur frequently, even in the positive elevations of Emerson and the celebrations of Whitman. The enthusiasm, of course, serves the disillusionment which is then found to follow in the next century. But the ambience of this American enthusiasm contributed in itself to a sense of exile in the writers of nineteenth century America. Although some — Cooper, Hawthorne, Melville, Twain — sought moments of physical refuge elsewhere, together with those who did not leave home — Poe and Dickinson[15] — they developed a fundamental core of meaning through the formative years of American literature. They produced, we might say, a literature of exile.

II

One of Poe's protagonists in an unfinished novel goes West but not for hunting and trapping as pretended; Julius Rodman rather was "urged by a desire to seek in the bosom of the wilderness that peace" he could not find among men. He "fled to the desert as to a friend." Of course, if Rodman would find peace in the desert of the American West, he would not be an exile, but his search is as much fated as Leatherstocking's. Rodman represents the American tradition of excessive individuality. He is fleeing society not so much because of its American peculiarities and certainly not in preference for another, but essentially because of its inacceptability as society *per se,* realized rather than dreamt.

Unrestricted adherence to an inner reality is the basis of America's individual excessiveness, or the American romance, as Lionel Trilling sees it: "The fact is that American writers of genius have not turned their minds to society . . . the reality they sought was only tangential to society."[16] Henry James is the only exception that Trilling allows. He might also have excepted Washington Irving at the other end of the nineteenth century. Although both acted upon a sense of exile, neither became exiles in America. Washington Irving lived in Europe for seventeen years, essentially as a tourist, and when he returned to America, accommodated himself to its society. James was raised in European schools and eventually settled in London although he never quite relinquished American possibility, not even in his late assessment, *The American Scene* (1907). James' possibility is a vision of European culture reinvigorated by fresh American virtues. The anticipated synthesis occurs in Europe with consequent corruption or destruction of the American character, the energetic innocent, or rejection of the old world society as corrupt. In England, however, he imagined the old world culture thriving without the decadence of the continent. There he found his home. Irving and James, at the beginning and ending of the century, may serve to frame our story of American exiles at home, although the case of James is far more complex.

Introducing the *Sketch Book* in 1819, Irving confesses his essential nature as tourist: "I was always fond of visiting new scenes, and observing strange characters and manners. Even when a mere child I began my travels, and made many tours of discovery into foreign parts and unknown regions of my native city." American attraction was in her sublime scenery while Europe's was in the refinements of a cultivated society. His longing was not to find a home, to belong, but "to escape, in short, from the commonplace realities of the present, and lose myself among the shadowy grandeurs of the past."[17] One commonplace reality he sought to escape was management of the family paint business, a real spectre that haunted him in America. Unlike T. S. Eliot, who also departed from middle class America for rather specific reasons a century later, Irving sought abroad "the accumulated treasures of age" rather than the authority sanctioned by the past.

During his seventeen year tour (1815-1832) he endeavored to "see the world in as pleasant a light as circumstances will permit." Nothing he discovers convinces him that Europe is "all that it has been represented by sneering cynics and whining poses."[18] Whenever he finds it so, he will abuse it also. Had he stayed at home, the good-natured satire may indeed have grown sneering and cynical, not only because of his distaste for the middle class life of a businessman, but also because of his fundamental aversion to popular movements, to democracy and to its serious tones. New Englanders were unacceptable to Irving somewhat because of their vulgar religions — transcendentalism, unitarianism, evangelicalism — but even more because they lacked congeniality.

Occasionally in the *Sketch Book* Irving expresses a feeling of loneliness but throughout Irving's work we can find only one candidate for the lonely exile — Rip Van Winkle, who awakes in post-Revolutionary America. The "village inn" is now the "union hotel" run by Jonathan Doolittle who lives up to his name. His place is run down, "rickety." A liberty pole replaces the great tree that had sheltered the old inn. King George on the inn sign is now George Washington, and the "very character of the people had changed . . . a busy bustling, disputatious tone . . . instead of the accustomed phlegm and drowsy tranquility . . . haranging vehemently

about the rights of citizens . . . a perfect Babylonish jargon to
the bewildered Van Winkle." But Rip's confusion is not sustained; it is transformed into pleasure upon learning that the
demise of his carping wife is among the changes. His good
nature restored, he rejoins society, whatever its altered condition. He had appeased the new democrats with stories of his
long absence which they accepted without believing, so now
he can assume a social role as a "chronicle of the old times
before the War." He represents a preservation of culture, a
more or less ridiculous parallel with George Lucacs' description of the post revolutionary individual and artist who is
engaged not in "concocting something 'radically new' but . . .
of assimilating all that is valuable in previous development
and adapting it," although Rip Van Winkle does not really
adapt in the way Lucacs would have it. [19]

Irving's notebook describes his discomfort in the uncertainty and transcience of post-Revolutionary America. He
was more attuned to the inhabitants of Sleepy Hollow enjoying their drowsy tranquility and resenting the new American
spirit, represented by Ichabod Crane, the man with an "ana-
conda" appetite. As Ichabod rolled his great green eyes over
the fat meadow lands of Katrina's father, "his heart yearned
after the damsel . . . and his imagination expanded with the
idea, how they might be readily turned into cash and the
money invested. . . . " Fortunately for the "country bump-
kins" whom he disdainfully ignored, Ichabod's appetite
extended to everything: "No tale was too gross or monstrous
for his capacious swallow." He had developed a gusto for
ghostly lore from his "perfect master," Cotton Mather. Thus,
the New England slicker is easy prey for Brom Bones'
headless horseman. Katrina is left to this country bumpkin,
who is nevertheless something of an aristocrat of the soil with
a "degree of rough chivalry in his nature." When Brom's
trumped-up ghost frightens Ichabod out of sleepy old

America, he flees, we presume, to start up the noisy machinery of Jacksonian America. And in the Hollow of the tranquil past, Irving wishfully concludes, Crane's schoolhouse is allowed to decay after his mysterious disappearance.

Irving admitted that his essential activity had been reverie, daydream, out of which came his spectral and whimsical stories, his extensive reading in German folktales notwithstanding. These stories, like his earlier satires, are of the past itself, not a sense of the past in the present, which would be akin to Lukacs' notion of adapting the past. Instead, Irving engages in pleasurable rearrangements of history. There was little he wanted in the present and though it threatened — "deliver me from all the pervading commonplace which is the curse of our country"[20] — he managed to defeat it, like Brom Bones, in his tales and reveries. In effect he never left home. When he returned from Europe he returned from the European past to the American past.

III

Henry James was eminently a man of the present. But his was a very selective present that continued the civilized past. Quite the opposite of Washington Irving, James was given over to the "actual scene." The concept of his realism, of creating the impression of the actual, stirred in his mind from the beginning, long before it was technically worked out in the Prefaces to the New York editions (1907-1917). At twenty, already a veteran of European schooling, he wrote of "the subtlest influences — birth, education, association —" that prejudice the imagination.[21] At twenty-six, on his first tour of Europe as a mature man, James speculated on the largeness of mind in the Venetian artists, the result of distance that dwarfed prejudice. Veronese "seems to have had in his head a perfect realization of a world in which all things are interfused . . . undramatic and 'impersonal' . . . not a whit of struggle, nor fever, nor longing for the unattainable, simply a glorious sense of the looks of things . . . "[22] In Tinteretto, the "actual scene" is conceived as a "great fragment wrenched out of life and history with all its natural details clinging to it and testifying to its reality."[23] It is the testimony that renders the appearances of reality and neutralizes the artist's prejudices. Here is James' artistic view of civilized society. The only excess it allows is art itself, homeless in America.

"We're the disinherited of Art," declares the narrator in "Madonna of the Future" (1873), "excluded from the magic circle . . . as void of all that nourishes and prompts and inspires the artist as my sad heart is void of bitterness in saying so! We poor aspirants must live in exile."[24] James, therefore, took his American — ignorant of the delicate amenities of civilization but also untainted by its sordid corruptions — to the "actual scene." In the old world, the "spiritual lightness and vigour" of the American, "looking to see something original and beautiful [could] disengage . . . from our ceaseless fermentation and turmoil."[25] American energy could invigorate the European conventions, forms, and manners, drained of their vitality through the centuries of usage. In James' first story of American confrontation with civilization, however, "The Passionate Pilgrim" (1871) is destroyed by his egoistic prejudices. His romantic cloud allows him to see nothing English except the landscape. The culture denies him and he is akin to the man James describes in his Preface to *The American* (1908) whose balloon of experience is cut free from reality. Yet, in dying, the pilgrim reinforces James' hope for the heroic strain in these young imaginations of the West, their promise to re-invigorate civilization.

Roderick Hudson (1876), however, is corrupted in the confrontation. Rather than observe and imaginatively recreate, this American sculptor plunges into the life of Rome. Characteristically undisciplined, he exhibits the uncultured freedom implicit in excessive American individuality. *Daisy Miller* (1878) is another undisciplined American innocent. Insisting on her freedoms, she violates the rules of propriety in Rome and dies as an indirect result. When the over-active American ego is neither corrupted nor destroyed in the confrontation, it is reinforced. Christopher Newman, *The American* (1877), knows exactly what he is after, the best wife possible. Rejection by the decadent nobility strengthens the resolve of his commercial ego which causes the rejection. Back in America, Newman can clearly see the distinction between right and wrong once more and renounce the opportunity for revenge; his dull American sense of decency triumphs over European corruption.

For all his enchantment with the continent, James moved from Paris to London in 1875. England was a place of civilized society rather than the unreachable culture Newman had found. "I feel how Europe keeps holding one at arm's length," James wrote home, "and condemning one to a meagre scraping of the surface."[26] England was an alternative to America. He felt the same uneasiness there as in Cambridge and New York, but in London the lonely state of the exile was easier to endure than at home. It was infused with culture: "I like feeling in the midst of the English world, however lost in it I may be."[27]

In *Portrait of a Lady* (1881), written just before he returned to America, James appears to be summing up, synthesizing, and refining what he had wrought in his first extended sojourn. Through this vigorous, unfettered American girl, James brings the three worlds of his experience together; America, unrealized potential; Europe, the finest culture but morally corrupt; and England, the 'reserve' that he first deprecates and then comes to appreciate as the basis for civilization because it respects privacy while continuing the culture of the past. Isabel rejects Casper Goodwood, the un-

cultivated American whose name describes him, and she also
rejects the orderly and civilized world of Lord Warburton. It
is the illusory world of enchanting culture she chooses, as
represented by the Europeanized American, Gilbert Osmond.
Osmond is a later-day Roderick Hudson whose life has become a series of dilettantish postures. Isabel's choice is itself a
sign that European culture has begun its corruption of the
fresh American. When she recognizes the falseness of the
world she has chosen, Isabel determines nevertheless to maintain social convention, the appearances of her marriage,
which is the defeat of her need for freedom and of her
honesty.

James returned to England in 1882, despondent over the
deaths of his parents, his sister's poor health, and quarrels
with brother William. Perhaps equally debilitating was his
lack of American popularity as compared with Twain and
Howells. He began to feel "orphaned" rather than cosmopolitan, and his opinion of the American innocent's high
moral quality and energetic potential declined. After devot-
ing *The Bostonians* (1886) to his native audience, James
turned away from the American character, dropped the international theme, and focused exclusively on the British, a
choice which inevitably invited American ghosts. He was also
dissatisfied with the results of his artistic method and scope,
which had produced only representational relationships, he
thought, rather than individual ones, and the scale was
limited. With others of his time, James was drawn to the experimentation of Daudet, Goncourt, and Zola, "in spite of
their ferocious pessimism and handling of unclean things,
they are at least serious and honest."[28] But *The Princess
Casamassima* (1886), focused on London's mean streets as
well as on its society of wealth and culture, was no improvement. Nor did it contribute to his popularity. Now James
questioned his sacrifices of life to art, the passion of the pas-

sions. His doubt is rendered in the equivocal response of the disciple in "The Lesson of the Master" (1888) when he learns his mentor has married his girl. It is his nature, the disciple dubiously reasons, which dedicates him to intellectual rather than personal passion, which exiles him from the lived life for the sake of art.

In the nineties, James reached out for living response, which "the usual imbecility of the novel" could not provide, "the reader never touches the subject, and the subject never touches the reader."[29] His efforts at stage drama were haunted by his ghosts, not only of his American past but of the abandoned life together. Even his art of fiction, neglected in his new pursuit of audience, had become a ghost; for example, the artist who prefers the model to the genuine article in "The Real Thing" (1892), and Lord Mellifont, a "style" in "The Private Life" (1893) who ceases to exist when he does not appear before others. Having stooped to the abyss of "vulgarity and platitude" in the theater,[30] and failing, James sought to confront the ghosts directly by returning to the novel, and finally, at the turn of the century, to the international theme. In the unfinished *Sense of the Past,* the protagonist is a ghost of his former self, but "it is not easy to concoct a 'ghost' of any freshness"[31] he discovers before giving up the manuscript. Unlike Cooper and Hawthorne before him or Twain and Faulker after him, James was not attempting to retreat into another time. His difficulty was simply being trapped in his own past, of repeating what he had already written. The solution of the problem, he told Howells, was to do "a neat little human—and not the less international novel."[32] He deliberately set out, that is, to penetrate the representations that resulted from prejudiced patterns of seeing the social atmosphere and to arrive at a real sense of individual personality.

In *The Ambassadors* (1903), a middle aged American

still innocent but less energetic than Christopher Newman, is able to strip away American prejudices and adapt to the pleasures of living in the old world, pleasures alien to his native New England. Yet Strether has the discipline to control his aroused spirit. When he dutifully returns home to Mrs. Newsome, a representative American, he returns to a spiritual exile, to lead also a representative life. In *The Golden Bowl* (1903) Maggie Verver is an advance even over Strether. She also recalls the ghost of the commercial Newman, referring to her royal fiance as a rarity to be obtained only in Europe. But she is also aware of European potential for corruption, unlike her predecessor in *The Portrait of a Lady,* and wants to be "called in," like the Europeanized American, Charlotte, who marries her father. Unlike either Newman or Archer, Maggie knows what she is doing.

Working to deepen American character by immersing it in "civilization," James ironically became nostalgic for New England smells and even sounds. His nostalgia had been increasing at least since the death of Victoria, an event he speculated would mark the end of British civilization. The nostalgia culminated in the trip of 1905 and his reaction in *The American Scene,* where the narrator's gratification with a few remnants of the older America is overwhelmed by the repellent sights of the newer America. In England again, he entertained a new set of ghosts; the returned ex-patriot of "The Jolly Corner" (1908) who is appalled at the image of the dreadful business type he might have bcome in America, and the ex-patriot of the unfinished *Ivory Tower* (1917) who finds his old memory of Newport unrecognizably distorted with the vulgar structures of the dehumanized American rich.

More and more James accepted "the essential loneliness" he had described when the British stage turned him away. The loneliness was "deeper than my 'genius', deeper than my 'discipline' . . . deeper, above all, than the deep counter-minings of art."[33] Henry James found his "lord" in his art but art was not a "gold lord"; it excluded him from the very life that his fiction proclaimed. He was an exile at home, but not an American home.

IV

Both Irving and James eschewed the American idea of freedom. It was uncivilized. For them people are free in the way D. H. Lawrence defines freedom, "not when they are straying and breaking away [but] when they belong to a living, organic, believing community . . . freest when they are most unconscious of freedom."[34] The freedoms within a society, controlled by society, were abused in the American tradition of excessive individuality. The exiles at home, following this American tradition, sacrifice whatever spiritual comforts societies proffer in order to continue their individualistic searches for an ideal alliance, societal or beyond, which would accommodate the demands of the self.

To the Adamic such as Whitman and Thoreau, the question of identity was an invitation to create a single, separate self. But for the exile at home the question was a painful ambiguity, the self had to be defined in terms of society but also in terms independent of it. Long before the Southern Agrarians proclaimed *I'll Take My Stand* (1930), the nineteenth century exile knew that the stance of unencumbered and direct relationships (rather than societal arrangements) was a lonely and empty one. Without community, freedom was irresponsible and selfish. The integrity of a self to be defined without community was abhorent.

Actually it was so from the beginning of American independence. "Whichever way I look nothing but the most frightful precipices present themselves to my view," Crèvecoeur writes in his last letter, "what is man when no longer connected to society?"[35] By 1800, Americans had no more moral purpose, Henry Adams decided, than the beavers they drove away; scum were rising to the surface. For all his hope of *Democracy in America* (1835), Tocqueville feared the danger of breaking the chain which aristocracy had forged from peasant to king. These apprehensions were reflected in the novels of James Fenimore Cooper. To cultivate the beautiful in America, Charles Dickens noted in 1841, makes one an outcast, which is the destiny of the typical narrator in Edgar Allan Poe and Hawthorne's "Artist of the Beautiful." Writing *Society and Solitude* (1870) in his later years, Emerson saw that a person needed to be clothed with society or would suffer bareness and poverty. Thus, Melville's sailor orphans in the end swim for the boat, however dismal they know the captain and crew to be. The process of democracy consummed its promise and resulted in those "plated people" whom Emily Dickinson excluded from her imaginary domain. *The Machine in the Garden,* abetted the process, as Leo Marx has demonstrated. It was the last of the exiling factors. Europe, impeded by its traditions, slowly made room for the industrial revolution while America immediately grasped the machine and adapted to its greedy pace. But the railroad of progress goes nowhere in Hawthorne's *House of the Seven Gables,* and the steamboat crashes through the idyll of Huck's raft.

Exiles at Home traces the process of exiling as it develops through six American writers into a major theme of American literature. It is not only the presentation of the exiled attitude but the story of that attitude, how it manifested itself in America, a continuation of an old world habit of vision. Nostalgia for the European past in particular was abetted of course by the democratic dust kicked up in the licentious scramble for material things. Yet, with the celebrators of American opportunity, these exiles at home took pride in their immediate ancestor's rebellion against this past. The nostalgia for it was highly selective, and can be viewed as a retreat to a familiar image, an alleviating interlude in the continuous search for the metaphysical idealization of mankind, often seen as Eden.

The story that begins with Cooper, ends with Twain, who reflects all the others. Cooper, and Hawthorne also, sought and then condemned European society for its aristocratic postures. Although they did not look upon American pretences and opportunists as European parodies, Cooper and Hawthorne were equally pained by "parvenues" overtaking America, their self-serving ambitions hidden in masks of social reform. Shades of Poe are evident in Twain's later loathing of the flesh of man and of the moral sensibility it embodies. Dickinson's evanescent Awe, occasionally perceived in a slant of light from the universe beyond her sentient circumference, is the wonder of existence that Twain reduces to mere thought or dream. Like Melville's *Confidence-Man*, Twain's *Mysterious Stranger* exposes the forlorn state of the human being in an empty eternity, suggesting the existential and absurdist universe that overcame American writers after World War II.

Chapter 2
COOPER:
America is No Place for a Gentleman

When James Fenimore Cooper sailed for Europe on June 1, 1826, he belonged to American society, to the landed gentry, and saw himself as a patriot. He had lost some health and most of his inheritance, and he was weary of the New York environs where he had established himself, after the publication of *The Spy* (1822), as a leading figure of the Bread and Cheese Club. With his wife's money he had built a home in Scarsdale a few years earlier. There he belonged to the Westchester County Agriculture Society and the Bible Society; he was a colonel in the militia. Upon his father's death (by murder) he inherited some money and a share of the estate at Cooperstown. But he also inherited his father's debts, and when his brothers died, one by one, mostly insolvent, he took on their debts and the support of their families as well.

Although early literary successes had improved his finances, he still needed money. Like Irving before him, Cooper went abroad seeking European publication protected by copyright laws, which meant more income. He intended to return within a few years, after publishing *The Prairie* (1827), the third and last, he thought then, in the series depicting the natural man's doomed struggle against the incursions of civilization which banish him. But he considered himself a man of civilization, and proud of his country. His ego had not yet allowed him to believe what his first novels suggested, the draining of American power from the landed gentry. He saw himself as an established literary figure, naturally and socially endowed to speak for the America in his mind.

Its culture was not an imitation of the British just as he was no imitation of Walter Scott. It was, perhaps, the other way. Scott was a British Cooper. Preparing to sail, he avoided any hint of self-expatriation by securing a counselorship at Lyon without duty or salary. As representative of the American people, he would be a living demonstration of his country's superior values in Europe. The Bread and Cheese Club sent him off with an elaborate bon voyage dinner.

Received as a triumphant man of letters, his response was more like that of Twain than Irving or James. Rather than succomb to the old world charm and allure of influential circles, he assumed the role of American innocent abroad. "What will you say," he wrote to Mrs. George Pomroy, "when I tell you that favoritism has permitted miserable, dirty, meagre shops to be erected against the sides [of Notre Dame Cathedral in Rouen] and in absolute contact with such an edifice!"[1] He was not impressed with royalty. ". . . If a servant of mine should presume to approach me with such dirty paws, as had this Excellenza [The Prince di Borghese] he would be in imminent danger of receiving his congé—Positively, they are begrimed!" (I, 210). Rather than seek society he was "compelled to draw back from it . . . " (I, 209). And instead of falling in line with European criticism of American culture as the later lost generation tended to do, he became a loyal defender. To counteract European ignorance of America, its arrogance and prejudice against it, he wrote, at the suggestion of his friend, Lafayette, *Notions of the Americans* (1828). The book promoted a vision of America as harmonious agrarian villages where freedom reigned under the republican leadership of landed gentlemen who were elected because of their distinctive virtues and their sense of *noblesse oblige* called Christian charity.

Notions was based on his confidence in man as a

reasonable creature. But Cooper was not describing America
as he knew it, nor even the America of his Leatherstocking
trilogy. He was setting up notions, a vision of what America
ought to be, just as his Leatherstocking was a notion of what
a man ought to be in nature, innately principled and thus
restrained only by God's laws. The qualities he had built into
Leatherstocking he imagined also in the American gentry,
which distinguished them from their European counterparts.
The basic notion was this ideally reasonable creature transplanted into a society where he was capable of enjoying a
freedom somewhat equivalent to that of the wilderness. In
this ideal portrait he prefers to see the great mass of man
elevated rather than the peaks of excellence leveled, the small
farmer learning to emulate the patrician gentleman and eventually sit beside him in Congress.

Perhaps what most alienated his readers, English as well
as American, was the placid picture of Templeton, the village
of *The Pioneers* (1823) now seen by his travellers, the English
narrator, Bachelor, and his American companion, as stable
and harmonious after the expulsion of Leatherstocking.
Although not distinguished, this American village is decent,
competent, and even intelligent. It is the triumph of mediocrity, and Cooper promotes it with pugnatious uneasiness:
"The country possesses neither the population nor the endow-
ments to maintain a large class of learned idlers in order that
one man in a hundred may contribute a mite to the growing
stock of knowledge."[2] Americans required training in the
"more practical and useful pursuits." Art is artificial and too
often the tool of despots: "Many nations excell in the arts but
none in the truths of human existence . . . they are desirable
so far as they temper society; but when they [nations] possess
it to the exclusion of still nobler society their dominion is
dangerous, and may easily become fatal" (II, 170). The excessive praise is often reaction to European condescension:

" . . . it is a fashion of Europe to talk a great deal of the leveling institutions of the United States . . . elevating would be a better word . . . I would defy any nation on earth to produce as many men (and women too) as the United States . . . who have reached a creditable moral elevation of character. I include manners, no less than principles, intelligence, and other requisites" (II, 294).

His American readers were alienated because they still measured culture by British standards. They still aspired to emulation, which he despised as slavish dependence: "We never shall get to be the thoroughly manly people we ought to be and might be, until we cease to look to European opinions. . . . This truckling to foreigners and eagerness to know what other nations think of us, is a fault that always disgusted me when at home, but it is a hundredfold more disgusting now that I know how utterly worthless are the opinions they republish" (*Letters* I, 287). He admitted, however, to a certain dryness of spirit that accompanied the moral elevation of the democrat. Although the "general taste of the reading world in this country is far better than that of England," there is a "poverty of original writers" (II, 99) and "of materials . . . no annals for the historian; no follies (beyond the most vulgar and commonplace) for the satirist; no manners for the dramatist [contrary to his earlier boast of American manners]; no obscure fiction for the writer of romance . . . " (II, 107). It is "most rare, that [the work of Washington Irving] has been shown in a state of society so cold and so restrained" (II, 111).

Americans were bland, very much alike, simple. Still he could not "conceive a state of society in which more of the attributes of plain good sense, and fewer of the artificial absurdities of life, are to be found" (II, 109). He had described them in his series of tales about Leatherstocking. Those portraits were intended to "elucidate the history, manner, usages,

and scenery of his native land" (I, 254). His further writings
would advance the literature of these independent people,
"thoroughly imbued with their distinctive principles and so
keenly alive to their advantages" (II, 122).

From first to last, however, his novels consistently
describe the failure of these distinctive principles in America.
As his three Leatherstocking tales had already shown and as
all his future work would iterate, the men distinguished by
principle, whether landed gentry or natural noble, would be
driven into exile by the mediocre, the ambitious, vulgar,
crude wasters of his American ideal, first in the wilderness
and then in the village. His *Notions of the Americans* would
never be realised.

I

Until he returned home, however, these *Notions* sustained his loyalty. He saw the European revolutions of the
1830's as counterparts to the American revolution, as natural
rights challenging artificial rights.[3] Old world aristocracy to
him was an invidious system of titled nobles controlling
government by patronage, not to be confused with American
Christian gentry who were elected to office by constitutional
law. So it seemed. In his first European novel, *The Bravo*
(1831), Cooper observed the oligarchical implications
beneath the charm of continental manners and the romantic
sheen of Venetian architecture. To maintain their powers,
privileges, and wealth, the hereditary class, essentially the
Senate of this "Republic" and its Council of Three, had
reduced the Doge to a figurehead. Under the lush surface of
Venetian life ran the labyrinthian passageways of a devious
city decaying in wealth. Here is the direct opposite of the
American wilderness, an oppressive social order without any
sense of divine law in nature, where conformity to despotic
aristocracy suppresses all individual qualities.

The oligarchy victimizes the upper class as well as the

lower but with more aplomb. Don Camillo Monforte has waited five years for the Senate to grant his claim of inheritance to a piece of the City. Since he is an outsider, independent of their rule, recognition of his claim would diminish the power of the tight oligarchy. The Council of Three prevent him from marrying Donna Violetta, ward of a senator, because of the influence such a match would yield. These aristocratic lovers are driven out and their property confiscated by narrow legalism, the application of a dead law.

The lower class fares less well. Antonio, a poor old fisherman, possesses essential Leatherstocking qualities, competent in the natural environment, humble, pious, and forthright in his demand for justice. He is not of sufficient worth to waste the senators' time with plotting. When he protests his grandson's imprisonment in the galleys, they simply murder him. But Antonio had friends. To placate them, the cynically adroit Council gives the old fisherman a grand funeral. They blame the murder on another state enemy, Jacobo Frontoni, who has fallen from favor for the same crime as Antonio. He too questioned the absolute authority of the Senate. When the Council learns that the Doge has been convinced of his innocence and is about to reprieve him, Jacobo is instantly beheaded. Venice continues in its beautiful misery unperturbed.

The two European novels following *The Bravo* examine other alternatives to American republicanism. In *The Heidenmauer* (1832) the feudal institutions of the baron and the abbott vie for power with a third contender, the burghermaster, who represents the new rising commercial class. In *The Headsman* (1833) Cooper condemns all societies limited by hereditary laws and customs. The headsman's son must inherit the loathsome job of his father as state executioner, and thus he is "condemned for no better reason than that he is born vile," just as the aristocrat is "exalted because his ancestry is noble."[4]

In all three novels, the aristocrats are condemned for hypocrisy in pretending to republicanism while practicing the singular principle of self-preservation. One aristocrat in *The Headsman* even asserts that self-protection is the essential business of government. Yet, Cooper relishes the minutiae of aristocratic society. Where his earlier attacks had been upon their manners, "not much superior to that of a Mohawk chief," his focus was now mainly on unprincipled politics. Later, in his *Gleanings in Europe* (1837) the attack is less on the old aristocracy than its dilution by alliance with the commercial class. And in *Excursions in Italy* (1838) he finds European aristocracy progressing towards republican enlightenment. This progress is stabilized, unlike America's, by respect for tradition and past refinements. Even before his return home, American critics had begun calling him aristocratic. And in the last bitter years, he also applied the once-loathesome term to himself.

American disapproval of Cooper had been increasing since the mild criticism of *Notions*. *The Bravo* and *The Heidenmauer* also received poor reviews, which Cooper characteristically blamed on American literati following foreign opinion in spite of his admonitions for intellectual and literary independence. He was convinced that the most cutting of these reviews by a "Cassio" in the *New York American* (June 1832), was the direct result of his "meddling" in foreign affairs. In 1830 he had joined his friend, General Lafayette, to urge French intervention in the Polish uprising on behalf of the insurgents. He had served on the Paris committee to raise funds, presided at dinners and drafted appeals to Americans for aid. When the French finance controversy arose two years later, posing a republican budget against a monarchial one, he again came to the aid of his friend. In his

Letter to General Lafayette (1832) Cooper argued that freedom was less costly than despotism, since no great standing
army was required. When the American Ministry in France
supported the Premier's side against Lafayette, Cooper felt
betrayed. This was his country's official response to his
patriotism. Later, in *A Letter to His Countrymen* (1834),
Cooper explained that Americans approved only when he
wrote of American things but not when he wrote of American
principle, what his work was about.

Since he was a man of principle, his future as a writer
was bleak; he decided to return home and "eke out an income" some other way. "The book on which I am now
employed (*The Headsman*)," he wrote William Dunlap in
November 1832, "will probably be the last. I can stand no
longer what I have received from home for the last four
years, and have made up my mind to retire while I can do it
without disgrace. Europe, I think, would sustain me a while
longer but I cannot forget that I was born an american [sic]
gentleman. The idea of becoming a hack writer in a foreign
land is not to my humour." (*Letters,* II, 360) Facetiously, but
truly as it turned out, he now identified an American
gentleman with the European aristocracy:

> In order to insure myself a reception [in America] that
> shall not be mortifying, I have serious thoughts of
> writing an essay on the beauties of Aristocracy, and on
> the blessings of exclusiveness in religion, politicks, and
> trade. . . . By puffing it myself, in the Quarterly, and
> forming an intimacy with all the bitterest enemies of
> America and of American principles, it is not improba-
> ble that all I have hitherto done on the other side of the
> question may be overlooked, and the elite of my coun-
> trymen may be persuaded to spare their insults when my
> back is next turned — I go home . . . to take a near view
> for myself, and to ascertain whether for the rest of my
> life I am to have a country or not. . . . I am tired of

wasting life, means, and comfort in behalf of those who
return abuse for services, and who show so much greater
reverence for fraud and selfishness than for anything
else. . . . I am heartsick and will say no more on the
ungrateful subject.

(*Letters,* II, 268)

He had gone abroad a member, fully joined, in American
society; he was returning home to self-banishment, exile, still
longing but unable to belong.

And after seven years abroad, he still needed money. He
could not live in New York. Even the fortune of Mrs. Cooper
(somewhat diminished) could not properly support his large
family there. "Besides, to own the truth, we have none of us
much heart to mingle in so heartless an affair as mere town
society. I shall probably be driven into the interior, but
where, Heaven only knows. . . . " (*Letters,* II, 360) In his despair, Cooper was identifying himself with Leatherstocking,
driven further and further west by the ambitious settlers. He
envisioned himself following the trail of his natural noble,
"Now my longing is for a Wilderness—Cooperstown is far
too populous and artificial for me and it is my intention to
plunge somewhere into the forest. . . . " (*Letters,* II, 89)

Leatherstocking, however, was romantic myth, possessed of "white gifts" but not the white man's burdens. The
family took quarters in the city while negotiating a return to
the deteriorated mansion his father had built in Cooperstown, his boyhood home. America had also deteriorated.
Pigs, literally as well as metaphorically, ran through the city
streets. He felt slighted by those who had been friendly and
barely recognized him now or weren't aware he had been
away. No one planned a celebration to match his bon voyage
dinner seven years earlier. "There may be better writers than I
in the country." he said, "but there is certainly no one treated
with so little deference."[5] Unable to accomodate to the bump-

tuous provinciality of Jacksonian America, he looked back to Italy with increasing nostalgia "for in that quarter of the world I am at least treated with common decency."[6]

II

In the tumult of his conflicts at home, Cooper's distinction between the cultural advantages of aristocracy and the political advantages of republicanism faded. The ideals he defended became his own rather than the Republic's. Like Leatherstocking, he eschewed the idea of American democracy as opportunity to seek a comfortable life. It meant aggressive ambition, capitalism, and proletarian mediocrity for most. In Cooperstown, the French furniture and Swiss servants he had imported and even the children's foreign manners offended the community. He was especially snobbish toward the new Whig party who opposed "King Andrew" Jackson. In a *Letter to his Countrymen,* Cooper had associated the Whigs with parliament who had fought not so much for England's freedom against the monarchy (Jackson) as for their own privileges and commercial interests.

When Cooper resumed writing, it was at a distance even greater than we sense in the Leatherstocking trilogy. In those stories, the process of Natty Bumppo's exile is depicted from the secure position of gentleman author, a proper inheritor of the land. The exploiters pursue and ultimately destroy the nature that is the home Leatherstocking's God intended for man. The old trapper was eighty-four when he called to his maker at the end of *The Prairie,* but Cooper was only forty-four when he came home in 1833. He was not ready to surrender his pen as announced, nor was his the sad but inevitable exile of Leatherstocking before the inexorable push of civilization. Cooper's exile was the outcome of the second cycle of the drama, not civilization against the wilderness but against itself, the vulgar overwhelming the refined. And this cycle was as ridiculous as it was sad. He appeared on the brink of exile somewhat like his John Paul Jones in *The Pilot* (1823), with a "smile of . . . bitter resignation."[7] Patrician trained, he was the disowned parent resigned now to the fact of intractable children who failed to understand their own principles of freedom. Explanation and instruction were futile. His immediate impulse was to satirize.

The Monikins (1835) is an allegory of two monkey kingdoms: Leaphigh, aristocratic England where tail length measures worth; and Leaplow, republican America where even the natural inequality of talent and intellect is curtailed. But Leaplowers put on false tails to show off their knowledge of foreign opinion and manners. A Leaplower never has a disinterested motive such as loyalty to class or country. Only selfish conduct is acceptable (a reversal of the patriotic ideal in *The Spy*). Principles are rules of a game. The greatest monkey of all is the one who can somersault from one party line to another without detection. (A slam at Jackson's spoils system.) The crux of the satire is a debate between the narrator, Goldencalf, possessed of enormous wealth and thus of the belief that the state exists for the protection of property and ought to be governed by property owners, and Downright, a disillusioned republican who appears to represent Cooper's views, at least at the outset. The argument is stalemated when both see that all who vote abuse their trust to their own advantage. Nevertheless, Downright remains adamant: even if men are monkeys, universal suffrage is right. But Cooper at the end has switched his bias to Goldencalf, who repudiates both ideas; he sees hypocrisy flourishing in all "ocracies."

Goldencalf's background indicates something of Cooper's ambiguous attitude towards his own. Neither were products of long genetic lines to the "manor" born. Goldencalf inherited his initial stake from his father who amassed it as stock jobber in a sordid commercial fashion; then he expanded his "social stake" by diversified investment, including slaves in America, and by getting himself elected to Congress, imagining that the process would also expand his human understanding. Goldencalf's father represents the Whiggish ways Cooper detests, but the younger Goldencalf is beginning to refine himself toward the Federalist image. Perhaps Cooper saw his father in both.

Judge Cooper was a land speculator who took advantage of his opportunities during the Revolution to acquire over 40,000 acres in Western New York. He became the patriarch of the district. His closest fictional representation is Judge Temple in *The Pioneers,* written a dozen years before *The Monikins.* Judge Temple is an established man of property when Cooper introduces him, a patriarch of Templeton who maintains social stability against the incursion of crude and ambitious newcomers, but somewhat hypocritically.[8] Cooper is not unaware of the contradition between the aggressive and ambitious behavior required for attaining wealth and position and the easy posturing of nobility that such wealth permits. Like young Goldencalf, Judge Temple comes onto the scene cleaned up, as does Faulkner's patriarch in *Absalom, Absalom,* Sartoris, also a judge, who admits a century later that he has accomplished his aim and now shall do a little moral housekeeping.

Temple also had a bit of cleaning to do. He had bought the land in a confiscation sale during the Revolution from loyalist Edward Effingham, and it was something of a steal. In the end, Judge Temple make amends when Oliver Effingham, who has come disguised as Leatherstocking's hunting companion but actually to investigate his lost inheritance, is allowed to marry daughter Elizebeth and thus regain the land by amalgamation. (Cooper also compensated for losses by marrying into the wealthy DeLanceys of Westchester.) Judge

Temple's code — nobility and Christian humbleness — is not
quite as natural as Oliver Effingham's who is Leatherstocking's social counterpart — nobility toughened by experience.
Oliver gently fingers a piano with one hand and the barrel of
his rifle with the other. Temple is more on the order of the
Goldencalfs, somewhat raw and unsure, newborn rather than
inborn.

But the Goldencalfs are more honest than Judge Temple. They tend towards uncertainty while the patrician, remaining rigid in his code, reveals himself to the reader as
rather duplicitous. And he is inept, almost to the point of
clownishness when he shoots Oliver while aiming at the deer.
His hypocrisy is equally clumsy. He staunchly asserts the law
as protector of God's wilderness against the excesses of axe
and rifle, yet joins in the wholesale slaughter of animals, as
does Oliver, "inflamed beyond prudence." His ineptness extends to the appointment of corrupt men to public office,
such as Doolittle the magistrate, whose avaricious abuse of
office the judge blindly protects as lawful. (Doolittle is an
early glimpse of the demagogues in the *Home* novels,
cunningly subverting the very laws they pretend to serve.)
Temple's deceptiveness mildly foreshadows the European
aristocrats Cooper later castigates. He excuses his landgrab
by asserting that he was merely holding the land in secret trust
for the Effinghams so they could claim compensation to the
British Crown for the loss. He seems unaware that cheating
the Crown is as much a violation of his code as vulturizing the
Effinghams. Nor is he aware that he is extending his assumed
elitist privilege when he offers to pardon Leatherstocking
because of his personal obligation to the hunter. And it is not
the breaking of the law — Leatherstocking's out-of-season
killing of the deer — that brings Temple to an adamant posture, but the protection of self. He insists on the letter of the
law only when Leatherstocking resists arrest, that is, resists

the law *per se*. His display of fellowship is also hypocritical; he is awkward and obtrusive when rubbing elbows in the tavern with the early settlers whose licentiousness he has to restrain with laws. His presence in the community church makes the people idolatrous; it is his church, not really theirs.

Although Cooper had idealized the natural nobility of Leatherstocking before he went to Europe, he had not idealized the patrician nobility of Judge Temple. Now as he drew back from republicanism in practice, he became more and more rigid in his ideal vision of it. He saw the patrician as the Republic's fundamental strength. He was noble and virtuous as Leatherstocking; and he was also being driven by his very principle into exile. Biographer James Grossman concludes that Cooper returned "out of step with his country," that Europe had "unfitted him for life in America."[9] It was more the shock of return, the experience of change itself, Jacksonian democracy at work on his own lawn, that actually unfitted the country for Cooper. America was not inferior by comparison with Europe but by comparison with his ideal. His image of America, unchanged by events, was a rare place on earth where principle prevailed. The actual America was a fraud compared to the country in his mind. He had returned to the democratic ideal in practice, the tyranny of public opinion and the common man, and rejection of the gentleman.

The poor reception of *The Monikins* was reassurance of his rejection. Cooper felt himself a negative factor in the American consciousness. The villagers in Cooperstown especially disliked giving up their shortcut across his property after the years of usage during its vacancy. But worse, they were outraged by his efforts to prohibit their enjoyment of his property at Three-Mile Point. This issue is ironical in view of Leatherstocking's attitude toward land as common property. The Point was a public picnic area on ground that Judge Cooper never sold. On the excuse of preserving the title for later inheritors, much as the senators in *The Bravo* excuse their self-serving acts as beneficial to posterity, Cooper asserted his ownership and warned trespassers they would be held accountable. The outraged villagers democratically resolved to hold his conduct in contempt and requested the local library to remove all Cooper's books. It was a classical example of the conflict between property rights and people's rights, squatters and owners, ultimately between haves and have nots. When the press spread the story, Cooper became known as the arch-aristocrat opposing the principles of democracy. His initial response was another effort to explain democracy to the democrats, in an "aggrieved tone," as Grossman says, that "reveals his need for their [countrymen's] affection," (G261) revealing, that is, the essential ambivalence of the exile at home.

In *The American Democrat* (1838) the people themselves are the most serious danger to the democracy. The majority tyrannize by substituting public opinion for law. They are not talented, not gifted with intelligence, and not educated. Such democracy drowns its proper leaders, men of natural talent, in mediocrity. But natural talent is no longer identified with a Leatherstocking operating in society, such as Andrew Jackson had first appeared to Cooper. It is associated instead with landed gentlemen, men of breeding and culture, who must be allowed the privilege of social exclusiveness; "It is unjust to require that men of refinement and training should defer in their habits and associations to the notions of those who are their inferiors in these particulars. . . ."[10] To demonstrate, Cooper returned to fiction, bringing the descendants of Judge Temple home from Europe where they meet the descendants of those licentious, obtuse, and wanton settlers for whom the laws were necessary. The offspring of Elizabeth Temple and Oliver Effingham—Edward Effingham—is now the family head in *Homeward Bound* (1838).

Edward, the American landed gent, is defined by contrast with his cousin John, who, like Goldencalf, derives his
money from commerce and speculation. A former Tory sym-
pathizer, John is now caustic about most things American.
Yet, he is essentially of the same spirit as the democratic
"adventurers" who so disgust him. Edward Effingham
derives his support from the land and is thus attached "to this
world of ours by kindly feelings."[11] Education and breeding
have "rendered him original and just by simply exempting
him from the influence of the passions" (63). He loves his
country, boldly praising its virtues abroad and gently apprais-
ing its excesses at home. Although the dichotomy between the
Effingham cousins may appear to be the fundamental split
between Jefferson and Hamilton, Effingham, like Cooper,
was not inclined to the Jeffersonian faith in uplifting the
masses through education. Rather he staunchly insisted that
people stay in their places. ("Let the cobbler stick to his last"
is the way Hugh Henry Brackenridge, another Jeffersonian
had put it in *Modern Chivalry* almost fifty years before.)[12]
Because the ambitious would not recognize the rules of the
gentleman's game in the burgeoning democracy and stay
where they belonged, Cooper's attitude grew more and more
towards the cynicism of cousin John Effingham.

Even before they reach American shores in *Homeward
Bound*, the Effinghams are affronted and offended by the
new American tyrant, the opinion-maker, Editor Steadfast
Dodge, who is briskly organizing the ship into committees in
order to run things democratically. The Effinghams avoid
him with such aplomb that he is not aware of the snub.
Public opinion establishes all Dodge values. It prevails over
the natural order of society, including the moral leadership of
the gentry. Although he is unable to form his own opinions,
he champions the equality of all opinions. To think one man's
opinion better than another is aristocratic. The way this

American democrat ought to behave is shown by contrast with Mr. Monday, an Englishman of the same class who drinks to compensate for his mediocrity. But Monday appears courageous while Dodge acts cowardly when Cooper stages a showdown by inventing some Arabs to spike the action with an attack. The ship's captain drives home the lesson to the ill-mannered, arrogant, and ignorant usurper of republican virtues. He is the essence of leadership, suppressing Dodge with his exulted knowlege and authority. When the captain seeks opinion, it is from Edward Effingham.

Arriving in New York City in the companion *Home as Found* (1838), Edward clings to his notion of America in spite of the evidence observed by his daughter Eve and cousin John—mainly the bland ugliness, the dullness, and the slavish imitation of European culture. Finally, at home in Templeton, they find the citizens bloated with liberty, insensitive to all other values, egoistic in their claims to equality, even with God who never intended for Americans to kneel. A conflict develops over the public use of Effingham land (here called Fishing Point) which Edward considers trespassing. Edward, however, does not deal directly with the people but through his agent, Aristabulus Bragg, a self-made man aspiring to the highest social position. Cooper does not consider his rather obvious talents as "natural," compared with those of Leatherstocking. They are merely promotional. Bragg does not know his place. When Eve Effingham refuses his proposal of marriage, Bragg calculatingly marries the French maid, the next best thing. Bragg charges through the life that is, while the Effinghams draw back from it, clinging to their unchangeable ideal of merit. Although the power to change had been the crux of the republic in his *Letter to Lafayette* and was reasserted in *The American Democrat,* his *Home* novels demonstrate his fundamental dilemma with change. If by law the majority could change the law, then freedom would destroy itself. Unable to resolve the dilemma, Cooper removed himself from it. When critics of his latest novel called him "slanderer," "traitor," and worse, "aristocrat," he retaliated with libel suits.

Although Effingham triumphs at the end of the *Home* novels and Bragg is driven out to attempt his fortune elsewhere, the sense of community has been replaced by a legalistic spirit which is fundamentally adversary, certainly not Christian. American democracy, in other words, had failed to provide the free life, just as his Leatherstocking trilogy predicts. The Effinghams might have triumphed this time but it would not be for long, as subsequent novels would show. The real winner was irrepressible Aristabulus Bragg, who heads west at the end, presumably and symbolically towards *The Prairie* in the wake of Ishmael Bush, the squatter, who has taken over the land from the old trapper.

III

Bragg is the best developed of all the social types Cooper attempted in this novel of "contemporary American manners," a hopeless task as he conceded in the Preface, because the nation was now comprised of mediocrities: "It would be indeed a desperate undertaking, to think of making anything interesting in the way of a *Roman de Societé* in this country."[13] In *Notions* Cooper had complained that America lacked the background to sustain a writer of romance although his own romances of the American wilderness and settlement already stood in world literature as absolute contradiction. But the woodenness of those incredible adventures may have been the result of frustrated motive. Only his first dismal effort at fiction, *Precaution* (1820) is an unadulterated novel of manners, that is, of acceptable established society, English manners. With his first examination of the American scene, the raw manners of the lower

classes overwhelm the effort to depict *Societé*. His realistic
sense directs his interest in what is there. Harvey Birch in *The
Spy*, like Leatherstocking in the novels that follow, is far
more developed than the Wharton gentry; and the lesser
characters like Betty Flanagan, the campfollower, and
especially Katy the housekeeper, are the most fascinating
elements in that book. When Birch's gold is confiscated by
the Skinners (irregular troops), for example, Katy worries
only that she will not be paid. Asked how anyone could have
the heart to plunder a man like Birch's father, who is near
death, Katy responds, "men like them have no bowels at
all."[14] As for the old man's dying after the Skinners' intrusion, "the chinking of the money made him get out of his bed
and the poor soul found the shock too great for him" (161).
With the old man dead she considers marrying Harvey Birch
in order to stay in the house respectably but decides that
Birch is not steady enough. Cooper is fascinated also with
Skinners, those early American rednecks, who are omens of
the future citizenry. After they have stolen the gold, burned
the home and turned over the spy to the American regulars
for hanging, the captain ironically and prophetically refers to
the licentious Skinners as "worthy children of America"
(220).

The gentry, on the other hand, are generally cardboard,
and Cooper often pokes fun at them. Henry Wharton, Sr., is
seen as more imbecilic than Judge Temple, occupying neutral
ground, fearful of taking a stand because he might lose his
wealth. The pretentious baggage accumulating about the elite
is spoofed even more openly. Dr. Archibald Sitgreaves who
reappears as Dr. Obed Battius in *The Prairie* and as Dr. Ergot
in *The Wept of Wish-Ton-Wish* (1829), is a man of sense
hovering on nonsense, "empiric in everything but his profession" (161). The baggage in *The Last of the Mohicans* (1826)
is artistic rather than intellectual: it is found in the puritan

singer, David Gamut and the gent he attaches himself to in the forest, Major Duncan Heyward, who is typically useless there. Leatherstocking must tell Heyward repeatedly to keep to the rear and avoid crossing the trail. In spite of his desire for a *societé* (really a contradiction of his own admonition against English imitation), Cooper displays from the start the American propensity of burlesquing the pretenses of class, intellect, and art. It was to emerge fully formed in Mark Twain.

Among the lesser classes, those who know their place, in spite of natural talents and in the face of opportunity, are nature's nobles. But such nobles — Harvey Birch, Natty Bumppo — are social exiles. They move aside, out of society's way. Cooper desired all creatures of lower status to exhibit the same noble behavior. An Aristabulus Bragg, taking advantage of democratic opportunity and attempting to rise, threatens the established order. Such ambition is ill-mannered, unprincipled, and thus unfit to succeed. Ambition itself perverts the natural talent. Bragg represents the outcome in Cooper's myth of the inheritors of America. The natural nobility of Leatherstocking, driven west by the gentry, is defeated there by the squatter, the new settler Ishmael Bush, who ultimately establishes law and becomes the new patriarch. In later representations, such as *The Crater* (1847), Ishmael's strength will be dissipated and ultimately destroyed by the Braggs, the toys of public opinion whose "plastic character had readily taken the impression of those things that are from propinquity alone pressed hardest on it."[15] Like Steadfast Dodge, his talent is to discern what is wanted by the majority and to rise by manipulating others to want it also. The majority can do no wrong.

The success of the Braggs destroys Cooper's *Notions* of America as a place of beautiful and thriving villages under the dominion of mild laws. Acceptable changes in this lovely image are only those implicit in its stasis — cycles, seasons, the repetition of ritual—the kind of motion that order tolerates compared to the irreversible changes of advancing civilization.[16] Cooper's America is one of Hemingway's good places, along with Spain, Cuba, Africa; ritualized rather than commercialized.

The sacrifice of Leatherstocking's freedom in nature was necessary to bring about this permanent state of beauty and political stability, where every man knows himself to be a part. Aristabulus Bragg shows Cooper what that part really is. Nostalgically he perceived that systems cannot endure, that all things are wasted, that the freedoms which provided his pleasant homeland would destroy it.

Nevertheless, Cooper himself was unchangeable. In spite of apparent contradictions, he clung steadily to his narrow views of republican leadership as the country changed about him. In *The Spy* Sara Wharton defends the rights of her countrymen against the rights of a sovereign by arguing that nothing could be clearer "than to obey those who have natural rights to command" (44). All the values Cooper renders in *The Spy*, in fact, he replays throughout his life. His ideas and convictions do not change, only his attitude which shades into deeper and deeper despair. Even before the country was established, Cooper sees the passing of stability. Northern slavery in *The Spy*, for example, is "giving place in every direction to that vagrant class which has sprung up within the last thirty years . . . and whose members roam through the country unfettered by principles, or uninfluenced by attachments" (66). Except for the noble principle, the sentiment applies to Natty Bumppo.

IV

In the range of Leatherstocking's fictive life, we can see that Cooper inaugurated the series at the crucial point, where the stability has been disturbed. In the two novels succeeding

The Pioneers, the author takes us further back, before stability was established and further on, after it was broken. *The Last of the Mohicans* takes place during the white man's struggle between the French and British (c.1757) in the least touched wilderness surrounding Lake George. Leatherstocking is a noble knight of the wilds, protecting forlorn gentlefolk who are prone to lose their way in the forest. He is clearly in charge of this world and he is at his best. It is in this novel that we become aware of his representative quality. What will happen to Leatherstocking has already happened to the Mohicans, the good Indians. The Hurons, on the other hand, who misuse their human nature, parallel the white exploiters who misuse the forest. When Leatherstocking appears next in *The Prairie*, the nineteenth century has already started and he is an old man who has suffered the fate of the good Indians. The white hunter, grown old and downgraded to trapper, can no longer flee society, represented now, not by Judge Temple or the Effinghams, but by the exploiters of nature who settle the West. The exploitatious society has overtaken him, cut him off from the forest, his homeland. In fact there is no forest, but rather an immense and vacant sky. Here buzzards prey and so do men. As Leatherstocking observes, "a band of Pawnees are outlying for these very Siouxes, as you see buzzards looking down for their food and it behoves us, as Christian men who have so much at stake, to look down upon them both."[17] The prairie is an early glimpse of the wasteland. Leatherstocking may be the first American character to perceive it: "the Lord has placed this barren belt of prairie behind the States to warn men to what their folly may yet bring the land." (28).

The prairie is a fit place for society's renegades, the family of Ishmael Bush, just as the majestic forest is the fit place for nature's noble. Ending the epic of Leatherstocking, *The Prairie* plays out the European romance of chivalry in

America (to be replayed in Mississippi by William Faulkner with Ike McCaslin as a sort of Effingham turned Leatherstocking.) The knightly code of Leatherstocking is essentially the code of the Effinghams and Judge Temple, that is, of the Christian gentleman. The code is ostensibly represented in this novel by Middleton, who is but a visitor to the prairie, seeking Inez, the flower of European gentility kidnapped and transported by the Bush family. The gentility are out of place here; so is Leatherstocking who first appears giant-size against the sky, more a legend haunting the place than a mere human inhabiting it. This land is earned by taking and occupying it. The conflict between individual freedom and social responsibility is not between classes that agree to the same values but within the lesser class whose values clash in newfound freedoms, as they pursue the Eldorado of their desires.[18] Regretfully for Cooper, distinctions of class dissolve in this redawning of the Western world. The representative man is Ishmael Bush who will grow during the course of the novel to patriarchal proportions and reestablish the ancient values. In the prairie we see the raw circumstances, the primitive stage, in the making of patriarchy. Ishmael wrests the land without moral considerations and then discovers moral responsibility, which the nature of even his tiny community thrusts upon him.

In contrast with the majestic sight of Leatherstocking, Bush is first seen in perspective against the prairie's level dullness, symbolic of American mediocrity, "the eye became fatigued with the sameness and chilling dreariness of the landscape" (15). He is dressed in the "coarsest vestments" (13), a gaudy silken sash, cap of marten's fur, and three worthless watches (mercantile contraptions), which dangle from his clothes. Richard Chase identifies Bush with Faulkner's Snopes.[19] But the Snopes' are more akin to the following generation, the Braggs, crass, greedy and legal.

Ishmael Bush is a "semi-barbarous squatter" (458), lawless, violent, epitome of the "fallen race." (80) He is an axe-wielder, violator of nature as well as civilization. He is fleeing from his past crimes and is in the midst of crime—helping in the abduction of Inez—when Leatherstocking first encounters him. But Ishmael claims the basic motive of the European immigrant for his flight westward: there is nothing in the civilized world for those who have no money but desire a better life than circumstances of birth allow. He does not seek ready-made bed and board, just water and wood. He'll care for himself and his own on the hungry prairie. Although he violates Leatherstocking's code of the Christian gent, he is as honest, stubborn, and in his way as principled as Leatherstocking.[20] Both seek individual freedom, appear proud of their illiteracy, appreciate instinct above reason, and scorn society's restraining laws. For both, the natural law of use takes precedence over legal deeds.

But Ishmael's aggressive and vengeful behavior reduces the principle of freedom and natural law to licentiousness and tyranny. Such behavior, however, results from his burden. He has not the restraint of the Christian gentleman, the "white gifts" of Leatherstocking, who needs nothing; he has the responsibility for the welfare of his clan. Leatherstocking can afford to succor the helpless as he chooses, but Ishmael must provide. For the sake of family, he must take and possess land while Leatherstocking can idealistically eschew possessions in the name of Christian humility. The virtues of community require the evils of possession. And ironically, Ishmael, who has fled the law, must reinstitute it to preserve the community. Even Leatherstocking recognizes the need of law, "when such as have not the gifts of strength and wisdom are to be taken care of" (32). When Ishmael reinstitutes law it is more severe than the law of his Eastern and elite prototype, Judge Temple. Learning that his wife's brother, rather than

Leatherstocking, is the murderer of his son, Ishmael condemns him, one of his own, to death as he would have condemned the old trapper. And further, Ishmael exhibits the
beginnings of compassion, leaving the poor wretch to hang
himself with these words, "Abiram White, we all have need of
mercy; from my soul do I forgive you" (457). Leatherstocking
is never allowed such sympathy. Although Ishmael does not
possess the divine and white gifts of Leatherstocking, he has
the capacity for subtle and ambiguous feeling that Leatherstocking lacks but which community requires. Ishmael's is a
classical social act of agonizing choice, beyond the graces of
gentility.

Ishmael is the new American patriarch, as raw and primitive as the country he conquers and, like the ancient
Israelites, his law is also raw and primitive, an eye for an eye.
His crude acts of acquisition are visible in the open light of
day as compared with the refined behavior of the Effinghams. Patriarchs of the genteel tradition are buffered by
generations from the Ishmael-like acts of their ancestors. It is
the distinction Faulkner defines by giving Sartoris a genteel
past while Sutpen springs out of nowhere. Cooper is reducing
the distinction to its basis. Ultimately, what patriarch did not
derive his land from some fortune-seeking adventurer? If
Ishmael Bush is a squatter, who ain't? he might say, as
Melville's Ishmael is to ask, "Who ain't a slave?"

The presence of Dr. Obed Battius in the Bush party
serves to emphasize the triumph of the squatters in the new
social order. They have arrived, complete with their symbol
of institutional knowledge and reason. In Dr. Battius, the Dr.
Sitgreaves of *The Spy* is transferred from the old landholder
to the new one. He is unnatural in his contrast with intuitive
and experiential knowledge. In *The Prairie* he assumes that
men like himself will become masters of God's universe
through science. The human mind and will are the standards

of judging all things. Dr. Battius is a caricature of human folly, but he is also a forerunner of B. F. Skinner in his behavioral view that science is the way to eradicate the evil principle in man.[21] Leatherstocking, of course, knows intuitively that man has an essential nature not to be tampered with: "human folly is not needed to fill up the great design of God," says the old trapper (302).

Throughout *The Prairie*, Leatherstocking appears as a garrulous old-timer full of dogma. The apotheosis of nature's nobleman with white gifts has decayed into a voluble relic. There is no longer any place for his spirit to go except back to its maker. He dies facing west, announcing his demise as "an end to my race."[22] Ultimately, Bush returns east, suggesting the spread of his "race" throughout the country, to be succeeded by the demagogues of the later novels.

After the disasterous reception of the *Home* novels, Cooper retrieved Leatherstocking. The use of proven material was the easiest way to restore his popularity. But *The Pathfinder* (1840) and *The Deerslayer* (1841) reveal deeper motivation. They offered him respite from the dismal present of triumphant Dodges and Braggs. These romances are powered mainly by a sense of nostalgia, the exile dreaming of an ideal homeland that never existed. In both, we encounter Leatherstocking as a young man contemplating marriage, settling down, and presumably fitting into some appropriate level below the gentry. Although he appears relieved when he fails to win Mabel Durham in *The Pathfinder*, he does suffer rejection. The action is appropriate; she is a touch above him socially. When he rejects the sensuous Judy Hetter because she is not up to his level in *The Deerslayer*, we see that he is seeking his proper place in the nature of things. It is this place, in harmony with both man's society and nature's that is disturbed in *The Pioneers,* where Leatherstocking's exile begins.

In *The Pathfinder*, Cooper nods to the possibility of education as the means for social adjustment if not advancement. Mable Dunham, the sergeant's daughter, who has been educated beyond her class, adjusts to a slightly higher social level when she rejects Leatherstocking in favor of Jasper Weston. The hunter is not quite good enough. If he is to become a member of society, his place is among the enlisted men, on the level of her father, Sergeant Dunham, with whom Leatherstocking identifies. "You're more befitting," he tells Mabel, "to be my daughter than to be my wife."[23] Education may set her a notch beyond enlisted men, Leatherstocking as well as her father, but fails to advance her to the officer class in this rigid military representation of social strata.

The only reason Lieutenant Muir, the quartermaster, even imagines himself suitable for Mabel is his fall from proper station through wanton liaisons and marriages. But his moral record, unsuiting him for his own class, also unsuits him for Mabel. Another suitor is Arrowhead, Chief of the Tuscarora. Racially unfit. Jasper Weston, the Great Lakes sailing captain, appears just right. He is a step above Mabel in her father's opinion but that is because the sergeant does not recognize her improvements through education. Leatherstocking is his choice. The hunter knows that education does count, not for any significant leap, but for some proper adjustment. It is a happy book in which people seek their own levels. Merit, represented by Mabel's education and Weston's competency, does provide some upward movement but never enough to tear or even stress the social fabric. Here is the ideal society in the wilderness, each in his own place according to talents and developments without disturbance by the unduly ambitious. When Jasper and Mabel move to New York City to join the larger society, it is not an abrasive assertion beyond capacity but a hopeful fitting into a proper place there. However horrible an urban prospect may be to Leatherstocking, he extends blessings. The proper place for Leatherstocking is on the border, where he is left at the end of this book, both weeping and laughing for his loss and gain. And here he is found in the opening of *The Pioneers* seventeen years earlier. He is never exiled from society since he has never joined it; rather he is exiled from that border position when society, which has borne his distant blessing via Mabel and Jasper, greedily encroaches.

The Deerslayer is a further reduction of society to skeletal simplicity. It is the beginning of things American — the serene beauty of the untouched wilderness and Lake Glimmerglass decades before Judge Temple settles there. This is "the ordering of the Lord,"[24] the home God intended for man. The wilderness "will not deceive you, being ordered and ruled by a hand that never wavers" (9). When the reverential spell of nature is cracked by an occasional rifle shot, it seems that mankind itself has become intolerable.[25] Leatherstocking, however, discovers the necessity of violence when he kills an Indian in self-defense, a natural act which almost kills him with remorse.

In contrast Cooper displays the unnecessary and therefore unnatural violence of Hurry Harry March and Tom Hutter. Harry is also a woodsman but the exact opposite of Leatherstocking. Proud of his good looks and physical strength, he throws tantrums when his ego is thwarted. Indians are mere animals to him and other men just obstacles. Hutter is much the same in moral outlook but he is also a prototype man of property, having built his Castle (hut) and Ark (boat) on the shore of Lake Glimmerglass, the only man-made objects disturbing its pristine beauty. Like the public at Three-Mile Point, he claims the property he squats upon as his own, and like the aristocrats Cooper found in Europe and the Whigs at home, he is motivated solely by money. They "knew no feeling of poetry, had lost their sense of natural devotion in lives of obdurate and narrow selfishness, and had little other sympathy with nature than that which originated with her lower wants" (269). Bounty hunters, paid by the civilized society for Indian scalps, women's, children's and men's, according to law, they have not even the possibilities of Ishmael Bush. They molest nature and make war, not to protect kin or establish home but to profit. They are the roots of America's commercial civilization.

Judith and Hetty Hutter, Tom's daughters, complete this skeletal society in the wilderness. Judith is a development of Cooper's dark lady of passion, Cora of the *Mohicans*, and Hetty is a reduction of Cora's sister, Alice, the light and the pure. Hetty is half-witted and as a result blessed with the virtue of candor, "one of those mysterious links between the material and immaterial worlds." (451) She has lost "the more artful qualities" and has retained the "love of truth" (43-44). Nevertheless, she loves Hurry Harry. To rescue him, along with her father, from the Mingoes, she pleads Christianity, asking the Indians to render good for evil. Why, then, responds the Indian Chief, has not the white man done this? Hetty bursts into tears, ostensibly for shame of her race. Although Leatherstocking is quite sophisticated by comparison, she is something of his counterpart, the natural woman with Christian impulse,[26] in harmony with the Lord's creation.

Judith Hutter is the unprincipled frontier woman, the counterpart of Hurry Harry March who pursues her as a beautiful object of passion. She is vain and alert to good looking men, even the Indian she throws overboard in the midst of an attack on her father's "Ark." Attracted to the glitter of the British officers who occasionally visit Glimmerglass, Judith is also an earnest pursuer of Leatherstocking. The matrimonial decision, given to Mable in the

The Pathfinder, is all Leatherstocking's here. Quite naturally he rejects the daughter of Tom Hutter. She may approximate his social level but falls below his moral level. He could not so demean himself as to marry her and join his own class. But any marriage would violate Leatherstocking's noble nature, which belongs in the woods. It would make him an exile in a settlement home, a man of family, property, and civil law.

The nostalgia of the ending is not the result of the young hunter's move into the wilderness but rather of our knowing his fate there, his ultimate exiling from the forest home. This is the end of Cooper's wistful dream and the author presents this last glimpse at its most promising moment, magnifying our sense of the lost ideal, a "being removed from the every day inducements to err, which abound in our civilized life" (vii). By the end, we have glimpsed the doomed future of the embyonic civilization on the shore of Glimmerglass, "a world of transgressions and selfishness and no pictures that represent us otherwise can be true" (462).

Hurry Harry and Tom Hutter are the new inheritors of American society rather than Ishmael Bush who was created when Cooper still retained a vestige of hope. We can find no trace in them of the responsible patriarch that develops in the avaricious squatter. They are the raw progenitors of the licentious majority who use their lawful freedoms in later novels to violate natural and moral law and to change the civil law. They wrest power from the narrowing class of the principled and distinguished, the landed gentry. This is the story Cooper tells in various forms and guises during the last decade of his life. It is the second cycle of his American myth, the exiling of the gentlemen from society, which follows the exiling of the natural man (with Christian gifts) from the wilderness. The men of principle in both cycles are defeated and the American promise evaporates in the decay of American civilization. Public opinion replaces principle as the demagogue replaces the European aristocrat, whose greed and selfishness are at least ameliorated by tradition and taste. If European society was unprincipled, at least it was stable; people knew their places.

V

Out of place in his own home, Cooper became fierce in defending his lost position. He fought court battles against the editors he thought had libeled him, had used him for publicity and profit. He wanted only to vindicate principle and himself in the eyes of a public he no longer believed in. But victories in his libel suits—twice over Horace Greeley— served to aggravate rather than soothe his feelings of abuse and calumny at the hand of his countrymen. Token awards by the courts were offset by public opinion; editors refused to mention his books at all. He found silence a more destructive enemy than calumny. Self-pitying and bellicose, Cooper picked even on the congenial Irving in spite of his influential contemporary's praise for *The Pathfinder*. He was especially piqued when Irving was appointed Ambassador to Spain in 1842, an ironic appointment for a man who had never shown particular loyalty to American culture abroad.

Such "humbuggery" contaminated the entire range of American politics, which had coalesced into parties and thus muffled the voice of the individual in violation of the democratic principle. The radical reformers epitomized licentious grasping, destroying what order existed. The Whigs acted always to make money, never with a sense of social obligation. The liberals held a fuzzy faith in popular opinion, adhering to the idea of the free press and trial by jury, which gave more power to the ignorant than the knowledgeable since they were greater in number. Alone, Cooper tended to become more strident, shouting for attention to his notion of rational behavior, which was now opposite Leatherstocking's.

He desired, rather, humble obedience to civil law and the preservation of the order established by the landed gentry. At the same time his fiction became more reflective, and with the exception of *Autobiography of a Pocket Handkerchief* (1843), even subtle.

The *Autobiography* is a clumsy satire serialized in *Graham's* in response to Greeley and the Whigs. (Greeley had offered Cooper a column in the *Tribune* to correct public opinion if he could.) In his attack on the Whiggish society, Cooper's patriarchal view of industry and commerce resembles a Marxist view. As the handkerchief tells its story, its maker, a seamstress, is the exploited victim of the profit motive, which stimulates cheating at every commercial transaction along the way to market from France to America. The handkerchief is purchased at an outlandish price by a New York speculator for his spoiled daughter but his motive is actually to bolster his sagging credit by the display of conspicuous consumption. The market crashes just then and he returns the handkerchief, also conspicuously. This display of honesty momentarily enshrines his reputation, allowing him to cheat his creditors and avoid bankruptcy. The daughter ironically stresses the point of commercial greed and lawful theft by prattling of the blessings of trade and the distribution of wealth it brings about. Here the Marxist parallel ends. To avoid undue sympathy for a mere seamstress, Cooper endows her with nobility; she is revealed as a fallen noblewoman.

The surety of satire is dissipated in the more serious novels of the 1840's where noble adherence to principle is itself submitted to examination. Loyalty, which Harvey Birch adamantly epitomized in *The Spy,* proves no simple-minded matter twenty years later in *The Two Admirals* (1842). It presents rather a dilemma as complex as those of the Greeks. And it is significant that the man of principle attempting the moral choice is no longer American. The British Admiral

Bluewater must choose between loyalty to his uniform and to
his superior, Admiral Oakes, or to the cause he believes in,
that of the Stuart pretender to the throne in the uprising of
1745. Loyalty in either choice would also be treachery. All the
other officers, even Admiral Oakes, are essentially indifferent to the problem; they exhibit the practical attitude
Cooper found in American Whigs. Oakes will accept whatever order society imposes as long as he is treated well. The
enlisted men are no different. Bluewater's underlings act only
in their personal interest — duty, pay, rations. Ultimately
Bluewater's choice is also practical. It is easier to act according to outward appearances — his uniform — than to oppose
them. It would have been easier for Cooper also to go along
with the expectation, to violate his inner ideal of what
America was supposed to be, and act as if loyal to the
America that actually was. But thirty years later, after
Bluewater had been honorably buried in Westminster Abbey
and his cause utterly defeated, his friend, Admiral Oakes, has
difficulty even remembering his name. In the endless vista of
eternity, does it matter what anguished choice he made? Does
principle or anything at all immaterial really matter? This is
the forbidden question, of course. It removes the questioner
from either idealistic or practical involvement with society. It
is an exile's question; not Bluewater's who is long dead, but
the author's.

Wing-and-Wing, his other novel that year, also presents
the complexity of conflicting principle, and again there is no
satisfying resolution. Once more characters are European,
lovers this time, a devout Catholic Italian girl and an atheistic
French rationalist. Neither can sacrifice belief for love.
Having discovered the complexity of moral choice, it appears
that Cooper can no longer associate the choice with
Americans, at least not with his contemporaries. The principled European lovers are contrasted with a Yankee sailor,

Ithuel Bolt, who has been pressed into service with the British fleet. Although Bolt's hatred of hypocrisy, British as well as Catholic, may at first represent Cooper's, his character is another example of the rising American demagogue—a Yankee sharpie, alert to the main chance. Ithuel Bolt returns to America with money acquired, we suspect, illicitly. The money grants respect and he assumes all the right poses as Deacon Bolt, preaching for abolition, temperance, and righteous religion.

The problem of conflicting values and principles is taken back finally to the American borderland during the Revolution where Harvey Birch, *The Spy*, has so unquestioningly performed the role of patriot. *Wyandotte* (1843) is almost a replay of *The Spy* in which altruistic patriotism is replaced with the self-interested treachery of the demagogue. Now the Revolution is a war without glory. Willoughby is the senior Wharton of this novel, as insensitive and obtuse as his earlier manifestation. Like Wharton he cannot decide which side will be most beneficial to him. He deplores both the English policy in America and independence. What he desires is law and order, but which law? The gentleman's law, which the British more or less have come to represent, or the people's law? These are epitomized by his son, a British officer (as is young Henry Wharton in *The Spy*) and by his demagogic overseer, whose name, Joel Strides, describes him. Strides deliberately stages an attack by the irregulars (the Skinners of *The Spy*) and the Indians so that Willoughby can be forced into a show of British loyalty by defending the village. Strides can then profit in the confiscation that follows.

Although he proclaimed himself loyal to America to the end of his years, Cooper had reduced his principle of loyalty to authority for its own sake. Strides' deceptive revolt against the village founder, Willoughby, is not much different in principle than the colonial revolt against the parent country.

And even within the parent country, Cooper had found the existence of a parliament was "legislative usurpation" that "terminated in the independence of the colonies. . . ."[27] A legislature was substitution of a "new and dangerous master for a prince who might be supposed to know no difference in his affection for his subjects."[28] Willoughby, the old patriarch, however obtuse, was at least a figure of authority, as the British monarch had been, an image compelling loyalty and thus order, as opposed to the divisiveness and demagoguery of party politics.

Willoughby is easily seen as another image of Cooper's father, especially since he is also murdered. His vacillations are taken more seriously than those of Wharton, his earlier manifestation in *The Spy*. He fears republican government but finds the Declaration of Independence "eloquently reasoned."[29] Yet, he desires America to remain a colony whose grievances he shares. The community he has established — the Hutted Knoll — is another glimpse of Cooper's lost ideal. It is a principality unto itself with its own undisputed patriarch reigning over a harmonious heirarchy, remote from the vulgar mess of commercial civilization. But isolated from the conflicts of the larger society, it cannot endure. His murder is the end of it all.

The murderer, Wyandotte, also known as Saucy Nick, is another noble Indian gone to drink. But more complex than John Mohegan of *The Pioneers*, he resurrects his decayed principles of noble savagery when Willoughby threatens to flog him. Like Leatherstocking, he had led the patriarch to the land Willoughby now possessed. Nick's murder of Willoughby is just vengeance for earlier floggings that had previously forced loyalty. After the Magua-like act of murder, however, he becomes an Uncas-like protector of Willoughby's daughters and wife (whom he calls Mother) against mutilation and death at the hands of Strides' Indians.

Wyandotte's resurrected behavior is a mere echo of dead principle. The hollowness of loyalty is emphasized when, nineteen years later, Robert Willoughby returns to his boarded up property, which he had retained through deceitful manipulation of deeds, and Wyandotte comes forth to confess the murder and offer his life in payment. Robert's forgiveness may demonstrate the spirit of Christianity but it violates the principle of loyalty. The author's despair of the lost ideal sifts through the shining moment of tribute to Robert as a man of liberty and independence, which he gracefully accepts from the very people who imprisoned him and who attacked his father.

VI

However confusing Christianity appears at the end of *Wyandotte*, it becomes Cooper's only respite from despair. In *Afloat and Ashore* and in *Miles Wallingford* (1844),[30] Cooper is effectively the main character, a garrulous old man who likes to quote the author Fenimore Cooper as he looks back over sixty years of destructive change in the young Republic. He longs for the old manners and customs of Clawbonny, his family estate on the Hudson which he had left to seek his fortune. On sea as well as land, he found men devious and nature capricious. Appearances could never be trusted. Chance and the actions of others often defeat the strongest will. Stranded on a raft in the midst of an ocean, Miles Wallingford is "alone, in the centre of the universe."[31] Here he comes to God and is saved. His chaotic and illusory world begins to come back into order. A major movement in the book had been the decline of the Wallingfords and the rise of the Hardinges, a poor family that had depended upon the Wallingfords. But in from the sea, with his humbling knowledge of the Christian God and his indifference to wealth, Miles Wallingford recoups all: money, friends, love, and possession of Clawbonny, including its former slaves.

Although Cooper shared Wallingford's Christian solu-
tion, it did not work to restore the author's faith in society.
And even in Wallingford's return to fortune and position at
Clawbonny there is the inescapable rumbling of the outer
world threatening his security. As the rumbling increases,
Miles, who had suffered life's vicissitudes far more than
Cooper, insists uneasily that "one thing is certain — there must
be a serious movement backward or the nation is lost" (440).
He had moved backward; why not the nation? The rumbling
is the noise of the latest tenant eruption in the Hudson Valley.
Possessing no land there, Cooper considered his involvement
altruistic. The anti-rent wars served to revive lost causes as
the uprising at Hutted Knoll served to resuscitate
Wyandotte's manhood. Psychologically, his opposition to the
moneyless tenants, refusing to pay rents and demanding
ownership, rivalled his libel suits as an outlet for vengeance.
It also provided a sense of allegiance with some acceptable
society, the Dutch patroons, and thus alleviated for a time a
bit of the exile's pain.

His fixation on the hereditary land rights of the patroons
is a direct contradiction of his attacks a dozen years earlier on
the aristocratic families of Europe. It is also a reversal of
Leatherstocking's position in the *Pioneers*, where the natural
man opposes his moral law to the civil law, and violently
resists arrest. Blind to the possibility of a tenant's moral law,
Cooper insists on exact execution of the civil law against the
anti-renters when, disguised as "calico Injins," they tar and
feather the sheriffs pursuing their duty. Speaking as Miles
Wallingford, Cooper had already violated the democratic
essence of Leatherstocking: "manliness of character is far
more likely to be the concomitant of aristocratic birth, than
of democratic, I am afraid. . . ." (215). But Wallingford also
twists the opposing forces together: "it takes an aristocrat to

make a true democrat."

In the Littlepage trilogy, Cooper nostalgically winds through the cycle of exile one more time, not of Leatherstocking being driven from his wilderness home but of the gentleman, the aristocratic democrat, from his village patriarchy. The ostensible purpose is to show the validity of the New York land patents and how subversion of them, even by legislated changes of the law, would erode American society and bring it to the brink of destruction. *Satanstoe, A Tale of the Colony* (1845) illustrates all that is to be lost, the home world of Wallingford's dreams. Like an early Faulkner, Cooper is looking back to a doomed past.

In the idyllic society of *Satanstoe*, the democratic impulse is limited to the mild exchange of British aristocracy for the American patriarchy. Cornelius Littlepage, who tells the story, fears he has little to offer Anneke Mordaunt, at least by comparison with British sophisticate, Major Bulstrode, fashionable possessor of wealth and title. Anneke is of slightly higher social position than Corny and her selection of the candid and humble American represents the triumph of Christian humility and superior talents (ghost of Leatherstocking) over European privilege and power. Insensitive to the democratic process buzzing all around him, Corny Littlepage believes that he is beginning a landed dynasty that will endure since it will provide the good life for all classes on his estate.

The seed of destruction in this idyll is Jason Newcome, the unprincipled Yankee who does not know his place among the lower classes. It is treacherous and unAmerican of Jason to take advantage of opportunity, to allow his ambition to expand when a mill site is leased to him on easy terms. Another leveling demagogue, he will use any means to achieve his ambition, preaching equality but wanting it only with those above him. He is deaf to the altruistic arguments of the land

owners, who have assumed risks of settlement in the Huron-
infested wilderness, have brought civilization (not corruption
as Leatherstocking saw it), have granted generous leasing
terms (to tenants who axed the trees for them), and have anticipated unending compensation not so much to themselves
as to their descendants. So far, Jason is less a threat than a
curious conversation piece to those confident and self-
justifying gentry at their firesides.

In *The Chainbearer* (1845) Mordaunt Littlepage, son of
Cornelius and Anneke, is less central to the agrarian society
his father founded and less confident. In parallel with the
British monarchy, for which he has little of his father's admiration, his personal influence has declined while the
shrillness of his tenants has increased. He appears to be a
Judge Temple with competence, sans foolishness, and
running scared. In the face of democracy's imminent threat,
Cooper's equivocation disappears. Without the patriarchial
powers of the Judge, Mordaunt fears the tyranny of the majority. He can act only as power of attorney on his father's
patents. But his attitude towards property rights is even
stronger than his father's. Having fought for them in the
Revolution, his rights of property are not only patriotic but
"sacred."[32] (A claim Cooper also made in a letter to the *Evening Post* concerning copyright laws.)[33] Violators of such
sacred rights were to be punished at the whipping post. The
major violators are Aaron Thousandacres, an outright squatter, and in the shadows, even worse, that Yankee lover of
liberty, Jason Newcome, the demagogue who gives license to
man's lowest passions. For those knowing their place,
however, Mordaunt is more accepting than his forebears. He
allows himself to love his chainbearer's niece, who properly
possesses the education and ancestry of a lady subdued by
misfortune.

Cooper's epitome of unpropertied virtue is the chainbearer, Andries Coejemans, a remodeled Leatherstocking now exerting his noble virtues within the confines of society and for its benefit. He is a celebate with reverence for God and Mordaunt Littlepage. The chainbearer's virtues are derived not from the vague Moravian education of Natty Bumppo but specifically from a proper blood line of Dutch gentry, which signifies Cooper's further rearrangement of democratic assumptions. Instead of rising, the line of Coejemans has fallen and the chainbearer has found his proper place for his intelligence. Although his hut is fifteen miles from the nearest settlement, he is chained in his place. His job is to measure the property and thus determine the exact rights of his employer. This latter-day Leatherstocking not only obeys but serves and defends the civil laws of property. The chain looped over his shoulder is the symbol of his employment and his duty and also of his self-imposed restraints, each man's binding in a workable society. The chainbearer is no exile. He is a man of loyalty, defending to the very death the interest of his master against the claims of squatter and demagogue.

And the master appears no less greedy than these opponents. Travelling in a sloop with prospective tenants, Mordaunt begins negotiating even before he arrives at his land patents. Too poor to purchase the land, the new settlers take leases, a necessary choice which is forever binding. They and their progeny are destined to remain tenants, as if a leftover Calvinistic God had so determined.

One of Mordaunt's opponents, Aaron Thousandacres, has squatted and milled the land for 70 years. The chainbearer, no match for Jason, the sly voice of the people, does take on the more forthright squatter in a great debate which is the center of the novel. Thousandacres has cut and sold every tree on every acre he could touch. Willful and competent in the woods, he adheres to the doctrine of use, as Ishmael Bush did before him. According to this principle, he takes the timber not used by others, ownership be damned. Civil law is a threat to his liberty.

The great debate occurs when Thousandacres takes Mordaunt a prisoner on his own land for no apparent reason other than being an aristocrat. Challenging the squatter's authority, the chainbearer is also imprisoned. Because of this arbitrary and unprincipled act, the reader tends to cancel the sincerity of Thousandacres as a man of principle and see him as Cooper desired, selfish and lawless. But the chainbearer, speaking for his master (since it would be improper for a gent to argue with a squatter) loses this advantage. He appears to oppose himself with the tired words of a Judge Temple. The words of Thousandacres, by contrast, are even more arresting than his arms. He has fought the king's soldiers to be free and depends on no man for his living. He has made his own hut from the timbers he cut and no servant of a gentleman, no chainbearer, is going to take it away. Along with Mordaunt's Indian friend, Thousandacres is absolutely baffled by the land deed, a piece of paper opposing the fact of physical possession. For the aged squatter, liberty exists "to let every man have as much land as he has need of, and no more. . ." (389). If Mordaunt is a true friend of liberty, as he says, then he will not claim land he doesn't use or need. If the squatter is greedy, what can be said of the absent owner?

The question is not civilization, yes or no, but whose civilization? The owner of the land will be the maker of its society. The issue is resolved by force, for the moment the force of the owner, which arrives in the form of posse and sheriff to arrest Thousandacres. But both lower class representatives, challenger and defender, are dispatched before the gentleman's rights are restored. The chainbearer is killed by the squatter's impatient son, and the squatter by Mordaunt's Indian friend in retaliation. But the presence of Jason Newcome among the possemen is clear indication that the owner's moment will not endure. Symbolically he has come to replace Thousandacres. Although Mordaunt can dismiss him now, it will not be long before his manipulation of the majority will allow him to change the law and triumph. For the moment, Cooper's cherished distinction between social equality and political equality is preserved. For Jason, natural rights are social rights and these include economic rights; every man has the right to equal opportunity in wealth as well as law. What else is political equality for?

In the last of the series, *The Redskins* (1846), narrated by Hugh Littlepage, grandson of Mordaunt, American life has been permeated with the social attitudes of Jason Newcome and Aaron Thousandacres: every man has a right to possess the land he needs and the rights of the majority are to do as it pleases. These attitudes have resulted in the anti-rent rebellions, which Cooper portrays as subversion of the civil law, and thus of social order now equated with the idea of principle. The anti-renters invoke moral law against the civil law, as Leatherstocking had done; "It's all owing to that accursed law, that the tenant can't set up a title ag'in his landlord. You see by this one fact, fellow citizens, that they are a privileged class, and ought to be brought down to the level of gin'ral humanity."[34] Cooper does not deny the privilege that goes with ownership; he denies only the privilege of political office, which is beside the point for the tenants. For them, the struggle is economic, haves against have-nots. Cooper acknowledges in the Preface that it may be feudalism he is defending: "We do not conceive this to be true; but, admitting it to be so, it would only prove that feudality, to this extent, is a part of the institutions of the State"(8).

There is no moral law left for Cooper, only civil law based on the Constitution. And if this law is "false principle," to change it would be a "far greater evil" than to "endure the original wrong" (528). A law that can change itself is no law. Legal change would destroy the patriarchy. At the end, Littlepage contemplates expatriation, to flee the arbitrary laws of the obnoxious majority. Perhaps in Florence he could reside "among the other victims of oppression . . . a refuge from republican tyranny" (538).

Home offered only exile. In his last years, Cooper was seldom seen outside of Cooperstown. His activity was restricted to church and family and his storytelling to the catastrophe of his fixated ideal of America, "country with no principles, but party, no God, but money, and this too with very little sentiment, taste, breeding, or knowledge" (*Letters*, III, 331).

In *The Crater* (1847), he fanticized the destruction of his ideal republic, which is not entirely recognizable as early American. His utopia, void of troublesome tenants, is a social hierachy of small farmers, all men of principle, living harmoniously in their places under the leadership of the original settler and chief landholder, Mark Woolston, and a Council of Three. The Council was elected unanimously and for life since the proper choice of government is clear to principled men unmolested by demagogues and their political parties. Here civil law and moral law are one. The Council of Three, which strongly suggests the arrangement of the despotic Venetian government castigated in *The Bravo*, granted each settler a deed of one-hundred-fifty acres to deal with as he would. The race begins, then, in equality and the outcome is determined by individual talents of virtuous men.

The patriarch—composite of them all from Temple through Hugh Littlepage—is of course community-conscious, establishing kilns, quarries, and mills for common benefit. And because he releases most of his holdings to the state, he cannot be accused of feudalism. He has faith in the people.

They will be grateful and offer deferential respect. To make sure, to avoid dissention and dreaded change (which in a utopia must be decay), lawyers are denied citizenship, school books are censored, and the sole minister is an upright Episcopalian. None of these rules are undemocratic since the settlers agreed upon them at the start. They had their chance. The idea of principle has been reduced to a singular code — stick to the rules.

In spite of all this precaution, trouble brews. A lawyer, a newspaper editor, and four dissenting ministers arrive. These demagogues are soon confounding the minds of the settlers. The Constitution is altered, the Council dissolved, the Governor dismissed. And worst of all, Mark Woolston is separated from his property, which finally makes God throw up; the volcano erupts, burying all.

In the end, like his exiled Leatherstocking, Cooper turns to God alone. Physically comfortable, his spirit was reduced to the barest level of existence. He becomes Roswell Gardiner in his *Sea Lions* (1849), alone in the antarctic, perceiving his proper place before the awesome power of God's immensity. That at least appears unchanging.

Chapter 3
POE:
The Demon and Psyche's Exile

Cooper laments the abandonment of individual and political qualities he cherished. His notions of political America estranged him. As the republic grew boisterously democratic, he clung to its principles so tenaciously that he distorted them. In Edgar Allan Poe, the estrangement is caused not by a political but an aesthetic notion, a country or region that could never exist. Not favorably born as Cooper, however, Poe was more obsessed with belonging. Essentially he was another ambitious spoiler of Cooper's American patriarchy but loathed the democrat as he did all ordinary existence. He pretended, rather, to be one of the aristocrats, Southern version, entitled to a social position one simply cannot earn. The pretense exiled him utterly.

The image of Poe's thirst to belong brings immediately to mind his "Man of the Crowd" (1840). The stranger, or wanderer as the narrator refers to him, is driven by extreme loneliness to seek any crowd that he can rub against. He is possessed to be enclosed, physically secured — we might say for Poe, 'entombed' — within a mass of people. At the end the narrator discovers that he is possessed also by "the fiend, Gin,"[1] which could be taken as the agent of exile as well as relief from its pain. But this information is imposed artificially upon the sketch, and though it serves biographical purposes it intrudes on the rendition of extreme loneliness. Also intruding are other Poe characteristics, principally his posture of erudition, in puffed-up language, in clumsy allusions to Eastern literature, philosophy, and art, and in his insistence on remote foreign phrases. If this posturing is not sufficient for identification of the narrator as Poe, and the man he is observing as himself, we can rely on the description, hardly of the man in the crowd but of the narrator's reaction. Comfortably sitting in a coffee house in London, the narrator describes the passing scene — it is one of Poe's rare objective views of an outer world. When he spots the lonely stranger in the crowd, the description turns immediately inward:

> I well remember that my first thought upon beholding it, was that Retszch, had he viewed it, would have greatly preferred it to his own pictural incarnations of the fiend. As I endeavored, during the brief minute of my original survey, to form some analysis of the meaning conveyed, there arose confusedly and paradoxically within my mind, the ideas of vast mental power, of caution, or penuriousness, of avarice, of coolness, of malice, of bloodthirstiness, of triumph, of merriment, of excessive terror, of intense — of supreme despair. I felt singularly aroused, startled, fascinated (*TS* 511).

Of the image outside the coffee house window we learn only that he was about sixty-five, and his tattered clothes were originally of quality linen "evidently second-hand *roquelaire*," an observation as unlikely as the narrator's glimpsing of a diamond and a dagger. (Worn where? How?) The location in London is more posturing; he can particularize only by reference to American scenes, "The street was a narrow and long one . . . the passengers had gradually diminished to about that number which is ordinarily seen at noon in Broadway near the Park — so vast a difference is there between a London populace and that of the most frequented American City" (*TS* 512).

Such posturing would ordinarily cost a writer the confidence of his reader, but it is part of the fascination of Poe,

who, in spite of his artistic protestations and his hard journalistic necessities, reveals the experience of his psyche, "the
hideousness of mysteries which will *not suffer* themselves to
be revealed" (*TS* 506-507), as the narrator announces in
the first paragraph. It is less his stories and poems and
theories that fascinate us than, through their transparency,
Poe himself. In his initial reaction to the man in the crowd the
narrator sketches the contours of Poe's mind. Peculiarly he
perceives no sense of social need in the outcast. Yet the outcast's longing for social contact is obvious in every movement, which the narrator observes but represses. Instead he
sees "mental power . . . blood-thirstiness . . . excessive terror . . .
merriment . . . supreme despair. . . ." (*TS* 511). These are the
qualities he wishes to see. They suggest the dreams of perverse vengeance he would harbor if he were the man in the
crowd that rejects him, which he is, in spite of the
gentleman's pose. The feeling of exile has been too extreme.
The longing has lost its original focus, and has been replaced
by solipsistic fantacizing. We are given projections on the inside screen of Poe's closed eyelids, an idiosyncratic consciousness seldom objectivized into our immediate world of
emotion and intellect.

"There is a certain flavor of provinciality," T. S. Eliot
found in the work of E. A. Poe, "the provinciality of the person who is not at home where he belongs, but cannot get to
anywhere else. Poe is a kind of displaced European."[2]
Baudelaire saw in Poe the "prototype of *le poete maudit*, the
poet as the outcast of society."[3] In the opening lines of his
early prize-winning story, "Ms. Found in a Bottle" (1833) Poe
sounds the exile's theme, which is repeated one way or
another by most Poe narrators: "Of my country and of my
family I have little to say. Ill usage and length of years have
driven me from the one, and estranged me from the other"
(*TS* 135). Had he asked the man in the crowd for an

interview, these might have been the opening words. They sound like the very essence of exile, yet the story bears less on estrangement than on the narrator's terror which he seems to relish, "hurrying onwards to some exciting knowledge . . . whose attainment is destruction" (*TS* 145). The direction of this exile's journey has turned into his own consciousness where he plays again and again with unresolvable conflicts. There is beauty in that exciting knowledge, which he seeks in the black whirlpool of approaching death. It would be rather clever to say that for Poe the other side of destruction is the homeland, but he is less in pursuit of the goal than of the terror itself. Poe's journey's are inner dramas, compressions of hostile external experience and vengeful desires. He journeys through the terrors of hell towards the unattainable, the beauty of heaven. Yet these inward journeys are peculiarly still, perfumed seas and dead cities in their depths; even the vast chasms, the whirlpools, the maelstroms and the white ashy curtain of mist through which Gordon Pym seeks the sensation of death are strangely static.

His theorizing deflects the quest towards abstraction — pure essence or music which are much the same. The "Human Aspiration for Supernal Beauty"[4] leads to the most perfect art object — the beautiful woman who is dead. Through such beauty he sought to escape the bounds of space and time and inhabit the place deep deep within the tomb or womb or black hole of himself where "Ulalume" slept and "Israfel" sang.

This unrestrained search of his internal world was engendered by external life defined in losses, of his actress mother at the age of two, his foster mother a decade later, a gentleman's education forfeited at Virginia and again at West Point, his first fiancee whose parents found him unsuitable, and the home of his foster father.[5] Marriage to his sickly thirteen-year old cousin, Virginia Clemm, was apparently

undertaken with anticipation of loss. By that time—1836—he
had become conditioned to it, masochistically or otherwise.
The record indicates that he was also a most unlikeable col-
league as working journalist and achieved his success only by
an overwhelming excellence. His pose as dispossessed southern aristocrat and as romantic rebel fighting in Greece (while
actually serving as enlisted man in the U.S. Army), and his
severe anti-abolitionist attitude are transparent shields to
hold off memories of loss in his external world. Unconsum-
mated at home and at work, the external life is abandoned for
the explorations into the "dark tarn of Auber," where he
could thrill in anticipation of a strange impending doom, as
he confessed to one of his later fiancees, Mrs. Whitman.

For Poe, "strange" did not mean novelty but abnormal-
ity and amorality, and there was no beauty without it,
"without some strangeness in the proportions." Natural law is
suspended in his tales. Most characters suffer conditions pro-
hibiting activity, forcing them to live in semi-trances and to
endure a "feeling for which I have no name." His poems and
tales offer a full repertoire of neurotic delights from simple
sadism in "The Cask of Amantillado" to elaborate perversities in "Berenice." Since there is no emotional norm there is
little sense of character motivation. In fact there are no
characters in any real sense, no affective exchange between
personalities. For Poe there was no world other than Poe. He
was the exile making his own society, his own home within
himself.

I

In *The Power of Blackness*, Harry Levin yokes Poe with
Hawthorne and Melville as examples of the typical American
"missing man," who, "having left his home behind, keeps
looking homeward, because he exists in a state of suspense
between wanderlust and nostalgia."[6] Later he finds it "hard
to say which conflicting impulse, wanderlust or nostalgia,

dominates the American temper."[7] It is hard to say because these are exiles at home. For Poe, especially, the wanderlust is directed to the nostalgia, memories suppressed and sublimated into dreams of the unattainable. Nostalgia for the notion of respectability, lost with the home of his status-conscious foster father, must have stimulated his elitist pretences. John Allan, a Richmond merchant with desires for aristocratic recognition and women on the other side of town, could also be a source for Poe's peculiar attitude toward passion, a fascination and loathing for the ambitious and sensual earth-self that imprisons his Psyche, his aesthetic soul.

His earthly ambitions were nurtured with great expectations, beginning with the potential of the blood in his veins. Grandfather was General David Poe of the Revolution. Appropriately Poe was schooled for five years in England with a view to a gentleman's finish at the University of Virginia. He was awakened from these ambitious dreams at seventeen when Sarah Elmira Royster's parents found his background insufficient for their daughter. Perhaps his other dreams — of unearthly beauty — helped to buffer the insult. He published a volume of them the following year (1827), but after John Allan withdrew support and he had resigned from the University and after his consequent enlistment in the U.S. Army. Within two years he had been promoted to the highest enlisted rank, Sergeant Major, an achievement of ambition that the exiled dreamer of his poems eschewed. In "Dreams" the poet wishes life to be a lasting dream, even if it were of "hopeless sorrow" rather than the "dull reality of waking life," which also has been "a chaos of deep passion from his birth."[8] Earthly ambitions — hopes — comprise the passion. He has been happier in dreams "Than young Hope in his sunniest hour hath known" (*P* 69). In "The Happiest Day, The Happiest Hour," the poet's heart has been "sear'd and blighted" (*P* 81) because it placed hope in power and pride, the passion of ambition once more.[9] Pride, however, poured venom on the poet. Now if he could live that life again he would refuse. Always there was the "dark alloy" in the winds of that happiness,

> . . . powerful to destroy
> A soul that knew it well (*P* 82).

Even childhood, the poet realizes, wasn't innocent of the ambitious passions which contaminate the earthly home and exile the poet. The nostalgia is for an existence undefiled by preparation for responsibility and achievement (power and pride). The notion is similar to the pre-birth paradise recollected by Wordsworth's youth in "Intimations of Immortality" (also by Milne in *Winnie the Pooh*), to Mark Twain's dream of Hannibal, Missouri, or to the memory of *Citizen Kane* dwelling on his boyhood sled, Rosebud, as he lays dying. It occupies Hemingway's Nick Adams in upper Michigan on "The Big Two-Hearted River." Like Nick, Poe's dreamy youth also encounters a duplicitous body of water in "The Lake: To —." Days it was lovely and lonely, a wild lake bound with black rock and tall pines. But night threw a pall and brought a mystic wind, and then he would awake "to the terrors of the lone lake" (*P* 85). The youth's reaction is directly opposite to Nick's. No taboo, this terror, but a "tremulous delight" (*P* 86). The lone lake is apparently the first of Poe's tantalizing black tomb images — the whirlpools and tarns and coffins and sepulchres and closets and walled-up niches. Here the poet confronts the vagueness of the chilling night wind in "Dreams" and the "dark alloy" (*P* 82) drooping the wings of "The Happiest Day, The Happiest Hour." The "Eden of that dim lake" (*P* 86) is not the place of ethereal dreams, but quite the opposite. It is delicious feeling, delight of terror, threat of extinction. He revels in this terror. This is Poe's passion — earthly. The dream of unearthly beauty is, on the contrary, devoid of passion. It is without terror because it is without life. It is pure. Static. An ideal to contemplate. Beauty.

Except for the beautiful dead woman as the ideal aesthetic object, all of Poe's literary ideas are formed in these teenage poems. For the rest of his short life he elaborated upon them. In "Al Aaraaf" (1829) the triumphant passions doom the earthbound. The dreamland here is an aesthetic realm suggested by a star once sighted by Tico Brahe.[10] It attains a stunning brilliancy and then disappears just as it appeared, mysteriously. The star is not yet the distant realm of beauty, but a medium, as the Arabs know, between heaven and hell where neither enjoyment nor punishment can exist because passion lurks there. In *Canto Two* the passion appears. Lovers. One lover is the subject of the ruler, Nesaces, and the other is Michelangelo. Their passion does not belong in heaven. Nor does science, another earthly contaminant. Poe might have been reading Shelley's "Queen Mab" and Milton's *Paradise Lost* but unlike those imaginary realms, "Al Aaraaf" suggests few earthly parallels, certainly no rebellions against war-mongering kings or tyrannical gods. Only earthliness itself is condemned, in terms of love and science. Poe's problem with science is not today's problem of technological suffocation, but its essence, its factuality and rationality. In "Sonnet — to Science" (1829), it is the scientific spirit that attacks the poetic imagination:

> Why preyest thou thus upon the poet's heart,
> Vulture, whose wings are dull realities?

Science represents the dismal experience of living an external life. It drags "Diana from her car" and drives "Hamadryad from the wood" (*P* 91).[11] The practical requirements for living — emotional and rational — contaminate or at least cloud the dreams. Even if the poet achieves the distant star of "Al Aaraaf," he cannot envision heaven (ultimately beauty which is ideal truth) because his sight is blurred by his earthliness, his remnants of dull realities. Universal experience is reflected here. Percy Bridgeman, Nobel-Prize winning physicist has expressed it as the modern physicist's prime insight ". . . it is impossible to transcend the human reference point," even to know our "dull realities."[12]

Two years later, Poe attempts heaven again and manages to sight "Israfel" whose heartstrings are a lute. He sings, "so wildly well" that even

> . . . the giddy stars (so legends tell)
> Ceasing their hymns, attend the spell
> Of his voice, all mute (*P* 175).

The poet has achieved the limbo of the giddy stars but not the heaven of the angel Israfel (*Koran*), which he cannot describe because he is confined to passionate terms of earth language. His effort reveals his contaminated vision:

> The ecstasies above
>   With thy burning measures suit —
> Thy grief, thy joy, thy hate, thy love,
>   With the fervour of thy lute —
> Well may the stars be mute!

Attempting to transcend himself, the poet even rationalizes his earthly limitations:

> . . . thou art not wrong,
> Israfeli, who despisest
> An unimpassioned song;

Finally he recognizes what he is doing and expresses his frustrations:

> Yes, Heaven is thine; but this
> Is a world of sweets and sours;
> Our flowers are merely — flowers, (*P* 177).

Yet the poet does not accept defeat gracefully. The poem

ends in a taunting rationale that soothes the ego. Change places, he challenges Israfel, and you would also sing a mortal melody while from his lute "a bolder note . . . might swell" (*P* 177).

"Israfel" appears in the 1831 volume *Poems*, along with "The City in the Sea" and "To Helen." These two poems represent a bifurcation in his vision, the two oceans his driven imagination was "wont to roam" (*P* 166). Unlike "Israfel" he presents here embodied images, as if he had accepted his human limitations. Helen's beauty reminds the poet of a wanderer coming home "o'er a perfumed sea" (*P* 165), and the home itself has precise historical reference:

> To the glory that was Greece,
> And the grandeur that was Rome.

These lines were added later and may have blurred the grammatical intent, but as the poem reads, it is the poet, as well as Helen, who is brought back "from the regions which are Holy-Land!" (*P* 166). Read only within the context of this single poem the Holy Land, the place from which he is delivered, is the Christian world. The Roman and Greek worlds (the grandeur no less than the glory) are home rather than the dull realities of the Christian society that confines him. But read in the larger context of other poems—"Al Aaraaf" and "Israfel"—the Holy Land is that unattainable aesthetic heaven he longed for. In either interpretation, Poe appears to be settling for less than heaven, at least for any uncomplicated or direct route there.

The last stanza reveals the inspiring image of Helen as an actual statue in a window niche. She holds an agate lamp that resonates with the bright intellect of the poet's Psyche, his soul, the perceiver of ideal beauty. The spirit of Helen is elsewhere, at home. This statue is the material suggestion of her, the earthly embodiment, the agent or vessel that might transport Psyche's imagination even beyond the glory and grandeur of the past to the attainable beauty of Israfel's indescribable heaven. Helen's statue in the window niche is the mother of all those intelligent dead beauties, Poe's women of marble passion. Unlike her offspring, however, the statue offers an image of brightness undistorted by the pallor of death. The others — Poe's perfect objects of art — have some "strangeness in the proportions" and dwell in necropheliac places, even those ladies who share the 1831 volume. "The Sleeper," is like a "window open to the night" (*P* 187) and "soft may the worms around her creep" (*P* 188). Contemplating her tomb, the poet is thrilled thinking of the dead who groan within. "Lenore" is less grotesque since the poet is concerned with the hypocrites who did not appreciate her in life and with the job of getting her to heaven. Nevertheless the images, if not ghastly, are funereal. Her "saintly soul glides down the Stygian river" (*P* 334), and lies on a "drear and rigid bier" (*P* 335). Evidently, something has blocked or blighted Psyche's journey and has driven the poet in another direction, to the dark, the other ocean where deep within lies "The City in the Sea." Here Poe seems more at home than in the Greek and Roman worlds. (These references were added "To Helen" in 1845, perhaps in response to the popularity of classical antiquity after Schliemann's excavation at Troy.)[13]

At first sight, "The City in the Sea" appears to offer consoling respite from the earthly passions that have clouded the poet's vision of aesthetic heaven. But here again something disturbs the tranquility of the dead in "their eternal rest" amid "the shrines and palaces and towers . . . [which] resemble nothing that is ours" (*P* 201). Of course not; "ours" is a turbulent, passionate death. To make it ours, a light appears, not the heavenly attribute of Helen's agate lamp but a hellish glow arising from the sea floor, making the city appear to rise toward the surface. But all is illusion: instead of rising the city sinks, apparently into the mire and,

> Hell, rising from a thousand thrones,
> Shall do it reverence (*P* 202).

The benign euphemism of souls at rest cannot be accepted anymore than the illusion of earthly existence as workaday tranquility rather than hellish death.

The something that blocks Psyche's journey, that directs the poet's imagination in "The City in the Sea" and then casts it into hell, is Poe's demon. It is not an arbitrary invention but a perception from the real past. He records the moment of perception in an early poem, "Alone" (c. 1829), where he muses on the realities of his childhood "in the dawn of a most stormy life" (*P* 146). Instead of seeing, as other children do, the red cliff of the mountain, the autumn tint of gold and the lightning and storm, he envisioned

> . . . the cloud that took the form
> (When the rest of Heaven was blue)
> Of a demon in my view. . . (*P* 147).

It is this unrecognized demon who stimulated the terror of the lone black-rimmed lake. Later, Poe identifies it as the imp of the perverse, although it displays no endearing qualities. Whether this perception is the result or the cause of disappointments in early social intercourse that established his psychic patterns and determined his "stormy life," it is certainly the agent of his exile, of his rebellious reaction to the materiality of living. The demon or imp lives in his passions, perverts them, directs them to nighttime flirtations with death and to other thrills — of vengeance and intellectual arrogance. The imp's irrational passion can strike back at those who have the power to hurt, subjugate, withhold. It empowers the vital forces within to destroy the artifices of social institutions, morality, beliefs. It is the devilish self, naked.

The demon is the dark counterpart to Poe's bright

Psyche. Each impells the poet to seek an opposing dreamland. Ultimately they confront each other in "Ulalume" (1847). But in the sixteen years between that poem and "Israfel" the demon grows dominant, Psyche fades. It is the demon-dominated Poe who writes the tales of terror, the criticism and literary theory, and who mockishly imitates scientific rationalism. The mind of C. Auguste Dupin, the science fiction, the hoaxes and puzzles and flat humor are all the work of this demon or perverse imp.

II

Frustrated in his reach for heaven, Poe retreated to an earthly home with his Aunt Maria Clemm — he called her "Muddy" — and "Sis," his sickly cousin, Virginia. Like other upright heads of house, he sought to provide. However odious, he submitted himself to the society of men without caste as he saw fellow magazinists. The imp within made it possible, directing his talent to popular forms of the German tale-tellers, the terrors of Hoffman and Tieck, popular yet deliciously suited for the perversities that vengeance required.

Once he had remarked that his "whole existence has been the merest romance — in the sense of the most utter unworldliness."[14] Now the work began to reflect the world in which he lived. Even "The City in the Sea" could be devilishly interpreted as a condemnation of American life. Given his loathing of democratic society, "a thousand thrones" (*P* 202) rising from hell could represent the authority of the masses intruding even on his dark dreams, which they have, ironically, darkened. Typically his first science fiction was a journey to the unknown: but an embodied one, the moon, unlike those out of space and time. It was empowered, of course, by the imp, who provided satiric thrusts at the dull reality of dismal economic existence left behind in "The Unparalleled Adventures of One Hans Pfaall" (1835). Styled after

Washington Irving—another aspect of his practicality—the tale reveals Poe's utter clumsiness as a satiric wit, beginning with Han's trade, mender of bellows. He teaches himself the technology for going to the moon in a balloon made of dirty newspapers and shaped like a fool's cap upside down. The flight takes place April First. The narrative device for the tale is a letter sent back with a moon man, two feet high, asking forgiveness for the death of three creditors who were killed in the launching, presumably by the hot air of the bellows mender. Poe's Rip Van Winkle is devoid of Irving's gentle humor and the significance of rebirth. Hans is just wearied with life.[15] The significance, as always with Poe, is in the journey itself, out of mundane existence.

He had already published five stories when the *Baltimore Saturday Visitor* awarded him its 1833 fiction prize for "Ms. Found in a Bottle." Giddy with this success, Poe described his Hans Pfaall and other sketches in that vein with such learning and enthusiasm that the editor, novelist John Pendleton Kennedy, took him for a man of science. Introductions from Kennedy swung open more publishing doors. Within two years, editor Thomas Wilkes White of the *Southern Literary Messenger* hired Poe as assistant editor of the best-known literary magazine in the South. Poe was on the road to success in the mundane world.

Artistically, too, he was not displeased. The "Ms. Found in a Bottle" is sent back to the world from an unknown place, a vast chasm enveloped by eternal night, "a black sweltering desert of ebony," where the writer's sensation is the "hopelessness of hope itself" (*P* 139). An even greater delight is "a feeling, for which I have no name" (*P* 141), occurring when a huge vessel washes down from a great height and the writer, somehow landing on the deck, finds himself invisible to the crew. The Ms. is then a message from a soul who has passed to another life. A more titillating interpretation could see the writer as a precursor to Ralph Ellison's *Invisible Man*, more titillating because of the irony in Poe's adamant racial prejudice.[16]

The success of *Ms.* encouraged him to repeat and refine the nightmare journey throughout his life. But the success of "Berenice" was less pleasing. The aesthetic ideal of the beautiful dead woman would not transfer from a poetic to a prosaic vehicle without damage. "How is it," he asked of this story, "that from beauty can I have derived a type of unloveliness? From the covenant of peace a simile of sorrow? . . . Either the memory of past bliss is the anguish of today or the agonies which are have their origins in the ecstacies which might have been."[17]

Five years later, Berenice will play the role of Lady Rowena while Ligeia will perform as the ethereal woman who can elevate all his passions. In the meantime he married his consumptive cousin Virginia, who at thirteen was not yet a real woman; who was wan, marked by death, not a sexual being of this earth, and so at least in mind sufficiently unattainable. (No evidence of her intelligence; perhaps her singing served as adequate substitute.) Outwardly secure in a home that appeared to satisfy both the earthly and ethereal passions, he now pursued his career as magazinist unabated. For the next eight years he devoted himself to the fierce criticism that built the satisfying legend of the aristocrat fallen on hard times and forced to expose his superior intellect. The legend is of a man set apart from others by virtue of his great learning, strange passions, and dark destiny, all contributing to his superiority which sanctions his opinions and contemptuous disregard of others. This impish pose must have provided at least some compensation for the neglect of his poetic imagination.

As magazinist he was thick in the battle for protective copyright laws which were a phase in the larger struggle for

American literary independence. He harangued audiences to buy American books, produced at the publisher's obvious risk. He reminded the American reader of a time when an American book was read "only after repeated assurances from England that such productions were not altogether contemptible."[18] But "on the reverse," we find "ourselves daily in the paradoxical dilemma of liking or pretending to like a stupid book the better because (sure enough) its stupidity [is] of our own growth, and discuss[es] our own affairs."[19] He was fearless of traditional restraints but the tradition was English, not American. He would attack the established, often deservedly, in both America and England, but on occasion would praise the sentimental goo of an unknown, usually American and usually a woman. He claimed English novelists were generally pretentious. Americans who followed in the English traditions—especially those in New England and New York—were even worse. They owed their reputations merely to the fact of being first in the field. "Is there any one so blind as not to see that Mr. Cooper, for example, owes much, and that Mr. Paulding owes *all* of his reputation as a novelist, to his early occupation of the field?"[20]

Perhaps his distaste for the novels he reviewed stimulated his own effort to try one. The first installment of *The Narrative of A. Gordon Pym* appeared in the January 1837 issue of the *Messenger* along with his review of Irving's *Astoria.*[21] He had read "An Address on the Subject of Surveying and Exploring Expedition to the Pacific Ocean and the South Seas," published that year by Jeremiah N. Reynolds, the same Reynolds who wrote *Mocha Dick, or the White Whale of the Pacific.* The effect must have been profound, since Poe on his deathbed inexplicably gasped the name, "Reynolds."

After two installments in 1837, Poe left the *Messenger* and took his family to New York where he finished the novel.

The work includes enough evidence of social criticism — especially in the relations of whites and blacks — and enough external adventure to suggest that he intended a portrayal of the essential American spirit, which may have seemed the way to wealth. When published in 1838, however, the novel was merely an elongated and therefore dissipated version of his journeys out of space and out of time, although Pym begins on more substantial ground.

He runs away from a Nantucket family, disguises himself and sets out for "some grayt and desolate rock, in an ocean unapproachable and unknown" (*CS* 619). Smuggled aboard a whaler by his friend Augustus, he is significantly stuffed into a dark hold to set up the first of several rebirths out of the suffocating conditions of life. The whaler departs from Edgartown on Martha's Vineyard, so perhaps he is sailing away from self. After several disasters, Pym and a companion set foot on the Isle of Tsalal, an "ultimate dim Thule" (*P* 344), which is not recognizable as the place of his nightmare dreams, not a place of terror but ludicrous satire. This thule is within the antarctic circle where all flora and fauna are black. (If the American South is black, the Antartic must be blacker). Even the teeth of the wooly-haired inhabitants are black. The water is purplish. White is a taboo color. So the antagonism is rooted in the very nature of things. After another rebirth — this time the companion catches Pym after he succumbs to the temptation of falling from a precipice — they escape the savages through a labyrinth of gorges and rocks. Finally they head towards the pole in a canoe. The more Pym suffers the more he seems to enjoy it. Suffering heightens his sensitivity and leads to ecstasy. The novel ends abruptly as the canoe approaches a rain of white powder, a misty whiteness that forms a curtain suspended between darkness and the glaring sea. Ecstasy is clearly indicated in the "embrace of the cataract, where a chasm threw itself open to receive us" (*CS* 735). Then a shrouded figure appears, also white but larger than any dwelling among men. An editor's note explains that the narrative is incomplete because of the recent accidental death of Mr. Pym.

In this practical effort to capture the popular interest, Poe appears to have broached the separateness of his dreamlands or at least attempted some relationship between them. The journeys in the earlier "Ms. Found in a Bottle" and the later "A Descent into the Maelstrom" (1841) lead to a vortex of "liquid ebony" (*TS* 591). These whirlpools that allure one to destruction are also "ultimate dim Thule," the black place that A. Gordon experiences and survives on his way to a white death. The experience turns out to be the American heart of darkness, racial hatred. Here, in one story at least, Poe penetrates the unknown within the whirlpool to find a concrete symbol for the black despair of enduring earthly life and passions. The journey to the aesthetic heaven, which the poet's imagination yearns for, must go through that black place and escape. By fleeing the utlimate thule, Pym frees or purifies his imagination so it can achieve the ecstasy, the embrace of the chasm in the white mist, that all absorbing glob of beauty to be defined in *Eureka*. This is Plato's old pain and pleasure process, or Poe's version of the fortunate fall. The pain of the primitive life on earth, we learn in "The Colloquy of Monos and Una," is the basis of the bliss of the ultimate life in heaven. So the forsaken poet still breathes, still hopes, in his prosaic prison.

Rather than recede from the pain of life on earth, Poe plunged into it and grappled as fiercely as any other opportunist in Jacksonian American. In *American Renaissance*, Matthiessen notes that Poe grovelled in the material world at least as much as any American writer. After the publication of *Pym*, Poe was offered the editor's chair at *Graham's* in

Philadelphia where he multiplied circulation several times over and enriched his employers but not himself. Graham had promised his editor a share in a new publishing venture but Poe's success apparently worked against him, "rendering that Mag [*Graham's*] a greater source of profit, rendered its owner, at the same time, less willing to keep his word with me."[23] His reaction was not another journey out of the cruel world but aggression in the opportunistic spirit of the air he breathed. He set about getting subscriptions to the new venture, sans Graham, to be called *Penn's Magazine*. To the end of his life he sought the goal of ownership, managing only briefly a third-share in the *Broadway Journal* in 1845. It failed within the year and Poe began to solicit subscriptions for another journal to be called *The Stylus*.

Poe's artistic imagination also grappled with the real world, but vengefully. If the society demanded scientific rationalism his tales would be overwhelmingly rational and scientific. This is the Poe that T. S. Eliot called "pre-adolescent," better at complications of "cryptograms, cy-phers, puzzles and labyrinths" than complications of life.[24] And this is the Poe that makes one pause. Is it all put-on? A pretense of innocence with a straight face like Mark Twain's tellers of tall tales? In "How to Write a Blackwood Article" (1838) his burlesque of popular fiction comes amazingly close to a description of his own. "Sensations are the great things after all," he declares. "Should you ever be drowned or hung, be sure and make a note of your sensations — they will be worth to you ten guinneas a sheet" (*TS* 340). He was not as good at laughter as ratiocination. Efforts at satire always ended in burlesque. "The Man that was Used Up" (1839) questions the qualities of an heroic Indian fighter who wishes to be President; he is revealed to be a synthesis of artificial limbs, wig, false palate, teeth and so on — a great mechanical blob put together to tell the mob about progress, also mechanical.

Perhaps too many clouds hung over from bad dreams to allow the sharp and steady focus on the external world required of satire. His hoaxes are usually science fictions, reflecting his interest in the latest fads, especially anything that simulates yet defies death such as mesmerism and suspended animation. As today's science fiction, Poe's was a vehicle for social criticism.

When Poe resumes his black journeying to the brink of destruction, science and rationalism are fused in the terror. The Norwegian sailor who returns from "A Descent into the Maelstrom" is not our basic lost poet getting his kicks and compensations by imagining another thrilling approach to death. He is our first glimpse of C. Auguste Dupin, the super ratiocinator of the detection stories—poet in his own right, yet man of this world. He analyzes the physical forces at play in the maelstrom, records them mentally with computer-like rapidity, and later can recall each detail leading to his conclusions and consequent escape. Reasoning that a cylindrical cask would descend more slowly than a boat, he leaps overboard and clutches such an object; cool operation, even though the evidence of his fright marks him ever after—the black hair has turned white.

In defense of Poe it is often claimed that his journeys are psychological probes into the forbidden territory of the unconscious where lurk our animal terrors and the horrors of inmost and utmost self. Critics frozen into Freudian patterns, such as Marie Bonaparte, find a singular image for this forbidden territory.[25] Struggling in the black walled whirlpool, the Norwegian feels himself on the very brink of eternity, which has been taken as the vortex of birth, the promise of reunion with mother. When Poe responded to critics of his day that his terror was of the soul, not Germany, perhaps he should have added, "nor mother," for some critics of our day. A more fulfilling view is of the journey to the uncon-

scious to expose by means of threatened extinction the hidden
sources of our impulses, longings, fears, thoughts, desires,
dreams and perversities. More fulfilling but equally artificial.
Such journeys are undertaken by the Bundrens, Ike McCaslin, and Joe Christmas in Faulkner country. But the only exposure we find in "A Descent into the Maelstrom" is to a thrill
of cheating death by human ingenuity. Even his three greatest
stories, all written within a single year and several years
before scientific rationalism out-witted "The Maelstrom," do
not yield experience of the unconscious. Rather, they portray
the conscious conflict of the imagination struggling to free
itself from its contaminating earthly confinement. In these
three stories even the narrator is aware that the conflict is
driving his poetic soul crazy.

III

In "Ligeia" (1838) the narrator attempts to resolve the
conflict of "Al Aaraaf" and "Israfel" through the imaginative
powers stimulated by opium. Although his bright-eyed Ligeia
defeats the conquering worm in his doped imagination, this
victory does not free him from the black house of the night.
In "The House of Usher" (1839), the narrator visits another
black house. He finds the inhabitant, an artistic and imaginative soul, in throes of despair, attempting to split off from his
earthy counterpart, his twin sister. But she reclaims him, and
the unity is foul destruction. The narrator runs in terror from
the vision. In "William Wilson" (1839), the narrator faces his
conscience, destroys that disturbing double, and finds
himself destroyed.

Except for a few paragraphs at the end, "Ligeia" is all
description, enlivened by the struggle of the narrator to
remember the ethereal one and thus transport himself out of
his gloomy and dismal Abbey. The narrator retreated to the
Abbey upon the death of Ligeia, who is not given any real life

substance. There is nothing to mourn for, since he cannot recall knowing even her family name, much less where she came from or how he met her. He merely knows that she was with him and was his wife. What he can do is long for her. He struggles to remember. (Later in "Ulalume" and also in "The Raven" he prefers to forget.) It is difficult to remember Ligeia because her qualities are all ethereal, supernal and sublime. She is, we remember, the demi-diety maiden of "Al Aaraaf." So how describe an unearthly apparition in the language of earthly creatures. As in "Israfel," "words are impotent to convey" (*TS* 317) such poetic visions, "the shrine of the most passionate devotion" (*TS* 311). He attempts to invoke the vision by getting himself "buried in studies . . . to deaden impressions of the outward world" (*TS* 310). Then by means of opium and analogies with "the commonest objects of the universe" (all that is available to the earthbound), he is able to perceive her as something like a butterfly, running water, one of two stars, certain sounds of string instruments, and Ganvill's assertion that "God is but a great will pervading all things" (*TS* 314). That she is dope-induced is also apparent — her face "was the radiance of an opium dream," her footfall had an "incomprehensible lightness and elasticity," her voice was of "dear music," her skin "the purest ivory," her hands "marble," her nose the graceful perfection of the Hebrews.

But she is Helen nonetheless, the giveaway is the "hyacenthine" hair. And the eyes, "the divine orbs." He was possessed to discover what "lay far within the pupils of my beloved" (*TS* 311-313). His passion at that stage of the dream is for knowing, not loving, her.[26] Although he speaks of her being "most violently a prey to the tumultuous vultures of stern passion," he is still in the context of her volition, not her sexuality: "of such passion I could form no estimate, save by the miraculous expression of those eyes . . . by the almost magical melody . . . of her low voice—and by the fierce energy . . . of the wild words which she habitually uttered." Not, however, by any other form of intercourse. Her learning was immense, including "*all* the wide areas of moral, physical, and mathematical science," as well as "the modern dialects of Europe" (*TS* 315). Ligeia was his guide to "the goal of a wisdom too divinely precious not to be forbidden" (*TS* 316). And that is why she cannot exist, at least not in any earthly place. This is the story of how "Ligeia's beauty passed into my spirit, there dwelling as in a shrine" (*TS* 314).

Upon her deathbed, Ligeia composes a poem (the sole and unconvincing evidence of her intelligence) in which the angels look down upon the human drama, the tragedy of man's futile acts and passions defeated by the conqueror worm. With her last breath, however, she shrieks defiance to the worm, in Glanvill's words. Her will can be stronger, can defeat the fate of flesh and its passions. But isn't she the writer of the poem? The shriek is not Ligeia's, of course, not anymore than the poem is Ligeia's. Her voice is low-volumed melody and gets even lower and sweeter as death approaches. The shriek is the narrator's state of mind at that point in the dream vision. This entire opium jag, we should remember, is taking place in the remote and dismal Abbey, his mind, which at this stage he had decorated with a "child-like perversity" in the hopes of alleviating his sorrows. The Abbey has become another black place like the whirlpools, the city in the sea, and the ultimate dim thule. He has penetrated inside, and it is costing him his sanity.

The decor, he realizes, reveals something of his "incipient madness." The only room described is the "bridal chamber" designed ostensibly for Lady Rowena, whom he marries in a "moment of mental alienation" (*TS* 320-321), but ultimately designed for Ligeia. Rowena's description consists of two items—fair hair and blue eyes. She is of this earth. But the bridal chamber is described almost with the relish of Ligeia's description. Rowena enters the dream for the same purpose as the furnishings, as preparation for the embodiment of the aesthetic vision, Ligeia. The chamber is a gaudy mishmash of riches from Venice, Turkey, India, Egypt and the funeral parlor. Behind the black and gold draperies a constant wind blows. The bridal couch is "solid ebony, with a pall-like canopy above" (*TS* 322). So quite naturally Lady Rowena "shunned me and loved me but little." And it mattered little, since he loathed her from the start. She disturbed his dreaming, his "wild eagerness" to "restore" Ligeia—"ah, *could* it be forever?—upon the earth" (*TS* 323).

Given the circumstances, Poe does not have to cite cause for Rowena's illness. The cause of her death, however, is presented ambiguously, a few drops in Rowena's wine placed by either the distraught husband or the spirit of Ligeia momentarily shadowing forth from her circulation behind the draperies. Since its all a dream, what matter? Ligeia reappears finally after the "pallid and rigid figure" of Rowena has gone through many painstaking birth pangs. Her "hair streamed forth" in a "rushing atmosphere." It is *"blacker than the wings of midnight"* (*TS* 330). This is not the stolid hycenthine hair she began with, not the hair of Helen. He does, however, recognize her wild eyes. The ethereal vision has become incarnated, but only through the contamination of earthly passion in that ghastly black hole of the diseased imagination. If he had not already admitted his insanity, the irony would be maddening. Later, Poe commented, "I should have intimated that the *will* did not perfect its intention."[27]

"The House of Usher" is a continuation of Poe's effort to probe implications of "Al Aaraaf" and "Israfel." It is more complex than "Ligeia" because it incorporates the characters of the previous story into that of Roderick Usher. Depressed by a "mental disorder" (*TS* 398), as he tells the narrator in his

plea for help, Usher resembles the teller of the previous story
who has become the house or shrine which Ligeia inhabits.
This Ligeia is not the ethereal spirit he had anticipated, but
the returned spirit in the cloddish flesh of Rowena. The story
is further complicated by the identity of Usher with his house.
Like Poe himself, Usher has closed himself in the house of his
mind. "The House of Usher" is organically one with its mad
inhabitant who contains all three characters of the previous
story — one within the other — and is therefore much like the
house that Jack built, disguised in a plethora of gothic cliches.

The narrator of "Usher," unlike the narrator of "Ligeia,"
is the writer's persona, a sane voice who steps into the house
of Usher as if to take another and much closer look at a terrifying dream, to redream it. The narrator is irresistibly drawn
to the house, as if he had visited the dream again and again.
This is not the dream of the opium eater in high gear, but the
"after dream of the reveller upon opium — the bitter lapse into
every-day life — the hideous dropping off of the veil" (*TS*
397). With a "shudder even more thrilling than before," the
sane narrator approaches the decaying house on the "black
and lurid tarn" surrounded by ghastly tree stems and possessed of "eye-like windows" (*TS* 398). Momentarily shaking
off the spell of the atmosphere "which had no affinity with
the air of heaven but which reeked up from the decayed trees"
(*TS* 399-400), etc., he examines the house more realistically
and finds it still stable in spite of the extensive decay; but
there was a faintly discernable fissure from the roof to "the
sullen water of the tarn" (*O S* 400). The significance of this
fissure is the terror of the dream, the exciting intimation of
knowledge whose possession is indeed destruction.

Usher's study is just as gaudily grotesque as Rowena's
bridal chamber, through less explicitly described: black
oaken floors, dark draperies upon the walls, the feeble gleam
of encrimsoned light. Unused instruments of music and

books are scattered about, but they "failed to give any vitality to the scene" (*TS* 401). The quote from DeBeranger that precedes the story refers also to a lute, which is Roderick Usher's heart as it is Israfel's. "His heart is a hanging lute; as soon as it is touched, it responds" (*TS* 397). For one brief period, Usher is freed of his depression and does play the lute. The sound of stringed instruments, in fact, is the only one that does not "inspire him with horror." His malady, he asserts, is a family evil. The deficiency was extreme inbreeding, as he puts it. He is the ultimate result of this family habit, a nerve-wracked thoroughbred, incapable of enduring most sensory existence. He could digest only the most insipid food. Even faint light tortured his eyes. "The odours of all flowers were oppressive" (*TS* 403). He is emaciated, like Poe's ethereal women, and if his eyes, "large, liquid, and luminous beyond comparison," are not sufficient to identify him with Ligeia, then his nose certainly is, "of a delicate Hebrew model" (*TS* 401).

The charge of the narrator is to alleviate the malady by bringing cheer from the outside world, so he is apparently a comfortable member of society, a rational, stable fellow. He is Usher's only personal friend, although they had not met since childhood. (This circumstance resonates with that in "William Wilson.") Usher's only other companion in life has been his twin sister, Lady Madeline, who now is dying. The long illness and "approaching dissolution" (how does he know?) of this "tenderly beloved sister . . . his last and only relative on earth" (*TS* 404), is admitted as the immediate cause of his gloom. But admitted only after a bit of fencing and then with hesitation. As Usher speaks her name, Lady Madeline conveniently passes in "a remote portion of the apartment" and the narrator feels an astonishing dread. Vaguely seen, she is not described, not even to the extent of Lady Rowena. The twin is obviously an organic part of Usher that is beginning to separate, as indicated by the faintly perceived fissure in the house, also Usher. She succumbs that very evening, "as her brother told me at night with inexpressible agitation" (*TS* 404), the narrator says, indicating at least troubled acceptance of the fact. Agitation rather than grief? Madeline is mentioned no more. Slowly, as Usher returns to his books, paintings, and his lute, the gloom lifts. Soon he is enjoying a new freedom, playing wildly well like Israfel within that dismal house whose dungeon still contains the seemingly forgotten body of Lady Madeline.

At the height of this surge towards aesthetic heaven, Usher sings "The Haunted Palace," encapsulating the myth he lives. Wanderers, (those poor wretches on the outside) peer into the radiant palace as the narrator sees into Usher, through "two luminous windows." Within they view spirits moving "to a lute's well-tuned law" and "Echoes whose sweet duty/was but to sing." And the song was of such beauty that it surpasses the "wit and wisdom of their king." Israfel revisited. But the vision cannot be sustained. "Evil things, in robes of sorrow," arrive and of course there can be no battle since such spirits would be contaminated by earthly passions if they had the ability to defend themselves. Their fall is so obvious the song does not even record it, but sings instead of the mourning for the "dim-remembered story" (*TS* 407). But what is the specific evil that blights Usher's vision? (Impaired even at its radiant best since Usher is still earthbound and thus limited to earthly metaphor.) The evil is specified in the very next event of the story—the return of Madeline who has never really died. Unlike Ligeia returning to join or inhabit the narrator, Madeline's is closer to the return of a Lady Rowena, a clod of flesh falling upon and smothering to oblivion her angelic twin half. He cannot escape the flesh, even by murder, since it is his. And the narrator, whose story it is, runs for his sanity, runs from his images of his own mind collapsing into the tarn as the house fissures and falls in a sudden whirlwind, the black destruction of the "Maelstrom."

The narrator is fleeing still in "William Wilson," (1839) the most autobiographical of Poe's fiction. He is now "outcast of all outcasts most abandoned" (*TS* 426), the wanderer. He does not run back to the aristocratic well being we had assumed for him in the "House of Usher." But aristocrat he remains, most ostentatiously, from the exclusive school of his primary days (actually the Manor House School which Poe attended outside London for several years) through Eton and Oxford, chased all the way. The pursuer is an aspect of mind we have not glimpsed before—conscience. Separated from conscience, the narrator is the flagrant demon conning and tricking his fellows at every turn. The narrator's impulses are obviously created by Poe's desire for retaliation, not only against the laws of the universe or the conditions of life that forever separate him from the radiant dreamland, but against that conscienceless society he aspired to, which rejected him and which he fundamentally resents—the pretentious aristocratic folk of Richmond and Baltimore and perhaps those literary illuminati and editorial snobs in New England, New York and even Philadelphia. Here, in this singular story, Poe reveals almost openly a resentful longing for a society that exiles him.

"William Wilson" is no spontaneous overflow of broody resentment however, but a deliberately planned fusion of mood, narrative technique, incident and character. The author, having progressively withdrawn from his narrator in "Ligeia" and "House of Usher," achieves enough distance in "William Wilson" to produce the effect of satire. The narrator is a caricature of the cavalier youth Poe had pretended to be. He represents Poe's mature view of the aristocrat, willful, selfish, arrogant, pleasure-seeking and rotten to the core. He dreams of no beautiful dying woman and only the faintest echo of a pre-birth unity disturbs his perverse mind. The satirical effect stems from a critical view on nonrational or nonsensical postures seen from a condescendingly moral distance. Fortunately, he has restrained his wit, always a disaster for Poe. "William Wilson" reflects his years as literary reviewer, which foster critical habits. It also demonstrates his submission to earthly existence, at least to the extent that he struggles with social conscience rather than escape through terrorizing or beautific journeys. Yet the impishness that passes from "trivial wickedness" (*TS* 426-427) to the demonic enormity of an "unpardonable crime" (*TS* 426) is rendered with too much delight. Poe is simultaneously relishing and mocking the object of his satire. A conscience-less individual is anti-social and the author assumes the proper moral stance, but his posture is overwrought and thus insincere. The genuine impishness is the duplicity of the author himself.

William Wilson tells his story retrospectively, with regret yet without guilt for the way he has lived. "Have I not indeed been living in a dream?" Was his conduct therefore not fated? Was he not "victim to the horror and the mystery of the wildest of all sublunary visions?" (*TS* 427). The immediate reference is to the vision of his conscience as his double, which he murders in the "unpardonable crime." The questions he asks are in themselves evidence of lacking conscience. With his mind so removed from the concerns of social creatures, Poe's external conduct must have indeed been without conscience, as his biographers have indicated. Now, after eschewing society, he longs for societal rewards, "its honors" (*TS* 426), and "the sympathy . . . of my fellow men."

His fate is the result of both genetics and environmental conditioning. From "earliest infancy" he gave evidence of inheriting the "family character." He grew "self-willed, addicted to the wildest caprices, and a prey to the most ungovernable passions" (*TS* 427). But his parents, possessing the same traits, did little to check his "evil propensities." Unlike the Poe of the biographies, this perverse imp was lavished with goodies. Life was pleasant indeed until "a high and solid brick wall" of his school imprisoned him. His Sunday outings were for the purpose of attending church, where he observed duplicity in the pastor, whose "demurely benign" (*TS* 428) pulpit continence was the same visage that administered the "Draconian laws of the academy." The duplicity, however, is prophetic, his own. "Oh gigantic paradox, too utterly monstrous for solution" (*TS* 429) is his reaction to the pastor.

Given his imperious disposition, the narrator quite naturally becomes the leader of "our set" but his leadership is not accepted by one rather shadowy member who was born on the same day and entered school on the same day. This troublesome fellow competes in all ways with the narrator, refuses to believe his assertions, does not submit to his will and interferes "with my arbitrary dictation in any respect whatsoever" (*TS* 431). The rebellious double was a constant embarrassment and worse; Wilson feared the double was truly superior since he equalled his own feats with the slightest exertion. The double lacks qualities, however, that allow the narrator to imagine himself superior in the eyes of others. He lacks "the ambition which urged, and . . . passionate energy" (*TS* 432), the qualities that trap the soul in earthly affairs. The double also has the power to bring to the narrator's mind "dim visions of my earliest fancy — wild, confused and thronging memories of a time when memory herself was yet unborn." In some "infinitely remote" (*TS* 436) time the two were one, before the shaping of personality, in a pre-birth oneness. Although these elements of mind are vagrant strains from previous stories, they do imply that even the social conscience, devoid of ambition and passion, can achieve something of ethereal beauty among men on earth. Poe reinforces this idea by adding affection to the qualities of conscience; he is disturbed by his double's *"affectionateness* of manner" (*TS*432). The double is also given a low whisper in which he advises the narrator of proper conduct. The voice of conscience is the same as Psyche's in "Helen" and "Ulalume."

When Wilson recognizes the double as himself, he runs away from the academy. Conscience pursues and appears increasingly in spectral visitations as the narrator graduates from Eton to Oxford and deeper debauchery. His life style is enabled, the wastrel glibly admits, by "the uncalculating vanity of my parents furnishing me with an outfit and annual establishment, . . . to indulge at will in the luxury already so dear to my heart." This is one of the few moments in the story where Poe's satirical touch veers out of control. Perhaps to assure no mistaking of his intention, he adds, "to vie in profuseness of expenditure with the haughtiest heirs of the wealthiest earldoms in Great Britain." He is forced to leave the University not by John Allan's refusal to assume his gambling debts, but the spectre's sudden appearance just at the moment Wilson wiped clean the fortune of a *"parvenu"* (*TS* 440) at a gaming party. The spectre blows open the heavy doors, enters in a "rushing impetuousity" (*TS* 442), and exposes Wilson as a cheat. His admonishment is in that "never-to-be-forgotten *whisper*" that "thrilled to the very marrow of my bones" (*TS* 443). Even the return of conscience is perverse, as is the cheating since he did not need the money. His host, John Preston, the actual name of a fellow student at the University of Virginia, requests Wilson to leave his rooms and quit the University.

He flees now to the continent and conscience doggedly pursues, stepping "between me and my ambition" (*TS* 445). The double thwarts revenge in Paris, passionate love in Naples, avarice in Egypt. Ultimately, the narrator perceives with "deep awe" that "the elevated character, the majestic wisdom, the apparent omnipresence and omnipotence" (*TS* 446) of his pursuer is threatening his will. In desperation, he raises debauchery to madness. The last intervention of the spectral conscience is at a fancy ball where Wilson is attempting to seduce the wife of his noble host. This time the narrator faces his conscience directly. The contest is brief since the conscience is no more able to defend himself than the angels. Nevertheless, Wilson plunges his sword into his conscience with "brute ferocity" (*TS* 448). But the spectre still speaks. A mirror suddenly appears, and there he is again, informing the narrator that he too is now dead, at least *"to the World, to Heaven, and to Hope"* (*TS* 448).

IV

Such death removes all restraint; the imp is now free to pursue a literary career of perversity with abandon, as the subsequent tales of horrific thrill testify: "Pit and the Pendulum" (1843), "Tell-Tale Heart" (1843), "The Black Cat" (1843), "The Premature Burial" (1844), "The Imp of the Perverse" (1845). At the peak of perversity, the unrestrained imp turns about to counter these wild violations of rationality with a disdainful display of super ratiocination in the character of C. Auguste Dupin, supreme outwitter of mundane minds. He is not a narrator's dream (the narrator is reduced to mere foil in the three Dupin stories) but the author's direct projection of his most admirable self. Another version of Dupin is the exile of "The Gold-Bug" (1843), a man of intellect scorned by society. Absorbed in cracking the code of the universe, he is even closer to Poe's self image than Dupin. The code he does crack leads to a pot of pirate gold, which was not his motive. He solved the puzzle for neither social nor selfish benefit but to solve the puzzle, as William Wilson cheats at a gentlemanly game of cards. Outwitting and winning. Dupin solves crime puzzles for the same rewards. But it is not enough for Dupin to prove his superiority to himself; he must flaunt it. With a gush of drivel on physics, mathematics and the reasoning processes, amply punctuated with philosophical references and allusions, Dupin demonstrates Poe's wide reading and his way of organizing it. His genius is defined by contrast with the merely methodical reasoning powers of the Prefect of Police. As the narrator in "The Purloined Letter" (1845) realizes, Dupin's whole method is "an identification of the reasoner's intellect with that of his opponent" (*TS* 984). Since the opponent in that story, Minister D_____, also has the powers of imaginative reasoning equal to those of Dupin, the Prefect was doomed to failure, in spite of his meticulous and thorough method of investigation. The poor Prefect could only identify with the reasoning of the masses, who fulfilled rational expectation. But Dupin knows Minister D_____ is both poet and mathematican, if only by the telltale signs of musical instruments and books in his apartment. Thus the Minister reasons imaginatively, like Dupin.

Dupin's "lucid reason" usually goes to the limit where "shadow and doubt" exist. It is in the darkness that Dupin's powers work. Problems "requiring reflection," he tells the narrator, are examined "to better purpose in the dark" (*TS* 975). So he lives in the dark with the narrator, in the familiar setting of the poet, a "time-eaten and grotesque mansion, tottering to its fall" (*TS* 532),[28] where the windows are shutted against the light, and the smoke (opium?) oppresses "the atmosphere of the chamber" (*TS* 974). They busy their "souls in dreams" (*TS* 533),[29] emerging only at night to walk the deserted Parisian street.

Because Minister D_____ is a poet, the Prefect takes him to be "only one remove from a fool." But Dupin, who admits to writing "a certain doggerel myself" (*TS* 979), recognizes himself in D_____, an initial that could signify both Dupin and double. In this double, however, ambition has replaced the conscience murdered by William Wilson. Given the ambition of his double, Dupin would appear as worldly and unprincipled as Minister D_____. His driving force appears to be vengeance rather than ambition. Without a specific target, vengeance is wanton and thus perverse. Poe's vengeance (most explicitly demonstrated the following year in "The Cask of Amontillado") usually appears undirected. Dupin is given a specific motive off-handedly in the last paragraph; "D_____, at Vienna once, did me an evil turn, which I told him, quite good humoredly, that I should remember" (*TS* 933). The perversity is felt even in the cunning tone of this remark. It is integral with his deviltry through the story—the baiting of the Prefect, the withholding of his solution while the Prefect blunders on for at least a month, and most pernicious, allowing the intended victim to suffer unnecessarily all that time.

The poet who condescends to live in doltish society will pinch it in vengeance at every opportunity. He is not an Israfel but a Dupin. "The Raven" and "The Philosophy of Composition," which analyses its construction syllable for syllable, could be taken as examples of Dupin's literary effort. Both were published in 1845, the year of Dupin's last splash of super ratiocination in "The Purloined Letter." The mechanical rhythms and monotonous chimings of sound certainly indicate that Poe was telling it straight when he claimed "The Raven" was meticulously planned, that nothing was left to chance or appeared through serendipity. The prosody and its explanation would be expected of Dupin, garrulous beyond recall once the coil of feigned reticence is sprung. The precise structure—a progression of moods from a desperation to forget, through trepidation and nervous humor to hold off memory, and finally despair at the torturous return

of memory—is also expected of Dupin's rational imagination. It is the theme—rememberance and longing for beauty
in the form of a dead woman—that may appear alien to his
mind. But that too, "The Philosophy of Composition" tells
us, was coldly calculated for effect in the Dupin manner: "I
say to myself, in the first place; of the innumerable effects, or
impressions, of which the heart, the intellect, or (more
generally) the soul is susceptible, what one shall I, on the present occasion, select?" (*SW* 453). The answer: Beauty. Super
ratiocination finds the way. First, tone. Since sadness "excites
the sensitive soul to tears" (*SW* 456), melancholy is the most
legitimate of all poetical tones. Subject? The most melancholy is death. Specific? When is death most melancholy? When
allied to beauty. The death of a beautiful woman is therefore
most poetic. "The Philosophy of Composition," which
capitalizes upon the success of "The Raven," throws back into the teeth of his lionizers their romantic notions of poetic
inspiration. Most impish.

"The Raven" was written three years after Virginia had
ruptured a blood vessel while singing and Poe had suffered
"again—again—again & even once again . . . the agonies of
her death";[30] after bouts with alcohol the previous year; and
within months of his failure as part owner of the *Broadway
Journal*. Such earthly straights dampened his ability to dream
visions of universal beauty. The "Dream-Land" of 1844 was,
for instance, an extremely bad trip to the "ultimate dim
thule" (*P* 344) from which the battered Psyche has "wan-
dered home but newly" (*P* 345)—probably his return to the
Clemm household from a job-seeking visit in Washington
that ended in alcoholic degradation. Instead of sweet pangs
of longing for unearthly beauty, he suffered now the despairing pains of "neverending oscillation between hope &
despair." The invention of Dupin as self-image, was a way to
quench the memories. And "The Raven" was indeed the prod-

uct of that super ratiocinator, a cynical set of artistic decisions aimed to please the popular mind, perhaps even the Prefect's. The poem offers a neat and insincere narrative of a struggle to find "surcease from sorrow" (*P* 365), and fails. Two years later, upon Virginia's death, Poe attempts a genuine probing with Psyche, his soul, instead of Dupin. His approach to "Ulalume" (1847) contradicts the icy deliberations in "The Philosophy of Composition." In "Ulalume," he confronts the problem directly, discovers the basic conflict, and recognizes his ambiguous human condition.

Between these poems, Poe relished the rewards of his success, sinking further into the tarn of ambition and other corrupting passions. He titillated scandal mongers with his attentions to Mrs. Frances Sergeant Osgood, a wealthy poet-taster who could perhaps set up his *Stylus*, and at the same time carried on with Mrs. Whitman, also a wealthy prospect. Shrewdly he attacked Longfellow for plagiarism, a ploy that could raise his esteem even higher in the public eye. He played the gracious role of the poet at home, inviting guests for walks in the woods about his cottage at Fordham. Within lay his wraith-like wife, whose long years of dying tortured his nerves. There was also Maria Clemm, tending to both. Virginia died finally in 1847. By that time, apparently, the home had become "Horror haunted," as "The Raven" states, yet on a "desert land enchanted" (*P* 368). It is that dichotomous image of horror and enchantment so glibly inserted in the earlier poem that he probes in "Ulalume."

The narrator of "Ulalume" begins his story in a state of seeming tranquility after many years of never-ending memory. He loses it at once as he recalls a "lonesome October" night of some "immemorial year" in a place he visited yet did not know. It is "hard by the dim like of Auber" (Jean Francois Auber, whose print, "Le Lac de F'ees," was popular that year) and in the midst of the "ghoul-haunted woodland

of Weir" (*P* 416) (Robert Walter Weir, another romantic landscape artist). The reader, however, knows it well by now—the
black vortex of the whirlpool, the ultimate dim thule, the city
in the sea, Usher's house in the tarn. But the narrator has
changed. Instead of the usual terror, this place now arouses his
sensual passion. In this ghoul-haunted woodland, the narrator
remembers openly and directly, without terror, the experience
of sensual excitement. His heart, which had been "ashen and
sober" as the sky and "withering and sere" (*P* 418) as the
leaves, now becomes "volcanic" as he strolls back into the
night. Lavas roll in "scoriac rivers" (*P* 416) (hot volcanic
coals), groaning as they roll. Although the imp does not accompany the narrator, he hovers about the scene,
manipulating the stars and directing the narrator to the tomb
of Ulalume. The narrator is accompanied by Psyche, portrayed here as angel whose wings droop to the dust in the
presence of passion. From Psyche's enchanted point of view,
the flesh is horrid. Thus the imp has a new target for his
perverse temptations; his old home, the narrator himself.

As the narrator recalls that night, he and Psyche were
not mindful of the dark tarn of Auber nor the woodland of
Weir, until night began to fade into dawn. Then Astarte's diamond crescent appeared with its duplicate horn. The horn
arouses sexuality:

> . . . —She is warmer than Dian;
> She rolls through an ether of sighs—
> She revels in a region of sighs.

But the brewing conflict is not the classical battle between the
spirit and the flesh. Astarte's horn is duplicate. Her eyes are
luminous, as Ligeia's were, containing all that ethereal intelligence and beauty, yet the "love in her luminous eyes" is
the main attraction. This intimation of sexual love quite
naturally terrifies Psyche. "Sadly this star I mistrust . . . "

The narrator is able to pacify his Psyche and subdue the resurgence of memory by focusing on the ethereal branch of the horn, which gives "crystalline light." This is a guide that will "lead us aright" (*P* 417) since it flickers up to heaven. But this is seductive reasoning and proves false the moment it succeeds. No sooner has Psyche been "tempted . . . out of her gloom" and "conquered," than the tomb blocks their path. No qualities of the dead woman are described, only his anguish at the sudden return of memory, of entombing her a year ago that very night. "Ah, what demon hath tempted me here?" It is the imp, of course, enticing his sexual passion and then perversely torturing it with memory of the unattainable. The treacherous imp has inspired the narrator's passion to seduce Psyche and then seduced the narrator with knowledge: "Well I know, now, this dark tarn of Auber," he cries, and Psyche, his soul, shares the knowledge, "Said we, then—the two' then" (*P* 418). Fused, they have discovered that the ethereal vision of beauty formerly sought in the heavens of "Al Aaraaf" and "Israfel" is entombed within the earthly passions of the human heart, the ghoulish woodlands. The ghouls of the heart he discovers now, have been pitiful and merciful in barring and banning the memory by drawing up the spectre of "This sinfully scintillant planet" (*P* 419), desires of flesh void of ethereal beauty. It is this knowledge that casts the poet from the enchanting "limbo of lunary souls" (*P* 418), which he had imagined for himself in "Al Aaraaf," to the horrid "Hell of planetary souls" (*P* 419) at the end of "Ulalume."

The desire for a beautiful woman—sensuous and ethereal at once—was an awakening for Poe. The beauty he describes in "The Poetic Principle," his last aesthetic statement, is no longer of dead women: it is "in the grace of her step—in the lustre of her eye . . . rustling of her robes . . . above all the divine majesty—of her *love*" (*SW* 484), as in a

Dantean sonnet. Alive and alluring, but the beauty still derives from "chastened voluptuousness," and it is still un-possessible. Possession destroys beauty, just as the attainment of knowledge is destruction. Beauty itself is "pleasurable elevation, or excitement, *of the soul*" (*SW* 471). Always extravagant, Poe could not merely acknowledge a discovery but had to exploit it. He lived the last two years of his life in a whirlwind of literary women. In addition to Mrs. Osgood, his collection included Stella Lewis, Anne Lynch, Mary Grove Nichols, and the formidable Mrs. Sarah Helen Whitman. There was also Sarah Royster Shelton, now widowed, whom he had not been able to forget. And Annie Richmond whom he met in Lowell, Massachusetts while lecturing in 1848. On his way to Providence to propose to Mrs. Whitman, he stopped at Annie's. His riotous conduct that night was a major event in the dissolute Poe story cast abroad by his literary executor, Rufus Griswold. Apparently he had attempted to alleviate the strain: "I procured two ounces of laudanum."[31] But "the laudanum was rejected from the stomach." Annie had nursed him and had promised to visit any future deathbed. When Mrs. Whitman accepted and then rejected him, because he had been in a bar room, Poe wrote "For Annie."

> Thank heaven! the crisis—
>   The danger is past,
> And the lingering illness
>   Is over at last—
> And the fever called "Living"
>   Is conquered at last (*P* 456).

"Poor Eddie," as Maria Clemm referred to him, simply could not handle all the pleasurable elevation his awakening demanded:[32]

> The moaning and groaning
> The sighing and sobbing.

A few stanzas on, the poem is into a reverie of exertionless desire. He lies happily in bed, bathed in succor:

> She tenderly kissed me,
>   She fondly caressed,
> And then I fell gently
>   To sleep on her breast —
> Deeply to sleep
>   From the heaven of her breast.

This "queen of the angels," he dreams on, covers him and shields him from harm. Quite clearly he wants home again, where one can dream that way without effort, confusion, or responsibility, and in safety.

On his last, fateful trip, still lecturing on "The Poetic Principle," seeking support for *The Stylus*, successfully engaging himself to Sarah Royster Shelton and suffering surges of love for Annie, he wrote Marie Clemm,

> The very instant you get this come to me. The joy of seeing you will almost compensate for our sorrows. We can but die together. It is no use to reason with me *now*; I must die. I have no desire to live since I have done "Eureka." I could accomplish nothing more . . . we must die together. You have been all in all to me, darling, ever beloved mother, and dearest, truest friend.[33]

He was returning to her, to home, when they found him on election night at Ryan's Fourth Ward polls in Baltimore. Poe died a few days later of alcoholic poisoning, "brain fever," or the bruises from an enraged husband.

Eureka, written the year before his death, was his grand resolution; but it did not resolve the enduring antagonism of his life, between earthly passion and beautific longings. Instead, it broke the tension. Poe had come apart. The "truly passionate self" wallowed in sensuous dreams of earthly women who were deliberately kept unattainable to prolong the excitement. The Dupin mentality, on the other hand, was passionless, pure. In leaps of super ratiocination it now synthesized the fundamental process of God's will, twisting and torturing almost every scientific bit of information Poe had acquired. *Eureka* is the revelation of the beauty intimated in "Israfel," the "supernal Beauty" (*SW* 470) that humans aspire to but cannot attain, and it is achieved after all, without women, dead or alive.

Universal unity is the subject of *Eureka*, in spite of its author's divided state of mind. Here the beautiful and the true are fused, according to dominant nineteenth century thought, but also space and duration are one as well as matter and energy, or material and spirit. All things that man apprehends and those he cannot apprehend in this universe are returning to unity in one great glob of God, which is perfect beauty, beyond perception. Although the process of return is God's will, it approximates the current push-pull theory of universal creation.[34]

Eureka works as a final rationalization for the author's conduct of life and for his art. Far better to be an exile from a universal Godhead than from insensitive Virginia aristocracy, from a vulgar democratic mass in ambitious pursuit of practical and passionate ends, or even from an elegantly decaying European past. Those early dreams of the poet reaching for the lute strings were not compensation, not fancies to escape the never-ending memory of the exile at home, but were blurred visions of the true and beautiful lost home, the imperceptible Godhead from which all men are exiled. And those beautiful dead women are worshipped not in fear of social and sexual incompetence but as vessels to transport the spirit home again. And the impulses to destruction were not vengefully motivated attacks on the society that rejected him, but surges of the imagination to transcend into the singular being that is the universe.

What he finds in *Eureka* is the answer to all those

nameless fears too terrible to mention. But the finding of it snaps the binds with earthly existence. He calls *Eureka* a poem, but it is totally abstract, philosophical, disembodied, while Poe himself had run amuck, totally embodied. All is found, all is nothing. In his final year of wandering, he could produce only the mundane fancy of "Landor's Cottage," a measured description of a vision with Annie standing in the doorway of the little house at Fordham; the thoughtless sounds of "Annabelle Lee"; or the meaningless chiming of "Bells." He died the image of the outcast that disturbs the narrator of "The Man of the Crowd." Perhaps he was home at last in his dreams and philosophy but still an exile among men.

Chapter 4

DICKINSON:
An Evanescent House of Usher

While Poe saw himself as an outcast from an American aristocracy[1] and his most successful characters were placed in European homes, Emily Dickinson had little awareness of either. Her home was in Amherst, Massachusetts and she seldom left it. Yet she did not belong there, among the college town gentry and their ladies. At home she was far more isolated than Poe and suffered longings that seem more genuine. In her mature years, Emily Dickinson was apparently the character of Amherst. Only five feet, she had grown corpulent and so referred to herself in late letters as "Jumbo," not quite the graceful wraith flitting between the bushes in white diaphanous gown, but she did wear the white steadily, at least since 1862, and hide she did from public view.

"Evanescence" was among her favorite words. Like the fading presences of flowers and birds, she allowed others only glimpses of herself. Amherst society, according to Mabel Loomis Todd, referred to her as the myth and the belle. In 1881, when Dickinson was fifty, Mrs. Todd wrote, "She . . . seems to be the climax of all the family oddity. She has not been outside of her own house in fifteen years, except once to see a new church when she crept out at night, and viewed it by moonlight."[2] On one occasion she was reported at her window lowering candy by string to a collection of children. The town attributed her reclusiveness, Mable Todd claimed, to a broken heart. Mrs. Todd, wife of an astronomy professor at the college, was a promoter of the arts with "a perfect passion all the time to write."[3] Dickinson managed to evade all her efforts to meet. Instead of an invitation to welcome the newcomer, the poet sent her a "tardy devotion," a bouquet from her garden with the explanation, "I have been unable to seek my flowers, having harmed my foot."[4] What an odd way to write! Like an alien transplanted in a different idiom. Mabel Todd managed an invitation to the house from the more outgoing sister, Lavinia. It was to play the piano for their invalid mother confined upstairs. Dickinson also listened, but also unseen. She sent a note into the parlor, a poem. "Elysium" was in "the very nearest room."[5] Mrs. Todd, who was to become Dickinson's first editor and with Thomas Wentworth Higginson, introduce her poetry to the world, did not understand that the Dickinson mode of social intercourse was written correspondence in which she recreated society to suit herself. After repeated failures to see her, Mabel Todd speculated that the recluse "became disgusted with society" and declared "she would leave it when she was quite young."[6] As supporting evidence, she offered names in the line of the broken heart hypothesis. Candidates included family friends, Dr. Josiah Holland, who had quit medicine for poetry and journalism, and Samuel Bowles, editor of the *Springfield Daily Republican*. Apparently such speculation had become an Amherst pastime.

Her correspondence and biographies indicate that Dickinson's choice was not against leaving but against entering adult society. In her circumscribed existence, she probed, expanded, and experienced as fully as possible the universe of her youth as the other inhabitants gradually withdrew. "I love so to be a child" (*L* 104) she wrote to former schoolmate, Abiah Root, at age twenty. In other letters, she signed herself with a little girl dimunitive, "Emilie," an affectation she maintained until age thirty-one. In a letter to her closest friend, Susan Gilbert, she revealed the exclusive alliances of girlhood, "but for our sakes, dear Susie, who please ourselves with the fancy that we are the only poets, and everyone else is prose" (*L* 144). A few years later, when Susan was about to become her sister-in-law, she was still able to write:

> Today is far from Childhood —
> But up and down the hills
> I held her hand the tighter —
> Which shortened all the miles — (*P* 14).

The earlier letter to Abiah Root presents a self-image of the poetic heroine resisting the establishment, "You are growing wiser than I am, and nipping in the bud fancies which I let blossom . . . the shore is safer, Abiah, but I love to buffet the sea." The occasion was her family's gentle pressure to join their church. Her friend Susan was more disturbed by her continuing refusal than the family. Emily took Susan's attitude as betrayal of their girlish pact to be poets and together stand against the prosaic horde: "Sue — you can stay or go — there is but one alternative" and she lived by it, "the lingering emblem of the Heaven I once dreamed" (*L* 305-6). The declaration could have been uttered by Poe, ensconced in clay and reaching for heaven.

Susan's marriage to her brother Austin was a severe blow to Emily's girlhood, but not enough to shake her out of it. Though Susan lived next door now, the distance that separated them was between the girl and the woman. In 1862, six years after the marriage, in the midst of the Civil War, which both seemed to ignore, and at her poetic peak, Dickinson still felt that her friend had dropped her. "Our Futures different lay," she wrote, and proceeded to contrast her sister-in-law's fulfillments with her own emptiness. Susan's future faced the sun, "Your Garden led the Bloom," while her own "In Frost — was sown" (*P* 631).

Dickinson's biographer and editor, Thomas H. Johnson, claims that she had not matured as a woman until she was thirty. But her correspondence and poetic fantasies reveal appropriate sexual stirrings well before that age. Perhaps Johnson has in mind the confused girlish attraction to her own sex as well as the other in which love and friendship are hardly distinguishable:

> Baffled for just a day or two —
> Embarrassed — not afraid —
> Encounter in my garden
> An unexpected Maid.
>
> She beckons, and the woods start —
> She nods, all begin —
> Surely, such a country
> I was never in! (*P* 17).

In another poem "There is a morn by men unseen / Whose maids upon remoter green" enjoy a holiday of "dance and game / And gambol I may never name" (*P* 24). Her valentines, however, were aimed at young men. If she failed to mature it was not as woman but as a person refusing the banalities and corruptions of established society: "the world is sleeping in ignorance and error," proclaims her first publication, a prose valentine in the Amherst Academy journal of 1850. With the fervor of the idealistically ambitious, it soars on: "and we must be cocking crow." (Not until four years later did Thoreau speak of awakening his neighbors to the dawning day.) Against this stirring appeal to society, she protested that existence was so great a gift, it was inconceivable for anyone to travel or to see visitors. Dickinson was never able to resolve this ambivalence.

I

Her correspondence leaves little doubt that she needed visitors. It also indicates a persistence, however masked in modesty, of youth's ambition for renown in the society she rejected. Whether or not she really believed that "Publication—is the auction of the mind of man" (*P* 709), Dickinson did take advantage of opportunities available to her, publishing four times in the *Springfield Daily Republican* (edited by family friend, Samuel Bowles), once in *The Round Table* (1864), and once, after a great deal of protesting, of wanting really to be wanted, in *A Masque of Poets*, an anthology compiled with the aid of Helen Hunt Jackson in 1878. That poem was appropriately titled, "Success." Although she declared "Fame is a fickle food" that "Men eat of . . . and die" (*P* 1659), she boasted to her brother Austin and Susan that she would yet make them proud.

In 1862, when *The Atlantic Monthly* printed Higginson's advice on how to write for publication, she responded with four poems and coy suggestion: she merely wanted to know if her poems "breathed" and were "alive" (*L*-403). Higginson rejected them but encouraged her to continue for private satisfaction. The rejection may have been take as a challenge: her productivity increased from 80 poems the previous year to 366 that year. (She had also fibbed to Higginson that she had written only one or two poems at the time when actually she had composed some 300). When Samuel Bowles published "A Narrow Fellow in the Grass" in 1866, he altered the punctuation, and she used the error as excuse to bring the publication to Higginson's attention, "Lest you meet my Snake and suppose I deceive, it was robbed of me—" (*L* 450). Such shrewdness was not beyond the shy Emily. On another occasion, she admitted having to be shrewd with God. In her later years she sent poems frequently to Helen Hunt Jackson, whose novels *A Century of Dishonor* (1881) and *Ramona* (1883) had achieved the fame Dickinson appeared to shun. Once she had asked the famous novelist, also born in Amherst, "How could you print a piece of your soul?" It was Mrs. Jackson, not Miss Dickinson, who discontinued the correspondence. As late as 1882, one of her poems was rejected by Thomas Niles, who later told Higginson, "it would be unwise to perpetuate Miss Dickinson's poems" for they "are generally devoid of true poetical qualities."[8] Two years before her death (1886), she wrote a young sculptor, "Success is dust, but an aim forever touched with dew" (*L* 822).

While she did not actively pursue the ambition her poems renounced, as Poe did, she never quite relinquished hope: "If fame belonged to me, I could not escape her" (*L* 408), she told Higginson. But the cost was too great. She was unwilling to compromise her cherished notion of the naked self in order to fulfill her desire. Late in life she confessed to a sense of nakedness before others. Social contact was exposure. Poetry and correspondence provided a surrogate society occasionally touched by visits of the real thing. On his famous visit of 1870, after eight years of correspondence, Higginson found her conversation, "wholly without watching its effect on her hearer."[9] She uttered words "in a soft frightened breathless, childlike voice," and talked "continuously—and differentially," mostly about the ecstacy of living. Yet she admitted to being frightened of strangers, "I . . . hardly know what I say" (*L* 473) meaning that she had no small talk. She spoke in aphorisms, and so intensely that she "drained my nerve power . . . I am glad not to live near her" (*L* 476). Perhaps it was this intensity that attracted him to her poetry, although the psalm-like rhythms were crude, the biblical references only private metaphors, and the art informed by few authors—the Brontes, George Eliot, and Mrs. Browning. "Of Poe, I know too little to think" (*L* 649), she told him. Whitman "was disgraceful" (*L* 404). Higginson suspected craziness as well as genius in this grown child. "I'm afraid," he wrote to his sister after his second (and last) visit, "Mary's [his wife] remark, 'Oh why do the insane so cling to you?' still holds."[10]

Her conversation was hardly distinguishable from her

correspondence. Frequently it turned homeward. "Can you tell me what home is?" she suddenly asked, or asserted with equal suddenness, "I never had a mother, that is, one to whom you hurry when you are in trouble" (*L* 475). Her mother did not care for thought, and her father was too busy although he gratified her desire for books which he imagined might "joggle the Mind" (*404*). The year before his death she wrote to Mrs. Holland that she was Lavinia's father and mother "and I have no Parents but her" (*L* 508). Yet she maintained a lifelong addiction to home. "I'm afraid I'm growing *selfish* in my dear home," she responded at age twenty-one to Jane Humphrey's invitation, "but I do love it so, and when some pleasant friend invites me to pass a week with her, I look at my father and mother and Vinnie, and all my friends and I say no-no, can't leave them, what if they die when I'm gone" (*L* 192). To another invitation for a brief outing, she responded, "I do not go out at all, lest father will come and miss me" (*L* 336).

Father may have been somewhat responsible for her addiction to home. Apparently he was possessive of all his children: he built Austin a house on the property as a wedding present. Edward Dickinson was a natural leader—lawyer, college administrator, congressman—fully involved and respected in the society. But he was remote. In the comings and goings of glittering guests Emily felt an outsider in her own home, beloved as it was. She certainly felt little unity in heart and soul with a family that addressed "an Eclipse, every morning—whom they call their 'Father' " (*L* 404), as she told Higginson. Her father was more awesome. "I always ran Home to Awe when a child, if anything befell me. /He was an awful Mother, but I like him better than none" (*L* 517-18).

She endured a year away from home at Holyoke Academy where schoolmates found her rather dramatic and hyperbolic. Although her way of saying things was unnatural for a seventeen-year-old girl, she was as concerned as the other young ladies with appearance. According to Austin, her homeliness played a significant role in her seclusiveness. Dickinson took a photo at Holyoke, put it away, and never took another. Earlier she had joked that someday she would grow into the belle of Amherst, but now she accepted her "gypsy face."[11] Anticipating valentines that year, she wrote Austin, "Every night I have looked and yet in vain for one of Cupid's messengers."

At home the following year she joined the Amherst Sewing Society. Here her opinions, especially of authors and books, were appreciated. And here she met Susan Gilbert, attractive, independent, graceful, and captivating conversationalist, most everything Dickinson had dreamed of being. Although they pledged themselves to poetic lives, social life was abundant — parties, candy-pulls, dances, sleigh rides, musical evenings and lectures. A great event was the publication of Charlotte Bronte's *Jane Eyre*. Jane also had a plain face and also desired to be attractive. She was Dickinson's exact age. Jane too longed for a power of vision, not for insights to nature, but for the busy world she had never seen.[12] Jane complained of women's lot in life, the drudgery of housework. Emily Dickinson began to complain also — of the narrowness of her Amherst neighbors who lacked vision and did what was expected of them. To demonstrate her new consciousness, she quit the Amherst Sewing Society.

By then she had already suffered her first loss, James Kimball, a ministry student (the calling of most men who attracted her) she had met at Society functions. He graduated and moved on. She wrote to him repeatedly for a year before realizing there would be no response. Wrapped in her own consciousness, she was prone to misjudge the intentions and motives of others, but she evidently desired rewards from the world of others just as Poe had desired them. Soon after Kimball, she lost Benjamin Newton, a 28-year old law student in her father's office, whom she called her "grave Preceptor (*L* 282) . . . who taught me Immortality" (*L* 404). He was the first of several preceptors who were mostly older men with mature minds that could sense the energies and rhythms of hers. She seldom took their advice but used them for the outer world's approbation. Except for the last and most enduring, Thomas Wentworth Higginson, she also fancied them as distant lovers.

Newton quit Amherst in 1849. He died three years later, but Dickinson had already lost another preceptor. Leonard Humphrey was only twenty-four, yet mature enough to have been a principal of the academy and now a tutor at the college. She referred to him as master. He died within the year and Dickinson wrote to her friend, Abiah Root, "How *precious* the grave, Abiah, when aught that we love is laid there" (*L* 103). The posture appears no less exaggerated than Poe's.

A fourth preceptor was found at home in the stream of her father's visitors — relatives, associates, or befriended young students. Apparently she had to take Henry Emmons more seriously than the others. Her brother Austin expressed approval of him as a suitor and so did her father. In a happy letter to Susan Gilbert in 1852, Emily foresaw her marriage and its erotic pleasure: "Those unions . . . can fill the heart, and make it gang wildly beating . . . we shall not run away from it, but lie still and be very happy!" (*L* 209). Lavinia noted to brother Austin that "Emily's hair was cut off and she was very pretty." But Emmons too graduated, and went off seeking someone else in another town.

Consolation this time was a project that involved the family. Lavinia had also been rebuffed by a Joseph Lyman and the sisters had each other's grief as comfort. They also

consulted the family minister. Finally their father took them
to Washington for a three week excursion while he attended
Congress. On the way home, they stopped to visit relatives in
Philadelphia and there Dickinson met the Reverend Charles
Wadsworth. Always living in paradox, her most intimate
friendships were most elusive. She saw Wadsworth three
times in her life, yet he became her emblematic lover who
provided the aim for longing she apparently required. At last
she could separate herself from those "Eastern Exiles" who
are "lonesome for they know not What—" (*P* 262). No more
was she "Adrift! A little boat Adrift!" At the moment
Wadsworth entered her life, she was "o'erspent with gales—."
Now she "Retrimmed its masts—redecked its sails—/And
shot—exultant on!" (*P* 30). But she had lost fancied lovers
before and feared it would happen again. As early as 1858,
her persona shakes a fist at God, envisioning repetitions of
His cruelty:

> I never lost as much but twice,
> And that was in the sod.
> Twice have I stood a beggar
> Before the door of God!
>
> Angels—twice descending
> Reimbursed my store
> Burgler! Banker-Father!
> I am poor once more! (*P* 49)

Who was this impertinent God, to make such an abject sup-
plicant of her? He was the God of the worshippers in the
church, the Amherst fathers who burgled and banked from
Sabbath to Sabbath just as He did, but His burgling was of
their real lives and His banking for judgment day. Her
prediction of God's burgling once more was fulfilled in 1861
when the Reverend Wadsworth announced that he had accepted a call to Calvary Church in San Francisco, and

although she had already suffered the loss in years of anticipation, her reaction now was that of a widow, as confided in these lines to Sam Bowles in 1862:

> Title divine—is mine!
> The Wife—without the Sign!
> Acute Degree—conferred on me—
> Empress of Calvary!
> Royal—all but the Crown!
> Betrothed—without the swoon
> God sends us Women—
> When you—hold—Garnet to Garnet—
> Gold-to-Gold—
> Born—Bridalled—Shrouded—
> In a Day—(*P* 1072)

The persona is here crowning herself Empress in the realm of her own consciousness. There is little evidence that Wadsworth, a stable family man, ever encouraged her, yet she imagines herself suffering the same fate as other women leading conjugal lives. Her respect and desire for the state of marriage is certainly revealed in its lofty identification with "Title divine." The metaphor of her betrothed's sacrifice at Calvary is not clear. But it is that event—the sense of his loss—which grants the Empress wife justification to exile society from her kingdom:

> The Soul selects her own Society—
> Then—shuts the Door—(*P* 303)

It is a majestic act that elevates her from the condition of "beggar/Before the door of God" (*P* 49) to the sovereign of her own domain. Sam Bowles recognized the psychological trick when he sent her an ironical greeting through Austin that year, to the "Queen recluse." And the queen also recognized her assumptions:

> The Day that I was crowned
> Was like the other Days—

Until the Coronation came —
And then — 'twas Otherwise — (*P* 356)

The difference between "other Days" and "Otherwise" was defined in reviewing her break with Susan Gilbert years before, seen now from a loftier position, " . . . one Summer, we were Queens — / But You — were crowned in June" (*P* 631). Emily Dickinson's crowning is in the fall, the season of evanescence, life's fading and dying.

II

With the departure of Wadsworth, the Empress donned her white mourning dress, her "white election" (*P* 528), and withdrew completely to home and garden, her kingdom in the shadow of Susan's. It contained all she required, except love, and this she came to crave. "I had rather *be* loved than be called a king in earth, or a lord in Heaven" (*L* 330), she confided to Mrs. Holland. So she invented it, as Poe invented lovers of marble passion, just beyond reach, "a lover/ Teacher to be longed for," eternally anticipated and thus exciting: "What would I give to see his face?" (*P* 247) . . . "Wild nights, Wild nights" (*P* 249). A few years later she came to understand that for her, "Expectation — is Content-ment — /Gain — Satiety — " (*P* 807), which explains why "I tend my flowers for thee — /Bright Absentee!" (*P* 339).

During the first year of his absence, 1862, she wrote at least a poem a day and invited Higginson to be her new preceptor, her safest friend.[13] When Wadsworth returned to Philadelphia in 1869, there was no reunion. Instead she wrote Higginson, "You are not aware that you saved my life." (*L* 460). Within her imaginary domain, she dressed as she wished, behaved as she wished and was cherished, at least by Lavinia, as she wished. (After her death, when Mabel Todd procrastinated over editing the poems, Lavinia cried out, "But they are Emily's poems!")[14] To the external world, she appeared an exile at home, exiled by immaturity, by fears of adult compromises. It was the refusal to compromise, her willfulness, that allowed her to play the game, to "close the valves of her attention — / Like Stone — " (*P* 303) to the external world.

Doors are shut frequently in Emily Dickinson's poetry, but not as tightly as "Stone" suggests. The queen sits regally in her lonely chamber, listening and hoping for intrusion:

> And marked by Girlhood's name —
> So Visitors may know
> Which Door is mine — so not mistake —
> And try another Key — (*P* 470)

The visitor most fervently desired was the lover whom she had lost without ever having:

> Except the Heaven had come so near —
> So seemed to choose My Door —
> The Distance would not haunt me so —
> I had not hoped — before — (*P* 472)

At times she is tempted to open the door herself, to return from her kingdom in exile to the communal life of her childhood which she imagines now as businesslike triviality:

> I Years had been from Home
> And now before the Door
> I dared not enter, lest a Face
> I never saw before
>
> Stare solid into mine
> And ask my Business there —
> "My business be a Life I left
> Was such remaining there?" (*P* 609)

The metaphors of her sovereignty are even more profuse than doors. Her kingdom is an "Undiscovered Continent" (*P* 832) and "indestructible estate" (*P* 1351), and

The Soul unto itself

    *   *   *

Secure against its own —
No treason it can fear —
Itself — its Sovereign — of itself
The Soul should stand in Awe — (*P* 683).

Awe is no longer confined to her father, but elicited by the sovereign soul which shares the mystery of nature. In its seclusion the soul can select anyone for its society, including other sovereigns, such as death:

Unmoved — she notes the Chariots — pausing —
At her low Gate —
Unmoved — an Emperor be kneeling
Upon her Mat — (*P* 303)

The fundamental color of her kingdom is purple, "The Color of a Queen, is this — " (*P* 776). It blends with amber at the setting of the sun, and with beryl at noon. This regal assumption was Dickinson's counterpart to Poe's aristocratic posture toward the society they both rejected and wanted.

Dickinson had deliberately and willfully reversed the process of exile. Declaring, "I am no longer their's," the queen cast them out. Society was exiled. It was too false for her kingdom. "They talk of Hallowed things, aloud," she told Higginson, "and embarrass my Dog" (*L* 415). She was subtle as acid in etching the women of Amherst society:

What Soft — Cherubic Creatures —
These Gentlewomen are —
One would as soon assault a Plush —
Or violate a Star —

Such Dimity Convictions —
A Horror so refined (*P* 401)

Henceforth, "My friends are my 'estate,' " she wrote to Samuel Bowles (*L* 338). The superficiality required for communal harmony prohibited the intensity required for the communion of the soul, for tasting "a liquor never brewed — ":

> Inebriate of Air — am I —
> And Debauchee of Dew —

The devout brewer in society could never "Yield such an Alcohol!" (*P* 214); he was a citizen, cast beyond the pale of her kingdom, "A Counterfeit — a Plated person — / . . . . what an Exile — is a Lie" (*P* 1453).

The worst lie of "Those fair — fictitious People — " was their easy and unquestioning assumption of immortality as prescribed, trusting " — in places perfecter / . . . . Beyond our faint Conjecture — / Our dizzy estimate — ," thus considering themselves "Blesseder" and "Esteeming us — as Exile — " (*P* 499). Not merely aware of her psychological turnabout, she insists upon it. The exiles include not only the devout brewers and business people who run society but clergy, mystics, makers of cosmologies, metaphysical dwellers and all far-sighted seers popular at the time. They were lumped together as "Eastern Exiles," which included her former unawakened self:

> The lonesome for they knew not What —
> The Eastern Exiles — be —
> Who strayed beyond the Amber line
> Some madder Holiday —
>
> * * *
>
> The Blessed Ether — taught them —
> Some Transatlantic Morn —
> When Heaven — was too common — to miss —
> Too sure — to dote upon! (*P* 262)

Within her own estate Dickinson's soul retains the unsoiled condition of Poe's "Israfel," but sings beyond no distant star. Heaven is here and now, "too common — to miss — ."

Its dimensions were those of her "Circumference," the reach of her consciousness. If it excluded the heavens of religious establishments, it also banned the repetitive trivialities of life's daily business, the earthiness that encumbered Poe's psyche. "I don't know anything more about the affairs in the world," she announced, "than if I was in a trance." (*L* 49). Even the causes blazing in the banners of the great War were only predictive banality to her, no more than the repetition of news in the penny post was to Thoreau:

> Color — Caste — Domination —
> These — are Time's Affair —
> Death's diviner — Classifying
> Does not know they are — (*P* 970)

Life within the chosen estate was intense, something like the inner life Thoreau endured for a short spell at Walden Pond. Dickinson dramatized the ordinary activity in her garden and home (her father would not eat bread baked by others) into momentous events and her acquaintances into friends and lovers. The anticipation of loss dramatized arrivals; the consciousness of death and the question of immortality breathed excitement into every living thing, the comings and goings, but especially the goings:

> I'd rather recollect a setting
> Than own a rising sun
>   *   *   *
> Because in going is a Drama
> Staying cannot confer (*P* 1349)

Evanescence was the key to her own behavior. After she assumed the role of widow, she faded even from her parlor upon the arrival of guests, including those her own letters had invited. She suffered stagefright but was a prima donna nevertheless, appearing for purposes of dramatic disappearance. "To escape enchantment," she once explained to Higginson, "one must always flee." (*L* 454). Fulfillment was self-destroying, unequal to anticipation:

Go not too near a House of Rose —
* * *
Nor try to tie the Butterfly,
Nor climb the Bars of Ecstasy,
In insecurity to lie
Is Joy's insuring quality (*P* 1434).

Her consciousness was a proscenium for "Drama's Vitallest Expression . . . the Common Day" (*P* 741). The morning anticipated noon, which was the moment of perfection, paradise achieved, but it faded into evening, which anticipated death. Transience, time, permitted only instances of inebriating joy, and even in the perfect instant, nature's "trembling emblems" intimated loss. To Dickinson, therefore, "Emblem is immeasurable — that is why it is better than Fulfillment" (*L* 773). The promise of the emblem is the thrill of suspense that the realized meaning attenuates. Anticipation is the soul of drama:

The Pendulum begins to count —
Like little Scholars — loud —
The steps grow thicker — in the Hall —
The Heart begins to crowd — (*P* 635).

And so exciting it is almost unbearable:

What fortitude the Soul contains,
That it can so endure
The accent of the coming Foot —
The opening of the Door — (*P* 1760).

On the other side of the door was Awe, the "Distance / Between Ourselves and the Dead" (*P* 949), the distance Poe had journeyed seeking his beatific heaven beyond space and time. For Dickinson, Awe was the mystery of existence that emanated from nature. Where Poe sought exciting knowledge whose attainment was destruction, Dickinson sought Awe, not to find it — that would be satiety of love and death, annihilation — but to anticipate its touch upon the soul, to long for the unattainable, as exiles are wont to do. Her journey was the "going / Of an inland soul to sea" (*P* 76). Not the self, as in Poe, her sea was all of creation that consciousness could circumscribe: flora, fauna, friends, and family. And more. Like Thoreau in his chinky house at Walden, Dickinson could see from her window "the sunrise on the Alps." Her estate included whatever her mind encompassed:

> Many cross the Rhine
> In this cup of mine (*P* 124).

It is created by her perceptions of the awesome in recognizable experience, the appearance of a bloom, the flight of a bird.

Platonically, she saw individual presences and events as emblems of a single essence, the ideal: "One bird, one cage, one flight; one song in those far woods."[15] Human beings were "trembling Emblems" (*L* 594) of love. Among her earliest poems we find, "Oh the earth was made for lovers," by which she means communion of these trembling emblems, no only with each other, but as in "the bee doth court the flower" (*P* 1), with nature. Her estate is made into heaven on earth by such momentous communions, her transports, exultations and inebriations. The communions occur through emanations of her consciousness into nature, transforming it into a garden, a paradise. Whether the body and soul inhabit heaven or heaven inhabits them cannot be discerned. Nor does it matter. "One is a dainty sum," and is only achieved at that heightened moment when the consciousness is spread to its circumference.

Mostly consciousness lives in the "center" of ordinary existence, aware and reflecting; heaven is too intense, an experience too rich to endure. And even at those rare extended moments, the consciousness does not encompass the universe. A circumference, after all, is a closure within a larger field. The emblems within that field enable "inferences" of the universe beyond:

> Invisible, as Music—
> But positive, as Sound—
> It beckons, and it baffles—

The universe is a riddle that utterly captivates:

> To guess it, puzzles scholars—
> To gain it, Men have borne
> Contempt of Generations
> And Crucifixions, shown—

It is most certainly unavailable by faith, which drugs instead of awakens the consciousness:

> Much Gesture, from the Pulpit—
> Strong Hallelujahs roll—
> Narcotics cannot still the Tooth
> That nibbles at the soul—(*P* 501).

Awakened, spread to its circumference, the consciousness does not solve the riddle, but experiences it, touches, feels the universe beyond the human reference point. It touches Awe. She celebrates this touching as "Circumference thou Bride of Awe" (*P* 1620). Her consciousness is the daisy touched by the sun, or the sea by the moon.

III

The exultation from the touching of Awe is no simple celebration of deity. It is closer to Poe's terrifying excitement in pursuit of beauty than to the joys of worshipping the paranoid God of Christianity:

> No vacillating God
> Ignited this Abode
> To put it out—(*P* 1599)

Awe is not cruel, not demeaning, but may have her father's "awful integrity," that "pure and terrible" heart, she described to Higginson (*L* 528). Awe is "so appalling—it exhilarates" (*P* 281). And at the same time, this "nearness to Tremendousness—/An Agony procures" (*P* 963). Awe "shames the petty differences between Happiness and Misery." In the riddle of Awe, Emily beholds her own impending doom, the urgent and unanswerable question of immortality.

The obvious answers were as burdensome as Poe's earthliness. For her as for Poe:

> Impossibility, like Wine
> Exhilarates the man
> Who tastes it; Possibility
> Is flavorless— . . . (*P* 838)

The obvious answers were Aweless, as fictitious as the plated people in society. No agony, no despair, not true. "I like a look of Agony,/Because I know it's true—" (*P* 241). That is the condition of the awakened consciousness, painfully and fearfully alive before the agitating riddle of death:

> How have I peace
> Except by subjugating
> Consciousness? (*P* 642)

To touch Awe was to perceive the terror of her own existence in the "momentousness" of creation. The terror, however, is seldom rendered, as in Poe's elaborate night journeys. Dickinson's terror is usually announced in rational, direct metaphors:

> One need not be a Chamber—to be Haunted—
> One need not be a House—
> The Brain has Corridors—surpassing
> Material Place—(*P* 670)

She has no need for the strange; there is terror enough in the familiar creatures of her own garden. And when she does choose to render rather than reflect, she succeeds more often in the mode of startling metaphor than story:

> Several of Nature's People
> I know, and they know me —
> I feel for them a transport
> Of cordiality —
>
> But never met this Fellow
> Attended, or alone
> Without a tighter breathing
> And Zero at the Bone — (*P* 986)

Nature is also "a Haunted House" as she told Higginson in 1876. But art plays at it, "a House that tries to be haunted" (*L* 554). The house of nature provides all the aesthetics she needs:

> A fairer House than Prose —
> More numerous of Windows —
> Superior — for Doors —
>
> * * *
>
> Of Visitors — the fairest —
> For Occupation — This —
> The spreading wide my narrow Hands
> To gather Paradise — (*P* 657)

To live in paradise is to live in beauty,

> For Beauty is Infinity —
> And power to be finite ceased
> Before Identity was leased. (*P* 1474)

Although Emily Dickinson refused definitions as she did doctrine ("The Definition of Beauty is/That Definition is none —" (*P* 288)), she evidently shares with Poe the Wordsworthian intimations of immortality, inklings of a preexistence for the unidentified soul not yet separated from infinity which is pure beauty. Refusing definition and thus the consistency of reason and system, she cannot be held responsible for a leap into disembodied existences elsewhere, in spite of "The Fact that Earth is Heaven — /Whether

Heaven is Heaven or not" (*P* 1408). As infinity, beauty must also be identified with truth. With the introduction of truth, however, Emily's consciousness more closely resembles Poe's, even in its necrophilia.

> I died for Beauty—but was scarce
> Adjusted in the Tomb
> When One who died for Truth, was lain
> In an adjoining Room—
>
> He questioned softly "Why I failed"?
> "For Beauty," I replied—
> "And I—for Truth—Themself are One—
> We Brethern, are," He said—
>
> And so, as Kinsman, met a Night—
> We talked between the Rooms—
> Until the Moss had reached our lips—
> And covered up—our names—(*P* 449)

Her longing for love carried beyond life, not to heavenly union but to the grave with the lover's corpse. Since she could barely face a lover live, she would take him dead:

> If I may have it, when it's dead,
> I'll be contented—so—
> If just as soon as Breath is out
> It shall belong to me—
>
> Until they lock it in the Grave,
> 'Tis Bliss I cannot weight—(*P* 577)

In a later poem (1868) her fascination is without the excuse of love, but with the dead body itself:

> Too cold is this
> To warm with sun—
> Too stiff to bended be,
> To joint this Agate were a work—
> Outstaring Masonry—(*P* 1135)

Her first published poem (1859) reflects the same macabre

fascination:

> Safe in their Alabaster Chambers —
> Untouched by Morning
> And untouched by Noon —
> Sleep the meek members of the Resurrection —
> Rafter of satin,
> And Roof of stone.

But here the intent is satirical. These are the unawakened, the unconscious believers in the Christian resurrection, stone dead, while life, which they never perceived anyway, goes on:

> Babbles the Bee in a stolid Ear,
> Pipe the Sweet Birds in ignorant cadence —
> Ah, what sagacity perished here! (*P* 216)

Without something of time and eternity the poem appeared frivolous, so Dickinson rewrote it in 1861, replacing the natural images with those of great world events "— and Doges — surrender —." But in the eternal firmament such events are "Soundless as dots — on a Disc of Snow". The grizzly humor is dissipated in her effort to make it profound.[16]

IV

Eventually immortality obsessed her consciousness. To the end of her days she questioned an answer she had occasionally assumed. "Is Immortality True?" she asked the Reverend Washington Gladder four years before she died (*L* 731). She was no more certain of her inferences from nature's emblems than of her ability to express nature's beauty: "So impotent Our Wisdom is/To her Simplicity" (*P* 668). But who could answer? Nature was a dwelling place that art imitates, a heaven realized by the living consciousness with intimations of Awe. She could not ask that frightening tremendousness; not unless it could be reduced to human proportions, personified into God. There was no other way to deal with that

> . . . certain Slant of light,
> Winter Afternoons—
> That oppresses, like the Heft
> of Cathedral Tunes—

This is where "the Meanings, are" in this "Heavenly Hurt."

> When it comes, the Landscape listens—
> Shadows—hold their breath—
> When it goes, 'tis like the Distance
> On the look of Death—(*P* 258)

Awe in a slant of light—the quickening recognition of life and the nostalgic tinge of its evanescence.

At times the Empress of Calvery desired "a cordial interview/With God" (*P* 844). But his presence was too intense, too awful to endure except in fleeting moments. These inebriating moments were always followed by the pain of the moment's passing:

> For each extatic instant
> We must in anguish pay
> In keen and quivering ratio
> To the ecstacy (*P* 125).

It was during the "ordinary hours" that she wrote to God, reflecting on those awful moments of bliss and anticipating future moments:

> Retrospection is Prospect's half,
> Sometimes almost more (*P* 995).

In these reflections she found "Eternity—obtained—in Time" (*P* 800). Eternity was the summing of time; The Infinite in the Finite (*P* 1695). And all of life itself was a "moment of Deathlessness" (*P* 1090), a color momentarily flashing out of the all-color, the white of the gown she wore. Life is infinite because it exists in time of which infinity is composed. The idea, she wrote Samuel Bowles, is to live in

paradise "constantly, instead of ultimately" (*L* 574). Eternity
and time were spirit and flesh:

> The Spirit lurks within the Flesh
> Like Tides within the Sea
> That makes the Water live, estranged
> What would the Either be? (*P* 1576)

Yet, on many occasions the body was mere "trinket" that the
soul discarded at death. Immortality was the mind alone
without corporeal friend, like a letter. At times she perceived
her contrariness and abandoned her reflections altogether,
declaring simply, "Instinct esteem/ . . . Immortality" (*P* 679).
And when love's craving inspired, it obliterated all other
definitions:

> Unable are the Loved to die
> For love is Immortality,
> Nay, it is Deity — (*P* 809)

Talking to God about immortality was talking to self.
Such correspondence was like writing a "letter to the
World/That never wrote to Me" (*P* 441). Impishly, she confided to others that letters to friends were a joy "denied the
Gods" (*L* 855). No made-up God could answer the question
of immortality. That truth was locked behind some "awful
doors" (*P* 160). Yet at times she could deceive herself, imagining her consciousness almost prying open these doors before
letting go:

> Just lost when I was saved!
> Just felt the world go by!
> Just girt me for the onset with Eternity,
> When breath blew back,
> And on the other side
> I heard recede the disappointed tide!

And she would deceive herself again if ever she got that close:

Next time, to stay!
Next time, the things to see
By Ear unheard,
Unscrutinized by Eye—

This is the impossible, beyond the human reference point. If she ever could gain the eternity concealed beyond the awful door, however, she would not behold the anticipated awesomeness, not even the indescribable unity of Poe's beatific Godhead. All she can imagine from this view out of time and space is looking back, "to tarry,"

While the Ages steal—
Slow tramp the Centuries,
And the Cycles wheel! (*P* 160)

Her previous answer that "Forever—is composed of Nows—" (*P* 624) was often a frail cover for despair in Dickinson's vacillations, another fiction, a way for lonely exiles to entertain themselves. At times her loneliness, "that polar privacy/A soul admitted to itself—" (*P* 1695) reduced her to the brutal Melvillean view that sees all searches as futile and all meaning as myth which is sham:

Finding is the first Act
The second, loss,
Third, Expedition for
The "Golden Fleece"

Fourth, no Discovery—
Fifth, no Crew—
Finally, no Golden Fleece—
Jason—sham—too. (*P* 870)

If heaven was in her garden, then why seek immortality elsewhere? If God had been here this summer, she boasted to a correspondent, he would think his paradise superfluous. But autumn came to her garden, then frost, and death. "Why—do they shut me out of Heaven" (*P* 248), she asks,

meaning either or both her frosted garden and the eternal
one. Realizing her bondage in human ignorance, she chides
God:

> Why Bliss so Scantily disburse —
> Why Paradise defer —
> Why Floods be served to us — in Bowls —
> I speculate no more — (*P* 756)

Clearly, the eternal heaven is second best. What she really
wants is her experience of heaven on earth everlastingly,
which would be unbearable.

Rather than appease an awful God, as she sensed her
own noon fading, Dickinson became saucier with him. He
had always resembled the Puritanical God of her father,
unloving and unlovable, but in her late poems he becomes a
"Bold Person," not to be trusted:

> Not if the Just suspect me
> And offer a Reward
> Would I restore my Booty
> To that Bold Person, God — (*P* 900)

He is the "supreme inequity" since he makes man and then
deceives him. Thus, she jeers, "We apologize to thee/For
thine own Duplicity." "To be human is more than to be
divine," she wrote Higginson upon the death of his wife, "for
when Christ was divine, he was uncontented until he had
been human." (*L* 592). God was so jealous he could not bear
to see "That we had rather not with Him/But with each other
play" (*P* 1719). This school girl taunt from an aging Dickinson may suggest her own suppressed desire to play. A little
further on, closer to death, she totally reversed herself. Given
his paradise of light, she would never "long for Earthly
Play/and Mortal Company" (*P* 1145).

V

The brief moments of bliss in her garden apparently were

not sufficient rewards for the loneliness of her life in which the major events were death and other loss imagined as death. Self-crowned queen in her made-up domain, she nevertheless endured the state of exile, dwelling on loss and yearning for the impossible. With Poe she shared the lonely fascination of anticipating death again and again. Nearly 600 poems, a third of her total, concern death. It is personified, like God, but not vilified. Death is variously a king "witnessed—in the Room" (*P* 465), a "supple suitor/that wins at last" (*P* 1445), a courtier politely guiding the queen to her destiny:

> Because I could not stop for Death—
> He kindly stopped for me—(*P* 712)

In the carriage they pass daily life, as a queen reviews the troops, until she is no longer passing but being passed by the setting sun and is growing cold. Although the dead one has gone to eternity, the focus is totally on the life that has been lost—glimpses of school children, grazing grain, setting sun—the loss of earthly heaven. Eternity is apparently an empty place where the soul longs endlessly for life. Death is the loss of consciousness, with its drunken, exhilarating moments of heaven. Thus, she hopes that even a coffin is

> Yet able to contain
> A Citizen of Paradise
> In its diminished Plane (*P* 943).

On the other hand the prospect of death's very moment is itself exciting: "Just let go the Breath—." It's so horrible, "it half Captivates," this "Gay, Ghastly, Holiday!" (*P* 281). Imagining the moment as "a Funeral, in my Brain," she perceives something beyond but cannot reach it. The treading of the mourners becomes the pounding effort of "sense . . . breaking through" at last. But constant drumbeats numb the mind and "Boots of Lead" creak across the soul. Although she hears all space begin to toll "As all the Heavens were a

Bell/And Being," but an Ear," she is excluded, an exile, member of "some strange Race/Wrecked, solitary, here." The final instant is a break in "a Plank in Reason" (*P* 280), a downward plunge and the end of knowing. In a following poem, even the thought of heaven is absent at the moment of death. Instead of the tolling bells, "I heard a Fly buzz—when I died." That's all. She has finished her earthly business, disposed of property, and now is still with anticipation for "that last Onset—when the King/Be witnessed—in the Room," but a fly interposed

> Between the light—and me—
> And then the Windows failed—and then
> I could not see to see—(*P* 465).

Death is an irritating nuisance that enlarges until it blots out the universe. Nothing follows.

Blacker still and bitter is her vision of death as "A Clock Stopped," where life itself is meaningless, a mere functioning of God's mechanism. When it wears out,

> Geneva's farthest skill
> Can't put the puppet bowing—
> That just now dangled still—

Here death is not personified. Instead, "An awe came on the Trinket," which then "hunched, with pain," and "quivered out of Decimals" (*P* 287). In this metaphor of living and dying, the poet has no more consciousness than "a plated person" (*P* 1453). She is also a trinket that has existed through

> Decades of Arrogance between
> The Dial life—
> And Him—(*P* 287).

Dwelling on death—by execution, warfare, sea monsters, once in an underworld guarded by a dragon—she had to resist the implication of life's absurdity, "could we see all we hope—there would be madness near."[17] Only man's arrogance makes possible the pretense of sanity. Most arrogant are the assumptions of importance in the face of Awe and the bloated notion of a certain hereafter. Poe too understood the vanity of human wishes, but screamed on, unsanely insisting on sanity, system, *Eureka*. Earth was the place for Emily Dickinson; a soul without consciousness was not much solace for the loss of her garden paradise. The sanity of system and society obscures the awareness of the living paradise:

> Much Madness is divinest Sense—
> To a discerning Eye—
> Much Sense—the starkest Madness—
> 'Tis the Majority
> In this, as All, prevail—
> Assent—and you are sane—
> Demur—you're straightway dangerous—
> And handled with a Chain—(*P* 435).

It was madness then that allowed life to be known, the sharing in eternity if only for an instant: "That it will never come again/Is what makes life so sweet" (*P* 1741). And so painful. The joy of life was the pain of loss:

> Joy to have merited the Pain—
> To merit the Release—
> Joy to have perished every step—
> To Compass Paradise—*P* 788).

Losses flooded her sensibility early in life and patterned her imagination. From the Reverend Wadsworth's departure she derived a source of poetry that welled over a dozen years. Most of her great poetry had already been written when the losses came again, beginning with her father's death in 1874, followed by Sam Bowles', Dr. Josiah Holland's, then Wadsworth's, her mother's, and most painful, Gilbert, the eight-year old son of brother Austin and Susan, who brought genuine, live love to "Aunt Emily" in her late years. During these years, she also had the love, and perhaps the offer of marriage, from Otis Lord, Justice of the State Supreme Court and family friend whose wife had died in 1877. She collapsed when Lord died in 1884 and remained an invalid until her own death two years later. Finding her "gold lord" had not proven the end of exile. She was habituated to loss, and her affair with Lord was hardly distinguishable from those she had imagined, longing for her absent lover and fearing his loss, "the withdrawal of the Fuel of Rapture," which "does not withdraw the Rapture itself." He was the temporary substance for the "loss of something ever felt";[18] his death, the moment of loss, was again the touching of Awe:

> Parting is all we know of heaven,
> And all we need of hell. (*P* 1732)

Her heaven was no beautiful vision beyond, but the consciousness of nature here and now which was forever. This was the home she encompassed but could not have for wanting, except in rare instants of joy, dampened by the melancholy awareness of the moment's passing.

It was for this ungraspable paradox that she had shut out the "plated person," who arrogantly assumed she was the exile. Her huge correspondence indicates they were not mistaken. Although she willfully refused the compromises to endure in society, her letters appeal for more intimate relations than her correspondents will give. Her barbs at the "Soft — Cherubic Creatures" (*P* 401) suggest more than casual concern for an abandoned society. Nor is she free of ambition for fame in that society. Closing the door suggests a touch of Poe's vengeance, just as her willful disappearances in the parlor before her guests, and her cavalier treatment of English idiom, grammar, spelling and punctuation suggest a touch of Poe's capriciousness if not perversity. Poe too selected his own phantom society, either in preference or as surrogate. Had she been rebuffed by the world as Poe had, she may have appeared just as petulant. And had she been forced into the rough and tumble of the workaday world, she also may have dreamed farther, of horrible night journeys to paradise beyond her own garden on earth. Yet the life she embraced was as awesome as Poe's ghouls; her consciousness as solipsistic as his reveries. In the loneliness of exile at home, her anticipations were also exciting and haunting as his.

The appalling spectre of death was to both the ultimate thrill of life; the extremity of the soul, she called it. Longing for knowledge of death was longing for the impossible, which perpetuated the excitement. A few days before her death, she wrote Higginson, "Diety—does he live now?/My friend— does he breathe?" (*L* 905). After the funeral, Higginson described Emily Dickinson's house and garden, decorated for the occasion, as " . . . a more saintly and elevated 'House of Usher.' "[19]

Chapter 5

HAWTHORNE:
Shadow and Sunshine and Shadow

"I am a stranger in this land, as you know," she said at length. . . . "I have left those behind me with whom my fate was intimately bound, and from whom I am cut off forever. . . . There is a weight in my bosom that I cannot away with."[1]

However mundane, inhibiting, or punishing the community may be, it is always salvation for Hawthorne's exiles, from this early revelation in "Hollow of the Three Hills" (1830) to his last romances. His overarching theme is the unveiling of the human heart so that it can be touched by love of another and through that touching join the magnetic chain of humanity. The heart is veiled by obsessive egos, whether in the scholar, scientist, or artist. These are cold realms for Hawthorne. No strain of imagination is necessary to see Coverdale in *The Blithedale Romance* (1852) realizing his human need for what he covertly observes and cannot open his heart to. Kenyon, the sculptor in *The Marble Faun* (1860) also observes the human condition, but with little heart of his own, like Hilda, with whom he retreats to the American homeland where they can mutually preserve a proud virginity beneath the mask of marriage.

In the year of his own marriage, 1842, Hawthorne recorded in his notebook:

The human Heart to be allegorized as a cavern; at the entrance there is sunshine, the flowers growing about it. You step within, but a short distance, and begin to find yourself surrounded with a terrible gloom, and monsters of diverse kinds; it seems like Hell itself. You are bewildered and wander long without hope. At last a light strikes upon you. You press toward it and find yourself in a region that seems in some sort to reproduce the flowers and sunny beauty of the entrance, but all perfect. These are the depths of the heart or of human nature, bright and peaceful; the gloom and terror may lie deep; but deeper still is this eternal beauty.[2]

We might expect to find the embodiment of this outline more readily in Poe than Hawthorne. It is never developed whole in any piece of his fiction but something of it is everywhere. In the opening scene of *The Scarlet Letter* (1850), Hester emerges from the cavern of the prison, a wild rose growing about its entrance, into the sunshine, having penetrated, we may presume, the gloom and terror. But the sunshine she enters is the Puritanical society, not the "eternal beauty" in the depths of the heart. The note he recorded in 1842 reflects Hawthorne's withdrawal after his disillusioning step into the sunshine at Brook Farm where he had hoped to escape a "false state of society." But "the real ME was never an associate of the community," he wrote Sophia.[3] After marriage, he found there was "no sunshine in this world, except what beams from my wife's eyes."[4]

Before the marriage, in the cavern of his chamber under the eaves where Hawthorne had submerged his social being, he yearned for the social sunshine. There was "no fate in this world so horrible as to have no share in its joys and sorrows. For the last ten years I have not lived but only dreamed of living."[5] He feared becoming "the Outcast of the universe," like his "Wakefield" (1835), who "stepping aside for a moment exposed himself to a fearful risk of losing his place forever." The evidence indicates that Hawthorne forced himself to the asceticism necessary for individual creativity. Actually, he broke his solitude with frequent trips to local taverns, and more extensive tours to the mountains, Niagara Falls and nearby villages.[6] According to Henry James, Hawthorne was not driven by any innate shade-seeking personality as the popular view had it and as Hawthorne himself often suggested.[7]

At college, Hawthorne's letters were more often bantering than sad-colored. "I have put on my gold watch-chain and purchased a cap so that with the aid of my new white gloves I flatter myself that I make a most splendid appearance in the eyes of the pestilent little freshmen."[8] Some letters revealed his concern for the future. He did not want to be a doctor and live by men's diseases, he wrote to his mother, nor a minister and live by their sins, nor a lawyer and live by their quarrels—so nothing was left but be an author.[9] The desultory tone of his decision is reinforced years later in a letter to Richard Henry Stoddard, "Year after year I kept on considering what I was fit for, and time and my destiny decided that I was to be the writer than I am."[10] Ambition motivated him; he found the way in writing and in his specific condition in Salem. He returned from Bowdoin to his mother's "abode . . . in which I had a room."[11] The only other occupants were his sisters. As he painted the scene, they hardly saw each other. They were all poor relatives under the surveillance of uncles elsewhere. A stranger in his own dwelling, Hawthorne became obsessed to earn his way back into the sunshine, "to open an intercourse with the world." Although such stories as "David Swan" and "The Ambitious Guest" (1835) warned of the accidents of life and the futility of ambition, and others, such as "the Man of Adamant" (1837) and "Lady Eleanor's Mantle" (1835) warned of excessive pride, Hawthorne appears nevertheless as the ambitious Oberon of "The Devil in the Manuscript" (1835) who burns his work in frustration and then exults to find his sparks igniting the town, "Here I stand—a triumphant author! . . . My brain has set the town on fire!"[12]

Although "fame was won"[13] with the publication of *Twice Told Tales* (1837), Hawthorne did not emerge into the sunshine of ordinary society until he had earned an established place with *The Scarlet Letter*. His sunniest writings followed from the seeming contentment of the Berkshires where he met Melville making his journey in the opposite direction, into the darkness of exile. His son Julian describes frequent visits of other admirers to the apparently happy Hawthorne circle, and wonders how this same genial man could be the fellow who regarded himself as the obscurest man of letters in America. But Julian also describes diffidence and restlessness. He notes that the weather bothered Hawthorne as he raced through *The House of Seven Gables* (1851), and the sight of the mountains themselves became detestible. "I hate Berkshire with my whole soul."[14] Moving to the Horace Mann house in West Newton, Hawthorne exchanged the mountains for the backyards and sullen streets of the city (reflected in *The Blithedale Romance*, partially written there). He moved on to the center of the New England intellectual movement, Concord, and on again, with the appointment as consul in Liverpool. England "touched a deep kindred chord in him," Julian observes, "which responded to nothing else. America might be his ideal home, but his real home was England, and thus he found himself in the end, with no home at all outside the boundaries of his domestic circle."[15]

Although America valued the artist merely as supplier of relief from materialistic pursuits, Hawthorne longed for its recognition. It was a sign of membership. But to earn that recognition, he had to suffer the sin of separation committed necessarily in artistic creation. This is the condition so many of his fictions investigate. He stages the early stories in the past to provide "suitable remoteness," a "theater,"[16] where

Puritanical obsession, imprisoning the "truth" of the human heart, reflects the alienating American present. And conceiving of the American future as the progressive idealism of Brook Farm, Hawthorne discovered there the same iron pride that prohibited the communion of opened hearts in the Puritan past.

In married love he imagined "that touch creates us — then we begin to be."[17] It is redemption from the obsession of the artist. But after a while even "all perfect" beauty in the cavern of married love grows lonely. He was drawn to a "theater" more remote than the Puritan past or future: "In the old countries . . . a certain conventional privilege seems to be awarded the romancer. . . . Among ourselves, on the contrary, there is yet no such Faery Land."[18] America was a place of untamed forests and licentious attacks upon them; but in the tame English countryside man and nature were balanced. And in the soft Italian moonlight on the aged marble, he could see what is human in the human heart and accept the imperfection that is called evil. He could see in, but he could not join in. He was the American, the artist Kenyon who must return with his copyist bride, Hilda, to exile at home.

I

Hawthorne's literary journey into exile begins with the artificial *Fanshawe* (1828). This romance served to wash his mind of eclectic stereotypes. Largely inspired by Scott, the action is standard abduction, pursuit and capture, suspended by withheld information and gothic machinery. From time to time the narrator appears to be mocking his own imitative efforts, rendering a comic effect rather than the gloomy one he intended to hang over the dark tale with its upbeat ending. The character of Fanshawe is supposed to be too sensitive for the action of life and the willful necessities of love. He is a preview of a type soon to be developed — the cold, intellectual artist, scholar, or scientist of the darkness who is chivalrous now but will be discovered as depraved, while the lady he loves but cannot embolden himself to claim is a prototype of the Puritanical maiden, later found to be made of sweets and steel.

With his sights cleared through the writing of *Fanshawe*, which he burned, the author now perches atop a steeple and assumes the role of a "spiritualized Paul Pry hovering invisible round man and woman, witnessing their deeds, searching into their hearts, borrowing brightness from their felicity and shade from their sorrow, and retaining no emotion peculiar to himself." (The familiar voices of James and Joyce, also exiles.) What the narrator sees in "Sights from the Steeple" (1831) is the community—a military parade, a funeral, young lovers, a crowd hurrying through the streets to escape a coming storm. In another sketch, "The Haunted Mind" (1835), the focus is inside the viewer. The mind enduring a wakeful night discovers in the "nightmare of the soul" that in "every human heart there is a tomb or dungeon, though the lights, the music, the revelry above may cause us to forget their existence and the buried ones, or prisoners, whom they hide." These two sketches render the boundaries of Hawthorne's focus. The journey into exile is into the hidden dungeons of the heart; the journey out of exile is to the open felicities and sorrows seen from the steeple. Deep inside the heart's hidden dungeons, the author discovers not perfection or eternal beauty as recorded in his journal entry of 1842, but the destructive dream of the artist's or scientist's excessive pride.

Hauntings of the mind occur in the tales of innocence and experience. Accumulated guilt is the haunter. When Reuben Bourne kills his son by fated accident on the very spot he left his future father-in-law to die in "Roger Malvern's Burial" (1831), his guilt is expiated; but another, more reasonable guilt, is incurred. Hawthorne attempts to break this chain in his tales associated with American independence. The people's governor, John Hancock, tells "Old Esther Dudley" (1838): "you have treasured up all that time has rendered worthless . . . and you are a symbol of the past. And I, and these around me — we represent a new race of men, living no longer in the past, scarcely in the present, but projecting our lives forward into the future." But in "My Kinsman, Major Molineux" (1832), Hawthorne cannot so clearly and freely align the individual's ambition with the new nation's. As a character in a story of American independence and of initiation, Robin learns that he must depend upon himself, but this lesson is equivocal since his dependence appears to be less upon himself than the opinions, mores, and customs of the others, the red-and black-gleaming mob of democrats.

The cityfolk — inn-keeper, prostitute, customers in a barber shop — share a secret knowledge that causes them to laugh at Robin's innocence, which floats in a dream-like fantasy. Seeking his uncle, Major Molineux, in the city and pursued by laughter, Robin retreats into memory of the happy domesticity he left at home on the farm, which serves only to make the present moment of alienation more bitter. Then the rumble of the crowd is heard approaching and a friendly stranger, speaking for the socialized personality, advises him that men have several voices as well as two complexions. A stranger with two complexions, black and blazing red, keeps an eye on Robin throughout the roaring laughter in which Major Molineux finally appears, tarred and feathered and on his way out. Robin is so confused, so emotionally in need to belong, to join the crowd, that his laugh seems loudest. For that moment he joins with the blazing red and black face and the red radiance of the church and the prostitute's scarlet skirt. He is with it now.

But his laughter is too shrill. Uneasily hypocritical, the laughter hides his kinship with the colonial past which is ap-

parently sinful (Why else ride Major Molineux out of town?)
The ambiguous laugh is essentially a huge question of direction—openly suffer exile with the sinful past (as Hester
Prynne is to do) or covertly suffer guilt for the sin of hiding
the past in return for social acceptance (as Dimmesdale is to
do). Equivocally, Robin turns back towards the farm, his
dream of home.

But if the new American city is an unlikely home, the
American farm is even less likely. Although "The Gentle
Boy" (1831) claims in the opening sentence "my home is
here," he finds it nowhere in the American wilderness. (He
dies as a result of Puritan cruelties and indirectly of his
mother's obsession to spread Quaker "truth" through the new
land. She is ostrasized, of course, since the Puritans have
already established ownership of the truth and are equally
obsessed in maintaining it.) The gentle boy's home is
elsewhere. The narrator suggests it is the old home, the same
that a previous generation had left "blooming like roses, and
like roses they had perished in a foreign soil." America also
has native roses, wild ones, like Pearl in *The Scarlet Letter*
who must be returned to England for taming.

When the sensuous joys of the old home are transplanted to American shores, the Puritans smother them. In
"The Maypole of Merry Mount" (1836), "Jollity and gloom
were contending for an empire," a contest abruptly ended by
the iron man, Governor Endicott, who represents the essential social condition that must be accepted, as the marriage of
Edgar and Edith, Lord and Lady of the May, symbolize:
"From the moment they truly loved, they had subjected
themselves to earth's doom of care and sorrow, and troubled
joy, and had no more a home at Merry Mount." Merry
Mount, however, does not represent the old home, only the
revelling element of it, led by vanity. It is a place where
"thought and wisdom" are "unwelcome guests." Rather than
an English tempering of care and sorrow and troubled

joy—"thought and wisdom"—the newlyweds are subjected t
a Puritanical tempering. Yet even the enforcer is subject to
his own humanity and must fight compassion for the joined
hearts he suppresses: "the iron man was softened" by the sight
of lovers and "almost sighed for the inevitable blight of early
hopes." Here is Chillingworth's "dark necessity."

Hawthorne sets these tales in the atmosphere of imagination or dream, more or less. In "My Kinsman, Major
Molineux" and "Roger Malvin's Burial," the dream atmosphere overwhelms the sense of external reality but in
"Maypole of Merry Mount" the reality of history dominates
the atmosphere. Amidst the revelry before Endicott appears,
Edith confesses to Edgar, "I struggle as with a dream, and
fancy that these shapes of our jovial friends are visionary,
and their mirth unreal, and that we are no true Lord and
Lady of the May." Her fears are prophetic. The frolicing is
soon defined as a dream in the Puritan sunshine. In "Young
Goodman Brown" (1835) the situation is reversed. The frolicing occurs in the midnight forest and although the reader
knows it is a dream, "the simple husbandman" defines the experience as real, and it shocks him forever.[19] He experiences
none of Edith's struggle with perception. He steps into pure
dream from the moment he sets "forth at sunset into the
street at Salem village" on his deliberate mission to test his
faith in the forest. (After which, he promises himself, he will
"cling to [Faith's] skirts and follow her to heaven.")

In the last two paragraphs the narrator awakens the
reader to the recognition of Brown's "dream and evil omen."
We are returned to the sense of the everyday social world but
Brown remains in his dream, which becomes his reality. He
lives ever after in the universe he or his Puritanical devil has
conjured. The devil, "peopling the heart of the solitary woods
at once" has revealed to Brown that his own suppressed
desires are shared by everyone. Brown sees them enacted not

only by the most respected townspeople, the deacon and minister, but also by the "shape of his own dead father," the "dim features of his mother," and most horrific, by "the slender form" of his wife, all in a "communion of evil" which the devil equates with "the communion of your race." All are witches. "Evil is the nature of mankind." Seen historically, Goodman Brown's imagination in the midnight forest describes the psychology of the witnesses whose special evidence condemned the accused in the Salem trials of 1692.[20] While young Robin hesitantly accepts his perceptions in the lurid night, if only for a moment, the Puritanical Goodman instantly rejects his, without a thought. He "was himself the chief horror of the scene." Being a simple husbandman he cannot accommodate the duality of nature which the devil has shown him as he has shown Robin. In Brown's vision, the duality is defined as social hypocrisy, the promoters of righteousness doing the devil's work. Thus Brown eschews human society and becomes a dour old man, devoid not only of charity but even of faith in anything upstairs. He commits the sin that Hawthorne later identifies as the unpardonable one, the sin of egoistic purity which exiles him in his human home.

The Reverend Hooper in "The Minister's Black Veil" (1836), on the other hand, comes to understand that hiding sensuous human nature is necessary. Such hypocrisy is the only way Puritanical society can maintain its social face. But he becomes obsessed with the notion of concealment. He dons the veil to expose to the secret sinner the commonality of his own "sad mysteries which we hid from our nearest and dearest, and fain would conceal from our own consciousness." Seeing on "every visage a black veil," he is driven to communicate by means of it, to force upon others a self knowledge of the shared secrecy. His veil is intended to serve the same "office" as the scarlet letter inadvertently comes to serve, not to shame Hester so much as to open the hearts of those who observe it. Hooper's outcome is ironical. Instead of joining society in a mutual recognition of sinful secrets, his obsession merely separates him from the others, including his betrothed. While the "dismal shade" is worn as a silent preachment against the sin of covertness, it also commits the sin. Although more complete than Brown's, the minister's reaction to his knowledge is driven by the same egoistic purity, pride.[21] This is the serpent that we find exiling Roderick Elliston in "Egotism; or, the Bosom Serpent" (1843), but unlike Hooper, who sacrifices himself in his obsession, Roderick accepts the love Rosina offers with the advice, "Forget yourself in the idea of another." This story was written just after the author's marriage.

The obsessions of his egoists were paralleled by the obsessions of whole communities in the new world, not only of the Puritans and Quakers in "The Gentle Boy," but also in the democratic mob of "My Kinsman, Major Molineux." Societies were obsessed most of all with repression. In "The Shaker Bridal" (1838), the whole populace "had overcome their natural sympathy with human frailties and affections." The protagonist was totally engrained in his society, therefore, when instead of embracing his bride, he removed his hand from hers and "folded his arms with a sense of satisfied ambition."

Hawthorne saw in the artist, as in the scientist, the same ambitious obsession. The heart freezes in all egoists when they neglect love and humanity. "Like all other men around whom an engrossing purpose wreathes itself," the painter in "The Prophetic Pictures" (1837) was "isolated from the mass of mankind. He had no aim, no pleasure, no sympathies, but what was ultimately connected with his art. . . . He did not possess kindly feelings; his heart was cold." The worship of art, like the worship of self or of the Puritanical zealot's

God — "O glorious art . . . O Potent art, am I not thy prophet?" — destroyed humanity and produced "the semblance,
perhaps the reality, of a madman."

The three major tales dealing with the semblance of
madmen — his obsessed scientists, artists, and scholars — were
written after Hawthorne's disappointments at Brook Farm
and after his marriage, both fancied as retreats into perfect
places. Actually he had created the image of marriage as
redemptory ideal several years before he met Sophia
Peabody. A certain Susan who had captivated him during an
extended visit to Swamscott in 1833 had also been a candidate
for his ideal of the woman savior. In "The Village Uncle"
(1837), Hawthorne pictures married bliss with Susan in a cottage by the sea. (A decade or so before Poe's "Annabelle
Lee.") A year after his marriage, in "The Birthmark" (1843),
Hawthorne condemned this vision of perfection; its fancier is
a destructive egoist. He condemned it again the following
year in "Rappaccini's Daughter." In "The Artist and the
Beautiful," also published that year, the vision of exiles
together in the cavern disappears and the egoist artist is alone
again, his art violated by the practical society whose love he
covets.

Alymer, the egoist of "The Birthmark," is a Goodman
Brown disguised as scientist. His faith is in the perfectability
of a human being and he insists upon it while Brown's lost
faith was in a perfection already achieved. Alymer kills his
wife in conquering her human imperfection, a mark in the
shape of a tiny hand, the human touch. The mark works
upon Alymer as the minister's veil and the scarlet letter are intended to work. He sees it as a "symbol of his wife's liability
to sin, sorrow, decay, and death." The mark extends to the
heart and to remove it is necessarily to remove life. The deep
bitterness in the dying wife's last utterance is too subtle for
the egoist: "you have aimed loftily; you have done nobly. Do

not repent that with so high and pure a feeling, you have rejected the best earth could offer."[22] The narrator must intrude to enforce the point that Alymer failed, as all humans must, to find the "perfect future in the present." The deepest penetration of the human heart leads not to the perfection of "eternal beauty" as he had imagined in the journal entry of 1842, but to death. Excluding the external world—represented by Aminadab, "If she were my wife, I'd never part with that birthmark"—Alymer seeks perfection instead of warmth in his cold cavern. This pattern is more explicit in "Rappaccini's Daughter." Results are equally disasterous.

In this tale there is a cavern actually allegorized, Rappaccini's garden of "thwarted nature." It is not yet perfect, and as in "The Birthmark," the scientist's obsession for perfection results in death. Although Rappaccini cares "infinitely more for science than mankind" as the outside world rumors and the tale demonstrates, the complete success of his experiment coincides with a remnant of human concern for the most beautiful of his poisoned beauties, his untouchable daughter, Beatrice. She is lonely. A mate must be captured from the outside world to accommodate her exile. But love is the variable Rappaccini has neglected in his experiment. Giovanni, his subject, is sufficiently manipulatable, but suffers the ambiguities of human emotion and perception. "Beautiful shall I call her or inexpressibly terrible?" His spirit was exulted to an "early enthusiasm of passion" but "groveled among earthly doubts." She had "instilled a fierce and subtle poison into his system. It was not love, although her rich beauty was a madness to him." It was passion, and when he finds that this poison has invaded his body, condemning him to the cavern with the beautiful Beatrice, Giovanni mistakenly accuses her, not as Adam would Eve for the loss of the garden, but for the loss of society: "thou hast severed me likewise from the warmth of life and enticed me into thy regions of unspeakable horror!" Beatrice, whose "grief was beyond passion," has actually protected him from herself so he could "go forth out of the garden and mingle with [his] race." Unlike her suitor, it was only her body that was poisoned, not her spirit, which "craves love as its daily food."

At last Giovanni perceives the idea of love in the cavern, but only momentarily. His "passion had exhausted itself" and "There now came across him a sense, mournful, and not without tenderness, of the intimate and peculiar relationship. . . . Ought not, then, the desert of humanity around them to press this insulated pair closer together?" But it is only a passing notion. With an antidote he will undo "the evil mockery of beauty" her father had wrought, purify her poisoned body and take it back into society with him. And as Rappaccini emerges into the garden "to gaze with triumphant expression at the beautiful youth and maiden, as might any artist who should spend his life in achieving a picture or a group of statuary," Beatrice swallows the antidote, which she knows is death to her poisoned body. "I would fain have been loved, not feared," she responds to her father's protest that he had tried only to protect her with the marvelous gifts the others would dread. Her last utterance is to Giovanni and it is not wasted in the subtleties of Alymer's dying wife, "was there not, from the first, more poison in thy nature than in mine?"

The poison of Giovanni's antidote is the concoction of Professor Baglioni, who is more than the Paul Pry of this story. He is society's symbolic tamperer, and Rappaccini's exclusiveness is "not to be tolerated by those who respect the good old rules of the medical profession." As he taunts Rappaccini with the outcome of his experimentation, the reader recalls Baglioni's previous musings, "It is too insufferable an impertinence in Rappaccini, thus to snatch the lad Giovanni out of my own hands. . . . Perchance, most learned Rappaccini, I may foil you where you little dream of it." Baglioni cannot tolerate social deviation and devises a scheme to bring deviants "within the limits of ordinary nature," even if it kills them. He is another early version of Chillingworth.

Hawthorne's introduction to this Puritanical tale in Italy associates Rappaccini's reversed garden with the nightmare vision of society the author (M. l'Aubepine, Hawthorne in French) had imagined in previous tales. It is the exile's view of his home society obsessed with unnatural and inhuman perfection: "Occasionally a breath of Nature, a raindrop of pathos and tenderness, or a gleam of humor, will find its way into the midst of his fantastic imagery, and make us feel as if, after all, we were yet within the limits of our native earth."

In "The Artist and the Beautiful" as in "Rappaccini's Daughter" the breath of nature is fatal to the achievement of perfection. Like Rappaccini, Owen Warland has retreated into an imaginative world where he has created a butterfly almost indistinguishable from nature's. Again, the intolerant external society, invited by the artist's need as Giovanni is invited by the needs of Rappaccini, destroys the artist's creation.

The perfection of this butterfly is in its imitation of nature's. "Is it alive?" asks Annie whose love the artist has sacrificed in his obsession. "Alive, to be sure it is," answers her iron-monger husband, an artison also but an utterly practical one as his society demands. "Do you suppose any mortal has skill enough to make a butterfly, or would put himself to the trouble of making one, when any child may catch a score of them in a summer's afternoon?" Actually, the iron-monger husband has exposed Hawthorne's own mockery of the artist whose vision is disassociated from the imperfect human condition. "In his idle and dreamy days he had considered it possible . . . to spiritualize machinery, and to combine with the new spirit of life and motion thus produced a beauty that should attain to the ideal which Nature has proposed to herself in all her creatures, but has never taken pains to realize." The husband who "spends his labor in reality," reveals Owen Warland as a mere copiest of reality, a useless artisan. The agent of destruction is nature's innocent creation. The child, "molded out of the densest substance," crushes the artist's "eternal beauty" with the clenching of his hand, while the artist looks on "placidly." The butterfly that took so many years to create is but a symbol of his art, "of little value." His spirit, however, is indestructable, which means he can do it again, and again, copy after copy. Such are Owen Warland's reflections as "his spirit possessed itself in the enjoyment of the reality," which neatly corresponds with the narrator's reflections on the painter of "The Prophetic Pictures" as the semblance, perhaps the reality of a madman.

"Ethan Brand," published in 1851 when Hawthorne had achieved a position in the sunshine, summarizes his view of all obsessed exiles who have neglected their place in the "magnetic chain of humanity." The lime-burner is obsessed with a single objective, to discover the unpardonable sin, and commits it by seeking it. He becomes a "cold observer," manipulating his fellow man like puppets in his experiment. Brutal and coarse as the others may be, they maintain some hold on human society, one in the local tavern, another in making soap for a neighbor, the doctor in his rounds. But Ethan Brand has emptied himself of humanity in his egoistic probing and at last looks back into himself, "But where is the Heart?" His cry of pain at the moment of suicide is for all Hawthorne's obsessed egoists who find themselves lonely exiles in the reality of a madman. "O mankind, whose brotherhood I have cast off, and trampled . . . beneath my feet."

II

A glimpse of light appears at the end of "Egotism; or, The Bosom Serpent," but it is not until after the sprinkling of sunshine through the forest in *The Scarlet Letter* that Hawthorne's fiction turns in that direction. He began the romance as another tale shortly after he was fired from his political appointment at the Customs House. It was intended to form part of a new collection of tales along with the Customs House introduction, but his editor, James Fields, persuaded him to make a separate book. His objection that it was "too somber" for a whole volume may be responsible for the humor, most concentrated in Chapter 20, "The Minister in a Maze." In *The Scarlet Letter*, Hawthorne relates themes and symbols he had been discovering in his dark tales, and completes the characters by deeper and more sympathetic probes.

Dimmesdale is a product of ego-guilt ideas variously represented in Robin, Hooper, and Roderick Elliston. His obsession for fame as scholarly minister of the people is similar to the obsession of Hawthorne's artists and scientists for perfection. But he is weaker than any of these, needing the strength of an iron system or the will of another human being to survive: "and what hast thou to do with all these iron men, and their opinions?"[23] Hester asks, knowing she is his alternative.

Chillingworth is shaped, or misshaped, from the Puritanical rigidity of Goodman Brown, the "Man of Adamant," and the outrage and revenge of Professor Baglioni. But he is driven by "dark necessity" and cannot help himself even as he sees his just revenge destroying him. His is the "fiend's office," the black flower of repression that blossoms "as it may" alongside the wild rose in America.[24]

Hester is a development of Beatrice in her human passion and her position as social untouchable. The only previous glimpse of her free will, her independent mind, however, which also exiles her spiritually, is in the obsessed outcast, the Quaker mother of "The Gentle Boy." But Hester's will is complicated by her uncertain perceptions of the real and the imagined, and is thus easily deceived, as is the community that ostracizes her. On the scaffold her sin is itself an illusion. Her mind escapes to the European past and then attempts to reason forward. How did she arrive at this unbearable moment? She must convince herself that she is what they say. She must touch that symbol "A" to make it real. What was happening to her was not happening to others. The "A" takes her "out of ordinary relations with humanity, and encloses her by herself" (54). But she shares the defiance of other exiles in American literature. Her clothes are "of a splendor in accordance with the taste of the age, but greatly beyond what was allowed by the suptuary regulations of the Colony. Her attire seemed to express the attitude of her spirit, the desperate recklessness of her mood" (53).

Pearl alone appears without precedent, a growth of sunshine that filters through forest leaves, and it is significant that we are told rather than shown her success in English society. Hawthorne has turned, has seen the filtered sunshine, but as yet has taken only the first step towards it. This is not the iron sunshine of Puritanical America, but the soft light of nostalgia upon the old world. And the step is taken almost playfully, with the *deus ex machina* of Chillingworth's fortune which transforms Pearl's life into a fairy tale of noble wealth and association in another country, dreamland for the exile.

Perhaps because of the setting, interpretations of this romance as a story of heavenly redemption from sin persist. But the sin is clearly social. It is of no value whatever that Dimmesdale bares his heart to his God in secret. He is hypocritical to his fellow men and women. And as Puritanical pursuer, Chillingworth is agent neither of heaven or hell but of social outrage and revenge. The attempt at heavenly consecration of the family on the scaffold in the middle of the night is mocked by supernatural fireworks, and the three souls appear connected by electricity as compared with the human warmth that unites Hester and Dimmesdale naturally in the forest scene that follows. The salvation in this story is Hester's recognition and acceptance of human society no matter how repressive, dark, and hypocritical it may be. Even though the society takes her confession and she takes her punishment, Hester is not allowed in, but remains on the edge of town, and even though the scarlet letter has come to represent *able* and to some, *angel*, yet in the very last chapter, "Hester Pryne was standing beside the scaffold of the pillory, with the scarlet letter still burning in her breast!" (250).

The events of this chapter occur in the open, at the place of public acknowledgement and here the iron sun of the Puritan shines. It "shone down upon the clergyman and gave a distinctness to his figure, as he stood out from all the earth, to put his plea of guilty at the bar of Eternal Justice" (254). Certainly that is what Dimmesdale thought he was doing, but he does wait until this final moment of his life when nothing is to be lost and all is to be gained. The iron sun shines nevertheless because the secret is revealed. Chillingworth, who lived only for revenge, which is justice in the Puritan context, can now shrivel away and the social order, no longer threatened by the hidden betrayer, can celebrate its restored wholeness. The meaning of this social reunification is punctuated by Pearl's tears, "the pledge that she would grow up amid human joy and sorrow, nor forever do battle with the world but be a woman in it" (256). But that cannot happen in America.

Pearl belongs in the old world where the history of the narrative begins with Hester's reflections of her native village and of the deformed scholar who was then working for "advancement of human welfare" (172). That world is still prominant in "the bright morning sun" of Boston's Prison Lane where the narrative itself begins. It "shone on broad shoulders and well developed busts, and on round and ruddy cheeks that had ripened in the far off island, and hardly yet grown paler or thinner in the atmosphere of New England" (50). The old world is also reflected in the Governor's hall, which "might have benefitted Aladdin's Palace rather than the mansion of a grave old Puritan ruler" (103). Within, the "serf" wears the "customary garb of serving men . . . in the old heritary halls of England" (104). The furnishings are English heirlooms. On a table Hester discovers a tankard with a foaming remnant of ale on the bottom, a token of old English hospitality. And the theocratic rulers themselves seem to live in nostalgia for their old home. "I have never seen the like, since my days of vanity, in old King James' time," Governor Bellingham exclaims upon sight of Pearl. And the Reverend Wilson connects the narrator's description of Pearl as "the scarlet letter endowed with life" (102) to the Catholicity of the old world. Pearl is "a little bird of scarlet plumage . . . shining through a richly painted window," in contrast with the plain glass of a Puritan church. She is "one of those naughty elfs or fairies, whom we ought to have left behind us, with other relics of Papistry, in merry old England" (109).

He connects her also with the red rose in the Governor's garden which grows on a neglected bush. Now the garden is given over to cabbages and pumpkins because the soil "on this side of the Atlantic" is "too hard" for the "ornamental gardening" of "native English taste" (106). The neglected rose bush is English, having been cultivated over many generations, in contrast with the wild American rose bush "rooted almost at the prison door" of the opening scene. A token of the "deep heart of Nature," it springs up in spite of repression and in defiance of it. The wild rose the narrator plucks from the bush outside the prison door is identified with Pearl when she tells Mr. Wilson that her mother had plucked her from the wild bush. Thus, her demands for the English rose in the garden anticipate her future acculturation. Pearl's dynamic nature will not be imprisoned or crushed, but as the baroque aspect of her name suggests, it will be shaped, however irregularly by the age-wisened forms of English tradition. She is the "sweet moral blossom" whose return to the old world serves to "relieve the darkening close of a tale of human frailty and sorrow" (113). No exile, Pearl will be at home in the old world.

But in this story she is only a blossom "that may be found along the track" (48). The central line of the drama follows the making of exiles in the new world. Of the major characters only Dimmesdale is a member of society, a stance he maintains at great expense of spiritual self-violation or so it seems. His obsession is with the notion of success as the spiritual instructor of an inhuman philosophy which is, therefore, impossible to follow.

Although Chillingworth associates himself with the role of Black Man, the narrator actually places Dimmesdale closer to that satanic figure, whose domain is the wild forest. The Black Man that Mistress Hibbons invites Hester to meet with a merry company in the forest can hardly be an associate of the wretched avenger, Chillingworth. When Hester does compare Chillingworth with the Black Man in her prison interview, she refers to a somber Satan who bargains for souls, not the spirit that releases repressed human nature; the fellow who guides Goodman Brown and young Robin. In Hester's mind, this Black Man has invaded Dimmesdale's soul as she confesses to Pearl, "Once in my life I met the Black Man. . . . This scarlet letter is his mark" (185).

For Hester, the forest is the place where natural loving has "a consecration of its own," and Dimmesdale fully agrees (195). But in the settlement, his character contains only professional traces of love for another human being. Her needs deceive her into thinking her lover is also an exile, that there is a heart beneath his trembling hand. The iron men have "kept thy better part in bondage too long already!" (197). Although he agrees to return with her to "our native land," his immediate response is selfish and full of self-pity, "I dare not quit my post," though his "sure reward" will be "death and dishonor" (197). Under no circumstances would he leave before the Election Parade and miss a final celebration of his sensitive intelligence. We witness the celebration through Hester's disillusioned eyes:

> Was this the man? She hardly knew him now! He, moving proudly past, enveloped as it were, in the rich music, with the procession of majestic and venerable fathers; he, so unattainable in his wordly position. . . . Her spirit sank with the idea that all must have been a delusion . . . there could be no real bond betwixt the clergyman and herself. And thus much of a woman was there in Hester, that she could scarcely forgive him . . . for being able so completely to withdraw himself from their mutual world; while she groped darkly, and stretched forth her cold hands, and found him not (239).

Dimmesdale may have deceived Hester, but not Pearl nor other children who see through lenses uncolored with adult needs and desires. His resultant fear of children, in fact, provides some of the story's comic relief, "little babes, when I take them in my arms, weep bitterly" (207). He would sooner encounter anything than Pearl's passion, save the wrath of "the wrinkled witch, Mistress Hibbons," with whom he compares the child. Pleading for protection, he cries to Hester, "Pacify her, if thou lovest me!" (210). And Pearl justifies his dread, "will he go back with us . . . hand in hand . . . into the town?" (212). She washes his trepid kiss from her brow. "Through it all," writes Hawthorne's contemporary, Anthony Trollope, "there is a touch of burlesque."[25] The touch is felt also in Hester's easy domination of him, "Wilt thou die for very weakness?" (196). What really frightens him is the prospect of going to England alone, but when she responds, "Thou shalt not go alone!" his fears instantly evaporate, and he is again the glorious man of resolve, "all was spoken!" Not quite all. There is the Election Day sermon, the ultimate payoff to his overwrought ambition.

Walking back to his home beside the burial ground (as opposed to Hester's cottage beside the sea), Dimmesdale vacillates between the dream of returning to the old world, secure in Hester's dominance, and the present reality, secure in his ego-feeding role as spiritual leader of the people. Except for that one passionate trespass, the minister has never gone "beyond the scope of generally received laws." He was safely within the social system, his sin serving to keep his conscience alive. Even the anticipation of his flight to England is checked by the systematic ambition his society nourishes. It is "most fortunate" (215) that the ship in harbor will not sail until the day following the Election Sermon. This "exemplary man" therefore can abet his ego by imagining he would at least leave his professional reputation untarnished, "they shall say of me . . . I leave no public duty unperformed." The narrator comments, "sad . . . this poor minister's [introspection] should be so miserably deceived!" (218). But "we have had, and may still have, worse things to tell of him," though none "so pitiably weak."

The worse things are not the playful temptations inspired by the sense of freedom he has taken from Hester's will, not the urge to utter blasphemous suggestions to the hoary-bearded deacon, nor to whisper arguments against immortality into the "rapturously attentive ear of an old widow," not even to veil himself à la the Reverend Hooper with his Geneva cloak and cast a wicked look into an adoring virgin's eye, nor teach wicked words to "a knot of puritan children," nor share a few "heavenly defying oaths" with a drunken sailor. The worse things are his ego-satisfying deceits and denials at the very moment of his death on Election Day.

His last day is his grandest. The parade preceeding the sermon exhibits American society in the "first stages of joyless deportment," casting a "dim reflection of a remembered splendor." Strains of old world gaiety, like Hester's emblem, give "grotesque and brilliant embroidery to the great robe of state" (230). Following the magistrates comes the successful priest, "of most aspiring ambition," and Hester now feels a "dreary influence come over her" (239), while Pearl's natural impulsiveness mocks the whole charade. She "would have run to him, and bid him kiss me now, before all the people even as he did yonder among the dark old trees" (240).

Dimmesdale's sermon is all tone and cadence as it comes to Hester standing outside the church at the foot of the scaffold. The words themselves would have "clogged the spiritual sense" (243), words only veiled the "complaint of a human heart, sorrow-laden." Without words, the sermon reached out to mankind, "beseeching its sympathy or forgiveness." Such are the thoughts of a woman easily deceived, listening with her own emotional needs. The narrator's derision of the sermon is subtle enough to be missed. The sense of Dimmesdale's sermon, he implies, is dazzling: "His subject, it appeared, had been the relation between Diety and the communities of mankind" (249). It differed from other such sermons in the "glorious destiny for the newly gathered people of the lord," which is ironically the Puritanical gloominess rather than the joyous heaven of the Jewish seers. The only freshness in the sermon is not spiritual whatever; it is the implication that Dimmesdale has determined not to run away, but stay and die, having achieved "the proudest eminence of superiority."

The narrator builds the image of pride until he cannot

resist the common jibe, "Did his footsteps, in the procession, really tred upon the dust of earth?" (251). As Dimmesdale walks back from the triumphant sermon, he even steps into Christ's march to calvary, "hardly a man with life in him that tottered on his path so nervously, yet tottered, and did not fall!" (251). He rejects assistance from Wilson and Bellingham, "nor would it have seemed a miracle too high to be wrought for one so holy, had he ascended before their eyes . . . !" This is the moment Dimmesdale chooses to publicly acknowledge Hester and Pearl. Inspired by his own exultation, he believes in the "will which God hath granted me!" (241), as though the deity had just that instant arrived on the scene to let this holiest of men out of the maze. His final account of his troubles on earth adhere to the apocalyptic myth. He accuses Chillingworth of fiendishness and so makes his confession an ultimate victory over Satan, although he has not displayed much of a struggle against the dark forces through the seven ambitious years of his hypocrisy.

The logic of the story shows that Chillingworth has inadvertently served him well. Out of his vengeful motive, the physician has managed to keep alive his patient's conscience, his guilt. But Chillingworth cannot help him now, and Dimmesdale goes to his end without conscience. " 'Is this not better,' murmured he, 'than what we dreamed of in the forest?' " (254). Hester is simply amazed at such blatant betrayal, almost dumbfounded, since Dimmesdale is not aware of Chillingsworth's interference with their planned escape. After a moment's fumbling, "I know not! I know not!" Hester is able to respond, "Better? . . . So we may both die and little Pearl with us!" Too bad for them. He answers, "be it as God shall order." Dimmesdale is not in charge, not responsible for others, and after all, he's through. "I am a dying man. So let me make haste to take my shame upon me." Even her quick compromise to accommodate his belief as he lay dying, "Shall we not spend our immortal life together?" is cut with his cruel security-seeking soul and accurate church law, "when we violated our reverence for the other's soul," now he tells her, "it was thenceforth vain to hope we could meet hereafter, in an everlasting and pure reunion" (256). In the forest, their union was not a violation of souls but had a "consecration of its own." His obsession now is dying well, "this death of triumphant ignominy before the people." Otherwise "I had been lost forever! Praised be his name!" And so Hester, Pearl, " 'Farewell.' "

If the reader has been deceived as Hester has, Dimmesdale's dying behavior should be an awakening. The worst sin in *The Scarlet Letter* appears to be Chillingworth's violation of Dimmesdale's heart; "revenge . . . blacker than my sin," the minister explains in the ambiguous light and dark of the forest and Hester agrees, failing to correct him to "our sin" for all her independence of spirit. As his character unfolds, the "my" proves to be accurate. The sin to which the reader is referred is their passionate transgression of social laws, but the sin Dimmesdale has actually committed is much deeper; it is the unpardonable one enunciated in "Ethan Brand," the sin of intellectual pride. Neither of the exiles in this romance, Hester or Chillingworth, are guilty of this one. Her confession has paid the great price and she has even been rewarded with Pearl, although she continues to suffer separation from society. And Chillingworth has no social transgression to confess. His only sin is vengeance, which is actually an office to be performed for the Puritanical society. He is the society's instrument as were the Furies chasing Orestes, all a "dark necessity," out of his control.

Had Hawthorne allowed him to develop as fully as Hester, Chillingworth would be capable of eliciting sympathy. Even as he stands, the narrator appears kindly inclined from time to time, seeing him as an aging scholar who has contributed to society and married a young woman to warm his September years. "It was my folly," he confesses to Hester. "My heart was a habitation large enough for many guests, but lonely and chill . . . And so Hester, I drew thee into my heart, into its inner-most chamber, and sought to warm thee by the warmth which they presence made there!" (74).

Even Hester is moved to admit, "I have wronged thee," and conclude a pact of secrecy with him in retribution. The narrator's insistence that vengeance transforms this "wise and just man to a fiend" stops further development as a character, although everything we learn of him is generous, including his obsession for revenge. Dimmesdale, after all, has wronged them both. Even after seven years of "the devil's office" (170), the narrator can refer to Chillingworth as "the unfortunate physician," who is shocked by the image of what he has become. Instead of self-pride, as the minister exhibits, the physician takes pride in Hester's qualities, "Thou had great elements . . . I pity thee, for the good that has been wasted in thy nature!" (173). And in the fairy tale conclusion of the romance we learn that the old physician has left his fortune to Pearl, in contrast to the contribution of her father. The inheritance allows her to escape the repressive prison of Dimmesdale's society.

The narrator deceptively colors our view of Chillingworth with Hester's unreasonable hatred of him, which grows in spite of her recognition that he is essentially generous. We must remember she is an easily deceived woman, a free spirit without social guidelines and therefore often in a maze of uncertainties. (For the brief moment Dimmesdale places himself outside social guidelines, he too is in a maze of uncertainties.) Hester's hatred grows out of the pain the old physician inflicts on Dimmesdale, and the hatred blanks out his qualities. She comes to blame him, rather than herself, even for their marriage, for persuading her to fancy happiness at his side. Blind to the actual deception by her lover, she rationalizes deception by her husband. She twists the circumstances of her marriage into betrayal. "He has done me worse wrong than I did him!" This, in spite of the obvious evidence that she has betrayed Chillingworth and that Dimmesdale has betrayed and continues to betray her. The narrator does offer the reader a sympathetic peek at Chillingworth beneath the veil of Hester's deceived rationale: "Let men tremble to win the hand of woman, unless they win along with it the utmost passion of her heart!" When others awaken her sensibilities, he will be "reproached even for the calm content, the marble image of happiness, which they will have imposed upon her as the warm reality" (176). Rather than the warm reality, Hester's perfidy makes an exile of her. Although she came to have "a part to perform in the world," there was "nothing that made her feel as if she belonged to it" (84). Yet she provided, in her exile, the only comfort her estranged husband could know on earth, "My home is where thou art . . ." (76).

Chillingworth's sin of vengeance seems to brand a private "A" over Dimmesdale's heart as society has branded a public "A" on Hester's breast. Revelation of the private "A" at the moment of death does not condemn Dimmesdale to the punishment of exile, as Hester's "A" condemns her, but frees him for the heavenly reward that the good Puritan prizes. And rather than harm his reputation on earth, the revelation enhances it. Seeing no "A" on his bared breast, the most respectable of deceived adorers interpret his act of exposure as a sacrifice for them. It is the enactment of a Christian parable, "in view of Infinite Purity, we are all sinners alike" (259). For the reader who may still be deceived, the narrator states outright that he has provided a version of "stubborn fidelity" which upholds a "character, when proofs, clear as the mid-day sunshine on the scarlet letter, establish him a false and sin-stained creature of the dust" (259). The victim, not the victimizer, is the villain of this piece, who trembles and quakes through a cowardly life, obsessed with ambition at the expense of those he owes allegiance. Although it is Chillingworth who is supposed to shrivel away like the bad witch of Oz, it is the man of God, the hero of the people, we see melting in the sunshine.

III

In *The House of the Seven Gables*, Hawthorne's narrator is as playful as sun and shadow in the forest of *The Scarlet Letter*. Where he somberly probed the problem of sin and guilt in the earlier romance, he now makes a game of it. After Pearl forces Hester to take up the scarlet letter she has flung aside in the forest, the narrator declares, "So it ever is, whether thus typified or no, that an evil invests itself with the character of doom" (211). This pronouncement is frequently repeated in *The House of the Seven Gables*, and to the very end, "no great mistake . . . is ever really set right."[26] Yet in the first chapter, the narrator assumes sin can be redeemed if an inheritor is so moved. Toying with the reader, he asks, "whether each inheritor of the property—conscious of wrong doing and failing to rectify it—did not commit anew the great guilt of his ancestor, and incur all its original responsibilities" (20).

In *The House of the Seven Gables* the only Pyncheon who even considered rectification was the Uncle whom the current Judge frightened to death and whom Clifford Pyncheon was convicted of murdering. The Judge's apoplectic death may serve as retribution but certainly not rectification. Nor is the marriage of the last Maule with Phoebe Pyncheon a rectification. On the contrary, Holgrave, the last of the

Maules, abandons his stance of social reform and becomes a conservative in the Pyncheon tradition. And the movement from the old house to set up anew on Judge Pyncheon's tainted territory in the country indicates a continuance of the past, not a rectification. According to Philip Young, the story "does not indeed, teach the bald and dubious lesson that it purports to" (the recurring sins of the past).[27] Hawthorne is more devilish than Young suspects. The story may toy with rectification, but does indeed teach the lesson it purports.

The new territory is essentially the social sunshine Hester confronts as she emerges through the prison door. As a prison, the house represents the sins of the American past. But it is also seen as a great heart, a diseased one that is abandoned for a fresh one, also diseased. The tiny group in the sunshine at the end of the book foreshadows the community that is doomed in *The Blithedale Romance* (1852). Essentially little is changed. There is no indication that Hepzibah has given up her habit of living in the past, nor that Clifford has joined his aesthetic romanticism to societal actualities. The only apparent change is Holgrave's, but it is backwards, into the past. Warmed by Phoebe's touch and a share in the Pyncheon fortune, the social reformer turns towards a conservative family life in the country sun, apparently towards a happy ending.

The story was written at a supposedly happy moment in Hawthorne's life, and seems to reflect the move from Salem to the Berkshires, from the dark past to the light of the present. In a letter giving his impressions of the new work, Herman Melville, however, finds his friend saying, "No! in thunder. . . . For all men who say *yes* lie. . . ." Melville refers to a "certain tragic phase of humanity which, in our opinion was never more powerfully embodied than by Hawthorne."[28] What Melville sees as tragic is implicit in the deceptive sun shine at the happy ending of the story. The historic conflict between haves and have-nots, Holgrave's "united struggle for mankind," is not resolved in his marriage with Phoebe. This bonding simply abandons the social problem along with the old house. But the problem will sprout again since the seeds of the struggle are in the soil of the tainted new territory. Significantly the aristocratic old chickens move with the family into the sunshine. What occurs in the narrative of this story is a phase, the tragic phase, as Melville calls it, of a cyclical history, which begins with Colonel Pyncheon in early Puritan times.

Initially, Hawthorne positions his narrator as he does in "Sights from the Steeple," on a perch looking down on the American parade. From this stance, the viewer can distinguish the "broad daylight" from the "legendary mist" which the reader may disregard, or allow . . . to flow imperceptibly . . . for the sake of a picturesque effect" (2). Craftily, the narrator emphasizes this effect — "the book may be read strictly as a romance," yet whoever chooses this option should be aware of the warning: "When romances do really teach anything, or produce any effective operation, it is usually through a far more subtle process than the ostensible one." The legendary view is not so easily discerned in the broad daylight, the romance of the past in actualities of the moment. It is in the attempt to connect, the narrator says, that "this tale comes under Romantic definition."

The meaning is neither in the romantic view which serves to "bring out or mellow the light and deepen and enrich the shadows of the picture," nor in the realistic view, the photographic close-ups of house and street, peddlers, dirt-scratching hens, the casual boredom of newspaper readers on the railroad car. The narrator claims he is "bringing fancy-pictures almost into positive contact with the realities of the moment" (3). The gimlet-eyed gentleman in the railroad car, for example, provides earthy contrast for Clifford's instant and overwrought ideality. Hepzibah is introduced in photographic detail as she reluctantly prepares for her day, exasperating the narrator in her meticulous fussing. "Will she now issue forth over the threshhold of our story? . . . First every drawer in the . . . bureau to be opened, and closed again . . . " (31). She is reluctant to step into the story, the romance to be told by the narrator. Mischievously the narrator asks, "What tragic dignity . . . can be wrought into a scene like this!" and consoles himself with the observation, "Life is made of marble and mud" (41). The meaning is in the connection between the romantic and the realistic views, between the past and the present.

In Judge Pyncheon's death scene, romance emerges as delusion in its play with reality. Having just related the Judge's history, the narrator places his fresh corpse beneath his ancestor's portrait, while in the present reality outside the house, the idea of Judge Pyncheon as a living entity continues. This scene is the ultimate demonstration of "an absurd delusion of family importance, which all along characterized the Pyncheons" (19). Hepzibah shares the Pyncheon pride but hers is not greedy, having little relation to the present moment. Her delusion is to create a present from the past. She looks down from her tower "upon forest, field, and town as her own share of the ancestral territory," although she is forced to open a shop for survival. With pretended pity, the narrator states that she possesses an inner "beauty and majesty which are compelled to assume a garb so sordid" (41), but nowhere does he show these inner dimensions. Her scowl is supposed to be an ironical opposite to the Judge's public smile, concealing his pinched personality, his greed and avarice. But the scowl masks no opposing qualities, nothing of spiritual grace or generosity, aside from the prideful matter of carrying for her own, Clifford. The cause of the scowl turns out to be nearsightedness, her singular focus on things past. Wanting nothing from society except support, she is no exile; even when she is moved out of the house into the sunshine, the past moves with her.

Beauty and majesty, the narrator tells us coyly, can only be discerned through the gift of "what is called poetic insight" (41), and this is the quality we are led to entertain in brother Clifford. This sybarite, however, can hardly stand to look at sister Hepzibah. Actually, his self-satisfying urges would drown all possibilities of perceiving inner qualities in anyone. All we can learn of his attachment to Hepzibah is need of creature comfort. The presence of Phoebe provides for his aesthetic needs. After thirty years of imprisonment he has changed only in appearance. The narrator defines him as "indeed, the most inveterate of conservatives" (163), another relic of the past to be connected with the current moment. Hepzibah pulls the curtain to cut off some of the offensive sunlight from his side of the table, an act which symbolizes her desire to keep him in the shadows of the past. But the decadent sybarite has developed an urge for human community, perhaps because of his long imprisonment and his residual childishness. Although he has a "shivering repugnance at the ideas of personal contact with the world," he is seized with a "powerful impulse . . . whenever the rush and roar of the human tide grew strongly audible in him" (165). This attraction of the "natural magnet" is induced directly by lovely Phoebe's plebian ministrations. It is she who suggests that he "look out upon the life of the street" (159).

His consequent experience is aesthetic, his arched window providing a frame as he observes the parade of mankind below. It is also idiotic, mixed with the emotions of Faulkner's Benjy: "at every pretty throb of his sensibility, turning for sympathy to the eyes of the bright young girl!" (160). Unlike Paul Pry viewing from the steeple, Clifford becomes involved, while the narrator sees it all as a latter-day Ecclesiastes, "we mortals, whatever our business, or amusement—however serious, however trifling . . . in spite of our ridiculous activity, bring nothing finally to pass . . . " (165). Clifford is impelled to fantasize the scene as an ocean of humanity and again as a river streaming from one border of his window frame to the other. He cannot philosophically resign himself to it as the narrator does but must plunge in, as he might thrust an appealing piece of cake into his mouth. Yet, he is aware that the stream of humanity, like the cake, would dissolve as he plunged and he would be in the midst of ugly actualities. He would be inside the scene with the "horrible ugliness" of the monkey he had spotted from the window, his greed for coins "symbolizing the grossest form of the love of money." But the mind is blanched of such detail when this "lonely being, estranged from his race, [feels] himself man again by virtue of the irrepressible instinct that possesses him" (166). The exile is restrained from leaping into the great center of humanity by Hepzibah and Phoebe. Had he actually plunged and survived, Clifford speculates, he would have emerged a different man, perhaps a democrat who could withstand the touch of his fellows, but perhaps, as the narrator speculates, "he required nothing less than the final remedy—death!" the realistic outcome (166).

Clifford's second attempt to enter his plebian fantasy is milder, an effort to join rather than plunge. He insists on including Hepzibah. They attempt church but before reaching it, the "warm sunny air of the street made them shiver." So they "shrank back into the dusky passageway," and closed the door," reaffirming their knowledge: "We belong nowhere," she says. "We are ghosts", he says. They "have no right among human beings—no right anywhere but in this old house" (169). At the end of the chapter, we find the romantic sybarite at his window again, no longer feeling the pain of the exile but content to blow soap bubbles in the air and observe how "the passers-by regarded these brilliant fantasies, as they came floating down, and made the dull atmosphere imaginative about them" (171). (Has Clifford come to represent the author in this symbolic assessment of his value?)

The duplicity of the story's ending is prefigured in Clifford's third attempt to realize his fantasy. The effort is not the result of an exile's urge to join humanity; it is rather an unplanned and fearful escape. Ostensibly, Judge Pyncheon's death releases all the inhabitants from the old house, or from the past, but Clifford's reaction is most immediate. He takes Hepzibah and flees wildly and without direction. They chance upon a railroad car, symbol of democratic progress. Although Hepzibah suffers "the wretched consciousness of being adrift," Clifford is exhilarated. He is being drawn at last into the great current of life, "moving at whirlwind speed," not towards a recognizable goal but "in a direction opposite their own" (256). Inspired to be among the commonplace riders, he addresses one of them, the "gimlet-eyed man," and garrulously expends a social philosophy which seems spontaneously conceived and which reflects both his own narrow experience and Holgrave's reform ideals: "It is as clear to me as sunshine — were there any in the sky — that the greatest stumbling block in the past of human happiness and improvement are these heaps of bricks and stones . . . which men painfully contrive for their own torment, and call them house and home," especially, he goes on, "a certain house within my familiar recollection" (261). The rider responds sanely to Clifford's loquacious and personal liberalism, "what can be better for a man than his own parlor and chimney-corner?" To this common citizen, Clifford is "all humbug." Undaunted, Clifford babbles on, revealing what are probably Hawthorne's social criticisms, " . . . the bank robbers . . . after all, are about as honest as nine people out of ten, except that they disregard certain formalities, and prefer to transact business at midnight . . . " (265). Clifford leaves the railroad car as impulsively as he entered it, but at "a dismal way station in the rain."

What Clifford brings to the new house in the country at the end of the story is his old childish self, enhanced by his freedom from the Judge's repressive shadow. He can now play without censure in his fantasies, using the practical Uncle Venner as his foil in place of the unyielding gimlet-eye on the railroad. His enfeebled love of beauty will continue the fading strand of culture inherited from Europe. A sense of the old world has been attenuating through the generations. *The House of the Seven Gables* has none of the old world brilliancy of Governor Bellingham's house with its servants and English roses, already neglected by the early Puritans. Before the idiotic Clifford, there had been the abused Alice, who was educated abroad and "could not take kindly to the New England mode of life, in which nothing beautiful had ever been developed" (192). Although her father also disdained anything American, he had enough Pyncheon in him to sacrifice his daughter for the possibility of wealth that might elevate him to the dignity of a "Lord Pyncheon!" At the end of the story, Clifford's enfeebled aesthetic sense, his residual European strain, will apparently be dominated by his reformist ranting, his new American strain.

If there is any hope that sin will be undone by American progress in the new country home, it is in the development of Holgrave, a young man of sense who takes the leadership role that Clifford cannot assume. But while Clifford, the "most inveterate of conservatives" appears in the end to mimic the reformer who "lacked reverence for everything that was fixed" (177), Holgrave has also reversed direction and so the hope is spurious. Through most of the story Holgrave is the narrator's portrait of the promising young American, "the representative of many compeers in his native land" (181). More traveled than read, he has labored in numerous occupations and organizations including a community of Fourierists. And pursuing a philosophy focused on the welfare of mankind, he hates the burden of the past with its arrogant class distinctions based on greedy acquisition. For Holgrave, "the moss-grown and rotten past is to be torn down . . . and everything to begin anew" (179). From the start, however, the narrator undermines Holgrave. He suspects the representative of young America possesses the "false brilliancy" of youth, which withers in the "sun and rain, and assumes a very sober aspect after washing day" (181). For all his reformist idealism, he is a photographer, a man capable of an open-eyed or realistic view which leads him to question his own idealism and to realize "that a man's bewilderment is the measure of his wisdom" (178).

Far from the adamant character of Hawthorne's historical tales, Holgrave is easily changed. He comes to fulfill, not the democratic promise of young America, but the "sober aspect" of the commonplace conservative in a new abode, "the elegant country-seat of the late Judge Pyncheon" (314). His only regret is that the house is not built of stone so that succeeding generations could not alter the exterior. It ought to give "the impression of permanance which I consider essential to the happiness of any one moment." Continued repetition of the past is emphasized by the portrait of the newly-dead Judge hanging in the new house just as the portrait of the cursed old Colonel hangs in the old house.

Playfully, Hawthorne sewed all over again the seeds of evil. Evidence runs through the story, in the direct statements of the instrusive narrator and in his tone, which mocks the action and the characters. Since the love and beauty of Phoebe serve as the agent of change, of movement out of the shadow, we would have to take her character seriously to agree with standard interpretations that Hawthorne overlooked his theme, "that no great mistake . . . is ever really set right."[29] But her silliness cannot be ignored. In early appearances that establish her character, the narrator does not fail to envelop her in some degree of absurdity. In her waking scene, Phoebe's breath mingles in the fragrance that floats past her window. She enters a musty old room and with "a touch here and there . . . in the course of half an hour, had succeeded in throwing a kindly and hospital smile over the apartment" (72). Her very dreams, "being such cheerful ones, had exorcised the gloom, and now haunted the chamber in its stead." The narrator even has Phoebe worry over her singular function in the story: "I have given them my sunshine," he makes the silly girl say, "but of course I cannot both give it and keep it" (214).

Working on Holgrave, her sunshine stirs romantic love which adopts its own metaphor: "Moonlight and the sentiment in man's heart responsive to it," says the stricken idealist, "are the greatest of innovators and reformers. And all other reform and renovation I suppose, will prove to be no better than moonshine" (214). Switching the focus of his romantic inclinations from social to personal benefit, the photographer suggests the outcome of the American promise. The demonstration of this outcome is among the burdens of the succeeding story, *The Blithedale Romance*. Before *The House of the Seven Gables* is concluded, however, the narrator has Holgrave remind us that this story has been staged and that he, Holgrave, is wizard still: "In this long drama of wrong and retribution, I represent the old wizard, and am probably as much a wizard as ever he was" (316). Obviously his wizardry has been shared with the narrator.

IV

In *The Blithedale Romance*, the most ostensible wizard

is Professor Westervelt. He is a murky version of Hawthorne's Black Man as scientist but lacks the deep down motive of his predecessors such as Chillingworth and Alymer. As a devil figure he is more innocuous than the informative red and black townsman of "Major Molineux" or the guide in "Young Goodman Brown." While Westervelt provides the gothic magic and machinery of the wizard, Hollingsworth provides the motive. And the hypocritical reformer has no trouble in dissolving Westervelt's mesmeric spell. "Come," he calls to the Veiled Lady. "You are safe!" and the Professor's spell is broken; Priscilla instantly unveils. Her affection is "too powerful for the jugglery that had hitherto environed her."[30] Hollingsworth's power to attract Priscilla is also hypnotic, as Holgrave's voice becomes for Phoebe: "A veil was beginning to be muffled about her, in which she could behold only him, and live only in his thoughts and emotions" (211).[31] But the reformer of *Blithedale* has none of Holgrave's restraint. Where Holgrave forebears indulgence "to complete his mastery over Phoebe's yet free and virgin spirit . . . and become the arbiter of a young girl's destiny," Hollingsworth has no compunction. Reform is his ploy, mastery his motive.

Hollingsworth is often compared with Chillingworth on the basis of similar name structure and the fact that Zenobia sees the fiend in him.[32] But the reformer acts to right no wrong and he attracts rather than repells. Once a blacksmith, he is more like his counterpart in "The Artist of the Beautiful" who wins the lady coveted by the artist, and he is also somewhat like the ambitious minister of *The Scarlet Letter*, a Dimmesdale of Blithedale. His magnetism draws not only Zenobia and Priscilla, the matched sisters of wealth and poverty, but also Coverdale, the minor poet who seeks to escape his exile through emulation of the reformer in the social sunshine. Hollingsworth is at least the equal of Dimmesdale in dissimulation. Their masks veil the same prideful concentration on self-aggrandizement. "It is all self . . . nothing but self, self, self!" (218) Zenobia shouts at Hollingsworth in a moment of unmasking. With the Puritan priest, he believes that man is depraved by nature, unchangeable, yet he dreams of changing man by reforming the penitentiary which binds him. He knows what is good for "the sluggish steers." His experience, like Coverdale's, taught him that intellectual and working man are incompatible: "The clods of earth . . . never etherealized into thought. Our thoughts, on the contrary, were fast becoming cloddish" (66). Nevertheless he pursues the egalitarian goal. His hypocrisy is more pervasive than Dimmesdale's but so is his retribution. Dimmesdale confesses and dies immediately, at the peak of his glory in the sunshine, while Hollingsworth lives on after Zenobia's suicide, a broken man under Priscilla's tender care. "As we do by this friendless girl," Hollingsworth had proclaimed at the height of his powers, "so shall we prosper" (30). In the ironical outcome of his prophecy, however, it is she who does for him. But she cannot save him from all-consuming guilt. "How many criminals have you reformed?" asks Coverdale on a visit twelve years after Zenobia's body was pulled from the Concord river. "Ever since we parted," the penitent tells him, "I have been busy with a single murderer" (243).

Although Hollingsworth and Holgrave play prominent roles in their respective stories, neither is the prime performer. That role belongs to the narrator in both romances. He is the only remaining exile at the end of *Seven Gables* and he steps into *Blithedale* as Miles Coverdale, a participant. Here he continues the main drama between the romantic and the real, shadow and sunshine. As announced in the Preface, the aim is to "establish a theatre . . . where the creatures of his brain play their phantasmagorical antics without exposing them to too close a comparison with the actual events of real

lives." The socialist experience at Brook Farm was "essentially a day-dream, and yet a fact" to Hawthorne as Blithedale is
to the minor poet, Coverdale, who seeks "an available
foothold between fiction and reality." He has been a "spiritualized Paul Pry" observing a corrupt society. The opportunity to play a role in an ideal society is as appealing to his
imagination as plunging in the ocean of mankind is to Clifford. And once within, the mirage dissolves in the same
confusing way. At Blithedale he encounters not an achieved
community, but an assemblage of other exiles, "estranging
[themselves] from the world" (55).[33]

In spite of the title, *Blithedale* is less a romance than his
previous novels. Yet Hawthorne cannot free his narrator of
wizardry, of the notion that he must manipulate the sensed
world in order to render the truth of the human heart.
Discovering the devil instead of the truth at work in the heart
of the ideal reformer, the narrator withdraws to his original
position as observer, and is unable even to reveal his attraction to the Veiled Lady he loves and so perhaps unveil her.
"Aloof from the possibility of personal concernment,"
Coverdale is similar to the naive disciple who unwittingly
loses his lady to the teacher in "Lesson of the Master," and he
is also something of James' timid lover in "The Beast in the
Jungle."[34] He looks back over a life of ambiguous longing,
aware of that "cold tendency between instinct and intellect,
which made me pry with a speculative interest into people's
passions and impulses, and which appeared to have gone far
towards unhumanizing my heart" (154). From the distance of
twelve years, Coverdale sees that lack of faith in the reform
society, in the idealism or romance of it, has usurped purpose
and "rendered my own life all an emptiness" (246). The minor
poet ends as a Goodman Brown tempered by self-knowledge.

Coverdale's intended journey from a corrupt society to
Blithedale is parallel with the Puritan journey to America.

Theological theory is replaced by social theory. The journey is also his own personal movement from the shadow to the sunshine and back into the shadow. It is from the shadow at the end that he tells his story of attempting the sunshine. He must "rake away the ashes from the embers in . . . memory, and blow them up with a sigh, for lack of more inspiring breath" (9). In that sigh is all the regret of disillusionment. Whatever the failings of the dream in actuality, he regrets his failure in not pursuing it:

> Yes, after all, let us acknowledge it wiser, if not more sagacious to follow out one's day-dream . . . although, if the vision has been worth the having, it is certain never to be consummated otherwise than by failure. And what of that! Its airiest fragments, impalpable as they may be, will possess a value that lurks not in the most ponderous realities of any practical scheme. . . . Whatever else I may repent of, therefore, let it be reckoned neither among my sins nor follies, that I once had faith and force enough to form generous hopes of the world's destiny" (10).

As he recalls the cold April day he set out from his comfortable quarters "into the heart of the pitiless snowstorm, in quest of a better life," he remembers also the beginnings of disillusionment. He finds Blithedale a cold Eden. Zenobia, its exotic Eve, wearing a hot-house flower in her hair, "caused our heroic enterprise to show like an illusion . . . a counterfeit Arcadia" (21). The kitchen and the housework are still a woman's lot and the fieldwork is closely supervised by a real farmer, Silas Foster, who exposes at every turn the idealists' ineptness and whose conversation centers on swine. "Pigs! Good Heavens!" Coverdale reflects silently, "had we come out from among the swinish multitude for this?" (20). He is particularly dismayed that after "separation from the greedy, struggling, self-seeking world," one of the first questions

raised should be "of getting advantage over the outside bar-
barians . . . we stood in a position of new hostility rather than
new brotherhood."

Coverdale can no longer see the social Eden he has envisioned because he is in it. He can no longer see romantically.
When Zenobia jokes about the cold weather, that she will not
be able to assume "the garb of Eden . . . till after May Day,"
Coverdale's reaction is a sensuous fantasy, " . . . these last
words, together with something in her manner, irresitably
brought up a picture of that fine, perfectly developed figure,
in Eve's earliest garment . . . when she was just made and her
Creator brought her to Adam, saying, 'behold! here is a
woman' " (17). To recover his idealistic vision, Coverdale
must undergo metamorphosis. He conveniently becomes ill,
and it seems he creeps "out of a life of old conventionalisms."
That life "is flung aside, like any other worn out or
unseasonable garment; and, after shivering a little while in
my skeleton, I began to be clothed anew . . . I was quite
another man" (61). But his new set of clothes restricts the free
play his imagination formerly enjoyed. It is a set of
Fourieristic ideals which encloses his vision, as Calvinistic
faith in eternal progress encloses the Puritan's vision. Wearing his new set of clothes, Miles Coverdale approximates his
namesake, the sixteenth century biblical translator whose imagination was also imprisoned by a set of clothes.

Coverdale's transformation is so superficial that his faith
is shaken even before he completes convalescence. He is confused when Hollingsworth, still his model, reveals that he
loathes the ideals of Fourier because the selfish principle is at
the base, "the principle of all inhuman wrong, the very
blackness of man's heart." Fourier has committed "the unpardonable sin," as monstrous an iniquity as the "Devil himself
[could] contrive" (53). And the more Hollingsworth condemns, the more Coverdale sees that the reformer is de-

scribing himself, "that he had come among us actuated by no real sympathy with our feelings and our hopes." Yet, from his tender treatment of Priscilla, it was obvious that Hollingsworth was "originally endowed with a great spirit of benevolence. But by and by . . . a cold, spectral monster which he had himself conjured up" wasted all the warmth of his heart, and at last, "as these men of mighty purpose so invariably do—he had grown to be [its] bond slave. It was his philanthropic theory" (55).

With this insight, Coverdale loses what faith he has. He sees the community bond now as negative, a quarrel with the old system rather than a unified vision of a new one. The peril was not that they should fail to become farmers but that they "should cease to be anything else" (65) except the "mirror of [Hollingsworth's] purpose" (70). Men like Hollingsworth, whose "godlike benevolence has been debased into all-devouring egotism" will "smite and slay you and trample your dead corpse under foot, all the more readily, if you take the first step with them, and cannot take the second . . . of their terribly straight path."

So Coverdale dresses again in the old clothing, the "old conventionalisms." He tells Priscilla, "my past life has been a tiresome one enough; yet I would rather look backward ten times, than forward once . . . I do not see much wisdom in being so very merry in this kind of world" (76). But Coverdale sounds a good deal more certain than he is. A short while later he admits, "I was beginning to lose the sense of what kind of world it was, among innumerable schemes of what it might or ought to be" (140). To regain this sense, he must leave Blithedale and seek the realities of the city. Pursuing a whim to bid the pigs farewell, the narrator muses, the "greasy citizens . . . alone are happy" in their "unctuous bliss . . . betwixt dream and reality" (144).

Just as the emigrants from *The House of the Seven*

Gables carry the dreary past into the country, Coverdale carries his confusion betwixt dream and reality into the city. He
is retreating from his flirtation with social idealism. Although
"empty of the beautiful," the flux of city life at first takes a
"sensuous hold" on his mind. "I felt as if there could never be
enough of it" (146). His Blithedale experience, however, has
so captured his attention that soon Coverdale can think only
of the entanglements he had fled. In the city he has returned
to the characteristic condition of the exile, longing for the
communion of a rejected society. The condition is reinforced
in the language by which he describes the city scenes. It is far
more concrete and sensuous than his descriptions of Blithedale. From his hotel window he looks through back windows
into other lives. "Realities keep in the rear," Coverdale explains, "and put forward an advance-guard of show and
humbug" (149). Without the patterning of his imagination,
the romanticising, his language renders only the details of his
observation, and these details do not cohere into sense or
story.

Among the inexplicable sights from his rear window is
Zenobia seen in the rear window of another hotel, with
Priscilla and then with Westervelt. Later, visiting Zenobia,
whose hot-house flower is now replaced by an altogether artificial one, he cannot discern whether the woman of
Blithedale or of the city is the real one. "In both, there was
something like the illusion which a great actress flings about
her" (165). Stunned by her flaming jewels and costly robes,
Coverdale asks, "Can it be, Zenobia, that you ever numbered
yourself with our little band of earnest, thoughtful, philanthropic laborers?" (164). Her answer comes later, at Eliot's
pulpit, in direct response to Hollingsworth's rejection of her:

> Of all varieties of mock-life, we have surely blundered
> into the very emptiest mockery in our effort to establish

the one true system. I have done with it; and Blithedale must find another woman to superintend the laundry, and you, Mr. Coverdale, another nurse to make your gruel the next time you fall ill. It was, indeed, a foolish dream! (227).

In the city, to Coverdale also, Blithedale and its characters have become a dream. Even old Moodie, who is merely associated with it, is immersed in the air of unreality. "His existence looked so colorless and torpid, so very faintly shadowed on the canvas of reality," that Coverdale fears the old man will disappear before his eyes (179). From Moodie he learns that Priscilla was called "ghost child" because she could vanish at will although she could never quite make herself visible. This disclosure positively inspires his voyeuristic tendencies. Compounding Priscilla's symbolic role as societal victim with her sexual role, both aspects of her "maidenly mystery," Coverdale "could not resist the impulse to take just one peep beneath her folded petals" (125).

Coverdale encounters the mystery of Priscilla again after weeks of hopping and fluttering "like a bird with a string about its leg . . . keeping up a restless activity to no purpose" (195). The event shatters his resistence to "inexpressible longings" for the three friends who had absorbed his life. He sees the Veiled Lady on stage, as in the beginning, under the mesmeric power of Westervelt. The name of the wizard now appears to take on the significance of "western world," perhaps most western or American, as he discourses on "a futurity . . . [of] one great mutually conscious brotherhood," which he describes "as if it were a matter of chemical discovery" (200) instead of love and sympathy.[35] Coverdale "detested this kind of man" when he first met him in the woods "because a part of my own nature showed itself responsive to him" (102). Like the Veiled Lady, however, he is far more responsive to the devilish powers of Hollingsworth, who rises now from the audience to counteract Westervelt's hypnotic power.

When Coverdale sets out again for Blithedale, he is no longer in pursuit of ideal community. He is following his friends. As he approaches, he fears "there was no such place as Blithedale . . . nothing but dream-work and enchantment" (206). The first glimpse of the buildings, however, reassure him and he perceives another purpose in returning. It is there he had "earned bread and eaten it, and so established [his] claim to be on earth . . . " At this moment Coverdale could as well have been Hester Prynne resuming life in Salem, an exile on the edge of town. "There was my home, and there might be my grave" (206). Having fantasized about the very existence of the place, however, he cannot bear the shock of realization, and so takes to his old hermitage on the edge, in the pine tree veiled by grape vines.

Before this hermitage parades the Blithedale society in masquerade, the figures "whirling round so swiftly, so madly, and so merrily, in time and tune with the Satanic music . . . " (210). At this distance from the human activity, Coverdale's imagination can view it whole and steadily. What he has seen as dream is now nightmare, the midnight frolic in the forest of "Goodman Brown." He emits a laugh, revealing himself, and the "whole fantastic rabble forthwith streamed off in pursuit of me, so that I was like a mad poet hunted by chimeras" (211). Outrunning them, he stumbles upon a scene at Eliot's pulpit. It is the "profounder region" where his friends dwelt. The scene is more masquerade, in reverse, the Puritan past in modern dress. Zenobia appears to be a dethroned queen on trial "or perchance, condemned already." The judge is Hollingsworth, "the grim portrait of a Puritan magistrate holding inquest of life and death in a case of witchcraft," and Priscilla is "the pale victim whose soul and body have been wasted by Zenobia's spells" (214). The narrator has led himself to another unveiling, and the reader may wonder if it is the final one.

Although the narrator has directed the mystery to Priscilla's veil, it is more Zenobia's veiling that intrigues us. In spite of all her championing of woman's independence, she would still subjugate herself to Hollingsworth's mastery if he loved and had not deceived her. She concentrates on an aggressive and insensitive man while neglecting a meek and needy sister. Even after rejection, this Oriental princess will not tolerate Coverdale's perjorative judgment of Hollingsworth as a "heart of ice," and a "wretch" (225). The criticism boomerangs. "Do him no wrong. . . . Presume not to estimate a man like Hollingsworth . . . " (225). The narrator has no inkling of the transaction he witnessed through the hotel window in which Zenobia gives Priscilla to Westervelt. Consequently, he cannot sense the possibility of a deeper complication in her defeat, the guilt, now that Hollingsworth has saved her sister from the wizard's usages. Even the gruesome sight of the suicide's face against the black water under the midnight lamp is veiled to Coverdale. She has merely exchanged one veil for another. "When you next hear of Zenobia," she had forwarned him, "her face will be behind the black veil" (228).

In July 1844, Hawthorne described in his notebook the suicide by drowning of an apparently ambitious farm girl. He blames the old bosom serpent, excessive pride, although he expresses the cause as Cooper might have seen it, "a penalty for having cultivated and refined herself out of the sphere of natural connections" (36). Zenobia is a reversal of the drowned farm girl. "Nature certainly never intended Zenobia for a cook" (48). At Blithedale, she is clearly out of her element and her demand on Hollingsworth's love is an expression of her excessive pride. It is Priscilla, the ethereal and wispy one, removed from time and space, who appears to have drifted to her "natural connections," the love and tender care of a diminished Hollingsworth. At the close of the romance, Coverdale observes the mundane seamstress' daughter physically in her element, nursing the former strong man in a "deep, submissive, unquestioning reverence" (242). And even as he observes this mystery in the outcome of the story, it evades him. In contrast to Zenobia's final veil, Priscilla wears now "a veiled happiness in her fair and quiet countenance" (242). So it seems to our narrator, observing from the periphery of life.

Love, the "natural connection" escapes Coverdale because he too is veiled. He does not attempt his own unveiling until the final hesitant line of the story: "I — I myself — was in love — with — Priscilla!" This sudden utterance is also a confession that the narrator's account has been prejudiced. Evidence that he has been preparing the confession is scattered through the story. While admitting to his "tendency towards the actual" and his determination to "take an exterior view of what we had all been about," the narrator repeatedly warns of his poetic license and fancy, which the reader can see is in the service of his prejudice. It is generated by his envy of Hollingsworth whose strength of purpose he had hoped to emulate. Coverdale's veil of prejudice is not lifted any more than any other veil in the story, but, along with Hollingsworth's strength, it dissipates in the telling twelve years later. At the end, Coverdale can enjoy the irony, "As Hollingsworth once told me, I lack a purpose. How strange! He was ruined, morally, by an overplus of the very same ingredient" (246).

Lacking purpose, Coverdale can never belong to anything. He is a nostalgic romancer, preferring even at the end of his narrative to dream of "our beautiful scheme of noble and unselfish life" (245). This is his thin cold art with no life of its own. Like Theodore in Zenobia's anecdote, his imagination will never unveil reality unless he commits himelf to it, never by observing from the shadow of a hermitage covered with vines, or a hotel window. Although he has spent his life "tolerably enough," he is a "poor and dim" figure in his own narrative, "suffering my colorless life to take its hue from other lives, but what, after all, have I to tell? Nothing, Nothing, Nothing!" (245)[37]

Whatever way the reader may respond to Coverdale's confession, it exposes the dark content of his mind and the vacuity of his heart. The artist-exile has never found the foothold between dream and reality. Without the opening and joining of one heart to another, the mind becomes the individual's reality in which the outside world is dreamt. The narrator's sad confession that he has nothing to tell ostensibly eliminates the assumed reader. It is a confession to himself alone, a lament that his heart is concealed, that community is not possible for him, nor love.

V

It was more than eight years before Hawthorne rejoined Coverdale in the shadows. Finishing *Blithedale* at the Horace Mann house in West Newton, the author extended his stay in the sunshine, like a hungry man at a buffet. "Shall I send him ten packs of visiting cards?" Melville chided. "And a box of kid gloves? and the latest style of Parisian handkerchiefs? — He goes into society too much altogether — seven evenings out a week should content any reasonable man."[38] Waiting to sail for his consulate position in Liverpool, a reward for writing President Pierce's campaign biography, Hawthorne found his fictional storehouse running dry and reworked the ancient myths, ostensibly for children, but now the old stories seemed "hideous . . . the sternest forms of grief. . . . How was the blessed sunshine to be thrown into them!"[39] In England, fictionalizing was suspended altogether, but his intentions re-

mained literary. In spite of a heavy social schedule and the
press of consulate duties, he began almost at once his English
notebooks, a replenishing of material that would provide in-
gredients for a work to which all the others had been
preparatory, a romance of the old world, the richer soil.[40]

The "old countries" provided the romancer the "Faery
Land" he had imagined in the Preface of *Blithedale*, "so like
the real world that, in a suitable remoteness, one cannot tell
the difference." While Hawthorne the counsel defended his
country's virtues, often by detrimental comparison with
England, Hawthorne the romancer, had returned to the old
world "Faery Land" he had promised himself. Excursions
into the countryside abetted his sense of coming home, from
a wild landscape to a civilized one. He searched through old
country histories as he had previously explored the histories
of Salem, especially alert to any possible family reference,
"even a gravestone in one of these old churchyards, with my
name upon it."[41] Although he wished still to be buried in
America, his notebooks contain little sense of longing for the
native land. On the contrary, "it sickens me to look back
upon America." Aside from the increasing competition of
"scribbling women," Hawthorne was sickened by the "tumult
and bad blood . . . we are the most miserable people on
earth."[42] It was only when Sophia went off to join the
O'Sullivan's in their near-royal existence at the Embassy in
Portugal that Hawthorne revealed any longing, "Nothing
gives me any joy. I have learned what the bitterness of exile
is. . . . Life seems so purposeless as not to be worth the trouble of carrying it on any further."[43] We can envision Sophia
protecting him from the relentless sunshine somewhat as
Hepzibah pulls the window shade to edge the light where Clifford sits.

English pretences—titles and other egoistic appurte-
nances—had annoyed him since his arrival. In his pique,

Hawthorne could attack anything British, even the Museum. Particularly annoying was the presumptuous blockishness of the English squire: "John Bull cannot make himself fine whatever he puts on . . . and his female is well adapted to him."[44] In his long walks through the slum districts, however, this Twainish attitude was subdued; Hawthorne reacted intensely to the squalor and disease and the tenacity of life he found in the streets of Liverpool. In a West Darby workhouse, an urchin, dirty and sore-ridden, pulled his coattails, demanding to be picked up. Glad that he was wearing gloves, Hawthorne could hardly bring himself to the touch, "yet I never should have forgiven myself if I had repelled its advances." Hawthorne had anticipated finding an ancestral trace in some manorial estate, not in a workhouse for the poor and deformed. But "out of all human kind, [the child] chose me to be its father!" Holding the urchin, Hawthorne felt a strange kinship as if he could "set down its affection to the score of blood recognition."[45] This was not the illusory stuff of the English romance in the mind's eye, but the opened heart compelling and upbraiding the closed heart of the returning exile he felt himself to be: "My ancestor left England in 1635. I return in 1853 . . . as if I myself had been absent these two hundred and eighteen years."[46]

A few years later, when he came to write the English romance, the dirt and squalor of Liverpool and the workhouse urchin were out of mind. He was in Italy and the image that fascinated him was the "bloody footstep," a dark stain in the smooth gray surface of Smithell Hall,[47] which he had visited. He could not use the legend that went with it, of a martyr responding to injustice by stamping the stone so hard his foot bled. He sought an embodiment in the American exile returning to stake his claim, but essentially found himself repeating *The House of the Seven Gables*. The returning American carries within him a secret sin, as Holgrave does, which is powerful enough to destroy the ancient family inhabiting the house. By the third version, the youth relinquishes his claim, rather than unleash buried sin, and takes a Phoebe-like lady back to America where the two will be fitting missionaries of a new social faith. After he encountered the Faun of Praxiteles, Hawthorne abandoned his English romance. It was time. By then his John Bull squire of the ancestral home had become an Italianate villain.

Hawthorne had seen an imitation Faun of Praxiteles in the Villa Borghese and then the real thing in the Capital gallery, and associated it with Guido Reni's painting of Beatrice Cenci in the gallery of the Barbarinnin Palace. Then, in a Capuchin chapel he was astonished with the sight of a monk laid out during a funeral service, his face flushed as if he had died of apoplexy, as the Pyncheons were wont to do. Blood oozed from the corpse's nostril and Sophia thought a bushy eyebrow twitched. The dead monk contrasted utterly with the intellectual and aesthetic richness of the Catholic heritage which enthralled Hawthorne in Italy. The "engineers who manage now [the church's] cranes and safety-valves,"[48] could not dispel the enchantment of the brilliant frescoes on the roof, and within the domes the gold and gems adorning the shrines; "nobody who has not seen a church like this can imagine what a gorgeous religion it was that reared it."[49] Glorious art brought the "deeper mysteries" closer to man's heart than the "most eloquent words of preacher or prophet" (340). Beyond the art was the confessional, "Man needs it so." In the comforts of Catholicism, an exile from "the dryness and meagerness of a New English Village" could find refuge.

The idea of an Italian romance forming in his mind carried the exile further back than the ancestral home, to the essential concept of being human. A human faun, simple and honest, void of principle, amiable, sensual and yet capable of pathos and even love, would join the human race through the commission of an innocent crime. The crime would be a natural result of his pathos and love, an effort to save a

Cenci-like figure; and the victim would be the principle of evil forever regenerating itself, the dead monk that still bled and twitched. The faun would develop into a man when guilt would enclose his heart, and Catholicism, not its clergy, would bless the confession and penance which opens the heart. This movement is Hawthorne's understanding of the human needs that bring the faith into being.

The Preface to *The Marble Faun* claims Italy as the "poetic or fairy precinct" Hawthorne longed for in *The Blithedale Romance*, the "atmosphere of strange enchantment . . . the American romancer needs." Here, "actualities [are not] so terribly insisted upon as they . . . must needs be in America . . . where there is no shadow, no antiquity, no mystery, no picturesque and gloomy wrong, nor anything but a commonplace prosperity, in the broad and simple daylight" (3).

But if the romancer was more at home in Italy, his story was certainly not. Transplanted to the richer soil of Rome, the wizard is more ominous than Chillingworth or Westervelt and even less embodied. He is the model monk and is nearly pure abstraction pared closed to the evil core. Hilda is now the proud and adamant Puritan. Her reaction to the knowledge of sin, unlike Goodman Brown's, is not permanently debilitating. And although the artist whose sensibility registers most of the story is no longer a minor poet seeking a foothold between reality and dream, nor a progress-minded daguerreotypist, he is still a Paul Pry. Instead of the actualities of the city or the romance of Blithedale, Kenyon offers the reader a travelogue through Hawthorne's statuesque fairyland. Hester can be recognized in the spirited woman exiled by the sins of her past, although Miriam's past is hidden, like Zenobia's. Even Donatello, the human faun, is not entirely fresh. In Europe he may be of noble family, but his innocence, although not his frolicsomness, derives in part from young Robin of "Major Molineux" and provides a displaced completion of the farm boy's story through sin and expiation in the Italian city.

Noticeably absent from *The Marble Faun* are the ambitious and hypocritical characters, Dimmesdale and Hollingsworth. They are partially subsummed by Hilda, although her ambition is not earthly and she is without hypocrisy since there is nothing to hide in her steely, unaccommodating heart. It is touching that she tries to soften and open her heart in the Roman church while tenaciously rooted in the Puritanical one. Unfortunately, her proud innocence will not submit to the experience of sin, not even second hand as befits a copyist. Her spirit is shut, therefore, to the possibility of penance and communion with the human race. And Kenyon is well aware of her virginal resolve as he follows her out of the wholeness of Europe to the vacuous New England home she symbolizes.

With Kenyon as the comprehending sensibility, the narrator's role is reduced to stage-setter and moral intruder. At the outset he attempts to induce the reader into a vague dream state in which "all matters that we handle or dream of now-a-days look evanescent and visionary alike . . . we find ourselves fading into shadows and unrealities" (6). And the characters are so intended, evanescent, shadowy: the model/monk is "dark, bearded, wild of aspect and attire, whom artists convert into saints or assassins, according as their pictorial purposes demand" (19); Miriam and Donatello fade in and out of scenes in their march of penitence; Hilda's copies have the "evanescence and ethereal life" (58) of their originals, and even she evaporates for a while. The reader is to be pulled out of time to live a spell in a romance where American values of progress are replaced by the mythically recurring past. Manipulating the story to sustain illusion, the narrator represses "actualities." The external scenes seem frozen, extensions of the sculptures and paintings.

The "actualities" are hidden beneath the surfaces in this

statuesque fairyland. Hilda refuses to see them even in the paintings she copies. In Guido's Beatrice Cenci, she sees only a sorrowful angel, "fallen and yet sinless" (66), until Miriam points out the history of her sorrow. "Her doom is just," pronounces the American virgin without another thought. And although Hilda witnesses Donatello's crime, she does not see it, the struggle, the falling body smashing onto the bricks below. Her mind, "the eternal adamant" (171), can permit only the abstract idea of a crime committed, and then it leaps immediately to the intolerable stain of her own second-hand involvement.

The hidden "actualities," however, become the substance of Donatello's mind, where they are replayed endlessly, the very essence of his transformation from the joys of innocence to the responsibilities of guilt. Before his crime, Donatello possesses an "infinite repugnance to graves and skulls, and to all that ghastliness which the Gothic mind loves to associate with the idea of death" (25). After the crime he is luridly fascinated with its ghastliness. The images spill out of his mind at one point into Kenyon's ear: "a fellow creature, breathing, now, and looking you in the face, — and now tumbling down, down, down, with a long shriek wavering after him, all the way. He does not leave his life in the air! No, but it keeps in him till he thumps against the stones, a horribly long while, then he lies there frightfully quiet, a dead heap of bruised flesh and broken bones. A quiver runs through the crushed mass, and no more movement after that!" (261). Eventually the repeated re-creations of the actuality resonate with mythical reality; through them, Donatello joins mankind.

Miriam emphasizes the disparity between the two innocents — Hilda and Donatello — in the church of the Capuchins following the murder. She criticizes Guido's unruffled archangel as he is depicted moments after his death struggle with the evil principle (whose face is later observed as the model/monk's): "I could have told Guido better. A full third of the archangel's feathers should have been torn from his wings . . . the battle never was such child's play . . . " (184).

The remark pertains to Hilda's adamant innocence, but also to the child's play on the bier, the model converted into the corpse of a Capuchin monk. This gothic metamorphosis shows no evidence of struggle or an actual fall onto hard bricks; it gives rather a sign of deathlessness, bleeding from the nostril in the presence of its murderers. Because she is capable of such experience, Miriam reads the sign symbolically as ageless evil, an accumulation of actualities into myth, just as she perceives the missing actualities in Guido's painting. "Farewell," she bids the deathless corpse, "till the next encounter" (191). Hilda can have no such sense of eternal evil in the fairyland. Refusing experience, she can only iterate abstractions. She is "Only visable by the sunshine in her soul" (63). To Miriam her "innocence is like a sharp steel sword" (66), and Kenyon uses the same image to descibe her powers of remorse, pursuing her nevertheless. The narrator finishes off his description of Hilda with a veiled reference to those "scribbling women" whom Hawthorne accused of dominating the American literary marketplace. She is capable of "pretty fancies of snow and moonlight; the counterpart in picture of so many feminine achievements in literature" (61).

The story is neatly divided two by two, the Europeans who engage the actualities in the fairyland and the Americans who do not and thus remain foreigners. Kenyon, however, like Giovanni looking into Rappaccini's garden, is capable of European experience. He can overcome his American conditioning enough to sculpt a Cleopatra which so completely captures womanhood that it astounds Miriam. She had considered him merely another plagiarist, but seeing that he could knead "a lump of wet clay from the Tiber" into a statue that was "all Cleopatra . . . fierce, voluptuous, passionate, tender, wicked, terrible, and full of poisonous and rapturous enchantment" (27), Miriam is tempted to share with him her heart-searing secret and thus relieve her unbearable loneliness. Then suddenly she draws back, sensing his residual barrier, his Puritanical "reserve and alarm," his question of propriety that he should listen, his fear that it might end in her hatred of him. "You are as cold and pitiless as your own marble," she offers instead of her confession. Although the narrator instantly intervenes to assure the reader it is not so, Miriam's intuition is partially verified in a later conversation at Monti Beni. Hilda has refused her the solace of confession and Kenyon defends the virgin's purity against even the threat of nasty words, "I shall tell Hilda nothing that will give her pain . . . the white shining purity of Hilda's nature is a thing apart; and she is bound, by the undefiled material of which God moulded her, to keep that severity . . . " (287). Miriam has no recourse but cynical irony. "You are right" she tells him, and if there were anything to forgive, which is nothing less than Hilda's unpardonable sin of selfish pride in her purity, "I do forgive her." In return for Kenyon's denial of comfort, Miriam offers a dubious blessing, "May you win her virgin heart."

Before Kenyon can win Hilda he must relinquish the artistic potential that created his Cleopatra, his heart momentarily opened and understanding in the old world. In that condition, he becomes a catalyst who brings about the reunion of those "wed in crime." Miriam and Donatello have penetrated through the gloom and terror that Hawthorne described in his notebook in 1842 and have come into the deepest region of that heart symbol, but the eternal beauty, similar to the sunshine and flowers at the opening of the cavern, is not theirs. They are not fulfilled, of course, because of the sin passed unto them at the moment of their wedding. It pressed the two hearts together "till the horror and agony of each was combined as one emotion and that a kind of rapture . . . closer than a marriage bond." There are no others in that cavern: "the world could not come near them; they were safe" (174). So they thought. On the streets moments later, the "paradise into which she and her one companion had been transported by their crime" dissipates. "Was there indeed, no such refuge, but only a crowded thoroughfare, and jostling throng of criminals?" (176).

Apart, Donatello is dejected in his tower, Miriam is forlorn in her obsession as a horror in her loved-one's eyes. Kenyon's role is to reunite the lovers and it is this activity which can potentially educate him in the human requirements of the fairyland. Kenyon succeeds in bringing Donatello down from his tower, where he has been reliving his crime to the extent of throwing earthworms over the battlement, and delivering him to Pope Julius' outstretched hand of marble in the open street. There Donatello is reunited with Miriam before thousands of wondering witnesses. But Kenyon himself remains as innocent of the mythical meaning as the witnesses, even as he pontificates: "your bond is twined with such black threads that you must never look upon it identically with the ties that unite other living souls" (322), a reference to the idealistic mating he seeks with Hilda. Kenyon is still an American artist looking in. For him, Italy remains a place to visit, where "papal despotism allows . . . freer breath than our native air," where we can "take a generous view of our associates . . . without ruining ourselves" (109). However long he resides, Kenyon is not a resident. "You have no guilt," Donatello explains, "to make you shrink from happiness" (323).

In the last third of the romance, the atmosphere of dream begins to affect even Hilda. She descends from her tower to seek comfort if not purgation from the stain of knowing about another's sin. The Roman streets have become "hot and dusty," the palaces, churches, and sepulchres dreary, the Tiber muddy "instead of a gold-brown rivulet." She becomes "acquainted with the exile's pain" (342), and yearns for a neat, comfortable house on an elm-lined street. Eventually Hilda unburdens herself in a confessional where the priest tries to bribe her into conversion in rather seductive language, "What have you to give in return for an old man's kindness and sympathy?" Nevertheless, she emerges "a figure of peaceful beatitude," as Kenyon sees her: "Saint Hilda, whatever church may canonize you" (364).

The confession lifts the burden of guilt for witnessing a murder, but Hilda has done little more than smooth a slight dent in her Puritan armor. Unaware of the deeper guilt she ought to feel, for willfully denying comfort to Miriam, she glories in her state of "infinite peace after infinite trouble." Her Puritanical experience in the Catholic church is symbolized by her refusal of the priest's absolution, "God forbid that I should ask absolution from mortal man" (359), and then by Kenyon's contrast of the New England church with St. Peter's. The clear glass allows "the pure, white, light of Heaven" into the New England church while the light streams into St. Peter's through "a brilliant illusion of saints and hierarchies, and old scriptural images, and symbolized dogmas, purple, blue, golden, and a broad flame of scarlet" (366). Similar difference exists between her copyist sense of art and the real thing.

When Hilda fails to make her appointment with Kenyon in the Vatican gallery, he loses ballast. He relies on her "perfectly transparent medium" to apprehend the sculptures. Chilled with disappointment, Kenyon wanders in the streets which had become uneasy for him as they had become dreary for Hilda. A carriage stops beside him and the grand lady within asks, "Is all well with you?" A shadow of a sallow-

faced Italian is also in the carriage, but all that Miriam wants
to say, in spite of her own troubles, is for Kenyon's comfort,
"when the lamp goes out do not despair" (397). He arrives at
the base of Hilda's tower just in time to see the Virgin flame
quiver and die, the only illumination in "his cold, artistic life"
(409). Now, through the "darkly colored medium of his fear,"
Kenyon saw the evil city, its priesthood with "red and bloated
cheeks and carnal eyes," its nobility "cultivating a viscious
way of life," its soldiery inheriting the foul licentiousness of the Gauls, Goths and Vandals, and its citizens "kneeling a little while at the confessional, and rising unburdened
. . . and incited by fresh appetite for the next ensuing sin"
(412). In the dark tide of human evil he felt over Rome, pagan corruption had been followed by perverted Christianity.

Finally, in the dreamiest episode of all, Kenyon descends
into a cellar-like cavity, or excavation, where he uncovers
fragments of an old marble statue which his imagination
must piece together, "What a discovery is here! . . . I seek for
Hilda and find a marble woman! Is the omen good or ill"
(423). The omen turns out to be ill for his pursuit of art but
good for his pursuit of Hilda. The assembled statue, suggesting Venue de Medici, falls into "worthless fragments"
again the moment Kenyon fixes his mind upon "something
dearer to him than his art" (424). At this moment of decision — between Hilda and art, America and Europe — Kenyon
is confronted with the myth of the fortunate fall. Miriam and
Donatello reappear at the scene of the excavation, dressed
now as peasants for the carnival which is to be the grand
finale of his dream-like existence in Rome. Explaining herself
at last, but omitting more than she reveals and assuring him
of reunion with Hilda, Miriam proceeds to the narrator's
main issue: "The story of the Fall of Man! Is it not repeated
in our Romance of Monti Beni. . . . Will not this idea account

for the permitted existence of sin, as no other theory can?" (434). Donatello has already fallen. The question for Kenyon is whether he should follow, not by virtue of murder, but art. Shall he fall into the life of art in sinful Rome or eschew it for Hilda's purity in America? There is no agonizing decision here. It is nearly automatic. The American artist backs away, "too dangerous, Miriam! I cannot follow you!" A few seconds earlier, he had confessed, "Ah Miriam, I cannot respond to you. . . . Imagination and the love of art have both died out of me" (427).

Thus, the Roman carnival becomes "the emptiest of mockeries" to Kenyon (437), until Hilda returns. Before he enshrines her as a household saint in the light of her husband's fireside, however, Kenyon must challenge her with his residual desire for the artist's involvement with life. "Did Adam fall," he asks his bride-to-be, "that we might ultimately rise to a far loftier paradise than his?" This question, of course, confuses the Adamic story, as Miriam presented it, with the Savior's story. Perhaps it is more amenable to Hilda this way. Miriam was referring to Donatello's fall into humanity, involvement with life. The rise was not to a paradise but to a "higher, brighter, and profounder happiness than our lost birthright gave us" (434). Even Kenyon's heavenly version, however, is a shock to Hilda. She takes the myth as creed, it mocks not only "all religious sentiment but . . . moral law" (406), not to mention criminal law. Begging her forgiveness for such speculations, Kenyon submits to her "white wisdom," which he now implores to guide him home, out of the Italian city, rich soil, ruins, arts, evils, catholicity, and all: for "Hilda had a hopeful soul, and saw sunlight on the mountain top" (462). Just as Hilda exchanges one tower for another, the narrator's tone suggests Kenyon exchanges one exile for another.

VI

Hawthorne returned to a war-threatened America in June, 1860, alternating "between a longing and a dread."[50] His aversion to English materiality and snobbery had not dampened his resolve to wring a romance from his English notebooks. The rapid pace of changing American values, on the contrary, enhanced appreciation of his spiritual home, including its materiality. He was drawn, he claimed, to the "class of works" written by Anthony Tollope. "They precisely suit my taste," he wrote Fields, "solid and substantial, written on the strength of beer and through the inspiration of ale, and just as real as if some giant had hewn a great lump out of the earth . . . with all its inhabitants going about their daily business, and not suspecting that they were made a show of."[51] He attempted to draw off this realistic impulse and increase his income by composing essays and sketches from his notebooks for the *Atlantic Monthly* while creating from the same source the serious romance that would crown his career.

From the manuscript he had abandoned in Italy, Hawthorne retained a tenacious new symbol of recycling sin, the bloody footprint of Smithell's Hall. It persisted through numerous studies and drafts, but would not meld with his old themes, new American ambiance, and English imagery into a narrative movement. The characters remained the symbolic puppets of his notes, however he shifted qualities, names, and story roles. The texture was always dense with atmospheric effects and influences, and the actions ran into multiple contradictions and melodrama. And adamantly, he plugged in the bloody footstep. It appears in all the drafts Julian Hawthorne edited and published as *Dr. Grimshawe's Secret* (1883), even when the action shifted to Salem, where a wizard, the old apothecary, Grimshawe, intrigues his ward, the claimant to be, with legends of his old home.

When Hawthorne at last turned away from his English

notebooks, he deliberately took up his early theme of immortal life, but the bloody footstep intruded. His imagination would not retreat to the simplicity of "Dr. Heidigger's Experiment." *Septimius Felton* searches for the elixir of immortality at first because a life-span is not long enough for a man to reform society, overcome the recurring sin of the long past, and achieve the final glory in the American Republic. The period is the American Revolution. As he perseveres, however, the search turns him into a cold, inhuman egoist, wanting the elixir for itself. One of the secrets of the elixir is its vulnerability to human passion. According to the old manuscripts he searches, the heart must never exceed seventy throbs per minute and the aspirant to immortality must shun women, great poets, good as well as evil acts, everything, in short, that makes life livable. Septimius, the would-be wizard, consequently, becomes the Puritanical man of adamant. But this development is invaded by Hawthorne's tugging memory of the ancestral home and so the bloody footstep of Smithell's Hall reappears, even in front of an Indian wigwam and on fresh leaves of American flora.

Although the search for the elixir remains Septimius' prime mover, the claimant theme provides the structure of the draft Sophia and then Hawthorne's daughter, Una, edited and published in 1872 (Sophia died the year before). The theme is ushered into the dreamy atmosphere via a sensuous English girl, Sybil Dacy, and her wizard uncle, Dr. Portsoaken, the Grimshawe of this fragment. They encourage Septimius to press a claim to his ancestral home with the bloody footstep in the hall. At the same time, however, they plan to kill him by contaminating the elixir they help him to perfect. Their unclear motive is presumably to gain the ancestral establishment for themselves. Just in time, love overcomes evil in Sybil. She drinks the poisoned potion and breaks the flask, saving Septimius. All that remains is rumor that he has gone abroad to claim his property.

Hawthorne "aborted" this romance because the pressures of war, the "Present, the Immediate, and the Actual," stifled his imagination. It was "utterly thrown aside"; instead he developed the sketches that were to be its adornment and background into *Our Old Home* (1863).[52] Before he finished, Hawthorne toured the battle scenes of war, though not battle, and in the essay "Chiefly About War Matters" (1862) proclaimed war so horrible that not even the abolition of slavery could justify it. The "actualities" of war served to reinforce his sense of withdrawal from his native land and his nostalgia for the old home. "I have never felt so "earnest a desire to be back in England," he wrote Tickner, "as now. . . ."[53] Although the American claimant to English inheritance becomes a "complete booby" in the sketches, his behavior is endemic, "this peculiar insanity lies deep in the American heart . . . we have still an unspeakable yearning towards England . . . evident in such wild dreams . . . about English inheritances" (18-19).

While American materiality repelled him, English materiality had begun to appeal. From a distance, he could fit even the heavy-witted and bulbous John Bull into a sympathetic image. Nostalgically he compared his native land with his distant home. In the "little nests" of English cottages where the "poor rustic laborers" lived, there was no "wholesome unfamiliarity between families"(53) that characterized New England. The ivy-grown churches, the gravestones, the very ground beneath them, "dug up over and over . . . until the soil is made up of what was once human clay" (54), are so familiar they seem "a recollection of some ancestral mind" and "the weight of all the past" (630). Ultimately the English soil stirs the same myth in his imagination that Donatello experiences in *The Marble Faun*, "the foul encrustation which began to settle over and bedim all earthly things as soon as Eve had bitten the apple" (277). *Our Old Home*, beneath the ruins, monumental houses, history, and ivy walls, is the soil itself. It begrimes the loathesome urchin in the West Darby workhouse, whose mission, Hawthorne reflects, is to remind the visitor that "he [the visitor] was responsible, in his degree, for all the sufferings and misdemeanors of the world in which he lived . . . the offspring of a brother's iniquity being his own blood relation" (301). Even John Bull is a fallen man. A "reflux of a common humanity pervades us all" (299). Here is the "moral truth" of the earlier tales and romances.

The manuscript placed in his coffin was the first chapter of yet another unfinished romance. In illness he had tried one more time, but after eight drafts the romance still refused his imagination. The only fresh image he was able to produce was a realistic portrait of the old apothecary, now Dr. Dolliver, who succeeded in concocting the elixir and has been growing younger as a result. The portrait is of Hawthorne's own aging self, " . . . he still retained an inward consciousness that these stiffened shoulders, these quailing knees, this cloudiness of sight and brain, this confused forgetfulness of men and affairs, were troublesome accidents that did not really belong to him."[54] The main event in the published fragment is the demonstration of greed by a Pyncheon-like aristocrat who must have the last privilege. He grabs for the elixir before Dolliver can prepare it properly and so dies on the spot, as the apothecary's grandson died before him. The only other character is a granddaughter, Pansie, held over from previous efforts. She will apparently point the way, for the rest of the romance, towards the ancestral home and the bloody footstep.

The same cast of characters vary their masks but essentially play out the same "moral truths" throughout Hawthorne's literary years. The inescapable evils of the past, of

greed and of adamant insistence upon perfection, produced
the exile at home in America, while human acceptance of sin
and retribution through opened hearts promised refuge. In
his last decade, Hawthorne kept returning from the sunlight
to the darkness, not the darkness from which he came, the
American past, but the European past. Perhaps there, the exile could find refuge. But, in effect, he was searching for that
romantic darkness with a new American candle.

Chapter 6
MELVILLE:
Games an Exile Plays at Home

The enfeebled light is extinguished at the end of Melville's last novel, as an old man, trusting his Bible and clutching his money belt and chamber pot, is conned into the darkness. "Something further may follow of this masquerade" are the final words of *The Confidence-Man* (1857). Only thirty-eight years old then, Melville was at the bottom of a fall from popularity as "the man who lived among the cannibals."[1] Without publishing another word of fiction he died thirty-four years later. He should not be confused with the trusting old man; Melville is the one who blew out the light. Other masquerades may follow, other fictions, not his. "Our comedy," as he called this satire, was no voyage of discovery but a bitter celebration of the journey's result.

In *Mardi* only eight years earlier, Melville had recognized that he was making a voyage "into the world of the mind" and if the golden haven was not gained, "better to sink in boundless deeps, than float on vulgar shoals."[2] Like his mythical authors of *Koztanza* and *Ponderings*, books within the book, Melville did not know what *Mardi* would become when he started, but wrote on, getting "deeper and deeper into himself" (595). It became a "sleep-walking of the mind" (596), lacking coherence, "wild, unconnected, all episode." But so is the world it reflects, "nothing but episodes; valleys and hills; rivers; digressing from plains; vines, roving all over; boulders and diamonds; flowers and thistles . . ." (597).

Such methodless method was necessary for his purpose. Partially it was his response to charges that his popular successes *Typee* (1846) and *Omoo* (1847) were not entirely true. This time he was after the real truth, "all that is romantic, whimsical, and poetic . . . it shall have the right stuff in it" (*L* 68).

After the failure of *Mardi*, which he thereafter called "a shelterless exile" (*L* 102), Melville resumed the more descriptive fiction that seemed truer to life for popular readers. With resignation he announced his new work as an "amusing narrative of personal experience—the son of a gentleman on his first voyage to sea as a sailor . . . nothing but cakes and ale . . . perhaps a fraction smaller than 'Typee' " (L86). *Redburn* (1849) and *White-Jacket* (1850), which followed without pause, were "two books which I have done for money—being forced to it, as other men are to sawing wood" (*L* 91). But he desired to write the sort of "books which are said to fail" (*L* 92) and Bartleby-like he did, returning to the stuff he preferred in *Moby-Dick*. The story of these fictions reflect the drama of Melville's exile. The tales and satires that follow *Moby-Dick* and its domestic counterpart *Pierre* (1852) are written from the exile's remote focus on the society he had yearned for and could not join.

A rhythm of withdrawal and return to the community spirals through Melville's fiction from the torturous descent into *Typee* to the vortex of the black stairwell at the end of *Pierre*. It is the spirit of the exile-at-home made manifest. The image of the vortex itself intensifies as Melville repeats the pattern of a disappointed, distraught, or culturally fettered and well-bred sailor setting forth to seek a new refuge for his spirit and ending usually in a swim for the boat, which is a surrogate of the society from which his idealistic individuality or prideful questing had exiled him. Again and again the adventurer pursues the ideals of love, beauty, morality, or universal knowledge that would make sense out of the inequities and ambiguities that are the flux of his life;

and again and again he is drawn back into the ambiguous, unjust and often cruel society that he fled by the powerful need for whatever love and belonging are available. The exceptions, Taji, Ahab, and Pierre, are swallowed into the vortex because they insist on penetrating its essential meaning, plunging into its void rather than retreating into the rings of energy that create it, rather, that is, than swimming for the boat.

The pattern is suggested even in the opening episode of Melville's first book, *Typee*. It is in Tommo's flight from the *Dolly* down into the imprisoning weeds of the jungle in the valleys and up into the freedom of the ridges, followed by the vacillation throughout the narrative of his joys and fears, the very wound of his leg responding to yearnings for home but healing when all seems well in paradise. It is in the haven Taji seeks in *Mardi* and the void he achieves in the swirling waters of the caves or vortices of Haitia. The connection of the vortex and Melville's doomed deep diver is suggested early in *Mardi* as the *Parki* sinks: "The hull rolled convulsively in the sea; went round once more; lifted its sharp prow as a man with arms pointed for a dive; gave a long seething plunge; and went down" (120).

In *Redburn* the exile's quest for home shifts to familiar society, the homestead of the old world and the crew of the sailing ship itself. The model glass boat his dead father brought him contains a dark and promising interior, concealing secrets as does the "Aladdin's Palace" in London where the statue of an old man forever cautions secrecy with his finger to his lips. The vortex of the *Neversink* in *White-Jacket* is a swirl of efficient maneuvers, pompous ceremonials and unjust cruelties with moral stillness at the center. In the last of the sea novels, Ishmael begins again, a seasoned sailor, feeling exiled on shore, setting out for the refuge of the sea and the community of crew. Vortices abound, beginning with

Father Mapple's rendition of God speaking out of the whirl-wind, punishing man for his pride. The whale creates a vortex in each dive; by implication it is what the deep diver dives in-to. Ishmael is himself a vortex, set into motion by the Ahab within him and saved from his own void by the urge for love and community, symbolized in the Epilogue by Queequeeg's coffin lid inscribed with the signs of a remote Polynesian culture but bearing Ishmael back to life in his own society.

Destruction, apparently, is not always the fate of plung-ing into the still center of the vortex. While acres of whales circle in the commotion of an external world in "The Great Armada" chapter, Ishmael penetrates to the very quiet center where he beholds love and nourishment in its purest form, mother whales and suckling whelps, benignity gleaming in their eyes. Love, the essence of home, like Whitman's kelson of creation, is found at the center of a vortex of whales, of dumb brutes ignorant of godliness, or of a primordial tribe of conscienceless savages. For such as these, earthly homes are possible. For prideful humans who adamantly persist in their challenge of knowledge and nature—the very pursuit that their tricky god built into their spirits—the center of the vortex is a destructive fate.[3]

Melville's adamant questers are quasi-extensions of Emerson's self-reliant men and their cosmic consciences. Basically European, their dreams could be enacted in the pristine and commodious American geography; but in the enactments come ugly aggrandisements of self—as rugged in-dividual, as captain of man's industries, as a force of in-telligence more potent than nature. Eventually the habit of such self-centeredness becomes a pattern of energy in itself, an American vortex with the still center sucking the ego with ever greater attraction until the ego plunges after itself to destruction. Such is the destiny of Taji, Ahab and Pierre. Ishmael, the orphaned surrogate of *Redburn* and *White-*

Jacket, resists the plunge into the void. Like his author, Ishmael draws back to the swirling walls of the crass American vortex. In the Epilogue of *Moby-Dick*, the vortex is the "devious-cruising Rachel," who finds instead of her missing children, "only . . . another orphan," another exile.[4]

Melville's exile is a defeated man, and beyond *Moby-Dick* and *Pierre*, he turns bitter. Ishmael is defeated by the whale as much as by Ahab. While Ahab dies in pursuit, Ishmael lives on in the commotion of whales, glimpsing their "visible truth" but unable to share it, the vortex of a culture not his, of nature itself.[5] Here is that wall of white, that cunning blankness of the whale's forehead that Ahab must strike through. Ishmael, however, is no harpooner, but a user of words. The visible truth for Ishmael can only be captured in language. The rings of the vortex in which he swims are all constructs of language, documents, myths, fictions, which veil the visible truth.

In *Pierre*, Melville tried once more. *Pierre* is a combination of Ishmael and Ahab, a writer who attempts truth by direct seige with words. He ends in ranting ideas and melodrama. His "great art of Telling the Truth" is but an art, a game of confidence, and the quester is but another hunter in the cannibalism of society. He returns in Melville's final novel as *The Confidence-Man*.

I

Like most American exiles at home, Melville was a family man. He was attached to his mother, brothers, and sisters and in communication with aunts, uncles, and cousins. Although he may have vaguely considered himself cast out of the good society by his father's bankruptcy, the young Melville was no exile seeking refuge. The evidence of his first book indicates rather a mindless adventurer imbued with the proprieties of home but properly critical of its excesses when compared with the paradise of Typee. He only plays with this paradise, however. And even here, at the start, it is the ambiguities inherent in the "art of Telling the Truth" that absorb him, that begin to exile him more than the actual conditions of life, which only later set him apart, wanting and rejecting.

The primitive society of *Typee* is another vortex, not his, and to see or "peep" in as the title tells us, the author has embellished his own experiences with the readings from other South Sea adventurers. The truth or rather factualness of his book, which he defended against accusations of readers and publisher, was at least diluted by these readings and also by the exigencies of art. By the time he came to write his third book, *Mardi*, the factuality of experience was separated from the effort to tell the truth, profoundly affected now by his readings of romance, poetry, and philosophy—Spenser, La Motte-Fouque, Burton, Coleridge, Hartley, Priestley. And he was looking into Shakespeare.

Melville was after the biggest fish and already conceived of himself in the model of the deep divers. Even Emerson, "a Plato who talked through his nose," now appeared to him a great man because he belonged to that "whole corps of thought-divers, that have been diving and coming up again with bloodshot eyes since the world began" (*L* 79). He had also experienced a marriage which was already turning troublesome, possibly because of his absorption into the world of mind, and possibly complicated because he installed his bride in a large house with his mother, four unmarried sisters, his brothers Allan and Thomas and Allan's wife while he sought company "among the literati" gathered about Evert Duyckinck, editor of the *Literary World*. Emboldened by the company he was keeping and his initial literary successes, Melville, it seems, placed himself into competition with the great authors he was reading, especially Shakespeare.

Because of the "muzzle which all men wore in their souls

in the Elizabethan day," Melville wrote to Duyckinck, "Shakespeare was not a frank man to the uttermost." To Melville, the American writer was unmuzzled and free to achieve what Shakespeare had the talent for, "the Declaration of Independence makes a difference" (*L* 80). Melville's wild fictionalizing, most notable in the Mardian *Koztanza*, may be the result of his self image as an unmuzzled American Shakespeare. It characterizes his work from the beginning: "Nothing but dark and fearful chasms," Tommo sees as he searches for the Happar Valley. "Could we have stepped from summit to summit of these steep but narrow elevations we could easily have accomplished the distance; but we must penetrate to the bottom of every yawning gulf, and scale in succession every one of the eminences before us."[6] This is Melville's declaration of purpose at the start of his career and the discovery of Shakespeare did not so much change it as reinforce it.

Although *Typee* mentions Shakespeare (198), Melville was not yet entranced by his "divine Wiliam." This first fictional voyage is quite the opposite of *Mardi*. It is a voyage out of mind rather than into it, fundamentally a travel essay about exotic primitives and a prisoner among them. The fictive conflict is between the prisoner's acceptance of a mindless paradise and his mindful responsibility to determine truth by confronting his ideas of the Typees with his actual experience of them. Tommo, like Melville, had read of the Marquesas and "felt an irresistable curiosity to see those islands which the older voyagers had so glowingly described." The very name induced "strange visions of outlandish things . . . Naked houris . . . tatooed chiefs . . . *heathenish rites and human sacrifices*" (5). If the descent into the valley is the rugged road to heaven or a torturous route to the womb, the cultural restrictions and the fears Tommo carries within him prevent acceptance. Not the questing hero of *Mardi*, Tommo

is rather muzzled by American propriety and sensibility (perhaps even more constricting than Shakespeare's boundries).

Escaping the hell aboard the *Dolly*, Tommo cannot accept the paradise he stumbles into because he is not free to accept it. Although he is more seasoned than the later Redburn,
who stretches the cord from home on his maiden voyage,
Tommo is yet no Ishmael "rushing from all havens astern."
His white man's home and civilization are carried within.
These imprison him in the Typee paradise as much as his captors. Perceiving Typee through the constructs of his own
culture, Tommo finds it utterly ambiguous. He is never at
ease, even among the family of Marheyo who adopts him.

Apparently the natives but not Tommo share the opinion of D. H. Lawrence and others who insist that the struggle down the horrible gorge is "an act of birth . . . or rebirth,"
resulting in a Lockean blank slate in the green Eden of
Typee.[7] He is treated as an infant and assigned a guard who is
a surrogate mother. Kory-Kory feeds him with his fingers,
supervises his bath among the river nymphs, and carries him
about until his wounded leg heals. But his residual fears are
never quelled, not even by Fayaway, "the perfection of
female grace and beauty" (85). As the senseless days dissolve
into one another, however, Tommo grows accustomed to his
fate and begins to appreciate his captors, especially their
freedom from getting and spending, from authority and
hierarchial rule, from sexual codes (at least those he knew),
and from their gods who tolerate disrespect. As his appreciation waxes, his leg heals. Typee becomes happy valley and the
civilization forbidden to him beyond the mountains is
"nought but a world of care and anxiety" (124). In his spell of
euphoria even cannibalism appears less uncivilized compared
to the Christian modes of executing enemies or evangelizing
natives into beasts of burden (196). The white civilized man
appears to him as the "most ferocious animal on the face of

the earth" (125). White men's stories and images maligned the Typees who were really as "pacific as so many lambkins" (128). He tries, however uneasily, to give himself over to the hosts' wild enjoyments. (But surreptitiously, he guts the raw fish before swallowing it.)

Yet Tommo cannot or will not relinquish his breeding. Frequently his "feelings of propriety were shocked." At the Feast of Calabashes, he expresses to Kory-Kory his dissatisfaction with the indecorous and improper customs. When he realizes Mahovi is the chief of chiefs, Tommo must compensate for the lack of "ceremonious pomp which usually surrounds the purple" by naming him King Mahovi (187-8). And his ironical jesting of his hosts' freedom of religious thought — "They are sunk in religious sloth, and require a spiritual revival" (179) — is doubly ambiguous, since the major activity of the Typees is sleeping. Mentally they are always asleep and so paradise bores, except for Fayaway. And even in her heavenly blue eyes Tommo seeks not ideal beauty but compassion for his exiled condition, "she appeared to be conscious there were ties rudely severed, which had once bound us to our homes; that there were sisters and brothers anxiously looking forward to our return, who were, perhaps, never more to behold us" (108).

His longing for home biased his values, and it was amplified by the Typees themselves. Their hominess "more than anything else, secured my admiration. . . . The natives appeared to form one household . . . bound together by the ties of strong affection. . . . it was hard to tell who were actually related to each other by blood" (203-204). Tommo's observation is an echo of the apparent desire in Melville's heart. The desire is manifested more directly in the flow of love between the hands squeezing the whale sperm on the deck of the *Pequod*, the love which is obliterated by Ahab's insensate questing. After "many prolonged, repeated experiences," Ishmael discovers, "man must eventually lower, or at least shift, his conceit of attainable felicity; not placing it anywhere in the intellect or the fancy; but in the wife, the heart, the bed, the table, the saddle, the fire-side, the country" (349).

Tommo's desire for home in the Typee paradise leads to anguish which overwhelms all pleasures, especially after the threat of Karky's tattoo, the language worn upon the face that would remake him into one of them. His anguish is less from the prospect of being eaten literally than the figurative cannibalism of passing away "my days in this narrow valley, deprived of all intercourse with civilized beings, and forever separated from friends and home," and eventually of his "inanimate form . . . blended with the dust of the valley" (239,243).

Tommo's departure is even more ambivalent than his fears. In freeing himself, he is obliged to throw a boat hook into one of his former hosts, Chief Mow-Mow, who opposes the departure. His act horrifies Tommo, as in *Mardi*, the killing of Aleema the priest horrifies Taji. But Taji's act is chivalrous — it frees beauty and ideal happiness, Yillah, from priestly captivity while Tommo's is selfish, freeing only himself. The slaying of Mow-Mow is not the killing of a dream.[8] Tommo never dreamt of a paradise in Typee until after he left it. His murderous departure signifies the treachery required to regain civilization and thus suggests the duplicitous barbarity of that civilization as opposed to the primitive simplicity of the Typees. The departure disappoints old Marheyo, Kory-Kory, and Fayaway. They weep on the beach while the perfidious white friend to whom they gave love returns it with murder and goes home regardless, the very emblem of the civilized marauders and missionaries he has condemned in his diatribes. Tommo's treachery fills Mow-Mow's last moment of consciousness and apparently

burns into his own: "I saw him [Mow-Mow] rise to the surface in the wake of the boat, and never shall I forget the
ferocious expression on his countenance" (252).

But in the first chapter of *Omoo*, he does forget. Safe on
the *Julia*, his leg medicated, his hair and beard clipped, and
"home and friends once more in prospect," he suffers but a
momentary melancholy, "the thought of never more seeing
those who, notwithstanding their desire to retain me a captive, . . . treated me so kindly."[9] In later life the South Seas
provided the images of persistent nostalgia for Melville; but
for Tommo, now narrator of *Omoo*, all was erased by morning: "the cool fresh air . . . at sea . . . was so bracing . . . my
spirits rose at once" (8). And not another thought of his
treachery, of Mow-Mow, Fayaway, Kory-Kory or old
Maheyo, nor home.

Conditions aboard the cockroach and rat-infested *Julia*,
whose Captain Guy is but a "Paper Jack," are worse than
those of the *Dolly*, which Tommo had fled. Now, however,
these conditions are taken as common experiences and thus
establish bonds among the rovers, and the bonds are
strengthened when the men are accused of mutinous intent.
Even the narrator's peculiar imprisonment is tolerable, being
shared in the open air. Confidence of belonging replaces the
fear of falling back into the "uncreate past."[10] In the com-
raderie of the rovers, he suffers but one threatening moment
in the entire book, when he is brought face to face with the
emblem of the fate he has just escaped, the tattooed face of
Lem Hardy. This "renegado from Christiandom and humanity" wears the "South Seas girdle," a broad band tattoo from
ear to ear and on his forehead a blue shark, a marking "Far
worse than Cain's" (27). Homeless, reckless, and impatient of
civilization's restraints, Hardy has found a place in the
primitive past as a savage war god with the sacred protection
of a "person inviolable forever" (28). His flesh under the tat-

tooing is evidence, however, of a civilized person forever violated.

Playing the game of war god among the savages, Lem Hardy could be another avatar of Melville's *Confidence-Man*. The loot in his barbaric home includes a princess, ten houses, four hundred hogs, and fathoms of tappa and split grass mats. The narrator's chum, Doctor Long Ghost, the extended shadow of a man, is another game player. Like the later avatars, he plays in response to a senseless existence and for meager stakes. His pranks and practical jokes gain his comrades' respect, his feigned illness gains privilege, and his "entertaining and instructive" wit (230) gain from his white bosses on the Imeeo farm a value as a "man of science" (231). Although the narrator has not generalized his observations, the missionaries are also seen playing the game and their native marks ironically play along but attend their own gods. The French Navy plays too, with their showy "brass plates and other geegaws . . . like baubles on a handsome woman" (109) and with their bluster, "constantly exercising yards and sails" in port and "running in and out the enormous guns" at sea (110). The acting British Consul at Papeettee, Wilson, representing Western society in general, is also in the game. He allows prejudiced evidence against the seamen but suppresses the seaman's affidavit of grievances as an "uncommon literary production", from which the men foolishly anticipate miracles. This language reflects the author's own judgment of his literary product as something of a confidence game and himself as a "Paper Jack," with the hollow authority of a Captain Guy.[11] "As a roving sailor, the author spent about three months . . . on Tahiti and Imeeo," lies the Preface of *Omoo*. Melville's time on these islands was closer to three weeks. At several points, the author blatantly interrupts the narrative to reveal the artifice of story-telling in this "true account." And the admission of occasionally using narratives of "previous voyagers" merely "in collaboration of what is offered as . . . the author's own observations," conceals his copious borrowings, not only to fill out the book as the publishers required but also to enhance credibility, confidence.[12]

If Melville is aware of the inescapable game of confidence in "the art of Telling the Truth," which later becomes the very fiber of *Moby-Dick*, *Omoo*'s narrator is not. He ships out as mindlessly as he shipped in, "weary somewhat of life in Imeeo, like all sailors ashore," (312) and with "the prospect of eventually reaching home . . ." (315). He leaves Dr. Long Ghost behind, echoing Tommo's ignoble departure. After the island goes down in the horizon, the wide Pacific cleanses all. Ahead lies the stuff of the mind.

Unlike Tommo and the narrator of *Omoo*, the hero of *Mardi* is a questor who plays the confidence game upon himself. Drifting "perhaps on the most unfrequented and least known portion of the seas," in a general westward direction, the sailor is drawn by gold and crimson clouds, "airy arches, domes and minarets." His spirit sails with the clouds "as in a trance . . . mild billows laving a beach of shells, the waving of boughs, and the voices of maidens." The clouds lead to islands a thousand miles westward, "invested with all the charms of dreamland" (8,7). So the stuff of the mind is foremost the stuff of dreams, a young sailor's fancy. He jumps ship in the midst of the ocean and the dead of night for this dream world, not because of shipboard tyranny that his predecessors had fled — his mates were "good fellows" and the skipper "a trump" (5). But they were "none with whom to mingle sympathies" (4).

Stimulated by sea vultures scavaging below but also nursing their young as "Hagar did Ishmael" (40) before she cast him out (a scene repeated with whales in the "Grand Armada" chapter of *Moby-Dick*), the hero's mind arrives at

simplistic thoughts of love and hate — love is delightful and
hate a thankless torment. These conclusions are tested soon
after the sighting of a ghost ship. Aboard is Annatoo, an
ugly, lustful nuisance of a wife hen-pecking her noble savage
husband, Samoa, and leading him as Cleopatra leads Mark
Antony. Such is the delight of love. He assumes command
without question and turning the prow westward, the narrator exults in his freedom and power as "owner, as well as
commander of the craft I sailed" (97). But his ballooning
egotism is disturbed by the covetness and willfulness of Annatoo, who will not allow the narrator to use her as he does
Samoa, her mate in "woeful wedlock," and Jarl, the
narrator's slavish companion.[13] He sheds the nuisance of
Annatoo in a storm and there is "no time to mourn" (117).
When he does have time, it is the sinking ship he mourns. In
the unfamiliar assumption of command over other lives and
in the heady freedom of his ego, the hero appears more and
more possessed with a touch of the schlemiel.[14] "I have loved
ships, as I have loved men" (120). Poor Annatoo.

It is by chance that Melville's hero blunders upon an object for his fatal quest. He sails into a secret rite of sacrifice.
The accident casts him into a myth, a pattern of lies, which he
lives to the end. A stolen glimpse of the beautiful Yillah, the
victim, transforms him instantly into an Elizabethan courtier.
Hotly swearing "precious blood of hers should never smoke
upon an altar" (131), the hero kills the old priest, a tattooed
authority, escapes with the maiden, and is immediately smit-
ten with remorse and questions of motive: to rescue her or
have her? Much the same question will plague Pierre a few
years later. Here the joy of conquest and the beauty of Yillah
throttle such mindfulness. The scene is similar to Leatherstocking's discovery of Inez, the jewel of civilization, kidnapped and transported under cover by Ishmael Bush as they
push westward through *The Prairie*. But Yillah of course is

the jewel of unreal dreams, not European civilization. And she is the proper white replacement for Fayaway, golden-haired and blue eyed. She represents idyllic, imaginative love instead of wedded responsibility, the "suicide" of bachelor-hood symbolized by Annatoo.

Taking advantage of her story, the hero reduces his Elizabethan chivalry to its fundamental nature as a game of confidence by assuming the role of Taji, a demigod from her own "fabulous Oroolia." He calms her fears with invention as quick as Huckleberry Finn's. The old priest, Aleema, the hero lies, was dispatched on an errand, leaving Yillah in his care. As if dreaming, Taji continues in fairy-tale language: he knew her as a child and "over the wide watery world have I sought thee" (143). The con game at the heart of this dream is no different than the tattooed priest's in his assumption of an old god's role, "and every night slept the maiden in the arms of grim Apo" (156). But Taji is not at ease in his game of con-fidence, no more than in the role of dominating egoist. His happiness is disturbed by the old priest's green corpse floating past and by phantoms, avenging sons of the old priest who are incredibly poor arrow shooters, and by mysterious flower messages from the jealous Queen Hautia. He is aware also of the serfs of host King Media brutalized by toil and scourged for cursing their king, but they are out of sight, hidden as death is in the sea. All these impingements, however, are countered by his burgeoning belief in the fiction of his own divinity and by the gratifications of Yillah. He suffers not an iota of longing or memory of any other life until, suddenly, the dream is gone, his love bower empty.

As he quests for her through Mardi, the world, Yillah's image blurs and he does not know what he seeks, except her "shade." The companions who join the quest can be taken as divisions of Taji's mind, as avatars similar to those of the cosmopolitan in *The Confidence-Man*. In this expansion of the quest, Taji's role fades. His mind becomes a stage and he appears upon it, mostly perfunctorily and in the third person, while the others, the categorical resources of his mind, dominate: King Media, practical despot; Babbalanja, idealistic philosopher; Mohi, factual historian; Yoomy, incomprehensible romantic poet. (All the staginess of the quest, the comic types, courtly language, jocose wit and chivalric pretenses reflect Melville's readings in Shakespeare.)

Ambiguities and games of confidence abound in the satirical journey of Taji's overloaded mind through the allegorical societies of sixteen dream islands, dogged by the avenging furies of the old priest's sons and by sensuous desire, Hautia, the seductress who taunts ("Bitter love in absence," 215) and promises ("Fly to love," 267).[15] As Taji fades from center stage so does ideal love. The notions of truth and political and religious posturings of Christian nations become satirical targets, largely inspired, as Melville wrote, by the revolutions of 1848 and by American imperialist actions. A Don Juan king on the Island of Juam grows morose in the luxurious sloth of his harem whenever the party ends because then he is reduced to the problem of truth. Each island is a crystallizing into form and to approach it is to approach the possibility of truth in that form, even if the form is a fiction. "What are vulgarly called fictions," Babbalanja asserts, "are as much realities as the . . . digger of trenches, for things visable are but conceits of the eye. . . . If duped by one, we are equally duped by the other" (283-4).

Even the distant land far on the other side of the lagoon, Vivenza, as promising as the morning, proved but a "braggadoccio in Mardi" (472). Yet it was a brave braggadoccio, and that bravery was inherited from the island of Dominora whose King loved dominion and hated relinquishing stolen nations. In the New Mardi, Vivenza, the confidence games are played by many kings. "We are all kings here," shout the throngs that greet the questing company (514). "In-this-re-publi-can-land-all-men-are-born-free-and-equal," reads the inscription on the temple, and below in smaller script, "Except-the-tribe-of-Hamo" (512-13). On the top of the temple of equality and freedom, a man with a collar and red stripes on his back hoists a "standard—correspondingly striped" (515). The substance and even the style of *The Confidence-Man* begin to emerge. Yet the sight of this new land is inspiring for Yoomi, the poet. In "this rejoicing hum of a thriving population," Yoomy laughs, "Yillah will be found" (523). The quest for ideal love—the *Undine* of La Motte Fouque or the Beatrice of Dante—has grown into a quest for the universal love of mankind in the new world.

But Vivenza is caught up in the spirit of old Mardi and goes warring without declaration. During the tumult, a scroll is pinned to a tree, making Paine-like pronouncements which Babbalanja suspects are the opinions of King Media and Media suspects issue from Babbalanja: "He who hated oppressors, is become an oppressor himself" (526). Here as elsewhere the wise lord it over the fools. There is cringing and suffering. In the southern regions are fiery and intractable people wielding thongs on the bloody backs of others. In the far west of Kolumbo, there is gold; haggard hunters murder for it in the pits and cry for "Home! Home! . . . with bursting eyes" (548). Instead of a golden haven, they have discovered a "golden Hell" (547). No Yillah there.

Babbalanja is the first to despair of finding her. He speaks for Melville as well as himself: "This Mardi is not our home. Up and down we wander, like exiles . . . 'tis not the world *we* were born in." That world is a domestic image of dreamt felicity, "where we once merrily danced, dined and supped; and wooed, and wedded our long-buried wives. Then let us depart. But wither?" (619) The philosopher settles for the next best thing, an island that promises the original Chris-

tianity before religious institutions perverted it. Here brotherhood may rebuke the arrogance of power, and although the
law of reason does not breed equality, "none starve outright,
while others feast" (627). (It holds more promise than the
Rachael, the ship Ishmael swims for in the Epilogue of *Moby-
Dick*.) King Media sees no possibility of Yillah in such a
place; men are the same everywhere.

But "then sweet Yillah called [him] from the sea," and
Taji sails on, his heart growing "hard, like flint; and black,
like night. . . . Hyenas filled [him] with their laughs . . . [He]
prayed not, but blasphemed" (639). He has become the
hunter that never rests, an Ahab in love, his monomaniacal
insistence forever pushing his goal ahead of his grasp.

His return to center stage at the end represents not only
the re-emergence of ideal love but also the rejection of all
compromises with ideal happiness. Dreaming ever more wildly he is enticed by sirens who promise the beloved shade of
Yillah in hated Hautia, Odysseus lured to Circe, with "sharks
astern." Her harbor is strewn with fragments of wrecks but
"swifter and swifter the currents now ran; till with a shock
our prows were beached." The sexual rhythm climaxes when
the "Two wild currents met and dashed him into foam"
(645-6). But "in the vortex that draws all in," there is no
Yillah. "Rave on," Hautia responds to his babbling for the
other, as might any woman so spurned, "Go, go—and slay
thyself. . . . There is another cavern in the hill" (652-3). The
swirling waters of that cavern lead to the open sea where Taji
suffers the supreme disappointment of being his "own soul's
emperor," utterly alone in the wide universe, and thus "my
first act is abdication! Hail! realm of shades!" (654) It was the
shade of Yillah he sought, the fiction he needed to live by,
that killed him. This is the final irony.

Something of a schlemiel he may be, but possessed of the
same "sane madness"[16] as Ahab, and of Poe's impossible

quest and Dickinson's, and later Hemingway's and Fitzgerald's and later still of Mailer's Rojack in *An American
Dream*, all unto death, titillated with the dangers of approach
and finding life's deep meaning there. It is the lure of the
sublime, the terror within the beauty that occupied the imaginations of primal America's earliest migrants. The at-
mospheres of Melville's three Polynesian novels are charged
with this terrible beauty, from the cannibalistic paradise of
Typee through the Yillah-Haitia spectre of *Mardi*. Befitting
Melville's view of ambiguity in all things, Taji is more
satirical than tragic. His bumbling quest exposes the games of
confidence that permeate both civilized and primitive
societies. As one of the two developments of Tommo (the
other is Ishmael) we see Taji hardening from the home-
oriented sailor, whose proprieties are shocked, through the
role of rover, and ultimately into the questor, adamantly
seeking a home the world cannot offer. It is an egoistic rather
than a communal ideal of love he must have, and even if this
world could offer the spirit of openness, charity and spontaneous affection, even then Taji would not accept it as Babbalanja does in Serenia because it requires some sacrifice of
egoistic will and independence. In searching for a lost dream,
Taji's ego, like Ahab's, rejects all possible havens the world
can offer, as the final sentence of the novel makes clear, "and
thus pursuers and pursued flew on over an endless sea." Such
ego is the ultimate object of the satire in *Mardi* and will be the
focus of the tragedy in *Moby-Dick*.

Meanwhile, Melville, no Taji nor yet an exile, has obviously identified himself with Lombardi, the Mardian
author of *Koztanza*, who "knew not what [his work] would
become," but when he finished "came out into a serene, sunny, ravishing region," and "sat within view of the ocean; his
face to a cool rushing breeze," having "created the creative"
(595), which is the form-free fiction ever closer to the truth.

Melville also sat, observing Taji, like a frieze on the urn, forever fading in pursuit of his stillborn ideal with the priest's green corpse and phantom sons in his wake. He sat until the tide of reviews came in to swamp him.

II

The adamant questor who has accrued guilt and fate by eliminating the communal (old priest Aleema) and passionate (Queen Hautia) components of human life, will be energized again, but later, to pursue a much larger mystery, also white, in hate and at the expense of love, and not in a dream world but one of social responsibility. In the meantime, to restore his reputation, Melville fell back upon proven material and mode, as Cooper had done after the disasterous reception of his *Home* novels. Melville's young brother, Tom, setting out on his first voyage, stimulated reminscence of his own initiation at sea. He prepared a fiction for market based on this memory but enhanced with readings and manipulated for the sake of easily recognizable form. In *Redburn*, the initiate that precedes Tommo is inducted into the seafaring society that Tommo fled as intolerable, but nevertheless returned to. The character he develops this time is an alternative to Taji. In *Redburn*, Ishmael is born.

The initiate wants to experience his dreams of adventure and he also wants to belong. Like the later Ishmael, Redburn begins in a negative mood, the consequence of an undisclosed "disappointment" that makes him feel at odds, alone. The feeling is easily associated with Melville's sense of separation from the society of established families as a result of his father's bankruptcy and death. The new milieu Redburn seeks is not an exotic other world at the farthest remove from his own but a more familiar strangeness of fellow seaman on a voyage to the near past, from the new world to the old. Most important is the milieu he expects to find when he gets there. He wishes to feel at home in the old world. Redburn is frustrated on the voyage out and at his destination, but succeeds in accepting his fellows and being accepted on the homeward voyage. The story is told with the residual irony that develops when a narrator looks back upon a completed past. It is thus shaped into a novel in which, "cakes and ale" notwithstanding, fiction confronts experience, as in most of Melville's work.

The fiction is Redburn's imagination. It is symbolically shattered when a figurine on a model glass ship his father had brought back from his sea journeys, and which stimulated the young man's dreaming, ominously breaks the very day he sets out. The world's toughness and wickedness display themselves almost immediately. Selling his rifle to support himself until the *Highlander* sails, Redburn is victimized by the pawnbroker. Then Captain Riga, whom he had anticipated as a surrogate father because he was so friendly in port, flings his cap in rage when the naive young man calls to pay his respects at sea. The voyage begins with a drunken sailor's suicide over the ship's bow, a horror made grotesquely foreboding when Redburn is assigned the dead man's bunk. His outlandish innocence, unlike the later Billy Budd's, compels derision from the heartless crewmen who find specific targets in his gentlemen's speech and his gentlemen's shooting jacket, which shrinks in the rain to become an emblem of his dwindling gentility. Rejected, he soon rejects. Before the *Highlander* reaches Liverpool, Redburn determines to resist the evil he has observed in the seaman he sought to join — their sneering, slovenly, drunken, obscene, misanthropy.

Robert Jackson is the embodiment of this evil. He regards the initiate with malevolence in his burning eyes, which have the power to extract tribute from the crewmen for whom he feels contempt. Through his long watches, Redburn

hears reverberations of Jackson's misanthropy, "nothing to
be believed, nothing to be loved, and nothing worth living
for; but everything to be hated in the wide world," and
discerns more "woe than wickedness" in his adversary. It is
here in *Redburn* that Melville glimpses the fearful spectre of
that wreck he invited in *Mardi*, the evil Jackson, diseased
from "every kind of dissipation and abandonment in the
worst ports of the world."[17] Observing him, Redburn imagines a man who has faced truth, been driven to lonely
despair by seeing and by experiencing the inhumanity of the
world. Redburn fears that he too will become isolated and
embittered. He sees a future self as a kind of "Ishmael in the
ship, without a single friend or companion, and I began to
feel a hatred growing up in me against the whole crew — so
much so, that I prayed against it, that it might not master my
heart completely, and so make a fiend of me, something like
Jackson" (62).

He compensates for the intolerable existence among his
cruel shipmates with entrancing visions of his destination, his
dead father's golden childhood home, and he hopes to realize
those visions with the aid of his father's guidebook to Liverpool. The city will restore the wholeness his humiliating experience on the *Highlander* destroyed; even more, it will
make whole the image of his father as he was before his
bankruptcy in the new world. The best families will open
their doors. His experiences in Liverpool, however, are more
grotesque, unaccepting and unacceptable, than any among
his mates. Horrible as the ship's society may be, he is
prepared to join it after his English encounters.

His father's England does not exist. Landmarks are
gone, a tavern replaces the old hotel, the library and reading
room will not admit him, and the outdated guidebook proves
a useless fiction in the intricate labyrinth of Liverpool.
"Guide-books" Redburn tells himself "are the least reliable

books in all literature; and nearly all literature . . . is made up of guide books" (157). His golden visions are replaced by a squalid slumland of polluted streets, prisonlike warehouses, and loathesome dens of vice. He witnesses a murder in a tavern, a woman nursing a dead baby. When he seeks help for another whose children cling to her rags, no one cares. Quicklime is cleansing the spot when he returns. If old England really existed in the countryside, he finds there "keep off" signs, and a farmer with a cudgel in his hand. The only friend he makes, Harry Bolton, is a would-be aristocrat who wants at the same time the democratic opportunities he thinks Redburn represents. Bolton appears to be another guide and proves to be another counterfeit. He shows Redburn the London aristocrat's counterpart to the Liverpool dens of iniquity, "Aladdin's Palace," which is also horrifying, "though gilded and golden, the serpent of vice is a serpent still" (234). Yet this serpent is the promise of some inner treasure, as within the hull of the glass boat that had dazzled Redburn at home, and as in Yillah and *Moby-Dick*. In a room adorned with mythological pornography, the statue of an old man is carved with a thin finger to his marble lips, "tremulous with secrets" (231). But the growth of Redburn is towards Ishmael, love and social acceptance at the expense of such forbidden knowledge.

On the return journey, Harry Bolton cannot endure the cruelties as Redburn can. By contrast and in reaction to his English guide, Redburn gains strength throughout the homeward voyage, meeting the challenges of his shipboard society such as it is. And it is made representative of society in general by the human cargo of emigrants herded into the holds without adequate toilet facilities or food. These conditions result in an epidemic, which panics the more privileged passengers. Thus, reflects Redburn, men kill other men for the price of passage. Yet he can now function in a society of such barbarity and even feel pleasure in his accomplishments within it, his manhood. He rejects the misanthropy of a "diabolical Tiberius . . . who even in his self-exile, embittered . . . yet did not give over his blasphemies" (276). Instead of misanthropy he can find joy in those instances where human love surfaces, as in the rapture of the Italian boy's organ music, "though the notes he broken . . . let me gaze fathoms down into thy fathomless eye . . ." This is an innocent prelude to the more experienced Ishmael's sense of communion as he glimpses the whales at love in the deep; "tis good as gazing down into the great South Sea and seeing the dazzling rays of the dolphins there" (250).

Redburn's achievement of a place in the only available society is somewhat in the direction of Babbalanja's decision, which offers another meaning of "cakes and ale." And Redburn's achievement is also Melville's, his "Priestley on Necessity."[18] As Redburn accepts restriction on human love and idealistic behavior, the author accepts restrictions of form and the requirements for consistency and verisimilitude, although they frustrate his need for direct metaphysical embodiment. However rankling, he obeys the dictates of society even in the most essential expression of independence from it, his book. The outcome was not as disastrous for Melville's spirit as he pretended to his acquaintances. On the eve of sailing for London that same year (1849) to complete arrangements for *White-Jacket*, which he had completed within a few months of *Redburn*, Melville wrote his father-in-law, "while I have felt obligated to refrain from writing the kind of book I would wish to; yet, in writing these two books, I have not repressed myself much — so far as they are concerned; but have spoken pretty much as I feel." Yet, Taji-like, he insists that his "earnest desire [remained] to write those sorts of books which are said to 'fail.' "[19] The journal of this English trip serves as a resonating footnote to *Redburn*; it records

London as a city of Dis, "clouds of smoke," "coaly waters," closed doors; even the British Museum was shut the "miserable rainy day" he wanted in.[20] He thought of writing about Israel Potter, the American exile who had more reason to feel even less welcome in England.

White-Jacket (1850) is based on Melville's last voyage as a seaman, and ends like *Redburn*, based on his first, with the narrator's return to society. But this time the developing Ishmael is an exile at the outset. *White-Jacket's* story reflects Melville's brief enlistment in the Navy to escape the fate of "something like Jackson," of becoming flotsam, less than a "Kanaka cab-horse" on a Hawaiian beach. The American frigate, *Neversink*, is homeward bound, which makes the voyage tolerable, and is also the representative of home itself, a floating hell, corrupt and enslaving. The narrator contrives the jacket to isolate himself from it all, a home unto itself. He refers to the jacket as his castle, "full of winding stairs, and mysterious closets, crypts, and cabinets."[21]

The jacket alone distinguishes him among the 500 men aboard but inadvertently as an object; he is known only as White-Jacket and refers to himself that way, even to the use of the relative pronoun 'that' instead of 'who.' "It was White-Jacket that loosed that main-royal, so far up aloft there . . . that was taken for an albatross . . ." (7). Somewhat in the way of Yillah and the whale, the white jacket accumulates phantom qualities in the eye of the crew. It conceals secrets from them and they shun it. Once mistaken for a ghost aloft, the narrator is nearly killed. He is excluded from the mess hall when the rainsoaked jacket drips on the table. Encased in his jacket, "white as a shroud," he is effectively a dead man in his society. Plunged into the "speechless profound of the sea" when he falls from the yardarm, he sinks "through a soft, seething foamy lull." As he and his jacket soak into the sea, the narrator is drawn to an oceanic universal, like Taji before him and Ahab after. Death seems as comforting as his jacket before the rain, when he "fairly hugged" himself and "revelled" in it (37). The experience is sensuous, of the self, and excessively poetic: "Purple and pathless was the deep calm now around me; flecked by summer lightnings in the azure far" (393). The choice to resist the "irresistible," to live, to rip open the jacket, is like "ripping open myself. With a violent struggle I then burst out of it, and was free" (394). Free, that is, to meld with the society that had repelled him because of the isolating jacket, free from everything that he imagined was his individual identity.

The white jacket is a barrier whose effect is the reverse of the white whale's. It conceals not the universal truth so taunting and tantalizing that Ahab must strike through to his death, but the opposite. It confines the limited human being, needing love of others, within his own ego. The narrator must rip through his white jacket to escape this inadvertant exiling into himself. And he is not motivated by any persistent urging but the threat of extinction. The impulse of life struggles with death in the deep which is here described as relaxed expansion into the all. As the ripped jacket sinks into the element to which it was always drawn, the narrator grasps a life-line from the *Neversink* and joins the living, ordinary and corrupt as they may be. His decision to live without his jacket, which he tried in vain to shed and disguise, is also the sacrifice of social ideals of justice and his acceptance of whatever passes as Christianity and democracy aboard the man-of-war, "This old fashioned world of ours afloat" (391).

Although the developing Ishmael who calls himself White-Jacket has metaphysical tendencies (he fears that man's total experience is circumnavigation in quest of the center of things), his thought is concentrated on describing and denouncing the official cannibalism of the world afloat that he ultimately accepts. The man-of-war is a detailed representation of the absurdly military isle of Diranja and the arrogantly fashionable isle of Pimminnee in the *Mardi* archipelago. It is a vortex, a pattern of energy maintained by the swirl of manuevers, pomp and ceremony with moral vacuity at the center. Wars are anticipated by the officers, the "overlords" of the "public", as chances for promotion, but for the "people," the enlisted men, as chances for death. Appeals to justice are made through the system to indefinite Navy Commissioners who are aloft, as far out of sight as gods. This society is forever preening as in "a childish parade of the old-fashioned court of Madrid" (164). When White Jacket chances upon one of the messages the Commodore passes with majestic gesture, he is amused to read, "Sir, you will give the people pickles today with their fresh meat" (21). Wanting clean kills only, the incompetent and tyrannical Captain Claret, who can't tell when to scud or run into the wind's eye, puts the "people" to polishing rusty cannon balls. And as with the French warship *LaReine* in *Omoo*, the men are in a constant show of furling and unfurling sails, which occasionally maims or kills one of them. Professional competence is parodied in the objective Dr. Cuticle who is also engaged in spectator sport. It was rumored he could "drop a leg in one minute and ten seconds from the moment the knife touches it" (255). The society White-Jacket must join is "charged to the combings of her hatchways with the spirit of Belial and all unrighteousness" (391), dedicated to the purpose of bloodshed, and sanctioned by the Articles of War with their ceaseless litany, "shall suffer death" (292).

Jackson's counterpart is Bland, the master-at-arms, whose scoundrelism approaches Claggart's in *Billy Budd*. He is deeper, more active, and less understandable than Redburn's nemesis; if his evil is not yet "innate" it is "organic," which to White-Jacket is symbolic of the society. His "wicked deeds seemed the legitimate operation of his whole infernal organization" (187), and his bland appearance gave the impression that he was innocent of his own evil. The "people" are themselves castaways and isolatoes who have found refuge in the Navy, "the asylum for the perverse, the home of the unfortunate" (74). They are capable of evils "so direful that they will hardly bear so much as an illusion," declares the offended White-Jacket, but cannot resist the temptation to allude to the "sins for which the cities of the plain were overthrown" (374).

But also aboard are a few poets and philosophers, bachelors who understand something of the good life, chiefly Jack Chase, "a sort of oracle of Delphi" (11). Chase, who presided over the maintop, had once defied authority but also distinguished himself in combat and is now influential enough to save White-Jacket from a flogging.[22] But Chase is himself no "deep diver." His feet are firmly planted on the deck, he is even "a bit of a dictator" (12). Jack Chase belongs. When commanded, he shaves his beard, "my manhood" (360), while the old sailor Ushant endures a flogging rather than surrender. "My beard is my own," he insists in a Bartleby-like refrain (364). White-Jacket admires Ushant's resistance and would have died himself rather than submit to flogging, but when he rips himself free of his individuating jacket and rejects death he is following Jack Chase, his masculine idol of virtue.[23]

White-Jacket's acceptance of Chase's man-of-war world has none of the triumph Redburn exhibits in his acceptance of shipboard society. It is a sickened acceptance, as he implies: "There is a fable about a painter moved by Jove to the painting of the head of Medusa. Though the picture was true to life, yet the poor artist sickened at the sight of what his forced pencil had drawn. Thus, borne through my task toward the end, my own soul now sinks at what I myself have portrayed" (386). But the portrait is no more "true to life" than the head of mythical Medusa. The major part of it, a polemical tract on tyrannical naval abuses, is inserted within the fictional elements of the first twenty chapters and the last ten of the novel, *White-Jacket*. And like the fictional elements, the tract is fabricated largely from accounts of voyages on a man-of-war besides his own.[24] If the portrait is as horrible as the head of the Medusa, it is also mythical, just as the articles of war are fictional within the society they sanction. They originated not in a republic but in the reign of a despot (Charles II) and they make the "declaration of Independence . . . a lie" (144). The book, *White-Jacket*, is put together like the white jacket the narrator fabricates: "I folded double at the bosom, and then by continuation of a slit there, opened it lengthwise — much as you would cut a leaf in the last new novel" (3).

The narrator is sickened not only by the society he has portrayed and his character's necessity to accept it, but also and mainly, by the realization that he has not and cannot escape the white jacket of fiction. His polemic, encased in fiction, is "true to life," but polemical nevertheless. From another point of view he sees that the official abuse of corporal punishment is justified by the need for order and expedience at sea. It is inflicted quickly and done with, and life goes on. If "you start from the same premises with these officers, you must admit that they advance an irrestible argument" (139). But that is the view of the yea-saying "public" whose Christianity and mock-democracy he had satirized. In the end, he portrays man sailing through this world "under sealed orders," hoping the "Lord High Admiral will yet interpose" (398) with the reforms his polemic urged, even though "his gospel seems lacking in the practical wisdom of earth . . . " (324).

III
When Melville encountered "Young Goodman Brown"

among Hawthorne's *Mosses from the Old Manse*, he felt
more than the "shock of recognition"; "this Hawthorne has
dropped germinous seeds into my soul."[25] His review of
Mosses in 1850, with its famous comparison to Shakespeare,
seems to concern Melville's own aspirations as much as
Hawthorne's tales. "Tormented into desperation, Lear, the
frantic King, tears off the mask and speaks the sane madness
of vital truth."[26] Later, he found Hawthorne's *Twice Told
Tales* "far exceed the 'Mosses' " but also that Hawthorne
"doesn't patronize the butcher — he needs roast-beef done
rare" (*L*121). And the Hawthorne that Melville met in the
Berkshires was certainly no Lear, but a man who apparently
had captured some of the beauty and happiness that
Melville's Taji pursues through *Mardi*.

Nor was Melville the man anticipated, although he kept
up the appearances of the adventurous sailor, enchanting the
Hawthorne children with stories of the South Seas and the
whale fisheries. Julian Hawthorne recorded that he was also
the "strangest being that ever came into our circle . . . restless
and disposed to dark hours."[27] When Captain Delano asks,
"What has cast such a shadow upon you?" Benito Cereno
answers, "The negro," but for Melville at this time the answer
was whiteness, the whiteness of the whale, and of hoary Lear
as well, tearing off the mask and speaking the madness of
truth.

Although *Moby-Dick* (1851) is inscribed to Nathaniel
Hawthorne, it contains none of the blackness from the past
and it ranges beyond hearts joined in the light of open day. It
is a description — humorous, tragic and lyrical — of Melville's
vortex in which the free American author has replaced the
confined Elizabethan and consequently the American Ahab
has replaced King Lear. Instead of humility seeking salvation
in love, Ahab's supreme ego seeks destruction.

Ahab can also be seen as a childish dupe in the American

folk tradition, but grown to epic proportions, taking seriously the tall tales of Moby-Dick. He is duped by his primitive
ego into a vendetta with an animal, "that inscrutable thing"
he hates. He imagines the animal, who "smote thee from
blind instinct," as Starbuck tells him, is also engaged in a
vendetta with him. "I'd strike the sun if it insulted me" (144).
He is even aware of his childishness, likening himself to a
schoolboy, on one occasion, and the whale to a bully who has
knocked him down; but rather than upbraid the whale to
"Take some one of your own size. . . , I am up again" (147).
That such a figure commands reasonable men is unfathom-
able to Ishmael, in whose imagination he exists: "How it was
that they so aboundingly responded to the old man's ire . . .
all this to explain would be to dive deeper than Ishmael can
go" (162).

At the end of *White-Jacket*, the man-of-war is seen on
the high seas as an emblem of the earth sailing through the
stars of space, "all wrongs remembered no more." The
voyage of the *Pequod* is the quest into the meaning of that
shipful of men through time and space, the one voyage that
would explain all the voyages, one ending only to begin
another. It is a voyage into the "art of Telling the Truth,"
which is neither art in itself nor truth in itself. Deeply
religious and dangerous, such a quest inhibits the flow of love
between men and violates the nature it attempts to uncover.
Pequod, the name of an aggressive tribe of Indians an-
nihilated in Massachusetts, means punishment, which is the
inevitable outcome of the quest, yet the quest is Melville's
dark necessity. Melville's narrator, Ishmael, expresses this in-
sistent urge in terms of the story of Narcissis, "who because
he could not grasp the tormenting mild image he saw in the
fountain, plunged into it and was drowned. But that same image, we ourselves see in all rivers and oceans. It is the image
of the ungraspable phantom of life; and this is the key to it

all" (14). (The reflection of self was also the key to it all for Emerson and Whitman, but for them it suggested vital American definition.)

Ishmael's chief reason for going to sea is much like Ahab's, "the overwhelming idea of the great whale himself. Such a portentous and mysterious monster roused all my curiosity" (16). Ahab is more violent in his explanation, since he is more than curious, seeking revenge and domination as well as ultimate truth, "How can the prisoner reach outside except by thrusting through the wall?" he asks, "the white whale is that wall, shoved near to me" (144). To Taji, the world of Mardi was also a "monster whose eyes are fixed in its head, like a whale." The white albino that Taji seeks throughout his imagined world, his symbol of ideal love, becomes for Ahab the whale, the world's meaning. But Ahab's motive is not unalloyed as Taji's. He pursues in the hatred Taji rejected. He is scarred, eaten in his encounters with the world; yet remnants of love, even nostalgia for home, surface at rare moments. In spite of his long exile at sea, his "forty years of privation and peril; and his "walled town of a captain's exclusiveness" (443), Ahab on occasion senses the comfort of human community: "let me look into a human eye," he asks Starbuck, "it is better than to gaze into sea or sky, better than to gaze upon God" (444). Ahab's monomania is the enormous swelling of festered psychic wounds, "Oh cruel," he cries out to his fiery father the sun, ". . . my sweet mother . . . What has thou done with her?" He was born of woman, of course, but a crazy one, and is thus homeless, as his father in the heavens, whom he imagines as lonely and exiled as himself, "hermit immemorial" (417).

Ahab is no fire-bringing Prometheus as some critics claim, nor a Satan, nor even the epitome of the American rugged individualist, as many critics claim.[28] (Prometheus grieved at Olympian neglect of mankind and was creative while Ahab eschews mankind and is destructive; Satan sought lost power by tempting God's minions through the pleasures of sin, while Ahab seeks universal knowledge as vengeance and is totally aloof from "the low enjoying power" (147); and the American rugged individualist is his own master while Ahab is in the employ of those hypocritical Quaker entrepreneurs, Peleg and Bildad, although he defies his duty to the profit-motive in chasing Moby-Dick out of vengeance.) Ahab is none of these. He most resembles the Titans of earliest myths, not Prometheus of course but those who also neglected mankind, like Enceladus to whom Pierre devotes a book. He is a hundred-armed giant fixating on his godly spirit which he personalizes. Good Christians like Starbuck also personalize their godly spirit. To Ahab, however, "The personalized impersonal" is prey and "practically assailable in Moby-Dick." Ahab "piled upon the whale's white hump the sum of all the general rage and hate felt by his whole race from Adam down" (160). Like the Jezebel that lured his namesake beyond the orthodoxy of Israel, the prey has lured Ahab beyond all "lovings and longings" (445). Not only has he abandoned wife and child but the smallest comforts, symbolized by his pipe and the very technology of his quest, the quadrant. He curses this instrument because it impudently shows him his minute place in the universe, not where he wills to be. It is "haughty," the instrument of commodores and admirals, a reminder of his own social position as mere whaling captain. Ahab will find his way himself, guided only by the leveling tools of self-reliance. With these, "the level ship's compass and the level dead reckoning" (412), Ahab will "strike through the mask."

The writing of the book is itself Melville's attempt to thrust through the wall, to dominate over the barriers of language, to break through that mask and grasp the ungraspable phantom, the "vital truth." Ahab may not care that Narcissus drowned but Ishmael does; he is aware of the danger. Yet like Queequeg in the submerged boat through the night of the first lowering, he pursues with his "imbecile candle in the heart of that almighty forlornness . . . hopelessly holding up hope in the midst of despair" (195).

Ishmael is Melville's quester, and the world he quests through is the sea room needed to tell the truth in. It is the sea of language as announced before Ishmael introduces himself, with the first word in the book, "Etymology." Ishmael's whale is every word he can gather about it, every legend, every myth, every fact, every experience, his and others; the etymological preface and extracts, the cetological expositions through the text. But the whole accumulation comprises the shapes of words, not truth, as his bookish classification of whales so comically implies: 'I. the *Folio Whale*; II. the *Octavo Whale*, III. the *Duodecimo Whale*" (120). The distinction between Ahab's quest and Ishmael's is shown in the American title, *Moby-Dick or, The Whale*, the specific white whale of Ahab's incarnation as opposed to whales in general, including that one.[29] Melville's imaginative and spirited narrator gets lost in the torturous paths of language as the author quests for a book about the whale, a more referential *Koztanza*.

The narrator begins by assigning himself a name, Ishmael, to symbolize his exiled spirit at home. He feels "a thirst in the great American desert" (13) while in his soul there is a "damp, drizzly November," the despairing pessimism that Redburn and White-Jacket feared would overcome them. When the drizzle becomes tempest, when he must fight impulses to knock off hats or commit suicide, as Jackson did, Ishmael knows enough to forsake the land, the "safety, comfort, hearthstone, supper, warm blankets, friends, all that's kind to our mortalities . . . [for] in that gale, the port, the land is [the] ship's direst jeopardy; she must fly all hospitality

. . . for the refuge's sake forlornly rushing into peril . . . " (97)

At sea, Ishmael's consciousness expands beyond the character he renders to us on shore. The quester of the truth must encompass it in order to penetrate it. Ishmael's consciousness becomes the stage containing the drama of Ahab, the crew, and the white whale, produced by "those stage managers, the Fates." He is also on that stage, a part of the "grand programme of Providence" (16). Awareness of his part and of the stage itself is lost from time to time as the drama expands like the breaching white whale himself, his bulk "piling up a mountain of dazzling foam" (455), while he is already somewhere else, still masked, somewhat in the nature of the Confidence-Man. Staging is how the confidence game is played. It is the deepest of the ironies in the book that Ishmael seeks truth through the only means available, his mind, which is a stage for acting out, recreating and rearranging our lives and our world in the medium of words.

The Ishmael who appears on the stage of Ishmael's drama finds at sea no ultimate escape from the conditions of the landlubber. Still on land, he asks, "Who ain't a slave?" (15) At sea, Ahab answers, "Who's over me?" (144). The social organization of men on land is essentially the same at sea, and more obvious there. But Ishmael's question applies also to the containment of the imagination by the vortex of language; "whereto does all that circumnavigation conduct?" Ishmael wonders at sea. "Only through numberless perils to the very point whence we started, where those we left behind secured, were all the time before us" (204). During his "Long exile from Christiandom and civilization," enduring the frustration of circumnavigation, of the vortex, the Ishmael upon the stage of his mind begins to identify with a fate that is not the narrator's, "your true whale-hunter . . . as much a savage as an Iroquois" (232). Through the invention of Ahab as alter-ego, however, the narrator actually avoids that fate.

His truth-telling spirit survives to tell the story of the true whale hunters.

Unlike Ahab, Ishmael accepts his limitations as a human being in the "grand programme of Providence," but such acceptance is not easily achieved for a spirited mind, as Father Mapple's sermon suggests. The sermon points to the basic ambiguity in Hebraic Christianity: "And if we obey God, we must disobey ourselves; and it is in this disobeying ourselves wherein the hardness of obeying God consists" (45). Ishmael can accept his human condition, if not Father Mapple's god, without disobeying himself. Ahab cannot. In obeying himself, Ishmael does not overreach his limitations nor personalize his universe, as Ahab does. He wants to know as much as Ahab but his is not a primitive intelligence having to start all over. He too would appreciate a finite world on the human scale directly accessible without the deceptive intervention of language and myth. He wants what Ahab wants but is willing rather than willful. Instead of the absolute assertion, "I am Ahab," we must remember he introduced himself with the tentative, "Call me Ishmael," as if to say it really doesn't matter. Language deceives. I am somebody else but at this dismal moment I feel like an Ishmael. Nor does Ishmael demonstrate the spirit of the good Christian that Father Mapple impresses upon his seafaring congregation. The Christian "gives no quarter in the truth, and kills, burns, and destroys all sin . . . " (51). Ishmael's providence is beyond religious myth while that of Ahab, the religious primitive, is ironically imprisoned by it, and thus Ahab is impelled to strike through. This is the godly ungodliness Peleg sees in his captain.

Ishmael transcends the constraints of Father Mapple's contradictory lore in his brotherhood with Queequeg. "Christian kindness has proved but hollow courtesy." The tatooed islander redeems his "splintered heart and maddened hand . . . turned against the wolfish world" (53). Ishmael, unlike Tommo in *Typee*, can join with the pagan as a "cozy loving pair" (54). (Concentration on sexual meaning here rather than human warmth and brotherhood is to miss the heart of it.) Queequeg is like a whale in his awe and mystery, "a riddle to unfold; a wonderous work in one volume; but whose mysteries not even himself could read . . . and these mysteries were therefore destined in the end to moulder away with the living parchment whereon they were inscribed, and so be unsolved to the last" (399). In Ishmael the mystery inspires love rather than hate and so the bitter shore personality, the exile, is dissipated and he is freed to find pleasure in his ruminations on the grandness of nature, the warp and woof of the mat-maker, the flow of love between hands in the squeezing of the spermaceti, and in the amours and suckling of whales in the deep. But he also observes the cannibalism of the sharks eating their own tails while disgorging their bowels. Even more shuddering, as he delights in the "enchanted calm which they say lurks in the heart of every commotion," the vortex of whales, his mind is capable of a factual note describing the hunter's lance cutting the precious nursing nipple, the "mother's pouring milk and blood rivallingly discolor the sea for rods" (326). Seemingly for his own delectation, he adds the information that men have tasted this milk and that "It might do well with strawberries." But the scene itself reflects his capacity for love of the mysterious universe even though its creatures, including himself, are such cannibals. The human brotherhood that he and Queequeg established beyond the barriers of Christian and pagan societies is part of this love.

The exile's aggressive anguish that drove Ishmael to sea now festers in Captain Ahab. If Ahab cannot belong to this world, he will make it belong to him. (Of course Ahab can be taken as imperialistic America attempting to engorge the

world in its outreaches of 1848 but such topical interpretation
is not central.) He is an exile but not from human society
since there is no longer anything he wants there. His crew is a
collection of isolated islanders, each "living on a separate
continent of his own," cut off from the common ground.
Like himself and Ishmael, they have little history. (Perhaps
they can be seen as representative of the American condition.)[30] However, these isolatoes do form a society aboard
the *Pequod*. And Ishmael finds in the crew the types offered
by the land society he fled, the good Christian like Starbuck,
the philistine like Stubbs, the plain fool like Flask.

It is not the hats of such fellows that Ahab is urged to
knock off. All human society is behind him. They are all
loose fish to be made fast as in the law where ownership
depends upon the power of the owner to keep it, "the Coke-
upon-Littleton of the fist" (332). Ahab is no longer an exile
from the human community but from the universe itself. He
is a perennial child of human history made perverse by denial
of his primitive "birthright, the May-day gods of old." He
will have what he wants regardless of responsibility to others.
So intently does this monomaniac crave knowledge and connection with a primitive reality that he twists his desire into
hate. Incomprehensibility is an insult to him. He justifies this
perversion in both the Hebraic and Puritanical way, avenging
a lost leg and making the symbolic object of his personal
hatred the evil of the universe: "The white whale swam before
him as the monomaniac incarnation of all these malicious
agencies which some deep men feel eating in them . . . " (160).

Such is Ahab's reading of nature's text. But the ultimate
reader in this drama is Ishmael and his reading contains
Ahab, who is seen as an abomination to nature, like his
wicked namesake. Nature will not tolerate such ego. Unfortunately, as the Bible story warns, nature does not follow any
human sense of justice; in scratching the irritation repre-

sented by Ahab, it happens also to eradicate Ahab's abject society, his crew. The Ahab on the stage of Ishmael's mind, however, is also like the whale, "a portentous and mysterious monster" that must be pursued. "Oh, Ahab! what shall be grand in thee, it must needs be plucked at from the skies, and dived for in the deep, and featured in the unbodied air!" (130). He is the greatest of players and so dominates Ishmael's stage that the narrator ignores his personal narration for five consecutive chapters and gives himself over to the drama utterly, "Enter Ahab: Then, all" are the stage directions for Chapter 36, "The Quarter-Deck," followed by the Chapter "Sunset" with these directions: "The Cabin; by the stern windows; Ahab sitting alone, and gazing out." The last of these staged chapters, "Midnight, Forecastle," is a complete dramatic scene in every detail, variety of characters, brisk dialogue, indications of sound, music and stage business. Here the dramatist fully sets his stage. In conjunction with the encyclopedic compiling of information, Ishmael's staging emphasizes the chaos of the material his language shapes. And all is determined by the shaper, who is confined to a cultural vortex and thus controlled in turn. It is all a stage play, a universal game run by an "unseen and unaccountable joker" (195).

With Ishmael, Ahab knows his universe to be a "turn round and round . . . like yonder windlass" (445). He hears the mad laughter of Pip, the boy who has dipped into the immensity which Ahab seeks, mocking his reckless ambition. He recognizes his own dependence on his "man-maker" carpenter and he knows that destruction awaits his "mechanical" men and his own mechanical willfulness. But he cannot turn back, although several times Ahab must push on against memories of his lost humanity. In "The Symphony" chapter, he drops a tear into the sea. And in "The Log and Line" chapter, his lost feelings are stirred by Pip as King

Lear's are by a proper fool. "I have one part in my heart," Lear tells the fool, "That's sorry for thee,"[31] and Ahab tells Pip, "Thou touchest my inmost centre, boy" (428). Ahab plays the willful and active part of the father that becomes entangled in the lines of his own creation. His tragic action, therefore, is tinged with comedy. On occasion, Ishmael's language appears to mock the action as melodramatic hyperbole: "Fate's lieutenant" (459), "Oh my captain, my captain, noble soul, grand old heart" (444), "Noble heart — go not — go not. . . . O Master, My Master, come back!" (462-63). In the mockery we can see Ahab as the satiric character of Taji enlarged beyond love's concern to the universal.

The structure of the truth seeker's drama also mocks the tragedy of Ahab's performance. Taking the freedom of a Shakespeare unmuzzled in America, the narrator allows characters established for significant roles to fade. Not only does his handsome sailor type, Bulkington, disappear, but even Queequeg dampens to no more significance than Tashtego and Daggoo, except to fashion a coffin lid before he dies. Although tension is established between Starbuck and his captain, there is none between Ishmael and Ahab, who represent the basic social opposition in the novel, the loving and hateful approaches to life and the universe. Also revealing is the moment of confrontation with Moby-Dick, certainly the climax of the novel's action, but the narrative of the last three days is no more intense than the black mass scene Christianing the harpoons. Instead, Ishmael's narrative returns to the form of the vortex established earlier in the "Grand Armada" chapter with the "tumults of the outer concentric circles . . . swiftly going round and round" (329). On the first day of the chase, the sea near Moby-Dick is described like the void at the center, still and smooth, as if a carpet had been drawn over the waves, and then the whale is seen as a beguiling god serene and tranquil "set in a revolving ring of finest, fleecy, greenish foam" (447). Above him, the birds wheel round in a vortex of their own. And after the whale attacks, Ahab's head moves absurdly in the heart of the whirlpool "like a tossed bubble" (450). In the final chapter, spiralling circles of increasing velocity "seized the lone boat itself, and all its crew, and each floating oar, and every lance-pole and spinning, animate and inanimate, all round and round in one vortex, carried the smallest chip of the *Pequod* out of sight" (469).

Ahab's defeat is also the defeat of Ishmael's quest. He had sought the meaning beneath the endless succession of voyages, but as the *Pequod* sinks he finds only that the "great shroud of the sea rolled on as it rolled five thousand years ago." The story of the truth contains the ungraspable phantom but the ungraspable phantom contains the truth which is ungraspable — all is story. The truth cannot be distilled from the vortex. It cannot be told. [32]

Just before he went to "drive" his "whale" through the press in New York, Melville had written Hawthorne, "Truth is the silliest thing under the sun." Nevertheless he will take his whale by the "jaw and finish him up in some fashion or other." What he "feels most moved to write is banned. It will not pay. Yet write altogether the other way I cannot. So the product is a final hash and all my books are botches" (*L* 128). Except for the Epilogue tacked onto the American edition, there is no evidence that Melville deferred to the market place in *Moby-Dick*. He had indeed written what he felt most moved to write. The masses of seeming digression — essays, sketches, technical descriptions, ruminations — are central to Melville's art of telling the truth and most certainly not aimed at sales. The failure he disguises in this letter is Ahab's — of capturing the whale, the elusive truth within the forms of art. Perhaps he would not have been so despairing had he known that in the next century Heisenberg and other scientists would encounter the same elusiveness in matter, which defies the prober by changing dimension in response to the measuring instrument.

IV

The Ishmael that emerges from the ocean in the Epilogue is akin to the earlier sailors ending the adventure in a swim for the boat, as rotten and deceptive as they know that home to be. The "devious-cruising" Rachel retrieves the orphan and another journey begins. But not Ishmael's. The reader has been to the heart of that sailor's endless voyaging. Melville returns us to the good mother's society. *Pierre* (1852) is a domestic voyage into the moral and intellectual nature of the willfully romantic soul. The son of plenty, born to a happy, senseless existence, has but to accept the good life offered by mother, who is lovingly called Sister, and by his fiance, who is no threat to mother. Like a resurrected Taji, however, Pierre is something of an Ahab in love. We discover him in the love bower of Saddle Meadow with the shade of Yillah defined into Lucy Tartan, his betrothed. This unlikely domestic sequel promises a melodrama that might have matched the popular successes of Melville's day, but he could not give up his questing, nor his propensity to satirize. The melodrama, therefore, is "botched" like all his books. He cannot write one way nor altogether the other.

The quest is drained of force because Pierre's mind, unlike Ahab's or Taji's, does not symbolize its object. He speaks of the abstraction as itself. Since he already possesses Isabel, the intruding half-sister, when he starts upon his journey, the quest is rather for intellectual justification of his moral choice. The choice exiles him from home because mother cannot abide it, being ignorant of its nature. The goal of the quest is somewhat objectified in the second part as the writing of a great book, not mentioned in the first part.

Pierre's mind is stufffed with romantic notions and myths of existence and he acts as a composite character of ideality made up from his readings, especially in Dante, Shakespeare and Greek myths. Robert Frost would call him a fool of books. Retaining an Ishmael bit of conscience, he is not absolutely certain of the adamant morality he opposes to the easy life at Saddle Meadow. He pretends to marry the girl who claims to be his half-sister in order to protect his family's reputation and correct his father's transgression. But is this a noble act or is he the victim of his own sexual attraction, perverted and distorted into an illusion of a noble act? If Isabel had been less beautiful, less sensual, would he have acted so nobly? If his European readings had not prepared him for a romantic cause? If he had not ached for some event to release his pent-up heroism, to work his lofty yearnings upon?

What this romantic narcissist desires above all is the willful defiance of a happy but hollow fate at Saddle Meadow, of the "dreary heart-vacancies of the conventional life,"[33] a defiance that Isabel stirs in him. She provides an immediate cause, revealing to him the fraudulence of his father's unbesmirched virtue. But his readings, or rather misreadings, confuse his aims. Instead of exposing the fraudulence, he hides it and rants defiance of the "Black Knight," whom the reader assumes to be fate, which confronts and mocks Pierre, a Moby-Dick of another color, "lo! I strike through thy helm, and will see thy face, be it Gorgon! — Let me go, ye fond affections; all piety leaves me; . . . From all idols I tear all veils" (65-6). But this monster is never concretized into a symbol for the dramatic conflict Pierre promises. Instead, Pierre exiles himself with pretended bride to Greenwich Village where representatives of the society he abandoned pursue and undo him.

In the transcendence of this domesticated Taji to the

"highest heavens of uncorrupted love" (142), the narrator vacillates in mood and meaning, frequently finding Pierre a fool and an ass, and from time to time the protagonist agrees. Isabel is first perceived as a phantom, disturbing his bliss with Lucy in the idyllic countryside. He feels her presence as the mystery of life, the darkness, the guilt, the grief. When the phantom who has corrupted his joy disappears, Pierre relaxes again into his idyll. But the "uncorrupted love" refers to Isabel, not Lucy. Uncertainly the reader wonders whether this is tongue-in-cheek irony or just the narrator's recklessness. The narrator's language is indistinguishable from Pierre's and appears to be a condescension, if not a parody, to the sentimental mode of the day. It is emotion-laden and hardly ever emotive.[34]

On occasion the story disintegrates into slapstick. After Lucy swoons at Pierre's announcement of his marriage to Isabel, the maid shoos him off, "Monster! incomprehensible fiend! depart!" (184) When his mother also shoos him, he goes with "idiot eyes," tripping over his feet and falling on his face, to symbolize the future. In New York, Pierre woos imaginary combat with the unspecified woes and evils of society and the narrator asks why he acts so ineluctably to so small a note. And why does he not have the sense, in spite of his romantic eagerness, to question the validity of Isabel's claim? "Pierre — foolish Pierre" (70). Before the tale is done, the narrator sees his hero as a "little soul toddler" who is "toddling entirely alone, and not without shrieks" (269).

This is the "regular romance" Melville described to his publisher (*L*150), Richard Bentley, and the "rural bowl of milk" he promised Sophia Hawthorne (*L*146). But it is also the "Krakens" that he implied would follow *Moby-Dick* (*L*143). It seems Melville could not proceed without mocking the romance he was trying to write, though krakens it might be. Perhaps he imagined he could fool the literary market place, giving what they think they want while actually retaining his distance and artistic integrity through the satire.

Books 17 and 18, "Young America in Literature" and "Pierre, as a Juvenile Author, Reconsidered," reveal one aim of mockery, American literature, which Melville saw as either melodramatic or excessively idealistic. The juvenile author is driven out, "an infant Ishmael, into the desert, with no maternal Hager to accompany and comfort him" (89). The common reference to lushly forested America as a desert had always been a cultural metaphor, but Pierre exiles himself to the city where he finds temporary refuge among artists and intellectuals at an abandoned church ironically called "The Apostles." Isabel, who stands by this infant for maternal needs in place of Hagar, is suggestive of Poe's "Ligeia" in her "death-like beauty" and "wild musicalness." Her hair undulates like "the phosphorescent midnight sea" (150). She seems to discern the voice of mother in her mysterious guitar, which suggests Charles Brockden Brown's *Wieland* as well as Edgar Allan Poe's Roderick Usher. Although she is Pierre's Jezebel, this earth-woman is also akin to transcendentalist seekers of higher spirits: "I hope one day to feel myself drank up into the pervading spirit animating all things. I feel I am an exile here" (119). And from her exile's point of view, Melville can criticize what he finds contradictory between the transcendentalist's self-reliant individualism and divine dependence: "I feel that there can be no perfect peace in individualism." Isabel is made into anything the author wants or needs in order to play with American literature.

Given Melville's penchant for wild journeying, even the precision of the external structure appears to mock. The twenty-six books are divided evenly into two parts, the idyllic life disturbed at Saddle Meadows as opposed to exile and death in New York City. This diptych (a new device that Melville will use in stories that follow such as "The Paradise of Bachelors and The Tartarus of Maids") is spliced with a mid-point book in which Pierre finds and reads Plinlimmon's pamphlet, offering him a basic philosophy of life. The structure brings to mind Hawthorne's *Scarlet Letter*, its twenty-four chapters also evenly divided and spliced in the middle, but fortunately with a symbolic scene (Dimmesdale, Hester and Pearl joined on the scaffold at midnight) that renders meaning rather than a philosophical tract that satirically seems to cover it.

The accidental discovery of Plotinus Plinlimmon's pamphlet on the way to New York serves notice that *Pierre* is another paper product. His country life is described as "a sweetly writ manuscript" (7). The moving forces of the action are mostly forms of words, epistles, beginning with Isabel's note disrupting his perfect happiness. In New York, Lucy's note disturbs the guilty fate he has arranged to live with, and Glen Stanley's letters first praise and then condemn. The ending emphasizes his failure to break out of a bookish prison, "Life's last chapter well stitched into the middle" (360). But it is not until the mid-chapter, "The Journey and the Pamphlet," that the reader fully recognizes Pierre as a paper fool. The pamphlet states the case of Christ-like men, "Chronometricals," too idealistic to exist in the practical and depraved world controlled by "Horologicals." (Emerson is often taken as this figure, although Melville's sympathetic satire appears more inclusive.) When the pamphlet gets lost in the lining of his coat, Pierre wears its wisdom unconsciously as he wears the literature he has read, and he cannot understand it any better.

Pierre's golden haven in the second half of the diptych becomes authorship of a great book, à la Plotinus Plinlimmon. In his innocence at Saddle Meadow long ago, he tells Isabel, he wrote fine and even famous poems and essays and was the easy darling of critic and publisher. That was the

Young American in Literature, "useless, fit for a time when poetry was a consecration." But in our "bantering, barren, and prosaic heartless age, Aurora's music-moan is lost" (136). Now in the Apostles, in the Europeanized America, the City of Dis, he must write the truth. Like the vortex of the Mardian author, his production is "built around a circle, as atolls" and his thought spins in culture's never-ending spiral (283). The golden haven, as in *Mardi*, is an idealistic book of love. But Pierre attempts to compose it with the ideas of other authors in his vortex. He did not see "that the heavy unmalleable element of mere book-knowledge would not congenially weld with . . . spontaneous creative thought. . . . He did not see, that it was nothing at all to him, what other men had written . . . that all the great books in the world are but the mutilated shadowings-forth of invisible and eternally unembodied images in the soul . . . if we would see the object, we must look at the object itself, and not at its reflection" (283-4). He has none of Ishmael's anti-intellectual sense to "throw all those thunderheads [Locke and Kant in Ishmael's case, whose opposition poorly trims the boat] overboard and then . . . float light and right" (*MD* 277). Obviously Pierre will not qualify as an Emersonian American scholar.

Nurtured by his readings, Pierre insists upon "the intrinsic correctness and excellence of his general life-theory" (209). He ignores the dilemma of his moral choice that saves Isabel but destroys his mother. Pierre even finds sanction for his incest in Dante's Francesca and Poala, Shakespeare's Claudius and Gertrude, and in the parentage of the Titan, Enceladus, of whom he dreams. Ultimately, the chain of reason goes, we are all products of incest and condemned to it. In a mixture of myths, Pierre's descent to the City of Dis ends with symbolic burial under a mountain, the same end suffered by Enceladus when the Titan attempts to storm the Olympians. For imprisoned Pierre, "The cumbersome ceiling almost rested on his brow; . . . the massive cell-galleries above seemed partially piled on him" (360). Pierre sees himself battling with gods also but not for mankind, only for himself, as Enceladus, not Prometheus.[35] And in spite of the strewn bodies at the Hamlet ending, Pierre is no more the indecisive Danish Prince than Prufrock. Rather than enlighten, Pierre's readings befuddle. Dante made him fierce and vengeful, but Hamlet "insinuated there was none to strike" (which Ahab should have realized) (170). So all the "fiery floods in the *Inferno* and all the rolling gloom in *Hamlet* suffocate him at once in flame and smoke" (171).

Pierre's failing is the same as Ahab's, the inability to accept his miniscule position in the universe. Humorless as Ahab, he cannot perceive the big joke in it all. Like Ahab, Pierre sees only the reflection of himself, his bookish self. The world's flattery of him at Saddle Meadow turns to hostility in the city and his reaction is vengeance, to return "Jeer for jeer and taunt the apes that jibed him" (398-99), especially the heartless publishers, Flint, Steel, and Asbestos, who had praised his early trivialities. But even the intention of writing the truth cannot circumvent the literary game, and Pierre is not defeated until he comes to this realization: "Like knavish cards, the leaves of all great books were covertly packed. He was but packing one set the more . . . " (339). As artist, however, Pierre is too obvious and uncontrolled, a mark himself "of all the ambiguities which hemmed him in" (337).

V

Pierre's domestic voyage is Melville's last journey. He probes no more. Little remains of the Ishmael squeezing the globules of spermaceti with his mates aboard the *Pequod*, finding love like a sort "sort of insanity . . . the very milk and sperm of kindness" (*MD* 323). Nor of the Ahab who must thrust through the hated wall of unreason to find the reason within. What remains is the vortex in which Pierre has been spinning, where the "endlessness is only concealed by the spiralness of the stair, and the blackness of the shaft" (289). As far as the eye can see into this black vortex, there the image of "Bartleby and Scrivener" appears, an exile from the dead letter office who refuses to scrive, which is to distort what is written, to trick by forms of art, to negotiate. So he stares at a wall, not challenged to strike through it as Ahab is, but in a near catatonic state, which may have symbolized Melville's condition after the disastrous reception of *Pierre*. (His mother and wife arranged a consultation with Dr. Oliver Wendell Holmes and sought an appointment in a foreign office to get him away for awhile.) "Ah Humanity," sighs the Wall Street lawyer at the conclusion of Bartleby's starved and imprisoned life. He does not know what to make of this irrational interruption which disturbed his negotiability and aroused his curiosity and sympathy. Since Bartleby prefers not to negotiate, it is the Wall Street lawyer who will ascend the spiral of the black shaft, as if re-emerging into life from the mysterious innard of the vortex, until, fully formed and totally conscious, he steps onto the *Fidele* as *The Confidence-Man*.

Bartleby is not quite the dead letter he comes to symbolize. In the Tombs he even shows a speck of emotion when he acrimoniously tells the lawyer, "I know you," and "I want nothing to say to you."[36] Is he at last responding to the world's misuse of him? He had arrived at the lawyer's door "incurably forlorn." Immediately he is isolated, placed in a corner with no view, a window facing a wall and screened from the rest. He is in effect returned to the dead letter office, reduced to a cannibalistic machine-man who "seemed to gorge" on the lawyer's documents (100). That he may desire more communicable quarters is indicated by his later rejection of other vocations the lawyer suggests as too confining. If he seeks reward for his diligence, which the lawyer acknowledges as "mechanical" rather than "cheerfully industrious," his disappointment is never given voice. Instead of reward, he is called upon for tasks and errands beyond his contract.[37] It is at this point he begins to "prefer not to." The machine revolts.

Given the lawyer's relaxed personality, had Bartleby explained himself, surely more satisfactory arrangements would be forthcoming. But his is not the language of other men. When he first preferred not to, "Not a wrinkle of agitation rippled him" (101). The lawyer can see nothing "ordinarily human about him." Nevertheless he feels "something about Bartleby that not only strangely disarmed me, but in a wonderful manner touched and disconcerted me" (102). Bartleby serves to awaken the lawyer to "a bond of common humanity" (110). The lawyer's office is also without a view of what "landscape painters call 'life' " (93). It exists between the "white wall of the interior of a spacious sky-light shaft" and a "lofty brick wall, black by age and everlasting shade." The lawyer walls himself in because he wishes to play safe, while Bartleby is not playing at all. He is outside of the human game of negotiation.

Bartleby can be fitted into the character of the Chronometrical described by Plinlimmon's pamphlet in *Pierre*, while the lawyer can be seen as the Horological.[38] Bartleby will surrender no details of himself, not even or especially his "native place." When the lawyer refers at last to the grass and sky as remaining pleasures even in the Tombs, Bartleby responds, "I know where I am," meaning the earth, which is an uncomfortable place for a Chronometrical. "The world seems to lie saturated and soaking with lies," says *Pierre*'s narrator, as he introduces Plinlimmon's pamphlet (208). Plinlimmon would see Bartleby as one of those "who finding in himself a chronometrical soul, seeks practically to force that heavenly time upon the earth; in such an attempt he can never succeed" (212). For the Horological, on the other hand, even when drawn by "the bond of common humanity", as the lawyer is, all is negotiation, including charity. The Wall Street lawyer admits, "to humor him in his strange wilfulness, will cost me little or nothing, while I lay up in my soul what will eventually prove a sweet morsel for my conscience" (105). Although he calculates the expanse of his humanity, the lawyer will not entertain the thought of sacrificing his reputation or practice for the sake of the other. When such sacrifice threatens, he withdraws, exemplifying Plinlimmon's description of the Horological: "certain minor self-renunciations mere instinct . . . will teach him to make, but he must by no means make a complete unconditional sacrifice of himself in behalf of any other being, or any cause, or any conceit." (204). The lawyer extends himself to a degree that satisfies his own soul, but never approaches Christ-like charity, which is beyond the human. To the end, the irrational and ascetic Bartleby is as mysterious and tantalizing to the Wall Street lawyer as Moby Dick is to Ahab. The lawyer is Ahab's opposite, playing safe, submitting to the will, and negotiating with his nemesis, but fooling himself nevertheless. "Ah Bartleby! Ah Humanity!" is not an appositional statement as the lawyer intends it, but an ironical one, for Bartleby, like Plinlimmon's Chronometrical is not quite humanity. The irony is emphasized by the grub-man when he identifies the prisoner as "a gentleman forger," the scrivener, that is, signing himself in on earth as human.

"Bartleby," published in 1853, reflects Melville's struggle against the conclusion that Western civilization is lost in negotiation and confidence games. "Cock-A-Doodle-Doo!" also 1853, "The Fiddle" in 1854, and "Jimmy Rose" in 1855, however, seek some root for a benevolent attitude, some possibility of making do with life as it is, which is essentially the lawyer's attitude. The narrator of "Cock-A-Doodle-Doo!" is reprieved from the engulfing gloom of his farming life by the glorious crowing of an irradient cock, the voice of the universe itself, it seems, singing, "Glory be to God in the Highest." His family is also enraptured by this glorious morning voice, even as it changes to a terrifying scream, and they die, one by one, in utter mystery. The narrator who experiences all this can nevertheless con himself thereafter to alleviate his depressions by singing "Cock-A-Doodle-Doo!" "The Fiddler" and "Jimmy Rose," two failures, also manage to trick themselves into acceptance of life. The musician recognizes himself as a genius even though society ignores him; and Rose, fallen from wealth, emerges, after many years of bitter exile in his own house, a "courteous, smiling, shivering gentleman," to become something of a social clown. He is a guest at the tables of those he had lavishly entertained in his earlier years. Jimmy Rose was too "thoroughly good and kind to be made from any cause a man-hater" (139).

The desire for the bright side of life fights the threat of "becoming something like Jackson," and insidiously invites the confidence game. In "The Encantadas" (1854), the "chief sound of life is . . . a hiss," but even here "the tortoise, dark and melancholy as it is up the back, still possesses a bright side" (236). But to see it, nature has to be turned upside down. The promise of the bright side is not only unnatural in the "Encantadas," it is also deceptive as in "Cock-A-Doodle-Doo!" The islands themselves shimmer with enchanting uncertainty some thirty miles at sea, but ashore are barren, inhabited by occasional castaways who are alien to each other, to the rock, and to the tortoise, as well as to the civilization that had abandoned them. The deception inherent in the human desire for the bright side echoes through the remainder of Melville's stories and most bitterly in the last, *Billy Budd* (1924), in the cherubic victim's final utterance from within the noose, "God bless Captain Vere."

Unlike the Wall Street lawyer, "The Lightning-Rod Man" (1854) is fully conscious of his deceptive staging. For him, playing safe is no mere attitude towards life but an active game. He sells a mechanism which will provide complete safety through insulation and thus isolation. He is a "False negotiator" who "drives a brave trade with the fears of man."[39] So does Scribe in "I and My Chimney" (1856). The chimney is sprawling, inefficient, possessed of "a warm heart" (168). Scribe, the architect, is for hire, either to the machine-efficient values of the wife who engages him to remove the chimney or the comfort-conserving husband who bribes him to leave it. To tear the chimney down might cause this house of human values to crumble, a fact ignored by the wife and of no concern to the architect who will employ any ruse, such as treasure hidden in the chimney, to win.[40] In the Scribe and the Scrivener, Melville may be examining the extremes of his own prospects—to write for a public, that is to negotiate, or not.

The negotiator's strategy, conscious or unconscious, derives from his assumption that men react mechanically in a mechanical universe. This is the assumption that disgusts Ahab even as he reduces his crew to mechanical functionaries and resorts to the carpenter for mechanical repairs of his own body. Ahab's fate is re-staged in "The Bell-Tower" (1855), where Bannadonna, a genius "mechanician," replaces the steely whaling captain and a mechanical artifact replaces the symbol of universal nature. At the casting of the great bell, when the "unleashed metals" cause workmen to recoil, Bannadonna forces them back to the job, striking and killing their chief. A chip of the chief, a bone fragment, gets mixed into the molten mass and this imperfection tolls the end of Bannadonna at the first sounding of the bell. Like the whale, the bell seems to have a will of its own. Although it is the human flaw in the mechanism that generates the vengeance upon its maker, the fundamental irony is the same in port as at sea, the turning upon the master whose will attempts to overextend his power or genius beyond human limits.

"The Bell-Tower" mechanism was to become the perfect serf, without personality, the condition anticipated for Bartleby. The condition is achieved finally in "The Paradise of Bachelors and the Tartarus of Maids" (1855). In this story, the bright side of life, carefree and mindless bachelorhood, is contrasted with the mechanical slavery that supports it. The bachelors, significantly located in London, wallow in pleasure, their door locked against "the thing called pain, the bugbear styled trouble" (213). Meanwhile, their counterpart in America, Old Bach, is at work mastering virgin maidens who labor in a white-washed factory, a "whited sepulchre" (216) within a desolate "frost-painted" valley (219). The only sound is the hum of the machinery, like "a living, panting Behemoth" (227). It resembles a female body pounded by a piston. The machinery appears to devour the souls of the blank-faced maidens who attend it, and after a nine-minute gestation produces blank sheets of paper. The observer, who was the guest of the London bachelors, now is a seed man who comes to the paper mill in the valley through torturous "cloven walls" in search of envelopes for his product. He flees the inhuman mechanics at the heart of this society, sighing, much like the Wall Street lawyer in reverse, "Oh! Paradise of Bachelors! and oh! Tartarus of Maids!" (229). The bachelors are an exact opposite of Bartleby. They prefer to play on the bright side, at the expense of the maidens who are de-humanized in the cloven American valley. This is no place for the narrator's seed.

Captain Amasa Delano in "Benito Cereno" (1855) is another bachelor on the bright side, on the sealer, *Bachelor's*

Delight. Unlike his London brethren, however, the American bachelor encounters disturbing experiences, and his reaction is much the same as the Wall Street lawyer's. He cannot comprehend the shocked awareness of the Spanish aristocrat, Don Benito. What casts the shadow upon Cereno's life? That he and his heritage are the ultimate causes of the atrocious slave revolt. Cereno is the representative oppressor of humanity throughout history and he has buoyed and justified such leadership by myths of historical, natural, or cultural superiority. His ship is now a "decaying relic of past glories," and the true nature of these glories is symbolized in the sternpiece, carved with "a dark satyr in a mask, holding his foot on the prostrate neck of a writhing figure, likewise masked" (6). The only unmasking that occurs in the story is for Cereno, who becomes conscious of the evil the leadership of his class wrought. The traumatic dispelling of illusion leaves Cereno in much the same state we find Bartleby. The righteous testimony of the events that follow Delano's deceived version of them is also illusion, another story for Cereno. Delano is saved from Cereno's black despair by his own obtuseness; he is unaware of the wall that entombs the truth and protects his illusions.

Becoming aware that he has unconsciously lived by the confidence games of his class, Benito Cereno is shocked into inertia, and so he is at the opposite extreme from the "false negotiator" who desires to take advantage of man's reliance on illusion but is not skilled enough. With Benjamin Franklin in *Israel Potter* (1855), Melville finally arrives at a full portrait of the "false negotiator," the confidence man *per se*. He appears to the altruistic Israel as a conjuror in black skull cap and a rich gown which is the gift of a female admirer. Immediately Franklin launches into an aphoristic and censorious lecture suggested by Israel's tight boots and high heels which conceal secret papers for Dr. Franklin. The American minister concludes with a note to himself, to produce a pamphlet on the subject. Nothing wasted. At dinner the deceptive American minister serves white wine of the very oldest brand, water. After more sanctimonious and duplicitous advice, Israel is sent to bed with an ambiguous warning against the temptations of the chambermaid. Franklin, who has been a successful jack-of-all-trades but has no poetry in him, teaches Israel, also jack-of-all-trades but far less successful, the ways to duplicity — as spy.

Israel is an echo of Cooper's Harvey Birch and of his Leatherstocking. He is fearless, self-reliant and mentally adept. Before going to sea as harpooner, he had been farm hand, surveyor, hunter and trapper. But he had also been a peddler in the frontier settlements, an experience which gave him some of the skill and bravado of the master. His abilities at disguise, however, are tempered with his inability to lower himself, to accept the station he must assume in society, and he resents Franklin's ease in doing so, in addressing nobility with proper title. He has no temperament for the social game. His American naval captain, John Paul Jones, is another confidence man. Like Franklin, Jones can also function as a citizen of the world, but one with poetry in his heroic soul. As a fighter, he is unprincipled, reckless and predatory enough to be honored even by the King of France, while Israel, who fought beside him, remains obscure. A contrast to both of these early confidence men, Franklin and Jones, is the true American hero, Ethan Allen. He is a native of the East but possessed of American qualities West, in line with Israel himself. Allen is seen as prisoner in Britain, where he answers scorn for scorn, refuses the honor of his rank, taunts superiors, denigrates old England, and defies the Philistines about him, apotheosis of the American promise in chains. Yet he too can charm. He "talks like a beau in a parlor to inquisitive ladies of Falsmouth." None of these American heroes are exiles at home or abroad. Israel on the other hand, spends most of his remaining years dreaming of home while working in a brickyard and wandering in "London deserts," Melville's City of Dis. Returning in 1826, he is no Rip Van Winkle but a Leatherstocking thrust out beyond any place in which he could exist. His home vanished, his country more foreign than England, the exile sees himself as a decaying cord of logs in the woods.

VI

With *The Confidence-Man*, the Melville exile re-approaches society, not in return but in revenge. Through his various avatars the confidence-man celebrates the absurdity of a social order in which truth is ridiculous and all is negotiation, confidence games. At the heart of the game is the cannibalistic nature of man. The marks are all types of hunters, "fame-hunters, heiress-hunters, gold-hunters, buffalo-hunters, bee-hunters, happiness-hunters, truth-hunters, and still keener hunters after all these . . . all kinds of that multiform pilgrim species, man."[41] The most gullible of these marks are the hunters of material things, the more difficult are the men of little faith who hunt for the satisfaction of the ego or the spirit. But if the confidence-man had also sought gain in either form he would not have been so effective. He is interested only in the game, like God and some earthly embodiments. He is so utterly interested that he cannot refrain even from conning himself. In the role of herb doctor, he cons the soldier of fortune whose crippled legs are the signal that he is really negotiating with one of his previous avatars, Black Guinea. He is like the sharks in *Moby-Dick* who bite and eat their own flesh. Only once is his skill matched, by Oliver Egbert, but the stalemate does not disturb him. It provides, instead, the singular touch of human appreciation for a fellow craftsman. In the second half of the satire the confidence-man settles into one mask, the cosmopolitan, "a true citizen of the world." Daniel G. Hoffman points out that the cosmopolitan is a "sartorial rainbow," suggesting " 'colorless all-color of atheism,' from which we shrink in 'The Whiteness of the Whale.' "[42] In effect the cosmopolitan is another spell-binding fish which may symbolize atheism, deity and humanity, all negative now, wearing the mask of reasonable charity, negotiating through a severely reduced universe, the society of fools, including the reader, aboard the *Fidele* steaming down the heart of America on "All Fools' Day."

From the start, the Mississippi, specific symbol of "the all-fuzing West . . . uniting the streams of the most distant and opposite zones . . . helter-skelter," is expanded into the whole universe of man, "one cosmopolitan and confident tide" (7). At the end, the cosmopolitan extinguishes the solar lamp in the center of the old man's cabin, surrounded by the "barren planets," previously extinguished lamps beside the sleepers in their berths (262). From the berths come universal voices questioning the cosmopolitan who has turned to the Bible of the trusting old man and reads from the Apocrypha to warn of himself, "believe not his many words — an enemy speaketh sweetly. . . . If thou be for his profit, he will use thee . . . Observe and take heed" (264). Here is the most cynical of all his tricks, which reduces trust to imbecility.[43] The warning is not heeded because the Apocrypha is not warranted. The cosmopolitan has no choice but to prefer "the folly that dimples the cheek" since the old man will not accept "the wisdom that curdles the blood." For "how can that be trustworthy that teaches distrust?" (265-6) And so the cosmopolitan, re-affirming the old man's confidence that a "committee of safety" exists in heaven, blows out the lamp.

The first avatar of the confidence-man to enter the tricky stage of the *Fidele*, which is America, the earth, and ultimate-

ly the universe, is a deaf-mute in the color of human kindness, cream. By reference to the Inca sun god, Manco Capac,
who also appears suddenly at sunrise, the deaf-mute becomes
the bringer of the light. His appearance is called an "advent,"
associating him also with the light-bringer of the Christian
world.[44] He is a stranger and seems to eschew all games of
confidence, perhaps because he has no capacity for negotia-
tions, being a deaf-mute. Thus, he can be mistaken as
something of a Bartleby, one who could not negotiate even if
he preferred. His message is charity, which thinks no evil,
believes everything, and never fails. The words are on a
placard held up beside another placard posted near the captain's door, as if in competition. The posted placard advertises a reward for a "mysterious Imposter," an "original
genius," who is of course the confidence-man.

Although his guises change, his message of charity does
not. This is the light that he consistently uses to deceive
mankind and in this act he is truly cosmopolitan. Pickpockets
weaving through the crowd reveal a need less for this savior
than for the money belts which a peddler conveniently
hawks.[45] Another peddler offers another response to the
message of the deaf-mute in cream colors. He hawks
salacious tales of thugs and cut-throats in the "new countries"
where the "wolves are killed off" and the "foxes increase" (2).
Confidence appears triumphant in America, West as well as
East. The light bringer, persisting with his signs of charity in
the midst of this crowd, is jostled aside and even trounced.
Finally, his direct message is answered directly by the barber,
later identified with the mute through his name, William
Cream. The barber posts his message, "No Trust," which is
acceptable to the crowd (3). The barber's action completes
the frame of narrative entrapment, the staging of life between
the poles of confidence, and as a total matter of confidence.

The guises of the confidence-man, most of them announced by the next avatar, Black Guinea, are necessary to play increasingly difficult games because the simplest game, the direct appeal of the deaf-mute, has been scorned. It is not sufficiently duplicitous. Whether all the avatars are essentially one or many does not matter, all are manifestations of confidence, central principle of societal man. And if the first appearance is not the confidence-man at all but a muted Christ, the point would be not that Christ failed in his simplicity but that Christ is a "mysterious imposter from the East," the "original genius" as the placard advertises. Nor is the confidence-man a false Prometheus, as Richard Chase claims.[46] The text implies, rather, that the myth of Prometheus is false, along with other myths. More puzzling than the deaf-mute is Black Guinea, the misshapen beggar with whom he is contrasted. Is this crippled beggar at the heart of our universe where a cream colored god ought to be? His is the only disguise that is tested. The black does not smear on his face when rubbed and his "bushy wool" will not be uprooted when tugged. But readers are never to know what they suspect.

Three times (Chapters 14, 33, 44) the narrator disrupts the story to remind the reader that he is reading, that fiction is contrary to fact, but also that fact or real life is also contrary.[47] The character who is inconsistent is therefore faithful to nature, which is the same point Mark Winsome condescends to make through his lofty double-talk with the confidence-man, whom he mistakes for an innocent, "full of all love and truth" (206). But Mark Winsome is himself consistent in his opinions and again in his actions. His inconsistency occurs in the opposition between these two consistencies. His thought consistently espouses the identity of beauty, truth, love. And his behaviour towards his fellows is consistently without feeling; he seems "more a metaphysical merman than a feeling man" (207).

Winsome and his practical sidekick, Egbert, are the cosmopolitan's most formidable marks, and they may be seen as the ultimate avatar of the mark, as the cosmopolitan is the ultimate avatar of the confidence-man. Their confrontation is a jumbled standoff, which is to be expected when deceived and deceiver are playing the same game. (The name can be read as a *mark* who *wins some*.) Victim and victimizer are now distinguished only by their skills. Totally wedded to what he thinks nature is, Winsome ignores a beggar poet's plea, perhaps suspecting another trick, especially since the cosmopolitan contributes cheerily. With an "expression of keen yankee cuteness" replacing his "former mystical one" he refuses to show "pity where nature is pitiless" (212). The beggar poet deserves no more pity than the bitten snake charmer of the Bible. So self-reliant Winsome can employ Biblical authority, like all the others, when it suits him, but his confidence is confined to himself and nature, both arbitrary. Nature means what he says it means. For purposes of negotiation, of contact with the world, the aloof Winsome introduces Egbert. Loaning is against Egbert's principles and a "friend" is above receiving alms. Thus are Winsome's ideals reduced to practice.

In the use of abstract idealism, Charlie Noble is less proficient than Winsome or Egbert, but he reacts with the same iciness to humanity. "Funny Phalaris!" he blurts unguardedly upon hearing the anecdote of a man's beheading for the amusement of the tyrant. "Cruel Phalaris!" the confidence-man quickly retorts, seizing the advantage (178). And when pressed to prove his charity by a beggar, Noble reacts as Winsome did, but with less finesse. Noble is preceded by still less proficient marks with Emersonian strains such as the immaculate man whose black servant does all his handiwork while he proffers a solution to the charity problem in the "Wall Street spirit" (42). He is described as a "stranger . . . of more than winsome aspect" (36) and is "charitable to the last, if only to the dreams of enthusiasm" (44).

Marks who are not Emersonian avatars are cynics in obvious contrast. The most emphatic of these are the student and Pitch. The student who reinforces his cynicism with Tacitus is easily jostled into enough confidence to speculate in the stock of the Black Rapids Coal Company. But Pitch, image of the Western American hero, is overcome only momentarily by a trick of confidence. He is preceded by a more violent prototype, "a kind of invalid Titan in homespun" (89), who responds to the confidence-man with a blow, thus combating the voice of negotiation with direct violence, as Billy Budd will do in Melville's last work. Pitch, the Missourian, is a more civilized version of the Western hero, clearly in opposition to the effete gamesmen of the East. His misanthropy is derived from the violence of nature in which he lives. He is aware of nature's games of confidence and applies them to men. He is the "coon," and tempts the confidence-man, "Can you the fox, catch him" (119). The Missourian is "A Hard Case," but nevertheless is worn down by the confidence-man's excessive loquacity. He is left with the reassuring pronouncement that "Confidence is the indispensable basis of all sorts of business transactions" (138). Realizing he has been taken, Pitch devotes himself anew to misanthropy in self-defense. And when he is once more disturbed from the "solitude beheld so sapient" (150), he raises his rifle, reverting to the violence of his prototype, the "invalid Titan in homespun."

The story of Colonel Moredock, the Indian hater, reinforces the message—that games of confidence breed the exile's hate and even violence. Like Pitch, Moredock is a frontiersman, somewhat closer to Leatherstocking, whom the story mentions and spoofs. He is a hunter living exclusively with the works of God but without a godly mind. He hates

Indians because they killed his mother, her several husbands and her children. And though he loves his own, Moredock finds that hatred exacts renunciation. Here is the American hero beyond the Alleghanies were Emerson's ideal America begins. Moredock's "instincts prevail . . . over precepts" (156), and his experience imbues him with hatred. Moredock and Pitch have become what Melville most feared, "something like Jackson."[48]

The Moredock story of withdrawal is balanced by the Charlemont story of return, of the "restored wanderer," which parallels the story of the cosmopolitan. When Charlie Noble asks if the story is true, the cosmopolitan replies, "Of course not," which means as true as he can make it. "Life is a pic-nic *en costume*; one must take a part, assume a character, stand ready in a sensible way to play the fool," as he tells Pitch (145). This is the "restored wanderer" talking, reentering society to play his vengeful game. Charlemont, the "Gentleman-Madman" of the cosmopolitan's story, is a reflection of himself, returning after bankruptcy (unlike Melville's father who never made it back). He is "gay, polite, humane, companionable, and dressed in the height of costly elegance" (201), another living lie like "Jimmy Rose," who was too good and kind to be a man-hater. The Gentleman-Madman appears as his society wants him, as Herman Melville appeared, writing gracious letters and suppressing vindictiveness, but "It was not well for friends to touch one dangerous string" (203).

The string is the ultimate concern with truth and Melville pulls it in the last episode where the cosmopolitan's vindictiveness is played upon a mark as simple and easy as his first avatar, the deaf-mute. The association of deity with games of confidence, introduced by the "advent" of the deaf-mute, is now reinforced scatologically. The cosmopolitan convinces the old man that his chamber pot is his life preserver and guides this "multiform pilgrim species" into eternity.[49]

VII

The Confidence-Man was poorly received and so the vengeance was futile. Again Melville's wife suggested a trip abroad and this time he went, stopping to see Hawthorne on the way to the Holy Land. Through the long years that followed at the custom house, Melville played the role of Gentleman-Madman, fighting with nostalgic poems and garden roses the rankling bitterness that threatened to make him "something like Jackson."[50] From the evidence of *Clarel* in 1876, he appears to be losing:

> The Anglo-Saxons — lacking Grace
> To win the love of any race;
>
> * * *
>
> Who in the name of Christ and Trade
> Deflower the world's last sylvan grade.

He was alone, having lost his wife to society, one son to suicide (1867) and within ten years, another. "I have no friends, I must live with myself alone."[51] Three years before the end Melville wrote bravely in the privately published *John Marr and other Sailors* (1888):

> Tho' lone in a loft I must languish
> Far from closet and parlor at strife
> Content in escape from the anguish
> of the real and the seeming in life.

But of course he was not content in exile. He was working until the last breath to render if not understand "the real and seeming in life," the game (or whale or deity).

Billy Budd, Foretopman (1924) is dedicated to the memory of Jack Chase, the sailor's sailor, who was a rational defender of the rights of man but also faithful to indomitable superiors whose life work was to threaten war. We see him at last in boldest relief as Captain Vere of the *Indomitable*, also called *Bellipotent*. Like Chase, Vere "loved books . . . free from cant and convention," writers who "honestly, and in the spirit of common sense, philosophize upon realities" (309). He too appears a trustworthy father-figure. But the narrator compares Vere with Admiral Nelson, a naval genius with a burning love of glory. In seeking glory, Vere is less obvious. This starry-eyed father-type, motivated by the "true welfare of mankind," converts almost instantly upon Claggart's killing to "military disciplinarian" (344). The killer, an "angel of God," must hang. Since Vere is "no lover of authority for authority's sake" (348), for whose sake, then, must Billy Budd die? For the true welfare of mankind? Or for his captain's necessity to exemplify vows of martial duty?

Vere maneuvers a drumhead court into a tragic view of the matter, urging them to ignore natural sympathy for Billy and adhere to the severest discipline. This court, which is his own creation, owes its allegiance not to nature, he argues, but to the king. Then Vere invokes the recent Nore mutiny to inspire a sense of urgency. But the hanging of Billy, a favorite among the crew whose nemesis he had just dispatched, would more likely provoke than ameliorate a rebellious spirit. Although Vere, "a martinet as some deemed him" (371), clearly saw what had happened, he arbitrarily judges Billy's act as mutinous homicide, and instantly applies the military code. He substitutes the myth of documents for man's responsibility to seek the truth, as in *White-Jacket*. Vere's perverted sense of duty even uses Billy's angelic self in his most subtle and ghastly appeal: Billy's "generous nature" won't mind the hanging, but "would feel even for us on whom in this military necessity so heavy a compulsion is laid" (357).

The military necessity is evaluated by the surgeon as he mulls his captain's peculiar reasoning: "The thing to do, [the surgeon] thought, was to place Billy Budd in confinement, and in a way dictated by usage, and postpone further action in so extraordinary a case to such time as they should again join the squadron and then refer it to the Admiral" (346). The surgeon wonders if Vere was "unhinged." There is no necessity and the forms of authority are not actually followed, since Vere had already condemned Billy before he called the drumhead court. When the exigency of life descends upon the starry-eyed philosopher, he reverts instinctively to his class, again as in *White-Jacket*, and makes his sacrifice, his negotiation, not with the Lord above, but with those ashore.

As a player of a confidence game, Vere is unaware of himself; the role is instinctive and it is unavoidable if one is to thrive in Christian society. Melville's satire has become so deep that this willful captain can be seen as an unequivocal Abraham or God sacrificing a son. But the satirical view is clear when the indomitable and altruistic believer in "forms, measured forms" (371) is ironically shot down by guns from the French *Atheiste*. Even dying he is a confidence-man triumphant, playing out the romantic tragedy of life. "Billy Budd, Billy Budd," he mutters, but "these were not the accents of remorse" (373).

Billy Budd is also a satirical target. He is a caricature, an abstract reduction of the Emersonian projection, sans sense, utterly natural, and thus sacrificial, Adam, Isaac, and Christ. He suggests all of these children, an "upright barbarian," "a young Adam before the fall," and aboard the *Rights-of-Man*, a "peacemaker," not by preaching but through a virtue that "went out of him, sugaring the sour ones" (294). He is another foundling, but one of noble strain, exchanging the *Rights-of-Man* for the *Indomitable*, where he represents the bright underbelly of the giant black tortoise crawling over the empty Encantadas. He rises out of Melville's nostalgic poetry of the last years where the handsome sailor was honed into a good-natured, loyal and apolitical simpleton. He is the sweet sunset in the holy land of *Clarel* (1876) which Derment sees in the midst of despair. He comes from the "Ravaged Villa" where the "weed exiles the flower." The Epilogue of *Clarel* suggests his potential: "When star and clod battle, spirit may rise above dust." This is the ultimate possibility, the desire and belief of the Christian faith and this is what Melville satirizes in the caricature of Billy Budd.

As in *The Confidence-Man*, no account of action or character is to be taken as true. All is negotiation, which is false by nature, including the fiction that contains the accounts. Billy appears an exception, but has no definition as a human being, and therefore is also a false account. "Goodbye to you," he says to the *Rights-of-Man* as he is impressed into service aboard the *Indomitable*. It is all the same to him. Now he is faithful to the king who impressed him. Unlike Hawthorne's Donatello, Billy does not fall into humanity upon the commission of his crime. He dies as innocent as he was born. He is so innocent, so beautiful and good, that the innate evil, or at least the imp of the perverse, would be aroused in most ordinary men. John Claggart, of course, is so extraordinary that he seems no more a real character than Billy. Also of noble strain, he is the exact opposite, the essence that man defines as evil in nature. It is "not engendered by vicious training or corrupting books or licentious living, but born with him and innate" (305). This account of John Claggart, however, is also false. His initials suggest that he may be intended as an inverted Jesus, the innocent soured by experience, as Redburn speculated about Jackson. There is longing mixed in the petty officer's malice. Watching Billy cavort with his mates, Claggart's expression becomes meditative and melancholy, his eyes "strangely suffused with incipient feverish tears." He looks a "man of sorrows." "Soft yearning" can be discerned in Claggart, as if "he could even have loved Billy" (333). Evil or not (and sexual or not), there is in him the humanity of want, as in Billy there is a capacity for violence, tainting his goodness.

For Billy, Claggart becomes the irrational mask which he must strike through, not to find any truth—the truth we remember is ridiculous—but to stop the false negotiation between Claggart and his mark, also a confidence-man, Captain Vere. At the crucial moment, Billy cannot speak because to speak is to enter the negotiation which is false in its very nature. His strike against the deviousness of language is more primitive than Babo's, who can practice deception himself, or Bartleby's, who merely withdraws. One result of this primitive strike is the immediate elimination of primitive evil. But another result is the generation of more civilized evil, starry-eyed Vere's imposition of his practical truth upon the officers of his drum court. The roots of Vere's practical truth, however, are still primitive, a sacrificial bribe ostensibly to maintain law and order aboard society's *Indomitable*.

The final depravity of this cannibalistic order, the narrator's bitterest irony, is the duping of Billy himself, which is one "Inside Story" of the title. "God bless Captain Vere!" he calls at the "penultimate moment" (367). This is certainly a turning of the other cheek, but Billy has been political goat in the story, not a savior. He is Christ-like in his purity of course, but Christ was not wanting for words in crisis, and his violence in the temple court was deliberate. Almost with spite, Melville tempts his readers with probabilities for a miracle, à la Christian mythology, and then confounds them. Billy's clothes glimmer as he sleeps serenely on the eve of execution, and there is no twitching in the noose on the morrow. His blessing of his captain is compared to a singing bird about to fly from a twig, and moves the herded crew to echo it, as Billy, "ascending, took the full rose of the dawn." Soon a ballad is composed, "Billy in the Darbies."[52] What the reader has experienced is the birth of a myth, the beginning of another spurious truth of ages. Meanwhile in *News from the Mediterranean*, still another "truth" is forthcoming:

> The enormity of the crime and the extreme depravity of the criminal, appear the greater in view of the character of the victim, a middle-aged man respectable and discreet, belonging to that minor official grade, the petty officers. . . . (373-4)

The meaningful similarities between the abstraction, Billy Budd, and the abstraction, Christ, is in the generation or recycling of myths. Billy is too good to be real. What exists is story.

Although Melville does not apply Billy's story to the myth of America we can align this figment of an alien with the new world dream, which has no more chance of fulfillment than the vision of Leatherstocking at Templeton. Billy's characteristics are partially shared with the frontiersmen who follow natural rather than civil law, such as Melville's own invalid Titan in the *Confidence-Man*. When they cannot escape the threat of negotiation, confidence games of the East, they respond as Billy does, with violence. But such natural actions are doomed in this social cannibalism, ensnaring with language and myth what it cannot directly devour as it gnaws to the ends of Christian civilization.

Five years after the publication of *Billy Budd*, Hemingway's Frederick Henry in *A Farewell to Arms* (1929) discloses a fundamental discovery of the lost generation:

> There were many words that you could not stand to hear and finally only the names of places had dignity. . . . glory, honor, courage, or hallow were obscene beside the concrete names of villages, the number of roads, the names. . . .[53]

The unbearable abstractions carry on the recycling myths, the human illusions of meaning that bind societies, duping believers and exiling those who perceive. But unlike Hemingway, who partially understood, the spiritual exile can declare no separate peace since he sees even in the word "dignity" another false negotiation, another story, the basis for another "pic-nic" in another country.

Chapter 7
TWAIN:
European Parody and The Absurd End of Exile

Mark Twain's *Innocents Abroad* (1869) asserts his
freedom from the constraints of Europe and its oafish offspring. Unlike other spiritual exiles of nineteenth century
America, Twain was not repelled by bad manners, shallow
roots, or an intolerably hollow culture. He was turned away,
rather, by his vision of America's residual Europeanism, the
myths and romances, the fabrications of Christian culture. In
Europe, where he spent almost a third of his adult life, he was
always an innocent abroad and in America he was an innocent at home. American culture was a bumptuous and often
unconscious parody of Europe's, whether in Hartford,
Virginia City, Washington, D.C. or Hannibal, Mo. The
agency of exile was not specific social conditions or frustrated
ideals as with Cooper, but Christianized man, either abroad
where he never wished to belong or at home where he longed
for membership but could not accept it. Twain's vision was
not a result of disillusionment. From beginning to end, he
reduced the human scene to its rudiments and always it appeared the same, absurdly pretentious and brainless.[1] And
yet there was a certain sentiment, a certain poetry, the innocence itself, also residual.

Whatever the range, from backwoods America to medieval England, the vision focused on the ways of Christian
gentlefolk and their victims. European culture and art are the
main targets in *Innocents Abroad*, religion and monarchy as
well as reason and progress are the targets in *Connecticut
Yankee* (1889), and ultimately in *Mysterious Stranger*

(posthumously 1916) the satire is directed at Christian man himself, who as democrat has the opportunity of choice and "in nine cases out of ten he prefers the wrong."[2]

Mark Twain was the embodiment of all that Cooper feared, the son of Cooper's ambitious settlers who had trampled the genteel code.[3] But Twain found the code alive and thriving even on the Mississippi shore, its polite greed permeating society. Twain's fictionalizing begins without any hope for realizing Cooper's political ideals. Instead, his caustic tones reflect the defeat of Cooper's republican instruction. Twain's innocents attempt faithfulness to their own visions in a society of rogues who have gained power, position, and pretensions. Of course, Huck Finn would not be as immediate a threat to Cooper as the corrupt politicians and demagogues whom we would easily recognize as descendents of Steadfast Dodge, Aristabulus Bragg, Joel Strides, and Jason Newcome. These are the new gents exercising the rights of the majority to do as they please. In time they become Dickinson's "plated people." Early in *Roughing It* (1872) and late in *The Autobiography* (posthumous, 1917), Twain describes the American democratic politician as "dust-licking pimps and slaves of the scum." He could tolerate them only as a universal joke, with an exile's bitter laugh.

With Melville, Twain saw the confidence game at the root of Christian culture, peculiarly outlandish in the fresh new world settings. Yet in Twain as in Melville there remained the befuddled poetry of innocence, the natural goodness of Billy Budd and Huck Finn, however beguiled by the need for membership in the damned human race. Even when they perceive society as a skein of lies, Twain's innocents remain innocent, including Satan himself, the most notable exile in God's universe. But Satan is not human and therefore does not have the problems of identity that Twain's vision forces upon his other innocents. He does not have to suffer with belonging and not belonging, nor lie and disguise himself in order to survive. After symbolic death, rebirth and the assumption of many masks, Huck Finn is mistaken for Tom Sawyer and is glad to find out who he is. Years later Satan provides another identity in *The Mysterious Stranger*, "a useless Thought, a homeless Thought." This response is the ultimate extension of Twain's vision beyond the hopeless societal masquerade. It reflects Poe's earthbound despair.

Most of Twain's celebrated masks demonstrate the quality of the exile at home confronting the society he cannot join. With the *Connecticut Yankee in King Arthur's Court*, the mask changes from the ignorant innocent to the knowing innocent, whose motive is similar to Melville's *Confidence-Man*, the exile returning to twit society for its incredible stupidity, corrupt pretenses, and greed. His knowledge drives the innocent into spiritual exile but he keeps returning to find ways either to belong or bitterly inform mankind of its abominable and futile condition. If the exile let go, he would be merely an isolato. Whether the miracle mechanic in King Arthur's Court, *Pudd'nhead Wilson* at Dawson's Landing, the man who corrupts Hadleyburg, or Satan visiting the drowsy Austrian village of Eseldorf, the knowing innocent is the stranger coming home to Hannibal, the picture book home, as corrupt as the external worlds from which the wanderer returns. Every place and time are the same, as the *Connecticut Yankee* remarks. "A privileged class, an aristrocracy, is but a band of slaveholders under another name."[4]

Twain was obsessed, it has been widely asserted, by guilts, mostly of family deaths, his brother Henry's, his firstborn Langdon's, his beloved daughter Susy's, and Olivia's even after her long illness.[5] But the guilt that moved his spirit was of another order. It was the guilt for being human, for belonging unavoidably and uncomfortably to the human race, "a race of cowards." His ultimate mask, Satan, was an effort to deny his membership, his own identity as Mark Twain or Samuel Clemens, who was "not only marching in that procession, but carrying a banner."[6]

"What is man?" he began to ask about 1882. Consisting of what? Training, the Connecticut Yankee had discovered, training in the moral rot of European Christian culture. It distinguishes Tom from Huck, the prince from the pauper and the white and black boys Roxana exchanges in *Pudd'nhead Wilson* (1894). The innocent creature of natural goodness untrained in Christian manhood is not an acceptable member of the race; nor is the race acceptable to him although he needs to belong. Here is the fundamental source of conflict in Mark Twain. It is the root of the dichotomies stressed in critical opinion; between the public funny man, Mark Twain, and the private brooder, Samuel Clemens, cultivating and resenting the audiences who laugh at him on stage;[7] or between the proper Victorian husband of Olivia Langdon and the roughhewn, swearing backwoodsman, enjoying his resistance to social correctness; or the dichotomy within the artist who failed because he could not resist the puritanical authority of his surrogate mother, Olivia, and therefore became an irresponsible child who "poured vitriol promiscuously over the whole human scene."[8]

His last mask, Satan, who is but a dream, could not solve Twain's problem of being a human stranger among his brothers any more than Poe's dreams of aesthetic purity could remove him from the prison of his earthly body. Wanting nothing, Satan's sole interest was in revealing what man is. He is the equivalent of Poe's demon, Melville's cosmopolitan, Dickinson's specter-lover, Hawthorne's devil advisor in "Goodman Brown" and "My Kinsman, Major Molineux." Unlike the figure of biblical lore, Satan is a disembodied conscience focusing on the ultimate cause of man's absurd moral sensibility, the root of his training, his Christian God, who is the ultimate con artist, feigning justice and mercy yet allowing senseless suffering and cruelty. After Susy's death in 1896, Twain told Howells that he was indifferent to everything but work, which was mostly from Satan's point of view. He recognized himself as mere "mud image."[9] There were rumors of him as drunk and sick and abandoned.

I

Outwardly, until those last years, Mark Twain acted as a fully integrated member of society. After he left Hannibal to seek his own world, the traveler was seldom without a companion. Ambrose Bierce lamented Twain's marriage because it would remove him from the bar, "Mark Twain who, whenever he has been long enough sober to permit an estimate, has been uniformly found to bear a spotless character, has gotten married . . . well that genial spirit has passed away: that long bright smile will no more greet the bar-keeper, nor the old familiar chalk it down, delight the ear."[10] As private secretary in Washington, D.C. he became a favorite among the coterie of journalists along newspaper row. (How could they resist a fellow who could see "no distinctly native American criminal class except Congress.") With the success of *Innocents Abroad* he discovered the sympathetic soul of William Dean Howells, a fellow backtrailer from the West (Ohio). After his marriage to Olivia and disastrous editorship of the *Buffalo Express* in 1870, he shared the charmed circle of artists and intellectuals at Nook Farm—Harriet Beecher Stowe, Charles Dudley Warner, William Gillette, Joseph Hopkins Twitchell. Even after Olivia's death, Twain was not alone. He could not bear it. His loneliness was relieved by inviting an admirer, Albert Bigelow Paine, to become his literary secretary and share his mansion.

Membership in the human race (meaning the Christian

culture of the Western world) was no great problem for the young Clemens; it was only later, after he had come to know the race as writer, that belonging was unacceptable. It was then he felt like "a banished Adam," returning in dreams and thought to "a half-forgotten paradise."[11] His wanderlust was typical of American writers, but Clemens was not quite Whitman's child going forth out of the cradle, nor Anderson's George Willard setting out from a Winesburg that he had outgrown. Unlike other literary wanderers, Clemens was going forth not only to discover the world but to capture it. He set out to win his fortune in money and status from that very Christian society he ridiculed and by means of that ridicule. In time success became the retribution demanded by the exile behind the mask.

Inevitably the art that was produced by a man with such motives would offend European sensibilities, especially those in American souls. Henry James found Twain's art limited to rudimentary minds. It incorporated the typically American vision of the deadpan narrator, an innocent outsider who can therefore see without assumption of what he ought to see. But this rudimentary vision is costly in romantic sensibility, as Twain laments in *Life on the Mississippi* (1883):

> The face of the water, in time, became a wonderful book—a book that was a dead language to the uneducated passenger. In truth, the passenger who could not read this book saw nothing but all manner of pretty pictures in it, painted by the sun and shaded by the clouds, whereas to the trained eye these were not pictures at all, but the grimmest and most dead-earnest of reading matter.

> Now when I had mastered the language of this water, and had come to know every trifling feature that bordered the great river as familiar as I knew the letters of the alphabet, I had made a valuable acquisition. But I had lost something too. I had lost something which

could never be restored to me while I lived. All the grace, the beauty, the poetry, had gone out of the majestic river![12]

The purpose of art for Twain was not art. That is why many readers find he wrote only one good novel and the last part of that flawed. Genteel literature to him was a polished lie, written and read through patterns dictated by ages of European aesthetic theory, as pretentious as the other artifacts in the cathedrals and museums of Europe. It was a great pity to Mark Twain that Jane Austen was allowed to "die a natural death."[13]

Van Wyck Brooks' assertion of a "tortured conscience," which "destroyed the meaning of life" for him, seems as true as James' assertion of rudimentary appeals.[14] The tortured conscience appears in the earliest years with the attraction of the forbidden fruit for the little Christian boy of Hannibal. It can be felt everywhere in Twain's work in spite of the external evidence, the emotional comforts of happy family life, of material satisfaction, even splendor, and of world-wide fame. But rather than diffuse his art, as Brooks has it, the tortured conscience can be seen as the generator, the force behind the shape, substance, and meaning of his work. He craved success, the means to respectability or honor; and he demanded integrity, the freedom of the individual from the dictates of honorable society. He was always looking for a class more respectable than the middle from which he came or the bohemian to which he drifted, and finding acceptance, even acclaim, he had to look further. His blatant self-interest was his means of becoming a member, of achieving honor, while his vision of the society available for membership repelled his sensibilities, ensnared his freedom, and blocked integrity. Twain's outrageous show of dress was itself a sign of this conflict—the dishevelled Bohemian effect in New York, the sealskins in Europe, the famous white suits in the late years.

What tortured his conscience was not a dual personality but the struggle for integration. His personality was no more divided than others who seek integrity and honor at the same time. Justin Kaplan's distinction, *Mr. Clemens and Mark Twain*, is true of many private people who lead public lives.

The story of Twain's exile develops as his voices of ignorant innocence become knowledgeable, as they generalize and name the elements of Christian civilization which offend their natural goodness. The earliest voices denigrate themselves more than the society, mainly through exaggeration. Yet they give a sense of reporting without preconception, without a guiding narrative pattern. The early letters and sketches distort experience by the way the character perceives and retells it, revealing his ignorant self more than the scene.

Snodgrass, always a funny name to Twain, was the earliest voice, Thomas Jefferson Snodgrass. Twain invented him in letters reporting his travels to the *Keokok Daily Post* in 1857, one from St. Louis and two from Cincinnati. He had been travelling since 1853, seeking more than Hannibal could offer and depending upon the journalistic training he had received from Brother Orion.[15] He had worked as a printer's helper in New York, Philadelphia and Washington. Now in Cincinnati he was boarding in a room with a Scotsman named MacFarlane, another self-educated man who entertained himself and Twain by expounding his acid philosophy through the winter of 1856 and 1857,

> that man's heart was the only bad heart in the animal kingdom; that man was the only animal capable of feeling malice, envy, vindictiveness, revengefulness, hatred, selfishness, the only animal that loved drunkenness, almost the only animal that could endure personal uncleanliness and a filthy habitation, the sole animal in whom was fully developed the base instinct, called *patriotism*, the sole animal that robs, persecutes, op-

presses and kills members of his own immediate tribe, the sole animal that steals and enslaves the members of any tribe.[16]

Twain records MacFarlane in his late years, in the autobiographical notes dictated to Albert Bigelow Paine, in which he could still remember a thing "whether it happened or not."[17] The words of MacFarlane are almost indistinguishable from the later Satan's. The character of Snodgrass, however, does reflect Satan's misanthropic feelings at the start of Twain's career, although he possesses neither the indifference nor conscience of Satan. Snodgrass is a backwoods bumpkin from the lower class river society, innocent of city ways, trying to find a place. Roughly, he represents young Clemens' naked ambition. He is cruel, insensitive and unprincipled. He has not even the humanity of Huck's Pap, who at least was bothered by good and bad angels. But the inhumanity of Snodgrass is conditioned by the world he observes; no better, no worse. He is without private conscience and his motive in life is not only to get along, but to find the main chance. In the last letter, an attractive woman dupes him into holding a basket until she returns. Waiting he day-dreams:

> Thinks I, I'll galant that gal home; and then (she's already struck with my personal appearance) she'll ask me to come again—spect she's rich as a Jew. No doubt that old man'll take a likin to me (changing the heavy basket to 'tother arm) and *he'll* ask me call around. *In course*, I'll come, and come often too, and when about dezen of that gal's sweethearts finds me a shinnin up so numerous, they'll get mad, and arter a spell they'll challenge me (changing the basket again)—I'll jist take 'em over to Kaintuck and shoot 'em down like polecats. *That'll* fetch the old man! He'll think I'm the Devil, himself. He'll come and tell me how many banks and railroads he owns, and ask me to marry his darter . . .[18]

Instead of the gal, Snodgrass gets to keep the contents of the basket, which he discovers, after "the counfoundest, damnationist kickin . . . (and) squallin," is a baby. But no standard dupe, Snodgrass the next night is "ketched by a perliceman . . . down to the river, trying to poke the dang thing through a hole in the ice."

From Cincinnati, Clemens set out for the Amazon, but got as far as New Orleans where he was distracted by the dream of every boy in Hannibal. Horace Bixby taught him the river and for two years Sam Clemens drew a licensed pilot's high wages. He learned the river but he lacked confidence, the tell-tale sign of one who wished to belong. The lack of confidence is reflected, however insincerely, in his self-deprication — the bumbler cub of *Life on the Mississippi*,[19] the tenderfoot inadvertently setting forest fires and just missing wealth in *Roughing It*, the harassed traveller intimidated by porters in *Innocents Abroad*. The schlemiel element is central even in the conscienceless Snodgrass. By laughing at himself as most representative of the damned human race, Mark Twain could endure his separation. But the self-deprication had another side, a pridefulness in being so bad and yet better than most of the others. It served his need for vengeance, which came in the form of material success, of beating them at their own game. "Bless me! What a pleasure there is in revenge!" he wrote to Orion in 1859:

> and what vast respect Prosperity commands! Why, six months ago, I could enter the "Rooms" and receive only a customary fraternal greeting — but now they say "Why how *are* you, old fellow — when did you get in?"

He had discovered money was the supreme value among his fellow pilots who had seemed so romantic a year before:

> Permit me to "blow my horn," for I derived a *living* pleasure from these things, and I must confess that when I go to pay my dues, I rather like to let the d----d rascals

get a glimpse of a hundred dollar bill peeping out from amongst notes of smaller dimensions, whose face I do not exhibit! You will despise this egotism, but I tell you there is a "stern joy" in it.[20]

The stern joy is discernible behind nearly all the voices, whether of ignorant innocence or knowing, beginning with the second Snodgrass series, ten letters written at the start of the Civil War between February and March, 1861. The second Snodgrass is no longer a crass backwoods son of the father of American democracy, but Quintus Curtius, refined old South descendant of the Republic who can look condescendingly upon the likes of Abe Lincoln and other pretentious social climbers. The change in Snodgrass reflects Twain's own ambivalent view of his elevation from vagabond printer to affluent river pilot. The occasion for the letters is advice to a new recruit from an esteemed member of the Louisiana National Guard, Snodgrass. His sidekick, a New Orleans dandy, describes military-life as a microcosm for society in general, which is divided into "the amiable victims and the worldly-minded but shrewd victimizers."[21] It is the same division we follow throughout Twain, masters and slaves, lords and vassals.

The recipient of the second Snodgrass letters, Charles Augustus Brown, is not explicitly described but he is the apparent victim being conned by Quintus Curtius. The lowbrow Brown persona later develops into the ignorant innocent who unconsciously exposes social pretension and hypocrisy. Eventually he becomes Huck Finn discovering an individual conscience that opposes the trained or social one. In these early letters, however, Twain is too concerned with revenge and the uses of self-deprication to explore the human potential in the Brown personality. This ignorant innocent appears merely stupid. Without the natural goodness that provides an individual conscience, Brown could turn from victim to victimizer as easily as Thomas Jefferson turns into Quintus Curtius.

The war that brought new opportunity to Charles Augustus Brown brought it also to Mark Twain. The only given explanation for his brief career in the Confederate Army is an anecdote in a speech to the "Ancient and Honorable Artillery Company of Massachusetts" in October, 1877,[22] after the success of *Tom Sawyer* (1876) and the beginning of *Huckleberry Finn* (1885). Listening to story after story of glory and gore by "honorable and venerable" veterans, Twain was moved to give his own account—about a group of recruits who play at being soldiers until they murder a man mistaken for the enemy, then ingloriously retreat from any contact and at last, unable to flee further, they disband and desert. Unlike Huck's decision to desert society, Twain's deserters are committing acts of herd cowardice rather than individual conscience.

The opportunity for another, higher place in the world, was not, as it turned out, in the Confederate Army, but in the American West, in the silver mines of Nevada, the Washoe. Offered the position of Orion's secretary, his euphoria was boundless. But he was no fool of dreams. Soon after the sublime freedom of "whirling along at a spanking gait, the breeze flapping curtains and suspended coats in a most exhilarating way . . . the cracking of the driver's whip . . . the spinning ground and the waltzing trees,"[23] the realistic Clemens writes home, "Don't you know it's all talk and no cider so far? Don't you know that people who always feel jolly, no matter where they are or what happens to them—are very apt to go to extremes, and exaggerate with four-horse microscopic powers?"[24]

He became fascinated with the tall tale as the only cohesive element besides the thirst for money in the Nevada community. The ability to tell or discern the tall tale was, in fact, the sign of the insider, who was actually an outsider back in the "States" from which he fled. The extra pleasure of the practical joke in the Washoe was the ingredient of revenge in turning the tables on the outsider, now Easterner and butt. As a member of the dominant culture, the Easterner is habituated to assume a self importance that the "older citizens of a new territory look down upon . . . with a calm, benevolent compassion, as long as it keeps out of the way — when it gets in the way they snub it. Sometimes this later takes the shape of a practical joke." It is in the playing of a practical joke on General Buncombe, who had been shipped out to Nevada as United States Attorney and "very much wanted to manifest" himself as a "lawyer of parts," that the tenderfoot of *Roughing It* begins to feel himself an insider (224).

"Jim Smiley and his Jumping Frog," composed from the lore in the Sierras, is ostensibly an insider's story. It was published first in the *New York Saturday Press* (November, 1865) and then copied in newspapers all over the country, even in California, ironically giving Twain the prestige of an Eastern writer.[25] The story is built as a narration within a narration. The sophisticated Eastern narrator is the dupe, and the duper is the teller of the story within the story. He is a garrulous old time Westerner, Simon Wheeler, who replaces the Brown type. The story celebrates the triumph of Western smarts over Eastern sophistication; the weapon is the tall tale. Although the Easterner is duped here, he actually loses nothing; he is merely caught in a provincial joke of insiders. The interest is not in the deceit of the Easterner but in the unconscious self-revelation of the deadpan deceiver, Simon Wheeler. Twain is laughing at himself as outsider, but he is laughing more at himself as insider and asserting his essential independence from it all, disassociating himself from his Virginia City past. (One San Francisco editor described him as a Bohemian from the sage-brush and an alcoholic bail jumper.)

In Hawaii, Twain saw into another world. He befriended Anson Burlingame, U. S. Minister to China who advised him in "refinement of association," to "Seek companionship among men of superior intellect and character. . . . Never affiliate with inferiors; always climb."[26] His Hawaiian connections opened opportunities: "I am thick as thieves with the Rev. Stubbings," he wrote home, "and I am laying for the Rev. Scudder and the Rev. Dr. Stone. I am running on preachers now altogether. I find them gay . . . I am taking letters of introduction to Henry Ward Beecher, Rev. Dr. Tyng, and other eminent parsons in the east."[27]

The posture of the effete narrator of "Jumping Frog" was continued in the Islands as travelling gentleman correspondent of the *Union*. For a companion, Twain resurrected the bumptious Brown whose crudeness makes him the fool among civilized people. But gentleman narrator and his fool are not altogether distinct masks. Twain is intent on separating and expunging the character of his Western bumpkin self, yet a good deal of his residual resentment lurks in Brown:

> I found twenty-two passengers leaning over the bulwarks vomiting and remarking, "Oh my God!" and then vomiting again. Brown was there, ever kind and thoughtful, passing from one to another saying, That's all right — that's all right, you know — it'll clean you out like a jug, and then you won't feel so ornery and smell so ridiculous.

And it is there also in the gentleman narrator:

> The chairs were not fastened to the floor, and it was fun to see a procession of gentlemen go sliding backwards to the bulkhead, holding their soup plates on a level with their breasts.[28]

Twain's mask of gentleman does not effectively screen

the vengeance on the cultured people who assaulted his character in Virginia City and San Francisco. He could not laugh at himself altogether, nor could he allow his Brown mask to show up the hypocrisy in the civilized point of view. Although the element of natural goodness is beginning to appear in Brown, he has not yet developed an individual conscience. But he is exhibiting the anti-romantic vision that will be realized in Huck Finn. When the narrator waxes eloquent on the Islands à la Don Quixote, Brown reduces him à la Sancho Panza. Honolulu, he reminds the letter-writer, is really a place of centipedes, scorpians, spiders, mosquitoes and missionaries.

In San Francisco again, Hawaii became an immediate lost paradise. "No—not *home* again," he recorded in his notebook "in prison again—and all the wild sense of freedom gone. The city seems so cramped and so dreary with toil and care and business anxiety."[29] Once he had boasted to his mother of knowing at least a thousand people in San Francisco.[30] Most of them, he now admitted, were disgruntled and defeated prospectors returned from the Washoe with empty pockets. Looking to the East, he rewrote an account of the *Hornet* disaster which appeared in a California journal and sent it to *Harper's Magazine*. When it appeared under the name Mark Swain he attempted to shoot himself but lacked the courage to pull the trigger. He signed on, instead, as roving correspondent for the *Alta California*, intending to report a trip to China at Burlingame's invitation. But instead, he headed for New York, the long way, around the cape. Mr. Brown was at his side.

II

In *Mark Twain's Travels with Mr. Brown*,[31] Twain is less remote, his Brownish qualities are more visible, and Brown is less cloutish. In spite of ambition to climb in the world, Twain's bohemianism is still evident in his dress, drinking and gambling and in his curiosities and sympathies. On one occasion the ship's purser chased him from the upper deck, mistaking him for a second class passenger, and he drew the criticisms he apparently relished from the stuffy socialities aboard. In New York, nevertheless, he pursued his ambitious goals with his letters of introduction. The result of the Beecher letter was an engagement to travel with a group of affluent pilgrims to the Mediteranean and the Holy Land.

When the *Quaker City* left New York Harbor, Mr. Brown was on board, but reduced in the letters to the original posture of the crude Western clown. When the correspondence was combined with notes and reproduced as *Innocents Abroad* (1869), Mr. Brown's commentary was deleted, perhaps to advance the author's suit of Olivia Langdon. Brown's function was transferred to Blencher and the doctor, but lightened to the point of insignificance. The useful qualities that had been developed in the Brown persona—the ignorant observation and interpretation—were now rendered through the voice of Mark Twain. In the narrator of *Innocents Abroad*, the Westerner lost his coarseness and the gentleman his polish.

By laughing at himself, the narrator is licensed to laugh at all the other gawking innocents as they compare the scene before them with memories of home, actually seeing nothing but programmed patterns, what they came to see or ought to see. In Milan they adore "The Last Supper" which they can barely discern. With his fellows, the narrator finds the native language funny. He prefers the expansiveness of Lake Tahoe to the snugness of Lake Como, and champions the cleanliness of American democracy over Roman sloth. But he has distance the others do not have, and perceives their motives, which are his own: "We wish to excite envy of our untraveled friends with our strange and foreign fashions which we can't shake off." The gentle reader will never know "the consumate ass" he can become until he goes abroad.[32] But the American traveller may also discover a "spirit of quietude and ease that is in the tranquil atmosphere . . . and in the demeanor of the people," and "begin to comprehend what life is for" (I, 243).

In France, "a bewitching land" where "all is orderly and beautiful" (I, 148), he begins to feel the pull of home. The train he is riding on becomes tedius and his mind conjures the "infinitely more delightful" stagecoach clattering across "the two thousand miles of grassy carpet," of "bewildering perspectives" and "dizzy altitudes among fog-wreathed peaks" (I, 150). The nostalgia induces mindless provinciality. With the other pilgrims he rushes to view a parade of royalty and sees in Louis Napoleon the image of an American entrepreneur, "genius of Energy, Persistence, Enterprise," and in his guest, the Turkish Sultan, "a genius of Ignorance, Bigotry and Indolence" (I, 176), the backwoods traits of the Tennessee hills and Mississippi shores. The idea of progress is vaguely associated with the Christian culture that Napoleon also represents and which Twain castigates as the travelogue proceeds. Twenty years later, Twain's Connecticut Yankee, another genius of enterprise, will directly confront the ignorance, bigotry, and indolence of Christianity.

For Twain, Christianity was always in the middle ages, even at that moment in France. Immediately juxtaposed to the glowing account of Louis Napoleon, the narrator offers the filth and poverty of the denizens of Faubourg St. Antoine. Napoleon's extravagant civic improvements do not change their lives although on occasion they call a king's head to account. Even Napoleon, therefore, this genius of enterprise, is one with the other kings of Europe, the great dupers in the Christian con game.[33] The evidence resides in the galleries. In the Louvre, "miles of paintings" display the "cringing spirit" of the artists in whom worship had replaced gratitude for their principle patrons (I, 185).

In the Holy Land he finds more games, the authentic tomb of Adam and the spot where the dirt was taken to make the first man, which is the center of the earth. At St. Vernoica's residence he sees the handkerchief the saint offered to wipe the sweat from the face of the first "mysterious stranger" (II, 257). He had seen it also in France, Spain and Italy.

Yet the narrator cannot forego the romance of it all. His vision separates him from the other pilgrims but he is still one of them. There remains a residual desire to enjoy illusion and he can see Venice "drowsing in a golden mist of sunset" (I, 277). But up close the gondolas are hearses plying water-filled ditches and he hears the "caterwauling" of the gondoliers in song (I, 280). By the time they sweep into the grand canal, however, it is moonlight, and all the poetry of Venice overwhelms his realistic sensibility. It was "soft and dreamy and beautiful" (I, 281). (Whatever Twain saw as beautiful was always 'dreamy' or 'drowsing' as in his visions of home on the Mississippi. The words almost always signify nostalgia. In the drowsy Venice moonlight, he sees the madonnas coming and going as Missouri belles do back home.) But in the morning, in the treacherous light of day again, Venice was rotting, and like the rest of Europe, poverty-stricken.

The popular success of *Innocents* was followed by literary recognition from the East, from Howells himself, and by another, more substantial reward, marriage to Olivia Langdon, entrance to the Eden of Eastern wealth and stature, target of his ridicule and object of his desires. But as his new Eden, Hartford, where he planned a magnificent mansion in a community of intellectuals and literati, gradually became another Venice awakened by daylight from its drowsy visage, he looked back further and further with increasing nostalgia for the lost Edens of youth and freedom. In the immediate past was the Washoe with its heavenly Lake Tahoe where "air is the angel's breath." A bit further back was the rot of Washington sweetened by very early memories of his Uncle Quarles' farm in Arkansas and of family myths of land in Kentucky, dreaming dupes and devilish dupers East and West. And further still was the river, the community of cubs and river men, dashed by the shoals and hidden dangers beneath the poetic surfaces. Ultimately he was carried back to the boyhood in Hannibal, an Eden again, to be destroyed by the vision of Huck's individual conscience.

The sophisticated narrator of *Roughing It* is the innocent of *Innocents* now immersed in the comforts of the East, recreating that brief moment of freedom when the stage rumbled across the prairie. He lets the reader know very early that he was traveled — "In Syria once at the headwaters of the Jordan" (55) — and has read a good deal and experienced a good deal. He knows the ways of the world and if he does not know the ways of the Washoe, he is quick to learn them and attempt community. As in *Innocents*, he travels with company; across the prairies, up the mountains, and into the mines it is "we." He sees the past as a member of a group. Only in the hard glare of day does the tenderfoot see individually, for himself as "I," and usually as a reminder of his present moment, "Even to this day," and "If I remember rightly, . . ." He remembers his ignorant awe of mechanical progress, the luxury of dining in the railroad car as it bounces over the barren prairie, but his comparison with Delmonicos reinforces his sophistication. Even this luxury is seen as communal, "the fastest living we ever experienced." This perfect arrangement of being free and yet belonging is possible only in recollection and only until he examines it as the pilot does the river.

The actual situation is symbolized for him by the "cayote" [sic] and dog in Chapter Five. The dog is a self-satisfied member of society but caught at the moment outside of it. (Somewhat like Cooper's traveling gentle folk,but the coyote is no chivalrous Leatherstocking.) The coyote possesses all the qualities required to endure in the amoral chaos of the West, but he is a "sorry looking skeleton" with a tail that sags in forsakeness and misery, "evil eye, sharp face, a general slinking expression all over" (66). "What an ignoble swindle," the narrator calls the coyote's "long calm soft-footed trot," which reduces the dog to the race of the duped, "taken in by an entire stranger" (68). This is not quite the birth of Bugs Bunny since the coyote, the "living, breathing allegory of want" (67) lives with the raven, lizard and jackass rabbit in the waste places of the earth on terms of confidence, and hates all other creatures. But Twain's sympathy is clearly with the coyote, wishing him a "limitless larder," at the end of the chapter, in his desolation and utter solitude (69).

The coyote's human counterpart is the stage agent, Slade, superintendent of the division. He is king of the territory, an absolute monarch — jury, judge, executioner — but also deceivingly genteel. For all his worldliness as traveler and reader of books, the narrator is as prone to deference for high position as the beggars of Italy:

> Here was romance, and I sitting face to face with it! — looking upon it — touching it — hobnobbing with it, as it were! Here, right by my side, was the actual ogre who, in fights and brawls and various ways, *had taken the lives of twenty-six human beings*, or all men lied about him: I suppose I was the proudest stripling that ever traveled to see strange lands and wonderful people (96).

He is especially impressed with the glittering gentility that covers Slade's cruelty. The agent hates restraint above all things, like Huck Finn and Twain himself, but with Slade, this hatred leads to more consequences than does the game of bad boy. In the end, on the gallows, Slade's courage fails. He "exhausted himself by tears, prayers and lamentations," this "bloody, desperate, kindly-mannered, urbane gentlemen" (104). No longer sympathetic, the narrator thinks "it is a conundrum worth investigating," and goes on to other kings, like Brigham Young of Mormon country, who leads a dog's life, harassed by his harem. The Mormons are not distinct from the rest of Christianity. In their Bible, he reads, "there had been slain two million of men, women and children, five or six million in all . . . and he began to sorrow in his heart." The narrator comments, "Unquestionably it was time" (133).

In Carson City he is also among royalty, "private secretary to his majesty, the Secretary" (163). But he is also free and feels as "rowdyish" and "bully" as a king, a "fine and so romantic" way to be. Giving up on schemes to get rich quick, the narrator becomes something of a Huckleberry Finn, nakedly observing his fellows in their ridiculous pursuit of wealth. Reduced to a laborer in a quartz mine for ten dollars a week, he determines never to work unless he has to. Like Huck, his goal of life would be leisure and pleasure, that is, kingly freedoms. His would be a "slothful, valueless, heedless career" (252). And yet, as he sums the failures of his life at that moment, how could he go home? To be pitied and snubbed. The West no longer seems the exciting place where free spirits found fortunes. It becomes a drainer of hopes, a place that made slinking coyotes of sociable dogs, or that leaves men broken and forlorn:

> By and by, an old friend of mine, a miner, came down from one of the decaying mining camps of Tuolumne, California, and I went back with him . . . the mere handful still remaining had seen the town spring up, spread, grow, and flourish in its pride; and they had seen it sicken and die, and pass away like a dream. With it their hopes had died, and their zest for life. They had long ago resigned themselves to their exile, and ceased to correspond with their distant friends, to turn their longing

eyes toward their early homes (386).

The Gilded Age (1873), written in collaboration with
Charles Dudley Warner, is an Eastern replay of *Roughing It*.
Twain's characters are thinly disguised members of his fami-
ly, beginning with Squire Hawkins, who moves from Eastern
Tennessee where "Shiftlessness and poverty reigned"[34] to
Missouri and becomes Judge as John Clemens did. Colonel
Sellers, patterned after his Uncle James Lampton, retains a
good deal of the Washoe tenderfoot. Innocent, ignorant,
living in abject poverty and bursting with the opportunistic
dreams of his day, Sellers is bold and deceitful enough but
not mean or selfish enough to succeed. "What you want,"
Sellers tells Washington Hawkins (patterned after Brother
Orion) when he seeks to warm himself at a stove that glows
with a single candle, "is the appearance of heat, not the heat
itself" (64).

Ambition propels the book to Washington. Here the
speculative atmosphere is just as crude, raw, selfish, and
violent as in the Washoe, but masked in a thicker veneer of
European manners. "Appropriation" was the strike in
Washington. If acquired with the spice of illegality, all the
better, like the saloonkeeper who had killed a man in the
Washoe. Here the European game was played by an
"Aristocracy of the Parvenus," and at the core of American
government (242), Twain relishes the duplicity of his
characters with their quickly donned air of moral responsibility: " 'Don't you think we want Cuba, Mr. Hawkins?' 'I
think we want it bad. . . . Senator Dilworthy says we are
bound to extend our religion over the isles of the sea' " (283).
Twain catches his pretenders at the very instant they assume
their imperialistic and aristocratic postures.

The disgust for American life in *The Gilded Age* is partially a reflection of a new admiration for England, where a

year before its publication Twain had been received with lavish praise. He had gone over with the intent of writing another satire, a kind of sequel to *Innocents*, but overwhelmed by adoration he returned and instead wrote his condemnation of American politics. This time abroad, he had fancied he was experiencing a stable government by a responsible elite and the practice of a gentleman's code by genuine gentlemen, qualities of life which made American pretenses appear even more hideous than he had portrayed them. In 1875 he proposed his version of the common nineteenth century solution to the problem of universal suffrage (that would have made Cooper proud): turn democracy into an aristocracy by giving men of education, property, and achievement ten votes each. By 1889 Twain's aristocratic passion subsided. He had gone abroad again, this time for a year and a half, and returned homesick. A *Connecticut Yankee in King Arthur's Court* reflects his earlier scorn of European tradition and customs, lies and myths that masters used to control slaves. It was during these years of external confusion that his exiled spirit sought home in Hannibal. There, cutting through the drowsy Eden of his boyhood, Mark Twain came upon the obvious medium for his innocent vision — the character of an uncultivated boy who develops an individual conscience.

III

The Washoe, Hawaii, even San Francisco for a day and Venice of an evening — all had served more or less as dreams of evanescent Eden, but his boyhood memories of Hannibal formed a more enduring dream. It was Twain's Templeton, the drowsy village on the shore of the big friendly river, home, beyond hope and challenge. No intrusions here of the adult world on the meandering freedoms of boys at make-believe. But in *The Adventures of Tom Sawyer* nostalgia does not quite mask the repressions of Christian civilization

The whole book was a lie, full of "stretchers" as Huck notes at the beginning of his own story, which corrects it. *Tom Sawyer* is a lie because Tom's imagination is trained and controlled by the civilization he mocks in his romantic imitations of it. The adults in this world are European parodies following Christian customs without question and quite free of the gloomy other-worldiness usually associated with American Puritanism. They are much the same bumblers we have met in Twain's travels. Tom does not quite manage to repress the adults but he does reduce them to children while he and his gang assume their roles, at least until they realize they have done so; in the midst of the pursuit of Injun Joe, for example, Tom shrugs off responsibility to go on a picnic.

In Tom's make-believe version of adult society, the members of his gang are thieves and crooks and always operate together, no brooding exiles here; always the prime value is loyalty. To avoid hated work, he must become an embryo captain of industry, getting others to work for him by varnishing the truth and appealing to vanity. He employs his leisure time in nonchalantly planning the slaughter of more innocents. He feigns affections and emotions — guilt, martyrdom, suffering, remorse — in order to gain attention and set the stage for his con games. Although an orphan, Tom Sawyer is born into a family which belongs and he is never an outsider. Because adults see in him their own reflections, Tom is acceptable, a good boy whose playfulness exhibits the characteristics required in society — manipulation, deceit, duplicity, acquisition. It is all honeyed over with the romance gleaned from European literature and myth which help the boy pretend to oppose his restraints — church, school, work — before he embraces them.

Tom hails Huck Finn, who is free of these restraints, as "nomadic outcast." He has "everything that goes to make life precious . . . so thought every harassed, hampered, respectable boy in St. Petersburg."[35] When this antithesis of human betterment does achieve material success by sharing in the reward at the end of *Tom Sawyer*, he is invited to join, that is, be imprisoned by society. But it appears he cannot take to such civilizing, "the widder's good to me, and friendly; but I can't stand their ways" (233). . . . Can't he though?

At the opening of his own story, Huckleberry Finn is trying to belong but still can't stand it. Nevertheless, he remains with the widow and her sister long enough to absorb the more subtle lies of the culture and reinforce his social conscience. Without that conscience he would hardly feel "scorched" when he decides to help Jim escape. Although he resists Tom's romancing he always succumbs to it. Tom is the maker of the society that Huck wants, its romantic authority. Only when he acts by himself, without Tom's authority to guide him, does Huck actually defy society. It is only without Tom that he could determine to help Jim escape and risk going to hell for it. And in spite of such determination, when Tom returns in the last part of the story, Huck immediately capitulates to the authority's romantic notions of freeing Jim, according to books, silly as they may seem. He is capitulating to the romances that pattern behavior of this pleasant society, where not even the slaves are expected to be unhappy, where everyone is genially engaged in the general business of bluffing and deluding one another within the common concealments of Christian culture.

Huck's training is into the standard patterns for boys in Tom's gang — romantic and chivalric — and into the standards of widow Douglas' pietistic society. The first time he lights out he returns, because of Tom's authority. If he wanted to join the gang, he needed a family. This movement is essentially a preview of the ending and points specifically to the author's intentions. In the ending Huck wants to free Jim and so puts up with Tom's circuitous way of doing it because he has become patterned that way. Before Pap steals him, mainly for money, Huck's training seems to work: "I was getting so I liked the new ones [ways] too, a little bit."[36] But taken to the backwoods where he can wallow in piggishness, he feels life there is also agreeable. His capacity for toleration of both conditions is a product of his natural goodness, but there are limits. When Huck lights out the second time, it is from Pap's barbarity, which proves even more inhibiting than the widow's piety. He has a slave in both situations. When he fakes his death, uncertainly wishing Tom Sawyer were present to provide the authority and artistry for this real-life deceit, to "throw in the fancy touches" (31), his aim is to "fix up some way to keep Pap and the widow from trying to follow me" (30).

Although he may be symbolically reborn on Jackson's Island, it is not into an identity but into undefined and unbearable freedom.[37] His dominant feeling is not exultation; it is loneliness. But "dreadful lonesome" was also his feeling when Pap brutalized him in the woods and he was "tiresome and lonesome" when the widow pecked at him. And alone, beside his window at the widow's, listening to the mournful woods that seemed almost calling for him under the shining stars, "I felt so lonesome I most wished I was dead" (8). It is the catcall of Tom Sawyer beneath the window that relieves his loneliness. When Tom insists on tying Jim to a tree for the fun of it, Huck succumbs and waits, "still and lonesome" again. On Jackson's Island, it is the discovery of Jim, the widow's other, legal slave, who relieves his loneliness.

They begin at once adjusting themselves into a home for two, based on natural goodness, nakedness, and free inquiry of mind. It is the opposite equivalent of Tom Sawyer's gang which required respectable family membership to play make-believe properly. In this community the shibboleths of primitive superstition replace those of Christian romance and myth. The superstitions of Jim and Huck are all defensive, warding off the dangers of nature and bad luck, but those of Tom Sawyer are aggressive, offensive, victimizing. "We got home all safe," Huck says after their adventure on the floating framehouse. It contains a dead man's body, actually Pap's, which is a symbol of the horror and brutality under the surface of life all about them, of civilization in the village or of nature in the woods. Like his other homes, the river proves alien and dangerous, its freedom deceptive, threatening with false distances and echoes, bewildering fogs, hidden snags and death floating by.

Huck desires community more than freedom, a home secure from brutality and duplicity. This desire is evident at the end of *Tom Sawyer*, perhaps awakened there. Hearing the word "welcome" directed at him, Huck "could not recollect" the word had "ever been applied to his case before." It was "the pleasantest he had ever heard" (201). Home and family come to his mind when he must instantly invent a lie. Seeking information ashore from Judith Loftus, Huck identifies himself as a girl needing help for her sick mother; he invents another family to save the gang of rogues from drowning on the *Walter Scott*; and another one polluted with chicken pox to save Jim. It is the realization of Jim's feeling for wife and children that allows Huck to see the slave as a human and a fellow. Often his imagination imperils or kills the families he invents: as George Jackson at the Grangerford's he is a survivor of a large family from Arkansas, as he is of the family fancied — Pap and brother Ike — for the Duke and Dauphin. When these prevaricating royalty stress their family connections (reminding us that aristocracy is a family affair), Huck's tolerance expands. It is to keep peace in the family, his raft community, however jarred by the intruders, that Huck agrees to go along with their chicanery.

The joining of Huck and Jim on Jackson's Island is not the instant creation of community but the promise of it. The beginning is easy and almost as playful for Huck as Tom Sawyer's gang. Home starts to form in mutual efforts to protect themselves against common enemies, the dominant society searching for them and the hazards of nature and hunger. It develops through the seeking of mutual beliefs in superstition and of a common tradition for authority. Huck reads to Jim of kings and dukes and earls until his "eyes bugged out." He is a surrogate Tom Sawyer playing to Jim as surrogate Huck Finn. "How much do a king get?" Jim wants to know. ". . . just as much as they want; everything belongs to them" (64). Using Huck's practical logic, Jim reduces the violent history of European culture to the absurd. "I see it warn't no use wasting words," Huck concludes in defeat, "you can't learn a nigger to argue. So I quit" (67).

Huck has not yet discovered the requirements for community: honesty and responsibility to the other. They are products of an individual conscience. He continues his pretenses in the way of Tom Sawyer when he rejoins Jim after their separation in the fog, dampening his companion's joy with a hoax. Jim, who has been calling Huck "Boss" is not fooled and his disappointment in Huck cracks the Tom Sawyer pose Huck has assumed. Huck's ensuing guilt is the first stage in the discovery of his own conscience. "It was fifteen minutes before I could work myself up to go and humble myself to a nigger" (71). He had felt no such remorse earlier when his prank with the snake disabled Jim for three days. Still as they approach Cairo and Jim's freedom, Huck is aware of a tightening of his social conscience, "it stayed with me, and scorched me more and more. . . . Consciousness says to me, 'What had poor Miss Watson done to you . . . she tried to be good to you every way she knowed how. *That's* what she done' " (73). The guilt of irresponsibility towards Jim the previous day is shifted. Huck now feels guilt for irresponsibility toward Jim's oppressor. Huck's dilemma is as unbearable as his former loneliness. Again, "I most wished I was dead." The dilemma is resolved not by a rational decision but by Huck's natural instincts, and therefore, has to be resolved more than once.[38] Each time he initially decides in favor of his social conscience and determines to turn Jim in. This time he heads for shore with that resolve but at the first opportunity protects Jim with a lie — the family with the smallpox inhabiting the raft where Jim hides — and blames his lax attitude, his wrong doing, on the thinness of his training, "a body that don't get started right when he's little" (76), as Tom Sawyer did. His last decision, at the Phelps farm, "forever betwix two things" (168), is his ultimate decision to remain an exile; but it is undone almost immediately with the appearance of Tom Sawyer.

Huck's responsibility, unlike Tom Sawyer's loyalty, is not learned from training in the chivalric code but intuited in necessary action. He is always "in a sweat"; for the Grangerfords, the Wilkes' and for those who more obviously oppress him, the widow, Miss Watson, even for the Duke and Dauphin. Soaking up responsibilities in contrast to the con games played up and down the river, Huck demonstrates his capacity for community. Ironically, Mark Twain could not avoid what his character was showing him. Huckleberry Finn, modeled on Tom Blankenship of Hannibal, was supposed to be memory's emblem of absolute freedom, not of responsibility, not of values that create community. Huck's love of freedom was turning out to be the biggest "stretcher" of them all, thus destroying Twain's last refuge, that idyllic image of the free flowing river and its drowsy shore villages. Twain had to retreat. Out of the fog he made a steamboat loom, like the monstrous society overtaking the river, with "red-hot teeth," unconsciously and irresponsibly pursuing its own course and "smashing straight through the raft," Huck's embryonic home. Within ten seconds, the boat started its engines again, "for they never cared much for raftsmen" (78).

Huckleberry Finn was put aside and although Twain dabbled occasionally with the material, he did not resume writing it until some five years later, after the shock of his return to an industrialized Hannibal in 1882. In the meantime his imagination sought more remote dreams, in a more distant past, in fantasy, even in scatology. But the violence and loneliness that comprise the milieu of Huck's mind refused to be dissipated, and the problem of Huck's individual conscience intruded like the pursuing phantom of Poe's "William Wilson." It appears suddenly in a story Twain published a year after he began *Huckleberry Finn*. "The Facts Concerning the Recent Carnival of Crime in Connecticut" is a surrealistic prelude to the darkness that pervaded nearly all his work in the last twenty years of his life. The individual conscience intrudes as the knowing innocent, as *Pudd'nhead Wilson*, "The Man That Corrupted Hadleyburg," and *The Mysterious Stranger*.

In "The Recent Carnival of Crime," the individual conscience appears unwanted as a "shriveled, shabby dwarf" of forty (approximately Twain's age). He is a "vague, general, evenly blended, nicely adjusted deformity" who "seemed to bear a sort of remote and ill-defined resemblance to me!"[39] The dwarf torments the narrator with his thorough knowledge of him—his lies, vices, arrogances, violences and guilts. At last the narrator recognizes his conscience as Satan, who is destroying the masks by which Christians live among their fellows. The conscience has been dwarfed by the narrator's neglect and abuse, having started precisely as tall as himself. The story ends when the narrator kills his satanic conscience.

And he does so with the exaggerated relish of a Poe or his William Wilson: "After so many years of waiting and longing, he was mine at last. I tore him to shreds and fragments. I rent the fragments into bits. I cast his bleeding rubbish into the fire, and drew into my nostrils the grateful incense of my burnt-offering. At last, and forever, my conscience was dead!" (300-301). An aunt, society's repressive representative—the widow, Miss Watson, Aunts Polly and Sally or Twain's own mother—appears during this internal act and is frightened by his external demeanor. As she flees in terror, a feeling of "unalloyed bliss" envelops him. It is the feeling of Huck's freedom on the river and suggests the feeling at the prospect of death in *The Mysterious Stranger*. But the freedom is used to indulge in a life of crime. The killing of conscience was, therefore, the killing of innocence, the goodness that we find in Huck and later in the Connecticut Yankee and Twain's Satan-like exiles.

Before going on with *Huckleberry Finn*, Twain had to face the implications of this fantasy. Unrestricted freedom was no more compatible with an individual conscience than with social conscience. Without individual conscience, Huck would become a Pap or one of the river rogues, or at the other extreme, a social rogue and victimizer like Tom Sawyer. Pushing the problem aside and seeking respite from his Hartford mansion, which had become a "monster" with its servants and streams of guests at large expense, Twain went off to Europe. Perhaps there the iconoclastic zest of *Innocents Abroad* would return and revitalize his spirit. Although he still found enough hatred for "travel . . . hotels . . . the opera" and "the old masters," as he wrote Howells; "in truth I don't ever seem to be in a good enough humor with anything to satirize it." All he could do was "foam at the mouth—or take a . . . club and pound it to rags and pulp."[40] *A Tramp Abroad* (1880), consequently, is a tedious travelogue in which the

European culture, notably German, is seen once more as a tissue of lies.

In Connecticut again, his mind drifted back to medieval England where he could flatten the roles of Tom and Huck into *The Prince and the Pauper* (1882) and substitute for the problems of social and individual conscience those of humility and pride. The book is a reversal of his affection for British elitism ten years earlier. Burlesquing British superstitions, traditions, and language and especially pretenses of class superiority, Twain sustains pollyannish images that Americans hold of their rags-to-riches virtue without a hint of the contradictions so prevalent in his stymied manuscript. It became the family favorite, showing that Papa was no mere humorist. He interrupted this benign storytelling to please his preacher friend, Joe Twitchell, who had been his companion in Europe, with a scatological diversion. *1601: or Conversation as it Was by the Social Fireside in the Times of the Tudors* was a spoof of polite Victorian parlor talk sprinkled with anal and genital references but erotically static. He was also initiating his definition, "What is Man?" a diversion from a diversion.

When Twain returned to *Huckleberry Finn* after his trip to Hannibal in 1882, it was to deepen Huck's revealing encounters with the slave society. With a renewed sense of European aristocracy as southern model, he continued down the Mississippi shores.[41] The meanness and deceits of the antibellum towns could no longer be covered by the poetry of young boys playing out adult romances. Until Tom Sawyer returns for the ending, the narrative focuses on the game playing of the adults as ready-made parodies of European aristocracy.

Immediately after his life on the raft home with Jim has been interrupted by the steamboat, Huck enters a world of deadly medieval feuding between the Grangerfords and

Shepardsons. Huck's individual conscience, arrested by Tom Sawyer in Hannibal and to be arrested by Tom Sawyer's return at the end of the journey, is still impeded by a residual longing to belong. Before Twain had put aside the manuscript Huck's encounters had been with fundamentally decent people, however hypocritical. But now he is downriver, where Jim was afraid to be sold. Yet, even here, the satire retains the quality of elegy, mainly because Huck's ignorant and innocent eyes predigest the violence and horrors. Although the Grangerford's is another "house beautiful," a "pathetic sham" of European grandeur, "the frame house painted white and porticoed like a Grecian temple," it evokes Twain's nostalgia, as do the establishments at the Wilks and the Phelps.[42] The Grangerford parlor with its imitations of European artifacts is the dominant society's counterpart to Huck's raft home of bare logs and wigwam. Beneath the reposes of gentility is violence — the bloody hands and murderous eyes of the feuding families, also European imitations, men along the bank shouting at two wounded boys, "Kill them, kill them" (94). When Huck regains the raft, he is soothed by Jim's voice, "Nothing ever sounded so good before" (95). The duplicity of this civilization, the horror of the house beautiful, stays with him in dreams, "I ain't ever going to get shut of them."

The raft home is as vulnerable as Poe's angel. It has no power to outmaneuver the steamboat; nor can it withstand the imposition of European civilization in its highest manifestations, a Duke and a Dauphin. Almost immediately the two rogues begin to jockey for the best position, very much in the manner of their parodic originals. Huck is unable to see the humor because, "What you want above all things, on a raft, is for everybody to be satisfied, and feel right and kind towards the other" (101). This is Huck's statement of the social goal. The Duke and Dauphin immediately demonstrate what most people really want: privilege and advantage. "All kings is rapscallions," says Jim and at once associates the European parody with the national image, "But dis one do *smell* like de nation" (124). With these parodies of aristocracy aboard, the raft becomes a farcical symbol of the shore society. The delights of freedom and even the concern for it evaporate in Huck's effort to get along, to accept what appears unavoidable. The Duke and Dauphin are grotesque versions of an adult Tom Sawyer, conning the gullible along the river banks with socially accepted conventions of Christian morality, stereotyped appeals to stereotyped desires. They are at once the rogue equivalent of political rabble-rousers and royalty, Cooper's demagogues and aristocrats rolled together. Even the more intelligent at the Wilks' place, who appear to be wary of habitual sentiments, are controlled by their manipulations of status symbols, gold above all. Thus, the society is held in bondage by the transplanted and distorted habits, myths, and values of European civilization

When the Duke and Dauphin are at last run off in their final costumes of tar and feathers, Huck displays none of his author's desire for vengeance. Instead, he feels sorry for "them poor pitiful rascals." He reflects not on the cruelties these rascals practice on Jim and himself but on the current cruelty of the mob (180). Huck has none of the later Satan's judgment which condemns all. But Twain has. In the posture of Colonel Sherburn, the author renders vengeance on the usurping subhumans of Brickville—the gullible mob whose slovenly ignorance, cowardice and prejudice invite their own gulling—without the slightest awareness of social injustice. The denizens of Brickville, Arkansas, are also the inhabitants of the Tennessee town where the Duke and Dauphin attempt their most heartless con game with the Wilks family. And by association with Pap—notorious for lying drunk among the hogs in the tanyard—these mobs "who trot along like hogs," also disturb the inviolable dream town of St. Petersburg. The drunken Boggs is reeling down the main street of all the river towns. When Colonel Sherburn reacts with a gun to his insults, his callous fellows crowd around to be entertained by his death throes as they were by his drunkenness. Only Huck and Boggs' daughter are distressed and their emotions also serve to entertain the mob. (The scene is replayed as a circus in the following chapter.) Twain's identification with Colonel Sherburn, who at least is not a coward, is obvious as he stands before the mob which has come to lynch him:

> The pitifulest thing out is a mob; that's what an army is—a mob; they don't fight with courage that's born in them but with courage that's borrowed from their mass and from their officers. But a mob without any *man* at the head of it is beneath pitifulness. Now the thing for *you* to do is to droop your tails and go home and crawl in a hole. If any real lynching's going to be done it will be done in the dark, Southern fashion . . . (118).

After this scene the swindles of the Duke and Dauphin seem less offensive. Having served to expose the greedy and violent innards of Southern society, these royal parodies of adult aristocrats are replaced with the young pretender, Tom Sawyer. The boyhood play he reinstitutes, painful as it may be to Jim, can once more provide cover.

When the Phelps' mistake Huck for Tom, we are back at the ending of the *Adventures of Tom Sawyer*; again Huck hears the words of welcome and "it was like being born again, I was so glad to find out who I was" (175). No longer the exile futilely seeking community with a runaway slave against his social conscience and the resistence of royal and common rogues, but a member, accepted and accepting. The Phelp's place, patterned on the Quarles farm, is more lax than the widow's, but it also requires lying violations of conscience in order to belong:

"Good gracious, anybody hurt?"
"No'm, Killed a nigger."
"Well, it's lucky because people sometimes do get hurt"
(173).

Upon Tom's arrival Huck is pleased to maintain his new identity, but is shocked and disappointed at Tom's willingness to help in the crime of freeing Jim, "Tom Sawyer—a nigger stealer!" (176). But as always, Tom is faking, playing safe, knowing Jim is already free. When the elaborate game of escape actually threatens Jim, life and limb, Huck challenges Tom but goes along with the way "the best authorities" do it for the same reason he tolerated the deceits of the Duke and Dauphin and the bigotry of Aunt Sally Phelps, to keep the peace, to make society possible. That, rather than freedom, is again his dominent motive.

The Phelps' farm provides Huck the security of home that Tom has always known. Within this security he can indulge Tom and even his own lingering sense of individual conscience. If *Huckleberry Finn* is the story of a boy's initiation into society, it is not the story of that boy's maturation, but of society's immaturity and its cruel consequences. The joining of society compromises the individual conscience. Huck ends where he begins. When he is reborn at the Phelps,' he is reborn into a parody of European myths and romances, the greedy and hypocritical society burlesqued by Tom Sawyer's make-believe. In spite of his brief moment of freedom and the glorious choice to go to hell, Huck capitulates in the end. His mature judgment is wiped out when he falls again under the spell of Tom Sawyer.

Huck's individual conscience was the essence of his exiling, but he could not sustain it against a social conscience because it came only in the form of "feeling right and kind." Had he attempted to acheive an abstract level, a stated ideal, it would then become another "stretcher" to be used in the

Christian lessons he had fled at the widow's. Yet the feeling for individual conscience remains in him at the end, and to that extend, he becomes an exile at home. This residual conscience is responsible for his talk of lighting out for the territory, but only "ahead of the rest," meaning Tom and Jim, who has been reduced to his place as "nigger Jim" when we pick them up again in *Tom Sawyer Abroad* (1894). For all his experience, Huck is still an ignorant innocent at the end of the book, not recognizing that he has already been to the territory on the river, as his author had been there in the Washoe, and that freedom does not exist as imagination has it. The territory is a romantic notion inviting the rogues and rapscallions and their American parodies of sophisticated European con games. Perhaps the individual conscience could survive freely only somewhere else and in someone else.

IV

Hank Morgan, *The Connecticut Yankee in King Arthur's Court*, is the first full treatment of Twain's knowing innocents. His individual conscience operates in the closed Christian world of Hannibal exposed by transporting it in time and place to medieval England. Here, as in the antebellum South, men and women were "slaves, pure and simple, and bore that name, and wore iron collars on their necks; and the rest were slaves in fact, but without the name" (111). To keep them in place and invincibly ignorant, the church taught them the divine right of things; it preached meekness, patience, and worship of rank. As an outsider, Hank has the moral distance of a Huck Finn, but his knowledge elevates his practical reasoning to technical methodology and induces in him an iconoclastic itch to destroy the shams and injustices that slaves are trained to accept and even adulate. Hank Morgan also retains Tom Sawyer's romantic sensibility which includes the heedless insensitivity to cruel consequences of his actions, a quality amplified in the queen who shares his name, Morgan le Fay. His fascination with kings and castles is subordinated to his greater satisfaction with the technological marvels that promise progress in his own age. A Tom Sawyer with the conscience of Huck Finn, Hank Morgan reflects the ambiguity of his author in the late eighties. He was invented on the eve of Twain's financial and domestic disasters when the author buried his disappointment at the poor reception of *Huckleberry Finn* with a renewed enthusiasm for investment and enterprise. Yet Twain despised the image of the robber baron this Yankee came to represent and later referred to him as an ignoramus. (This northern counterpart of the Southern aristocrat was even more monarchial, controlling America's institutions through serreptitious webs of connections.) Hank is thus ambivalent, at the same time the loyal friend of the monarch and the fomenter of rebellion against his institutions. If the exile, driven by the need to belong, cannot join society as it is, change it. And if not in the extant world, then in dreams.

Fundamentally the Yankee's dream can be seen as a didactic sequel to *Huckleberry Finn*, a correction to the correction of *Tom Sawyer*. The dream home is now reduced through historical distance so that it can be manipulated and reformed by a wizard of technology who is nevertheless another innocent. If he were not an innocent, Hank would hardly hope to free the slaves from the Christian bondage that deludes them "to grovel before king and Church and noble" (111). What the "dupes needed" was a "new deal."[43] Although he lacked poetry, he could make guns, revolvers, cannons, boilers, engines, all sorts of labor-saving devices. His list however, suggests war-wasting rather than labor-saving. Thus his effort to transform the "human muck" Colonel Sherburn described at Brickville into "men" by means of his technological powers is defeated by his own myopia, which is also the Colonel's. What his technology and rationality wrought was an exchange of one set of delusions for another. In practice his rationality and his machines proved as dehumanizing as the Grangerford's religious chivalry.

Composed of Tom and Huck, he is the Mark Twain of that moment speaking almost directly to his audience from inside his thin fantasy. The actions of the Connecticut Yankee are quests to oppose the author's condemning observations of Christian civilization and thus hold back his inexorable progress into spiritual exile. Like Tom Sawyer, the Yankee delights in showmanship, a con man in love with his work. His magic incantations, fire works, and elaborate ceremonies provide a circus aura that elevates his technical achievements into miracles. They are intended to arouse more sensation than Merlin's and thus win away the superstitious minds of the population. As "Boss," the Yankee is the American version of king and saviour. He has come to deliver the people from their stupor. But the way to human dignity that he promises is a modern paradox of industrial slavery, "a Factory, where I'm going to turn groping and grubbing automata into *men*" (203). He succeeds in abolishing slavery, equalizing taxes, building steamships, railroads and factories and putting knights to work selling soaps and stovepolish rather than wasting time saving damsels in distress or seeking the Holy Grail. It is reason he hopes to inculcate, working against his own knowledge that "training is all there is to a person," except for an original bit that could be "hidden by the point of a cambric needle, all the rest being atoms contributed by, and inherited from, a procession of ancestors that stretches back a billion years to the Adam-clam or grasshopper or monkey from whom our race has been so tediously and ostentatiously and unprofitably developed" (208).

That original bit is what defeats the Yankee, the Huck in

him, his natural goodness, his individual conscience. Much in the manner of Huck at the sight of the Duke and Dauphin tarred and feathered, Hank feels sorry for the queen after he has conned her out of another cruelty. Like Huck he responds with sympathy to human scenes of sentiment, even to the pilgrims at the restoration of the fountain, kissing the water as if greeting a lost friend, "it was pretty to see and made me think more of them . . . " (270). Hank is obviously a member of the race and exemplifies his own observation: "There is no accounting for the human being" (250). When his cold rationality indicates that a reign of terror and a guillotine are needed, his sentiments also indicate that he is the wrong man for it. But he is the Boss and his rational reforms end in the dehumanized horror of modern warfare.

With fifty-two boys remaining loyal because they were brought up under him, the Boss is a prisoner of his own technology, besieged by the Church in a holy crusade. His fortress contains "the prettiest garden that was ever planted" (468), consisting of torpedo bombs and gatling guns and fenced with electrical wire. This is the garden of reason and knowledge, the alternative to the medieval garden of superstition and ignorance outside the fortress where chivalry had flourished. Now it is fouled with the stench of twenty-five thousand electrocuted and machine-gunned knights. With such victory in sight, Hank's individual conscience suddenly erupts. He turns off the electrical fence and goes forth to help the knights who are only wounded. Meligraunce, playing coyote, stabs him, and he allows himself to be further deceived by Merlin, disguised as an old woman, whose potion delivers Hank Morgan from his fantasy. Returned to the present moment he has no more taste for it than Gulliver home from his travels; he dies a lonely exile. His rationality and knowledge had succeeded only in disturbing the stupid, superstitious civilization he had hoped to reform. Had he been totally dehumanized, he would have achieved his progressive utopia, but it would also be dehumanized.

Twain's financial world caved in a few years after the collapse of his Yankee's dream, which was intended as his "swan song" as he told Howells, "my retirement from literature permanently." After a singular success with the Grant memoirs, his publishing firm suffered a series of flops and eventual bankruptcy. Much worse was the Paige Typesetter catastrophe, in which he eventually lost over $200,000 and his Hartford mansion. When Henry H. Rogers, a literary admirer from the "gang of robber barons" offered to straighten his financial mess and advised that he go to Europe and devote his energies to writing and lecturing, Twain grasped the opportunity. "If *Connecticut Yankee* were to be written again," his letter to Howells continued, "there wouldn't be so many things left out. They burn in me; they keep multiplying and multiplying, but now they can't ever be said; and besides they would require a library—and a pen warmed up in hell."[44] What he left out is mostly amplification as his exiles return to various surrogates of Hannibal, their innocence blackened with knowledge and their individual conscience utterly frustrated. Ultimately the exile becomes all conscience, the inhuman Satan, an absurd dream.

The outsider arriving at Dawson's Landing in *The Tragedy of Pudd'nhead Wilson* (1894) is no longer the effete Easterner to be outdone by the shrewd Western low brow, the likes of Simon Wheeler. He is rather an exile with the Yankee's rationality and fascination for "every new thing that was born into the universe of ideas."[45] But he is drained of social hope. His sarcasm escapes from him upon arrival in the "sleepy and comfortable and contented" village. It is a chance remark denigrating a dog and is taken at face value by village idiots, numbers one through six, who classify Wilson, after due consideration, as a "pudd'nhead." Denied a livelihood as an attorney, the outcast installs himself at the edge of town where his major expression is a calendar on which he records acerbic aphorisms condemning the nature of man. Apparently taken from Twain's notebooks and placed at the head of each chapter, these utterances are outside the story, and Pudd'nhead has no more connection to the society at the center of the story than his aphorisms.

The tragedy in the title is not Wilson's. It is Roxana's, the beautiful and robust slave who bears one of her master's children on the same day his wife bears another. She defies fate by exchanging them in their cradles, generating a plot intended to demonstrate, as in *The Prince and the Pauper*, how environmental chance and training determine one's morality and fate and the arbitrariness of social identity. Roxana's son is brought up as Thomas A. Beckett Driscoll, heir to the fortune with ironic English monicker, while the all-white boy becomes a slave, more appropriately named Valet de Chambre. The names of the slave-holding gentry serve also to parody British pretensions in the Mississippi valley; York Leicester Driscoll, Percy Northumberland Driscoll, Colonel Cecil Burleigh Essex, Pembroke Howard. The parody is honed with the finer distinction of the F.F.V.'s (First Families of Virginia), whose prime duty in life is the preservation of honor. Italian twins add flavor — "How romantic . . . and they're all ours!" — but quickly become scapegoats through Tom's mental manipulation.

As a result of his training in the gentry, which includes Eastern polish at Yale, Tom Driscoll becomes another parody of the parody of aristocratic pretension as the Duke and Dauphin do in *Huckleberry Finn*. The bogus heir becomes a wastrel, thief, and even murderer, and when his mother threatens to expose him, he sells her down river, the worst of fates. The original bit in him that is not the product of training and chance is what Roxana calls, "De nigger in you. . . .

Thirty-one parts o' you is white; en only one part is nigger, and that po' little one part is yo' soul" (139), which she blames for his degeneracy, indoctrinated as she is in the dominant white code, "dupe of her own deceptions." On the other hand, his white half brother, Chambers, is brought up a slave and becomes one. Restored to his proper position through Pudd'nhead's ratiocination, Chambers' "gait, his attitudes, his gestures, his bearing, his laugh — all were vulgar and uncouth, his manners were the manners of a slave" (224).

Rather than contradict the genteel code of honor, Thomas A. Beckett's reversal of fortune reinforces it; he is after all, not one of them. Through Pudd'nhead's luck, evidence and logic, this scum of aristocratic training is proven a "nigger" and murderer, returned to his creditors as a slave and sold down the river. The society goes on, blithely unaware of its false and paradoxical values. Pudd'nhead's fortune is also reversed, from outcast to hero, demonstrating a fickleness in this honorable elite equal to that of the piggish herd in *Huckleberry Finn*. And the acceptance of such honor — he becomes mayor in fact — reveals the depth of Wilson's desire to belong, which had been perverted into those acerbic aphorisms. His is not the homecoming from exile of an ignorant innocent like Huck Finn, but the knowing surrender of conscience, a Pudd'nhead indeed.

The "fiction of law and custom," however, which rigorously defines who is slave and master, is not so frivolous. This fiction forever condemns Roxana, all white to appearances but one-sixteenth black. This is her tragic situation at the outset. It is ironically amplified by her adherance to the chivalric code which enslaves her. When Tom refuses to challenge the man who kicked him to an honorable duel, she is disgusted and blames his cowardice on the "nigger" in him; and when she sells herself back into slavery for six hundred dollars in order to save Tom, the model of her sacrifice

is the genteel white woman who, of course, is not subject to
slavery; "Dey aint nothin' a white mother wont do for her
chile . . . " But her mother's passion extends far beyond the
code:

> "It's lovely of you, Mammy — it's just — "
> "Say it ag'in! En keep on sayin' it! It's all de pay a body
> kin want in dis worl', en its mo' den enough" (159)

At the end, she becomes a tragic figure in the classical sense
as well. Through her moral choice — exchanging her child for
the all-white one in the crib — she has come to suffer the reversal of her intention. She is victimized by the capricious cruelty
of her sacrificial object, and finally grieved by the loss of the
same worthless child: "Roxy's heart was broken . . . the spirit
in her eye was quenched, her martial bearing departed with it,
and the voice of her laughter ceased in the land" (224). Roxana is at the core of the story where the tragedy — hers and
that of her race — has replaced comedy. Pudd'nhead is the
title figure but — his bitterness soothed and his conscience
abrogated — he remains what Twain intended: "I have never
thought of Pudd'nhead as a character but only as a piece of
machinery . . . with no dignity above that."[46]

V

Although he attempted revivals of his most successful
characters — *Tom Sawyer Abroad* (1894), *Tom Sawyer, De-
tective* (1896) — Twain's fictive imagination was now focused
by this piece of machinery. In more pure and less human
form, it could be manipulated to reveal his despair of human
existence. And he wished to distinguish existence less and less
from his dreams of it, perhaps because the dreams no longer
offered escape. "I dreamed I was born and grew up and was a
pilot on the Mississippi and a miner and journalist . . . and
had a wife and children . . . " The dream is so real "I wonder

if it is."[47] The purest dream of escape was published in 1896, the year of daughter Susy's death. It had been with him since his printer days in Hannibal when he chanced upon a stray leaf from a book about Joan of Arc. She had always meant exquisite purity to him. Joan was the counterpart in beauty of the individual conscience disembodied, another piece of machinery.

Moving restlessly from city to city and writing furiously from 1896 to the end of his life fifteen years later, Twain played with the question, "Which was the Dream?" Had everything been illusion? His family and its tragedies but dreams? And who was the dreamer? The content of reality was of course absurd, as his works had shown, but now the very idea of a reality seemed in itself absurd. The reversals of prince and pauper, master and slave, were more than devices of plot, they were expressions of this vexing problem. What was illusion? What was not illusion? And to be aware of the illusion was necessarily to be outside of it; outside, therefore, of the illusionist, the dreamer. Such awareness was total, not human. It was the way out of exile since a non-human stranger wants nothing, longs for nothing.

In the fragment Bernard De Voto has titled, "The Great Dark," the stranger appears as the Superintendent of Dreams to a Twain-like father contentedly asleep after the celebration of a daughter's birthday. The high point of the celebration had been the gift of a telescope which had revealed the wonderous world in a drop of pond water. Under the guidance of the Superintendent of Dreams, the father, Henry Edwards, is soon sailing with crew and other passengers on that great sea, harassed by microbe monsters. Vaguely they are seeking some lost land. He believes in the reality of the adventure and yet he is dimly aware that he is dreaming. Besides the sea monsters, the humans aboard the ship suffer a white hot lamp that burns down upon them without mercy, an obvious symbol of determinism inescapable even in dreams. The world that he knows awake is the dream in this waterdrop world.

His daughter's death apparently moved Twain's imagination beyond its concentration on the ugly nature of Christian civilization. But only momentarily. And even this fragment contains undercurrents of his criticism. "You come from a small and very insignificant world,"[48] the Superintendent of Dreams tells Henry. This version of the mysterious stranger is without vengeance; he is interested only in exposing the common notion of reality. In "The Man That Corrupted Hadleyburg" (1900), Twain returns to a seemingly human stranger who extracts vengeance with such rationality that he resembles Poe's Dupin more than a character on the banks of the Mississippi. He is an exile deliberately returning to his home of "commercial integrity" in order to expose the corruption thinly veiled in the most moral and well-intentioned citizens who inhabit the village, now a "mean town, a hard stingy town." And exposure is ridiculously easy. The temptation to acquire wealth dishonestly unhinges their integrity. None is exempt. Mary Richards, among the best of them, however, has the capacity to stand aside and wonder, like Twain, "how strangely we are made."

Twain was also the stranger returning home that year. His notebook referred to life abroad as "this everlasting exile," which apparently continued at home, "the 20th Century is a stranger to me."[49] Although he had been received as a literary hero and the publication of his world lectures, *Following the Equator* (1897), had restored some of his fortune, he brooded in his knowledge of the world and his own personal losses. Daughter Jean had now been diagnosed as epileptic and Olivia was often bedridden. Yet the advent of another century, for all he had experienced, rekindled his outrage at Christian civilization. Polemics flood his fictional efforts and fragmented reminiscences. The pamphlet becomes the appropriate form, the one he could complete. Most popular was *King Leopold's Soliloquy* (1905) in which "civilized" Europe piously exterminates some ten millions of the "uncivilized" in the Congo. The *Autobiography* contains extensions to the Czar's systematic exterminations in Japan. But those "unspeakable Belgians" outmassacred all, the English in South Africa, the Germans in China, all except the American "Killing of the Moros" in the Phillipines, also found in the *Autobiography*: "We abolished them utterly, leaving not a baby alive to cry for its dead mother. *This is uncomparably the greatest victory that was ever achieved by the Christian soldiers of the United States.*"[50] Christianity, which comforted Cooper's last years most ironically gave solace to Twain's. His obsession with the horror of Christian civilization assuaged his financial and family losses.[51] Vengeful, unrelenting attacks satisfied his lonely outrage.

"I know the human race," says King Leopold, and that knowledge is his power. Human cowardice and stupidity even amaze the Czar:

> With this hand I flogged unoffending women to death and tortured prisoners to unconsciousness; and with the other I held up the fetish towards my fellow deity in heaven and called down blessing upon my adoring animals. . . . To think that this thing in the mirror — this vegetable — is an accepted deity. . . . Is the human race a joke? . . . Has it no respect for itself?[52]

Leopold and the Czar are hideous extremes of the Christian aristocrat, the premier European models, the originals, beyond any American imitation, any Mississippi Duke or Dauphin or adult Tom Sawyer that Twain feared to imagine. His response to such Christian deity is development of their opposite extreme, the Superintendent of Dreams. This stranger is even more knowledgeable but he is outside of the domain that Christianity had defiled, and therefore innocent.

In all versions of *The Mysterious Stranger*, Satan's indifference is easily perceived as a mask over Twain's or Huck's innocent conscience.[53] The popular version, edited and first published by Albert Bigelow Paine in 1916, describes Satan showing up in Eseldorf, Austria in 1590.[54] An earlier fragment of nineteen pages is set in St. Petersburg in the 1840's but the story could just as well occur in the waterdrop world of "The Great Dark," beyond time and place, "far away from the world and asleep. . . . Some even set it away back centuries upon centuries and said that by the mental and spiritual clock it was still the Age of Faith in Austria. . . . I remember it well, although I was only a boy; and I remember, too, the pleasure it gave me."[55] The narrator, Theodore (also called August), is floating in the exile's reverie through the centuries to the good place forever lost. The waking world no longer intrudes as in "The Great Dark." Theodore is a spiceless fusion of Tom Sawyer and Huckleberry Finn,[56] a shadow of a character, a "thought" as Satan tells him, containing the "dream" which is Satan or Philip Traum.

Young Satan pretends to no motive, but his visitation is obviously for the same purpose as that of all other strangers, to instruct at least the somewhat juvenile conscience that dreams him. Ironically, this nephew of the angel exiled because of rebellious pride, teaches humility, Christ's fundamental instruction most especially violated by Christians. The effect of every miracle young Satan performs, and every word he utters, is to reduce Theodore's world to the tiny waterdrop of "The Great Dark." Young Satan, whose presence enthralls Theodore, has known the vacuous serenity in heaven and the writhing torture in hell and knows that human religious notions are irrelevant, of "paltry poor consequence" (51). Young Satan is without sin, which is a notion confined to the human's insignificant speck in the universe. His family cannot do wrong, "for we do not know what it is." Although young Satan admits his uncle sinned, "before the Fall he was blameless" (48). Had his uncle not been innocent, we must assume, he would not have revolted, but joined in silent acquiescence with heavenly corruption.

A prototype of young Satan appeared as early as 1867 in the *Alta California*: "Jesus and the other boys play together and make clay figures of animals. Jesus causes them to fly, and eat and drink."[57] Young Satan is a more developed character; he can destroy as well as create. When he demonstrates by squeezing life out of workmen he had just moulded, Theodore responds in Huck's language, "It made us sick" (50). Satan's company is a forbidden pleasure and would therefore appeal more to the Tom than the Huck in Theodore, except for its essential satisfaction of castigating Christian culture. That pleasure is Twain's and it is the pleasure of his own company, of the adult Twain returning with knowledge to the juvenile Twain.[58]

Satan's mask of indifference is frequently dropped, reducing *The Mysterious Stranger* to a fictional version of *What is Man?* Man is dirt with a moral sense and can thus perform atrocities no beast could imagine. Man is also a "museum of diseases," his life a "continuous and uninter- rupted self-deception," duped "from cradle to grave," which he enters in stench (55). The progress of man's Christian his- tory is unrelieved horror. The sophistication of his weaponry is the basic measure of his progress. And the purpose of it all is to serve some noble, monarch, or other leech who really despises him. The first man was a hypocrite and coward and all after are the same. Although most humans have no wish to inflict pain on others they are cajoled into it by kings, a "closed corporation of land thieves." Happiness is possible only for the insane, and laughter is the only weapon of the sane. Only laughter can blast the pretensions of the human animal. But the general run of the race are myopic. They may see "the comic side of a thousand low-grade and trivial things . . . grotesques, absurdities, evokers of the horse-laugh," but they see nothing the performer wants them to see: "the 10,000 high grade comicalities which exist in the world are sealed from your dull visions" (164).

Here Satan speaks directly for Twain. And directly to the juvenile whose sensibilities are not yet subjugated by reason or warped by the moral sense. With his mask dropped, Young Satan is the exposed innocence of Twain, not destroyed but enraged by the experience of Christian civilization. It is his indestructible innocence that produces acts of natural goodness. His kind miracles save Father Peter and Margot from the avarice of church hypocrites. In another version, as Number 44 on Schoolhouse Hill in St. Petersburg, Satan fights like superman against the bully Henry Bascom and his slave-trader daddy, and later saves people against all odds in a deadly storm. At the end of this version he appears among the slaves and wins their respect. In a third version, Number 44 appears as a pauper and becomes an apprentice in a printshop, also in remote Eseldorf. He is the miracle worker in disguise seeking the good person who will be known by his charity. The angel is humanized inside as well as out in this fragment. When the master offers friendship, his eyes gleam with happiness. Number 44 restrains his powers for self defense against the human ugliness and cruelty directed at him. He employs only creative powers — to return kindness such as running the presses by magic when the workers strike. This natural goodness, however, is not confused with human nature; when human innocents offer good acts, they get hurt. Johann Brinker, for example, becomes a paralytic deaf-mute as a result of saving the life of corrupt Father Adolph. For good measure, Father Adolph condemns Johann's mother to the stake as a witch.

Before he abandons the human race in the concluding chapter, Young Satan promotes death as the only alternative to laughter or lunacy. It was Twain's increasing preference for himself, beginning as early as Pudd'nhead's calendar. For Young Satan, Christ's world is not worth saving. Nothing is lost when he departs for another corner of the universe. But for August, the loss of Satan is the loss of joy, of the boy's world, of innocence. Unlike Christ's departure, the lost joy was the mischief of deviling the ordered society. The mischief results from seeing things as they really are. Satan's departure portends the onset of adult life, the acceptance of the deceits, lies, repressions and cruelties of Christian civilization. But Young Satan's ultimate lesson shows August how to avoid that fate. It is the revelation of his deepest knowledge, which can preserve August's innocence and condemn him to exile in the adult world:

> It is true, that which I have revealed to you; there is no God, no universe, no human race, no earthly life, no heaven, no hell. . . . Nothing exists but you. And you are a thought, a homeless thought, wandering forlorn among the empty eternities (405).

Twain's satanic voice is a lifetime removed from the clownish innocent at the end of *Roughing It* who glimpses the earthly Eden of Hawaii and instead of joy feels "like the Last man, neglected of the Judgment, . . . a forgotten relic of a vanished world" (486). Knowledge separates these voices. The ignorant innocent has the balm of nostalgia for a vanished world — the incorrigible Christian culture — but the knowledge of that world makes such nostalgia absurd. To Twain, as well as to Young Satan, "God, and the Universe, and Time, and Life, and Death, and Joy and Sorrow and Pain [are] only a grotesque and brutal dream evolved from the frantic imagination of that insane 'Thought.'"[59] Twain's satanic voice

echoing through earlier American dreams lacks the solace
even of Leatherstocking, alone in the desolate prairie, calling
to his Maker, or of Cooper's last exile in the *Sea Lions*, the
patriarch shorn by democracy, alone in the antarctic, secure
only in the awesome power of God's immensity. If Cooper's
literary anomalies offended the realist in Twain, these last
comforts would be absurd to his Young Satan. So would
Poe's feigned or mad and self-consuming devotion to *Al
Aaraaf*, Dickinson's frightened adoration of Awe beyond her
circumference, and especially Hawthorne's salvation of social
openness for the embittered or hypocritical hearts of his
egoists.

Among those lonely exiles in America's ebullient nineteenth century, Young Satan resonates singularly with
Melville's *Confidence-Man*. He is the "Something further"
that "may follow of this Masquerade," which ends the
Melville satire. Although the confidence-man becomes the
cosmopolitan, his ship of fools is confined to America.
Young Satan, more obviously a cosmic exile, returns the ship
of fools to Europe at an arbitrary time and all Christendom is
abroad. The innocent narrator, however, can be freed by the
Cartesian knowledge Satan has passed on to him, that existence is a thought. He can, therefore, "Dream other dreams,
and better," beyond Christendom.[60] But only a moment
before, Satan had told August, "There is no other life" (403).
The ultimate lesson from the knowing to the ignorant innocent, from the late to the early Twain, is thus a deception, a
satanic trick, the ultimate con. It is in our dreams we most
deeply and inevitably deceive ourselves. Conning is human
nature, at least in Christendom. August's satanic dream has
left him "appalled," without even the nineteenth century
grace of Melville's cosmopolitan who leads his last mark, an
old man clutching Bible and wallet, "kindly" into "the
darkness which ensued."

In Satan's ultimate lesson—the absurdity of innocence itself—American literature leaps over the latter-day verities and determinisms of the Hemingways and Fitzgeralds and Farrells to the loveless funhouses in the middle of the twentieth century where absurdity has "become natural and a thing to be expected."[61] Absurdity obliterates the nostalgia that V. S. Pritchett found in Mark Twain, the "channel of the generic emotion which floods all really American literature . . . not only harking back to something lost in the past, but [suggesting] also the tragedy of the lost future."[62] Looking back through *The Sound of the Fury* we can behold William Faulkner replaying Twain's tragedy. Quentin Compson just before his suicide finds "was" the "saddest word of all there is nothing else in the world its not despair until time its not even time until it was."[63]

Nearly all American exiles at home have by now joined in the Western world's absurdity. It is "natural and a thing to be expected."

Chapter 8
Merely Absurd

By the time Ezra Pound proclaimed that "Tradition is the Artist's capital," it was not news. From the beginning of their independence, American writers felt themselves cut off from "centuries of race consciousness, of agreement, of association."[1] Henry James summed the reaction to the American claims of literary independence when he stated in *Hawthorne* (1879) that art blooms only where the soil is deep, that history is required to produce literature and a complex social machine to set a writer in motion. And Hawthorne himself, after early visions of authoring the American scene, expressed the same need, "Romance and poetry, like ivy, lichens, and wallflowers, need ruins to make them grow."[2] Cooper had also been troubled. The American needed history, heritage and tradition to fix his place in society. The paucity of America's past even drove the genial Washington Irving to complain that America "unfortunately cannot boast of a single ruin."[3]

If there were no ruins nor "paraphernalia" of the past, as James saw it,[4] there was Puritanical inheritance. Not only did this inheritance endow Americans with psychological problems of moral behavior but it also reinforced their ancestors' habit of looking away from the society at hand, to reject the place of actual experience as home. They looked East and West, backwards and heavenwords: Poe to a beautiful beyond; Dickinson to an awesome one; Melville to exotic places; Cooper and Twain to a virgin beauty in an imagined past. The American inherited the propensity to be exiled and fulfilled it with romantic visions.

But why so little love? Leslie Fiedler asks in *Love and Death in the American Novel*. His answer—homo-eroticism, especially between white Europeans and the native Indian or imported Black as the surrogates of human bonding in the new country—appears a mere displacement of the question. In the novels of Europe there is also homosexual love, but love between men and women has been central. The theme of romantic love, it appears, was overwhelmed by another, the more pressing concern with identity: "Who am I?" is the recurring American question of the nineteenth century and continues into the twentieth. Romantic love leads to social responsibility, integration with society, procreation, family, "centuries of race consciousness, of agreement, of association." The question of identity results from denial of such love and its consequences. The question seems inevitable, given the romantic vision that removes one from society where identity is naturally defined.

Early answers to the question of identity—Crèvecoeur's independent farmer, Franklin's business opportunist, the folk humorist's shrewd Yankee, Cooper's morally innocent and God-trusting pioneer—self-consciously excluded European culture. They concentrated on native intelligences and powers. Emphasizing individuality, these visions of American identity are nevertheless backgrounded by society. Cooper is largely occupied with the rendition of American village society and the ideal but doomed way his hero might accommodate to it. Disappointment with the discovery that such an individualistic society is an unsurmountable contradiction leads subsequent exiles to the consolation of other illusions, mainly the old European home.

To Cooper, Hawthorne and Twain, who lived abroad for extensive periods, the vision of Europeon society as refuge was indeed illusory, as unassumable as the past was for *The Great Gatsby*. The illusion for Melville was a dream of truth, rather than tradition, which he sought primarily in the sea and its islands. Dickinson and Poe, seeking ephemeral realms, remained at home; she a recluse on family grounds, and he a journalistic grind erratically providing for mother-in-law and child wife.

All these illusions were rooted in the European tradition of visualizing ideal worlds where the individual would have room to realize notions of self-fulfillment in a subordinate society, one that is background to the self. In America, Richard Poirier has observed, individuals "actually believe in their power at last to create an environment congenial to their ideal self."[5] It is the nature of societies, however, to suppress such selves. The vision, nevertheless, continues. Pursuing it, American writers have insisted on the individual's integrity, an ideal oneness of thought, action and feeling, at the expense of society's recognitions, of honor.

Although the distinction between integrity and honor has been obscured in the absurd modernism of the twentieth century, it is still conspicuous in the fictions of William Faulkner. In his idealized vision of the lost home—the old South—integrity coincides with honor. But in the contemporary South, the recognized virtues of the old home are displaced by greed and perversity and consequently honor is no longer available to the individual who maintains these virtues. Quentin Compson's psychological injury, for instance, his inability to accept the incest to which neither sister nor father object, is a wound of honor, "Compson honor," while Quentin's brother Jason foregoes integrity to preserve an absurd illusion of honor in the new South. The individualistic determination of the black outcast, Lucas Beauchamp of *Intruder in the Dust*, on the other hand, is an assertion of integrity. In *Sanctuary*, Popeye is a puppet of the ugly mechanical civilization that rapes the old South, but he is also the outcast of that new civilization, bent on retaliation. His twisted sense of integrity is fed by his violence, and these gestures justify in his mind society's opinion and banishment of him. Faulkner's term for such absurdity is repudiation. Joe Christmas' murder of Miss Burden in *Light in August* is his repudiation. In the ante-bellum South he had a place at least as "nigger." Absurdly his act of repudiation destroys another exile at home, one who offered him some of the essential values — love and caring. In a distorted way, the criminal's violent attack on society's moral ambience defends shreds of integrity. In the social eye repudiation is always absurd, but not always perverted or destructive. In "The Bear" Ike Mc-Caslin's repudiation is to deny his inheritance, his property, and seek an ideal sanctuary in the wilderness where once, he imagines, the human being lived in harmony with nature. He even enjoys the companionship of a sort of Chingachgook in Sam Feathers.

Repudiation was also a motivating force in the nineteenth century exile at home, often in the form of vengeance. In some poems of Dickinson and in the later fictions of Cooper, Melville and Twain, vengeance rises almost to the textual surface, and in Poe breaches it. The exile repudiating society in the nineteenth century, however, is more easily seen as mad rather than criminal or merely absurd. In contemporary literature, repudiation has become commonplace. "In the context of our present pervasive madness, that we call normality," R. D. Laing has observed, "sanity, freedom, all our frames of reference are ambiguous and equivocal."[6] When the nineteenth century exile repudiated society by exposing a private world in acts of speech instead of violence, the society would find that he had lost touch with reality, meaning societal agreement on what shall be acknowledged as real. This is the "sane madness" Melville attributed to King Lear and found in Hawthorne's exiles, and it is, of course, the sickness of his own "Bartleby."

The American idea of freedom, the tradition of excessive individuality, is manifested in the narratives and lyrics of all our exiles at home. In all of them the fiction of self deludes the American character: Cooper's demagogues and patricians swim in the same ocean of delusion as Colonel Sellers in Twain's Washington, D.C. and his Judge Driscoll in Dawson's Landing. The all-encompassing ego of Melville's Ahab deludes him into taking the symbol for the thing, which he must have, though language forever masks it. Hawthorne's Dimmesale extends his ego, over the expanse of nature, seeing the "A" of his conscience in the electric night sky. Even Poe's Gordon Pym reads phenomena with his ego, perceiving a human figure in the great white mist that confronts him at the end of his journey. With Wallace Stevens, the nineteenth century exile may also say that everything is fiction. It was for ludicrous re-arrangement of external reality that Twain castigated Cooper and then, nearing the end of his life, asked "Which was the Dream?"

The literature of exile is a fantastic literature, as Tzvetan Todorov defines fantasy, texts that create a tension of uncertainty between fact and illusion, that oblige the reader to "consider the world of the characters as a world of real people, and to hesitate between a natural and supernatural explanation of the events described."[7] In contemporary literature, the sense of the fantastic may be deadened since we no longer recognize a common base for distinguishing the possible from the impossible. The nineteenth century, however, shared an understanding of the familiar as real in their metaphysical distinctions between actual and imaginary worlds. In the twentieth century, it appears that only the imaginary is significant; historical man has been replaced with structural man who creates himself and his future according to pattern. But the prime American question is still "Who am I?" Although stressing relationships between the imagination and its structures, our twentieth century literature continues with the nineteenth century concern of identity in relation to society. There is little essential difference, for example, between the multiple personalities of Rinehart in Ralph Ellison's *The Invisible Man* (1947) and the cosmopolitan in Melville's *The Confidence-Man* published ninety years earlier. Commenting upon his own imagination, Ellison appears much the same as Ishmael and, even more, Ahab. His aim is to create an imaginative world that might "challenge the apparent forms of reality . . . to struggle with it until it reveals its mad, vari-implicated chaos, its false faces, and on until it surrenders its insights, its truth."[8]

In the end, Ellison's invisible man burns the papers that define his past in terms of culture's institutions; they inhibit "possibility" in his resolve to recreate himself out of his own experience. He is an avatar of the nineteenth century exile at home, an outcast from the society he could not abide yet needed, not only for the comfort of belonging but also for his identity. In the second part of the twentieth century, where the idea of society has attenuated into fragments and shards, such exile is so common it is merely absurd.

NOTES

CHAPTER 1

1. Charles M. Kennedy, trans. *An Anthology of Old English Poetry* (New York: Oxford University Press, 1960), p. 5.

2. (New York: Viking Press, 1951), p. 240.

3. *Portrait of the Artist as American* (New York: Harcourt Brace, 1930), p. 294.

4. *A Home-Made World: The American Modernist Writer* (New York: Knopf, 1975), p. 18.

5. *A Hugh Henry Brackenridge Reader*, ed. Daniel Marder (Pittsburgh: University of Pittsburgh Press, 1970). pp. 70-71.

6. For account of Pound's vorticism and its relation to the vorticism of Wyndom Lewis, see Hugh Kenner, *The Pound Era* (Berkeley: University of California Press, 1971), pp. 232-247.

7. *Exile's Return*, p.8.

8. Quoted by Cowley, *Exile's Return*, p. 244.

9. "The River," *Collected Poems*, ed. Waldo Frank (New York: Liveright, 1933), p. 18.

10. For example, see Alfred Kazin, Preface, *On Native Grounds* (New York: Harcourt Brace, 1942, rpt, Doubleday Anchor, 1956).

11. Alexis de Tocqueville, *Democracy in America*, trans. George Lawrence, eds. J. P. Mayer and Max Lerner (1835 rpt. New York: Harper and Row, 1966), p. 12.

12. *City of Words: American Fiction 1950-1970* (New York: Harper and Row, 1971), p. 427.

13. For elaboration, see Irving Goffman, *The Presentation of Self in Everyday Life* (New York: Doubleday Anchor, 1959); Manfred Putz, *The Story of Identity: American Fiction of the Sixties* (Stutgart: J. B. Metzler, 1979); Richard Poirier, *The Performing Self* (New York: Oxford University Press, 1971).

14. Cited by James R. Mellow, *Nathaniel Hawthorne in His Times* (Boston: Houghton Mifflin, 1980), p. 326.

15. Actually Poe attended school in England the five years his foster parents lived there.

16. *The Liberal Imagination* (New York: Viking, 1940, rpt. Doubleday Anchor 1950), p. 206.

17. "The Author's Account of Himself", *The Sketch Book*, ed. Haskell Springer (Boston: Twayne, 1978), pp. 8-9.

18. "The Author," *Braceridge Hall*, ed. Herbert F. Smith (Boston: Twayne, 1977), pp. 6-7.

19. *The Historical Novel*, trans. Hannah and Stanley Mitchell (London: Penguin Books, 1969), pp. 13-14.

20. Cited by Margaret Denny and William Gilman, eds. *The American Writer and the European Tradition* (Minneapolis: University of Minnesota Press, 1950), p. 45.

21. Edel, *Letters*, I (1974). p. 45.

22. Edel, *Letters*, I, pp. 138-9.

23. Edel, *Letters*, I, p. 140.

24. *The Reverberator* (London: Macmillan, 1921-3), pp. 397-8.

25. Edel, *Letters*, I, p. 77.

26. Edel, *Letters*, I, p. 428.

27. Edel, *Letters*, II, p. 86.

28. *The Letters of Henry James*, ed. Percy Lubbock (London: Macmillan, 1920), I, p. 105.

29. Lubbock, *Letters*, I, p. 168.

30. Quoted by Leon Edel, *Henry James: The Treacherous Years* (New York: Lippincott, 1969), p. 107.

31. Lubbock, *Letters*, I, p. 363.

32. Lubbock, *Letters*, I, p. 365.

33. Quoted by Edel, *The Treacherous Years*, p. 350.

34. *Studies in Classical American Literature* (1923 rpt. New York: Viking Press, 1951), p. 6.

35. Hector St. John de Crèvecoeur, *Letters from an American Farmer* (New York: E.P. Dutton, 1912), pp. 198-9.

CHAPTER 2

1. *The Letters and Journals of James Fenimore Cooper*, 4 vols., ed. James Franklin Beard (Cambridge, Mass: Belknap, Harvard University Press, 1960), I, p. 150; subsequent references parenthetical.

2. *The Travelling Bachelor, Notions of the Americans*, 2 vols., ed. Robert E. Spiller (New York: Frederick Ungar, 1963), p. 97.

3. "Now to the American it is just as inconceivable how one man can

yield precedency, or respect, or submission to another, merely because he happens to be born an eldest son. You see all this is artificial. . . . In some few instances, change has been attempted by revolution; . . . The Americans had no revolution strictly speaking; they have only preceded the rest of Christiandom in their reforms . . . " *Notions*, II, p. 339.

4. James Fenimore Cooper, *The Headsman* (New York: D. Appleton, n.d.), p. 198.

5. Quoted from Lewis Leary, Introduction, *Home as Found* by James Fenimore Cooper (New York: Capricorn Books, 1961), p.v.

6. *Correspondence of James Fenimore Cooper*, ed. his grandson James Fenimore Cooper (New Haven: Yale University Press, 1922), I, 334.

7. James Fenimore Cooper, *The Pilot* (New York: D. Appleton, n.d.), p. 383.

8. Marius Bewley, among others, finds Cooper's patriarchs ambivalent rather than hypocritical. The ambivalence, according to Professor Bewley, represents tensions between the individual and society in the American experience. *The Eccentric Design* (New York: Columbia University Press, 1959), Chapters II and III.

9. James Grossman, *James Fenimore Cooper* (New York: William Sloan Associates, Inc., 1949), pp. 257-259. Subsequent reference parenthetical.

10. James Fenimore Cooper, *The American Democrat* (New York: Minerva Press, 1969), p. 86.

11. James Fenimore Cooper, *Homeward Bound* (New York: D. Appleton n.d.), p. 13.

12. Hugh Henry Brackenridge, *Modern Chivalry* (New York: American Book Co., 1937), p. 11.

13. *Home As Found*, p. 6.

14. James Fenimore Cooper, *The Spy*, ed. James H. Pickering (New Haven: College & University Press, 1971), p. 159.

15. *Home As Found*, p. 238.

16. Thomas Philbrick argues that the design of *The Pioneers* follows Thompson's *The Seasons* in "Cooper's *The Pioneers*: Origins and Structure." *PMLA*, 79 (1964), pp. 579-593.

17. James Fenimore Cooper, *The Prairie* (New York: D. Appleton, n.d.), p. 258.

18. Or as Cooper has it, the "El Dorado of the West." *Prairie*, p. 12.

19. Richard Chase, *The American Novel and Its Tradition* (New York: Doubleday, 1957), p. 61.

20. For more elaborate comparison see John P. McWilliams, Jr., *Political Justice in a Republic* (Berkeley: University of California Press, 1972), pp. 263-264; Henry Nash Smith, Introduction, *The Prairie—A Tale* (San Francisco: Rinehart Press 1950), pp. xvii-xviii.

21. Frederic Burrhus Skinner, *Walden Two* (New York: Macmillan, 1948).

22. Warren S. Walker, like Roy Harvey Pierce before him, asserts the old man dying on the prairie has been "martyred," that he offered himself for sacrifice: "in the figure of Natty Bumppo, Cooper gave America its first distinctive messiah image." *James Fenimore Cooper* (New York: Barnes and Noble, (1962), pp. 336-38. But whom, we might ask, does this messiah save? To whom does he point the way? And quite unlike the Christian messiah, he learns to kill when threatened, rather than turn the other cheek.

23. James Fenimore Cooper, *The Pathfinder* (New York: D. Appleton, n.d.), p. 523.

24. James Fenimore Cooper, *The Deerslayer* (New York: Chas. Scribner's Sons, 1925), p. 17.

25. Donald A. Ringe *James Fenimore Cooper* (New York: Twayne Publishers, Inc., 1962), p. 83.

26. David Howard emphasizes the similarity. In *The Deerslayer* the "actions are really showing Natty to be too good for frontier life, which in effect means too stupid." The evidence is Leatherstocking thoughtlessly "giving his opponent a second chance to an absurd degree" and living up to his word as he returns to the Indians for "certain death and torture." *Tradition and Tolerance in Nineteenth Century Fiction,* eds. David Howard, John Lucas, John Goode (New York: Barnes and Noble, 1967), p. 33.

Howard sees Natty Bumppo as Mark Twain's fool who takes society at its own evaluation.

27. James Fenimore Cooper, *The History of the Navy of the United States of America* (Upper Saddle River, New Jersey: Gregg Press, 1970), I, p. 31.

28. *History of the Navy*, I, p. 32.

29. James Fenimore Cooper, *Wyandotte* (New York: D. Appleton, n.d.), p. 231.

30. Originally published as *Afloat and Ashore*, or *The Adventures of Miles Wallingford*, (1844).

31. James Fenimore Cooper, *Miles Wallingford* (New York: D. Appleton, n.d.), p. 337.

32. James Fenimore Cooper, *The Chainbearer* (New York: D. Appleton, n.d.), p. 123.

33. August 6, 1842, *Letters*, IV, p. 304.

34. James Fenimore Cooper, *The Redskins* (New York: S. Appleton, n.d.), p. 275.

CHAPTER 3

1. *Collected Works of Edgar Allan Poe*, 3 vols., ed. Thomas O. Mabbott (Cambridge, Mass: Belknap, Harvard University Press, 1978), II and III, "Tales and Sketches," p. 515; subsequent references parenthetical, *TS* followed by page number.

2. *From Poe to Valery* (New York: Harcourt/Brace, 1948), p. 9.

3. *From Poe to Valery*, p. 22.

4. *Selected Writings of Edgar Allan Poe*, ed. Edward H. Davidson (Boston: Houghton Mifflin, 1956), p. 483; subsequent references parenthetical, *SW* followed by page number.

5. From West Point he wrote to his foster father, John Allan, " . . . it was my crime to have no one on Earth who cared for me, or loved me." *Letters of Edgar Allan Poe*, 2 vols., ed. John W. Ostrom (Cambridge, Mass: Harvard University Press, 1948), I, p. 41.

6. *Power of Blackness: Hawthorne, Poe and Melville* (New York: Knopf, 1958), p. 4.

7. "Castles and Cultures," Appendix, *Power of Blackness*, p. 245.

8. *Collected Works of Edgar Allan Poe*, 3 vols. Thomas O. Mabbott (Cambridge, Mass: Belknap, Harvard University Press, 1969), I, "Poems," p. 68; subsequent references parenthetical, *P* followed by page numbers.

9. This poem is frequently interpreted as a reflection on Poe's leaving the Richmond foster home with the Allans in 1827.

10. The poem's title is derived from Tycho Brahe's astronomy. It was the name that Arabian astronomers gave to Tycho's nova or constellation. Although Poe was involved here with Greek myth — especially the goddesses Nesace (commissioned to spread imaginative powers among earthlings), Ligeia (commissioned to distribute melody and harmony below), and Ianthe (bright thing of Al Aaraaf who condemns herself by loving an earthly being) — the poem has been interpreted in terms of Christian mythology, the fall of man. For example, see Floyd Stovall, *University of Texas Studies*, (July 1929) pp. 106-33.

11. Images borrowed from Bernadin de St. Pierre's *Studies in Nature* (1808). "Sonnet — To Science" immediately preceded "Al Aaraaf" in

the second edition of Poe's poems (1829) and is understood to be a prelude.

12. "Philosophical Implications of Physics," *American Academy of Arts, Bulletin*, III, 5 (February, 1950) quoted by James B. Conant. *Limits of Language*, ed. Walker Gibson (New York: Hill and Wang) p. 21.

13. John Augustus Shea's "The Ocean" includes the lines, "The Glory of Athens/The Splendor of Rome." It was composed, according to Shea's son George, at West Point, during Poe's time there. "The Ocean" was published in the Boston *Ariel* of May 1, 1830. Poe's obituary for Shea in the *Broadway Journal* (August 3, 1845) referred to the poem as "one of the most spirited lyrics ever published." (*P* 170, note 9-10).

14. Quoted by Richard Wilber, "Edgar Allan Poe, An Introduction," *Major Writers of America*, ed. Perry Miller (New York, 1966), p. 181.

15. *Complete Stories and Poems of Edgar Allan Poe* (New York: Doubleday, 1966), p. 527; subsequent references parenthetical, *CS* followed by page numbers.

16. Yet Poe referred to a black, Armistead Godon, as the most interesting man he had ever talked with, according to Thomas O. Mabbett, Introduction, *The Selected Poetry and Prose of Edgar Allan Poe* (New York: Random House, 1951), p. xiv, note 4.

17. Defending "Berenice" to Thomas Wilkes White, Poe stated that whether or not it was "in bad taste is little to the purpose. To be appreciated you must be *read*, and these things are invariably sought after with avidity." *Letters*, I, p. 58.

18. Poe's review of Joseph Rodman Drake, *The Culprit Fay and Other Poems* and Fitz-Greene Halleck, *Alnwick-Castle, with Other Poems (Southern Literary Review*, April 1836). Cited by Davidson, *SW* 418.

19. "Review of New Books," *Graham's Magazine* (January 1842).

20. The review in *Graham's* goes on, "We might at any moment have as many Mr. Coopers as we please." Cited by Edwin Fussell, *Frontier: American Literature and the American West* (Princeton: Princeton University Press, 1965), pp. 139-140.

21. He admired the Irving book for its exclusively American material. Edwin Fussell looks upon *Pym* as Poe's effort to deal with the American West, noting his description of the sea as a "wilderness," pp. 141. But the direction is towards the pole, south, not west.

22. Always a scientific faddist, Poe must have been aware at this time of the theory of Captain J. C. Symmes which proposed that the poles were openings into the earth connected by a tunnel through the core. The theory is the source of "Symmes Hole" in Thoreau's *Walden*. (The

case for Poe's awareness could be strengthened by the similarity of Pym and Symmes, especially since Poe's initial replaces the "S" of the Captain's name.)

23. *Letters*, I, p. 205.

24. *From Poe to Valery*, p. 19.

25. See Bonaparte's *The Life and Works of Edgar Allan Poe, A Psychological Interpretation* (London: Imago Pub., 1949).

26. D. H. Lawrence makes a fundamental distinction between Poe's knowing and loving. He claims that wanting to know was Poe's essential aim. *Studies in Classic American Literature* (New York: Viking, 1964), pp. 65-81.

27. *Letters*, I, p. 118.

28. As Dupin's house is described in "The Murders in the Rue Morgue."

29. Also in "The Murders in the Rue Morgue."

30. *Letters*, II, 356.

31. *Letters*, II, 401-402.

32. While Poe signed his letters to Mrs. Whitman, "Edgar," he frequently signed those to his mother-in-law and to Annie Richmond, "Your own Eddie." For examples, see *Letters*, II, pp. 426, 448, 461.

33. *Letters*, II, 452.

34. God, who willed himself into being, was at first non-atomic—a primordial mass of energy. Some unexplained necessity caused God to radiate himself into space, individuating and diversifying until the universe reached a maximum of diffusion and differentiation. For some time the atomized universe has been contracting towards its original unity. The diversity is an abnormal state: the unity normal. "Unity. This is a lost parent. This they seek always—immediately—in all directions." The seeking of the unity is at once the yearning for supernal beauty and for universal truth, which is the urge to reconstitute God. This process, of course, appears as destruction of the extant universe. Disunified, the human particles fell into perverse ways. They are "infected with system and abstraction." Practical science has "deformed as with the ravages of some loathsome disease." It has permeated taste and repressed imagination. Consequently, human beings cannot see or contribute to the reassembly of God. But occasionally, in dreams or reverie, the poet has glimpsed the universal condition of self in the godhead. But even the poet, like all humans, is captive in the fallen world of passion and scientific reason, which pervert the imagination into nightmare journey and false desire.

CHAPTER 4

1. So did the French poets who found inspiration in Poe. According to the account of Floyd Stovall, "They were inclined to think of him as a displaced European whose genius was stifled in an unfriendly environment." Introduction, *The Poems of Edgar Allan Poe* (Charlottesville, The University of Virginia Press, 1965), p. xxix. Stovall appears to be paraphrasing Leon Lemonnier, *Edgar Poe at les poètes francais* (Paris, 1932) whom he previously cites.

2. Quoted by John E. Walsh in *The Hidden Life of Emily Dickinson* (New York: Simon and Schuster, 1971), p. 26; Richard B. Sewall in his *The Life of Emily Dickinson* (New York: Farrar, Straus and Giroux, 1975), p. 216, also quotes this letter (dated November 6, 1881), and a passage from Mrs. Todd's journal (dated September 15, 1882): "She has not been out of her house for fifteen years," (p. 217).

3. From Mrs. Todd's diary. Quoted by Walsh, p. 36.

4. *The Letters of Emily Dickinson*, ed. Thomas H. Johnson (Cambridge, Massachusetts: Belknap, Harvard U. Press, 1958), p. 781; subsequent references parenthetical, *L* followed by page number.

5. *The Poems of Emily Dickinson*, ed. Thomas H. Johnson (Cambridge, Massachusetts: Belknap, Harvard U. Press, 1955), Poem 1760; subsequent references parenthetical, *P* followed by the number of the poem in this edition.

6. From Mrs. Todd's journal. Quoted by Sewall, p. 217.

7. Quoted by Thomas H. Johnson, *Emily Dickinson, An Interpretative Biography* (Cambridge, Massachusetts: Belknap, Harvard U. Press, 1955), pp. 162-163.

8. Quoted by Richard B. Sewall, p. 221.

9. In "Emily Dickinson's Letters," *The Atlantic Monthly* lxviii (October, 1891), p. 452.

10. *Letters*, p. 519; see Johnson's comments to *L* 405, p. 517-18.

11. Walsh, p. 67.

12. See Walsh, p. 68.

13. As Johnson says in Chapter V, Part Two of his biography: "She wanted to find someone to whom she could 'recite,' yet who affinitively was 'safe,' " (p. 120).

14. Northrop Frye, in "Emily Dickinson," *Major Writers of America*, gives a different version of this incident: "Lavinia took the packets to Sue [Susan Gilbert Dickinson], with a demand that they be transcribed and published immediately, meeting all complaints about the length and difficulty of the task with: 'But they are Emily's poems!' Sue

proved to be indolent, and perhaps jealous, and after a long wait Lavinia took them to Mrs. Mabel Loomis Todd. . . . " (New York; Harcourt, (1966), p. 651. Sewall writes about the same incident: "When, after Emily's death, and despairing of Sue, Vinnie finally took Emily's poems to Mabel Todd for editing, the reason for her secrecy, for the nocturnal visits and clandestine arrangements. . . . was fear of Sue's anger" (p. 148) and "she tried vainly, with 'fierce insistence' (according to Mabel), to get Sue to edit them" (p. 219). Sewall also quotes from Mabel Todd's journal, an entry dated November 30, 1890: "Susan is afflicted with an unconquerable laziness, and she kept saying she would, and she would perhaps, until Vinnie was wild. At last she announced that she thought nothing had better be done about it, they would never sell — there was not money enough to get them out — the public would not care for them, and so on —, in short, she gave it up. Then Vinnie came to me" (p. 219). Mabel Todd, however, wrote another version of the same incident, published in *Harper's Magazine*, March 1930: " . . . Lavinia came to me, as usual in late evening, actually trembling with excitement. She told me she had discovered a veritable treasure — quantities of Emily's poems which she had no instructions to destroy . . . these poems, she told me, must be printed at once. Would I send them to some 'printer' and how quickly could they appear?" Walsh adds: "The process, she [Mabel Todd] thought, would take a year at least. Vinnie in despair at the prospect of such a delay, Mabel said, could only urge pathetically, 'But they are Emily's poems!'" (p. 40).

15. Cited by Frye, p. 655.
16. Ronald A. Sudal, on the contrary, sees Dickinson "rejecting the consolation of immortality" in later years and finding "comfort in the intrinsic value" of life, beginning with the elegy written upon her father's death in 1874:
    Lay Laurel on this One
    Too intrinsic for Renown —
    Laurel — vail your deathless tree —
    Him you chasten, that is He." (p. iii, 1393)
See "Elegy and Immortality": Emily Dickinson's 'Lay this Laurel on the One.' *ESQ*, 26 (1st Quarter, 1980), pp. 10-14.
17. Quoted by Frye, p. 660.
18. Quoted by Johnson, p. 65.
19. Quoted by Johnson, p. 132-133.

CHAPTER 5

1. *The Centenary Edition of the Works of Nathaniel Hawthorne*, ed. William Charvat et. al., vol. IX, *Twice Told Tales* (Columbus: Ohio State University Press, 1974), p. 200.

2. *Centenary*, VIII, *The American Notebooks* (1972), p. 237. Subsequent references parenthetical.

3. To Sophia, September 3, 1841. Cited by Randolph Stewart, *Nathaniel Hawthorne, A Biography* (New Haven: Yale University Press, 1948), p. 60.

4. *The Heart of Hawthorne's Journals*, ed. Newton Arvin (New York: Barnes & Noble, 1967), p. 90.

5. Quoted by Austin Warren, ed. *Representative Selections* (New York: American Book Company, 1925), pp. xiii-xiv.

6. Newton Arvin finds the "physical necessity" of his solitude broken frequently by jaunts to the village of Swamscatt, to Vermont and New Hampshire, and to a place near King's Beach where he was interested in a young lady. *Hawthorne* (Boston: Little-Brown, 1929), p. 35.

7. *Hawthorne* (London: MacMillan, 1879), Chapter II. James, however, misses the restlessness, finding in Hawthorne's notebooks "serenity and amenity of mind."

8. Letter to sister Elizabeth, October 1, 1824. Cited by Randall Stewart, p. 24. Horatio Bridge described Hawthorne at Bowdoin as "taciturn" yet "invariably cheerful with his friends," while another college mate, Jonathon Cilly, noted an isolating "world of thought and imagination which he never permitted me to enter." Mark Van Doren, who cites both of these sources in *Nathaniel Hawthorne* (New York, 1949), pp. 20, 21, concludes that Hawthorne was a typical college man of his time, "Taverns, idle shows, cards, billiards, liquor, tobacco, fireworks, shooting and fishing were forbidden by the college rules. . . . Hawthorne broke many of these rules, as most of the students did." p. 19.

9. Stewart, p. 11. He wrote more than one letter to this effect. See also James R. Mellow, *Nathaniel Hawthorne in His Times* (Boston: Houghton Mifflin, 1980), p. 25.

10. Cited by Van Doren, p. 24.

11. Julian Hawthorne, *Nathaniel Hawthorne and his Wife,* , I (Boston: Houghton Mifflin, 1884), p. 96.

12. For a legend of Oberon as American quester, see Hugh McPherson, *Hawthorne as Mythmaker* (Toronto: University of Toronto Press, 1969), pp. 3-34.

13. *Hawthorne's Lost Notebook*: 1835-1841, transcription, Barbara S. Mouffe, (University Park: Pennsylvania State University Press, 1978), p. 25. This exclamation was entered in the notebook of fall, 1836, but *Twice Told Tales* was not published until March, 1837. James R. Mellow suggests the occasion was actually Park Benjamin's highly favorable review of Hawthorne's *Token* stories in the October issue of

the *American Monthly Magazine,* a review that brought Hawthorne's name to the public for the first time. *Nathaniel Hawthorne in his Times,* p. 95.

14. *Hawthorne and His Circle* (New York: Archon Books, 1968), p. 37.

15. *Hawthorne and His Circle.* p. 240. Hyatt H. Waggoner explains "the well-adjusted Hawthorne, we begin to suspect, is the man he would have liked to be, and no doubt partly succeeded in being, but it is not the man he knew from within." *Nathaniel Hawthorne* (Minneapolis: University of Minnesota Press, 1962), p. 11.

16. *Centenary,* III, *The Blithedale Romance and Fanshawe* (1964), pp. 1, 2.

17. Quoted by Malcolm Cowley, ed. *The Portable Hawthorne* (New York: Viking; 19 –), p. 613. Married love must be distinguished from love. Hawthorne had strong affections also for Sophie's sister Elizabeth and somewhat earlier for Mary Silsbee of Salem.

18. *The Blithedale Romance,* pp. 1, 2.

19. H.J. Lang draws attention to Hawthorne's concern with reality as perception while serving as editor of *The American Magazine of Useful and Entertaining Knowledge* (1836). An article Hawthorne edited, "The Doctrine of Colors," contains this passage: "The gay coloring in which the Almighty has decked the pale marble of nature is not the result of any quality inherent in the colored body or in the particles by which it may be tinged, but is merely a property of the light in which they happen to be placed." "How Ambiguous is Hawthorne"? *Hawthorne, A Collection of Critical Essays,* ed. A.N. Kaul (Englewood Cliffs, N.J.: Prentice-Hall, 1966), p. 89.

20. David Levin examines Brown's imagination in terms of its historical significance in "Shades of Doubt: Spectral Evidence in Hawthorne's Young Goodman Brown," *American Literature,* XXXIV (November 1962), pp. 334-352.

21. In a note to the story, Hawthorne appears himself to be veiling its meaning. The idea, he says has been taken from the life of a Reverend Moody of York, Maine, who also hid his face until the "hour of his own death," but was guilty of a specific sin, the accidental death of a friend.

22. Along with other critics, H.J. Lang takes these words as absolution. Alymer "is absolved by the dying woman." "How Ambiguous is Hawthorne"? *Hawthorne, A Collection of Critical Essays.* p. 95.

23. *Centenary,* I, *The Scarlet Letter* (1971), p. 201. Subsequent references parenthetical. D.H. Lawrence read the romance as triumphant story of man and wife conspiring to seduce and torment a flawed agent of

348Exiles at Homethe iron denomination. *Studies in Classical American Literature* (New York: Viking, 1923), Chapter VII.

24. Q.D. Leavis, among others, reads Chillingworth's "old faith" and "dark necessity" as original sin. "Hawthorne as Poet," *Hawthorne: A Collection of Critical Essays*, p. 51.

25. "The Genius of Nathaniel Hawthorne," *North American Review* (1879). Cited by Richard H. Fogle, *Hawthorne's Fiction: The Light and the Dark* (Norman: University of Oklahoma Press, 1952), p. 119.

26. *Centenary*, II, *The House of the Seven Gables* (1971), p. 313. Subsequent references parenthetical.

27. Preface, *The House of the Seven Gables* (New York: Holt, Rinehart and Winston, 1970), p. xiii.

28. *The Letters of Herman Melville* eds. Merrel R. Davis and William H. Gilman (New Haven: Yale University Press, 1960), p. 123.

29. Among them, F.O. Mattheisen in *American Renaissance* (New York: Oxford University Press, 1941).

30. *The Blithedale Romance and Fanshawe*, p. 203. All subsequent references parenthetical.

31. In an insightful criticism of *The Blithedale Romance*, Frank Davidson is among the first to see the symbol of the veils as a unifying element. The symbolic veils include the veiled lady, Zenobia's "sort of mask," Fauntleroy's eye patch and his pseudonym "old Moodie," the veil of the narrator's twelve-year retrospection, Coverdale's hermitage, and Zenobia's final "black veil of the river," "Toward a Re-evaluation of *The Blithedale Romance*," *The New England Quarterly* XXV, (1952), pp. 374-383.

32. James R. Mellow also sees similarity between Dimmesdale and Coverdale in names as well as covertness. p. 400.

33. In his notes on Brook Farm, Hawthorne refers to other members as "these people," "this queer community," "their enterprise." See May V. Hillman, "Hawthorne and Transcendentalism," *Hawthorne and His Contemporaries*, ed. Kenneth Walter Cameron (Hartford, Conn., 1968), p. 539.

34. It is surprising that James was not more attracted to *The Blithedale Romance*, Hawthorne's only complete effort to render a story from an observing participant's point of view. The "finest thing" he found in Blithedale is Zenobia, "the nearest approach that Hawthorne has made to the complete creation of a person." *Hawthorne,* p. 134.

35. Among the names of the victims of the Fire Island boat disaster in which Margaret Fuller drowned was Henry Westervelt, notes James R. Mellow, p. 402. He uses this discovery to help construct a case for Fuller as the model of Zenobia in spite of her plain appearance.

36. *Centenary*, VIII, *The American Notebooks*, p. 266. Martha Hunt, the 20-year old teacher who drowned herself in the Concord River was more of a Priscilla than a Zenobia, coming from a humble farm family. Hawthorne had taken part in the night search for her body. His description in the notebooks is more gruesome than the version in *Blithedale*. See. 262.

37. Roy Male reminds us that in New England's legendary history, the classic attempt to make love by proxy is associated with the names Miles and Priscilla. "Toward the Wasteland: The Theme of *The Blithedale Romance*," *College English*, XVI (1957), pp. 282-283.

38. *Letters*, p. 146.

39. *Centenary*, VII, *A Wonder-Book and Tanglewood Tales* (1972), pp. 178-9.

40. In *The Shape of Hawthorne's Career*, Nina Baym claims the motive for going to Liverpool was money alone, "not at all . . . a supposed attraction to Europe." The proposition is not argued. (Ithica: Cornell University Press. 1978), p. 207.

41. Letter cited in James T. Fields *Yesterdays with Authors* (Boston: Fields and Osgood, 1890), pp. 73-74.

42. Letter to Horatio Bridge, March 30, 1854, cited by Mellow, p. 494. To Longfellow, he wrote "I do love my own country; but for all that, the honest truth is that I care little whether I ever set eyes on it again . . . I have had enough of progress . . ." August 30, 1854, cited by Mellow.

43. *The English Notebooks by Nathaniel Hawthorne*, ed. Randall Stewart (New York: Russell and Russell, 1962), pp. 271-272.

44. *The English Notebooks*, p. 197.

45. *The English Notebooks*, p. 276.

46. *The English Notebooks*, p. 8.

47. *The English Notebooks*, p. 143.

48. *Centenary*, IV, *The Marble Faun* (1971), p. 345. All subsequent references parenthetical.

49. Passages from *The French and Italian Notebooks of Nathaniel Hawthorne* (Boston: Houghton Mifflin, 1899), I, pp. 46-47.

50. *Yesterdays with Authors*, p. 88.

51. Letter to Fields, February 11, 1860. Huntington Library. Cited by Mellow, p. 527.

52. *Centenary*, V, *Our Old Home: A Series of English Sketches* (1970), pp. 3-4.

53. *Letters of Hawthorne to William D. Ticknor* (Newark, N.J.: Carter Book Club, 1910), II, p. 114.

54. Works, XI, *The Dolliver Romance* (Boston: Houghton Mifflin, 1882), pp. 130-131.

CHAPTER 6

1. *The Letters of Herman Melville*, eds. Merrell R. Davis and William H. Gilman (New Haven: Yale University Press, 1960), p. 130. Subsequent references parenthetical, *L* followed by page number.

2. *Mardi and a Voyage Thither*, eds. Harrison Hayford, Hershel Parker, and G. Thomas Transelle (Evanston and Chicago: Northwestern University Press and The Newberry Library, 1970), p. 557. Subsequent references parenthetical.

3. Melville's vortex is a concept quite apart from Ezra Pound's, which is a radiant cluster of ideas constantly rushing into, through and out of a stable shape of movement, a patterned integrity of a culture and a tradition. It is an image caught by words, as Pound derived it from Wyndam Lewis, for whom the idea is magical and religous, an energy of correspondance between gods, nature and man. Melville's vortex is closer to that of Wyndam Lewis, but less a concentration of magical energies than a universal whirlwind of destruction. At the center, however, he occasionally finds love, as in "The Great Armada" chapter in *Moby-Dick*.

4. *Moby Dick*, eds. Harrison Hayford and Hershel Parker (New York: Norton, 1967), p. 470. Subsequent references parenthetical.

5. In a letter to Hawthorne, Melville defines the "visable truth" as "the apprehension of the absolute condition of present things as they strike the eye of the man who fears them not, though they do their worst to him, — the man who, like Russia or the British Empire, declares himself a sovereign nature (in himself) amid the powers of heaven, hell and earth." *Letters*, pp. 124-5. (Compare with sovereign attitudes of Emily Dickinson, Chapter 4.)

6. *Typee: A Peep at Polynesian Life*, eds. Harrison Hayford, Hershel Parker, and G. Thomas Tanselle (Evanston and Chicago: Northwestern University Press and Newberry Library, 1968), p. 53. All subsequent references parenthetical.

7. Lawrence sees Melville as "mad with hatred of the world." He was "born hating it. But was looking for heaven." *Studies in Classical American Literature* (New York: Thomas Seltzer, 1923; rpt. Viking, 1964), p. 134.

8. Milton R. Stern finds the blow to Chief Mow-Mow "an acutely conscious thing rather than mere physical reflex. . . . With identity itself

staked upon the outcome, the world of mind physically utilizes sheer will in order to defeat the physical world of external circumstances. . . . Tommo rejects isolation and his own former escapist role." *The Fine Hammered Steel of Herman Melville* (Urbana: The University of Illinois Press, 1957), p. 59.

9. *Omoo: A Narrative of Adventures in the South Seas*, eds. Harrison Hayford, Hershel Parker, and G. Thomas Tanselle (Evanston and Chicago: Northwestern University Press and The Newberry Library, 1968), p. 7. Subsequent references parenthetical.

10. D.H. Lawrence, p. 136. "I could not go back on myself so far," Lawrence declares in apparent agreement with Tommo, "Back to their uncreate condition." p. 137.

11. William B. Dillingham stresses the Captain's duplicity. He sees Melville making the same distinction between Captain Guy and authentic sea captains as Hemingway makes between two kinds of doctors in *A Farewell to Arms*, or two bullfighters in *The Sun Also Rises* or two kinds of fishermen in *The Old Man and the Sea*. Captain Guy is essentially a landlubber who "should be in a baker's shop or in a tavern sipping ale." The acting counsul, Wilson, is also an example of "a man pretending to be something he is not." *An Artist in the Rigging* (Athens: University of Georgia Press, 1972), pp. 100-101.

12. The only source the preface mentions is William Ellis' *Polynesian Researches*. Gordon Roper's "Historical Note" in the Northwestern-Newberry edition of *Omoo* lists other sources, including those Melville employed most heavily in *Typee*. See pages 322-325. A pertinent study of Melville's use of documents as authority compelling the reader's belief is Benjamin Robert Dellavedova's "The Carnivorous Word: A Study in Herman Melville" (Unpublished Ph.D. dissertation, University of Tulsa, 1977).

13. This passage could not have escaped the eyes of Elizabeth Shaw Melville who copied out the manuscript for publication. Leslie Fiedler, Leon Howard, and others have found in such passages of *Mardi* a reflection of Melville's agitation in the binds of marriage. See Leslie Fiedler, *Love and Death in the American Novel* (New York: Stein and Day, 1960), pp. 292-8; and Chapter Six, "The World of the Mind," Leon Howard, *Herman Melville* (Berkley and Los Angeles: University of California Press, 1951).

14. Leslie Fiedler finds the shlemiel characteristic also in other "rejected sons" of Melville. *Love and Death*, p. 357. It is amusing to note that Melville later owned a 1874 translation of the popular 19th Century fantasy, *Peter Schlemihl* by Adelbert Von Chamis.

15. In *Melville's Mardi: A Chartless Voyage*, Merril P. Davis divides the romance into three sections: The Narrative Beginning, Chapters 1-38;

The Romantic Interlude, Chapters 29-64; and The Travelogue Satire, Chapters 65-195. (New Haven: Yale University Press, 1952), p. 140. Apparently only the last part is seen as satire. Other critics, such as Newton Arvin, agree, taking Taji as a non-satirical hero. Admitting the allegorical nature of Yillah, Professor Arvin yet insists she is "too tenuous and too pretty to be anything but an artistic miscarriage." The satirical point, however, is in the realization that there is no Yillah except as an emblem for an impossible quest. Also in Professor Arvin's view, it is remorse over sexuality with Hautia that "drove Melville, in *Mardi,* to an act of symbolic suicide." The only symbol of remorse in the end is the relentless pursuit by Aleema's sons, whose terrible aim joins them to the satire. See Arvin's *Herman Melville: A Critical Biography*, (New York: William Sloane, 1950), p. 95.

16. "Hawthorne and His Mosses," rpt. *Shorter Works of Hawthorne and Melville*, ed. Hershel Parker (Columbus Ohio: Charles E. Merrill, 1972), pp. 225-26.

17. *Redburn, His First Voyage*, eds. Harrison Hayford, Hershel Parker, and G. Thomas Tanselle (Evanston and Chicago: Northwestern University Press and The Newberry Library, 1969), p. 57. Subsequent references parenthetical.

18. See *Mardi*, p. 21.

19. *Letters*, pp. 91-92. A letter to Richard Henry Dana, Jr. also indicates the significance he gave to *White Jacket* in spite of his protestations to the contrary, "Would to God, that every man who shall read it, had been before the mast in an armed ship, that he might know something himself of what he shall only read of." *Letters*, p. 93.

20. *Journal of a Visit to London and the Continent*, ed. Eleanor Melville Metcalf (London, 1949), pp. 22, 66. He describes a November rainy day in much the same way as Ishmael described the dismal November soul that drove him to the sea.

21. *White Jacket: or the World in a Man-of-War*, eds. Harrison Hayford, Hershel Parker, and G. Thomas Tanselle (Evanston and Chicago: Northwestern University Press and The Newberry Library, 1970), p. 36. Subsequent references parenthetical.

22. Chase is almost the reincarnation of an Elizabethan courtier, reciting verses and performing sea duties with equal felicity. "Jack would have done honor to the queen of England's drawing room" (p. 14). In Jack Chase, Melville is obviously reflecting his enchantment also with "St. Shakespeare," whose influence is also evident in the comic creations like Lensford, the poet, and Dr. Cadwallader Cuticle; and in the names of the low-life personae—Baldy, Tubbs, Priming, Cylinder, Pounce, Pills. Compare with Shakespeare's Quince, Snug, Bottom, Flute, Snout, etc.

23. Howard P. Vincent sees the "construction of the jacket as a parody in metaphor of Melville's own method of writing. . . . and when his hero rips the jacket from him to let sink into the sea, Melville is rejecting even old literary forms." "And Still Fall From the Masthead," in *Hawthorne and Melville in the Berkshires: A Symposium*, (Kent State University Press, 1969), p. 149.

24. Willard Thorp was perhaps the first to find in *White Jacket* "an increased independence of the remembered facts of his own nautical adventures and a firmer reliance on his imagination." Cited by James E. Miller, "*Redburn* and *White Jacket*: Initiation and Baptism," *Nineteenth Century Fiction*, 13 (1959), p. 274. A year later, in 1939, Charles R. Anderson's *Melville in the South Seas* proved that a great deal of the novel had come from secondary sources and that Melville often bordered on plagiarism in many instances. However, he showed how Melville altered drab passages into poetic ones. Major sources were apparently Nathaniel Ames, *A Mariner's Sketch*, James Mercier's *Life in a Man Of War and Scenes in Old Ironsides*, and Samuel Leech's *Thirty Years from Home*. The most complete assessment of Melville's borrowing is given by Howard Vincent, *The Tailoring of White Jacket* (Evanston: Northwestern University Press, 1967). Others are: Keith Huntress, "Melville's Use of a Source for White Jacket," *American Literature*, 17 (1945), pp. 66-74; Page S. Proctor, Jr., "A Source for the Flogging Incident in *White Jacket*," *American Literature*, 22 (1950), pp. 176-178; Thomas L. Philbrick, "Melville's Best Authorities," *Nineteenth Century Fiction*, 15 (1960), pp. 171-179, and "Another Source for White Jacket," *American Literature*, 19 (1958), pp. 431-438; Robert C. Lucid, "The Influence of *Two Years Before the Mast* on Herman Melville," *American Literature*, 31 (1959), pp. 243-256; Daniel W. Green, "Melville's *Neversink*," *American Notes and Queries*, 5 (1966), pp. 56-58; John D. Seelye, "Spontaneous Impress of Truth: Melville's Jack Chase, a Source, an Analogue, a Conjecture," *Nineteenth Century Fiction*, 20 (1966), pp. 367-376.

    Matthiesson sees Melville reshaping materials from these sources somewhat in the manner of Shakespeare; "relieved of the necessity of inventing," Melville could "release all his energy to imagine the sensation as a whole," *American Renaissance* (New York: Oxford, 1941), p. 394.

25. *Shorter Works of Hawthorne and Melville*, p. 231.

26. *Shorter Works of Hawthorne and Melville*, p. 225.

27. *Hawthorne and His Circle* (Hamden, Conn: 1968), p. 32. The Hawthorne children referred to Melville as "Mr. Omoo."

28. For Richard Chase, Ahab is "the epic transmutation of the American free enterprizer." *Herman Melville: A Critical Study* (New York:

Hafner, 1949), p. 101. He is also a "false Prometheus" (p. 46). To Alfred Kazin, however, Ahab is struggling, Prometheus-like, to "reclaim something that man knows he has lost. He is "exiled from his 'birthright, the very May-day gods of old.' " He is searching to restore the broken covenant, and this search represents "Ahab's real humanity." Thereby, he becomes the emblem of "the aristocracy of intellect in our democracy." Introduction, *Moby Dick* (Boston: Houghton Mifflin, 1956), p. x.

For the most extravagant case of Ahab as Satan, see Henry A. Murray, "In Nomine Diaboli" *The New England Quarterly*, XXIV (December 1951), pp. 435-452. Marius Bewley also sees Ahab as satanic in "Melville and the Democratic Experience," *The Eccentric Design: Form in the Classical American Novel* (New York: Columbia University Press, 1959).

29. On observation of Dellavedova in "The Carnivorous Word," p. 56.

30. Richard Chase sees the entire book as an American epic, consisting of types and tales and major American problems such as race relations, aggressive self-reliance, and puritanical restraints. See "Melville and Moby Dick," *Melville*, ed. Richard Chase (Englewood Cliffs, NJ: Prentice Hall, 1962), pp. 49-62. The novel has also been taken more narrowly as a democratic anti-slavery fable. See Charles Firster, "Something in Emblems," *New England Quarterly* XXXXIII (March 1961), p. 21. ("Benito Cereno" would perhaps be a more likely candidate.) Among other Melville critics, Newton Arvin finds the novel in line with the Greek epic, while Natalie Wright finds it more of a Biblical epic. See Arvin's *Herman Melville* and Wright's *Melville's Use of the Bible* (Durham, NC: Duke University Press, 1949).

31. *King Lear*, Act III, Scene 2.

32. This is the essential tragedy in William Ellery Sedgewick's *Herman Melville: The Tragedy of Mind* (Cambridge, Mass: Harvard University Press, 1944).

33. *Pierre, or the Ambiguities*, eds. Harrison Hayford, Hershel Parker and G. Thomas Tanselle (Evanston and Chicago: Northwestern University Press and the Newberry Library, 1971), p. 90. Subsequent references parenthetical.

34. Edgar A. Dryden sees *Pierre* as mockery of the sentimental novel in *Melville's Thematics of Form* (Baltimore: The Johns Hopkins Press, 1968), p. 129. For comparison of style with that of *Moby Dick*, see R. P. Blackmur, "The Craft of Herman Melville: A Putative Statement," *The Lion and the Honeycomb* (New York: Harcourt Brace, 1955), rpt. in *Melville*, ed. Richard Chase, pp. 75-90.

35. The basic mythical images of Pierre's personality, according to

Richard Chase, are Prometheus and Christ, but with Ahab, he is a "false Prometheus." *Herman Melville*, p. 114.

36. *Selected Tales and Poems by Herman Melville*, ed. Richard Chase (New York: Holt, Rinehart and Winston, 1968), p. 128. All Subsequent references to Melville's tales and poems are to this edition.

37. In *Typee* and *Omoo* Melville is much concerned with strict adherence to seamen's contracts.

38. Bartleby has often been seen as a Christ figure and the Chronometrical is a Christ-like spirit, but the stress is on his unsuitability for earthly life. Bartleby has also been seen as a schizophrenic, most recently and most minutely by Morris Beja, "Bartley and Schizophrenia," *The Massachussetts Review* (Autumn 1978), pp. 555-565.

39. p. 153. Richard H. Fogle sees the "Lightning Rod Man" as "Fear itself." *Melville's Shorter Tales* (Norman: University of Oklahoma Press, 1960), p. 57. To Richard Chase, however, he is Zeus himself, who inhibits or corrupts the "moral, aesthetic, civilizing creativity of sex." *Herman Melville*, p. 103.

40. Merton M. Sealts interprets the story autobiographically, seeing in it a reflection of Melville's resistence to Dr. Holmes medical examination. "Herman Melville, 'I and My Chimney,' " *American Literature* XIII (1941), pp. 142-54.

41. *The Confidence-Man, His Masquerade*, ed. Hennig Cohen (Holt, Rinehart, and Winston, 1964), p. 7.

42. "The Confidence-Man: His Masquerade," *Form and Fable in American Literature* (New York: Oxford University Press, 1961), rpt. in *Melville*, ed. Richard Chase p. 131.

43. Richard Chase, however, finds the old man "Old God and Father of all the planets," as well as Uncle Sam. *Herman Melville*, p. 205.

44. In *The Wake of the Gods* (Palo Alto: Stanford University Press, 1963). H. Bruce Franklin sees the conflict in *The Confidence-Man* between Vishnu (life preserver) and his avatars, Siva (destroyer) or Krishna (blackness). The cosmopolitan represents all the world's savior gods. In the end Vishna as Buddha extinguishes his own light, the solar lamp.

45. In *A Cheerful Nihilism*, Richard Boyd Hauck interprets the deaf-mute as God and Satan in one. And he sees the confidence-man as educative rather than destructive. He "teaches the reader, if not his audience, that since there can be no perfection in an imperfect world, mere faith in some Perfection is the only possible source of hope . . . that confidence is what holds the world together. . . . " (Bloomington: Indiana University Press, 1971), p. 115. Elizabeth Foster also sees the con-

fidence-man as educative by showing life as a masquerade. That is the light he brings. See the Introduction to her edition of *Confidence-Man* (New York: Hendricks House, 1954).

46. *Herman Melville*, p. 187.

47. For an analysis of the book's structure, see John C. Cawalti, "Some Notes on the Structure of *The Confidence-Man*," *American Literature* 29:3, pp. 278-88.

48. Roy Harvey Pierce equates Mordock's blind hatred with blind confidence, which is a peculiar reading; Melville points to the motive rather than the blindness of the hatred. "Melville's Indian Hater: A Note on the Meaning of *The Confidence-Man*," PMLA 68 (December 1952), pp. 942-48.

49. Daniel Hoffman sees the old man as "America grown old in ignorance of evil." *Form and Fable*, p. 307 f.

50. "I begin to indulge in the pleasing idea that my life must needs be of some value. . . . I consume a certain amount of oxygen." *Letters*, p. 216. Even "the problems of the universe seem a humbug." *Letters*, p. 256. "Life is short, and so ridiculous and unrational." *Letters*, p. 260.

51. Quoted by Richard Chase from Melville's marking in his copy of Alger's *Solitudes*. *Herman Melville*, p. 288.

52. Already composed in 1888 and included in *John Marr and Other Poems*.

53. (New York: Modern Library, 1932), p. 196.

CHAPTER 7

1. "Assfulness" is a choice Twain term, especially useful in describing politicians. See for example, "Banquet for a Senator" in Janet Smith, ed. *Mark Twain on the Damned Human Race* (New York: 1962, Hill and Wang, 1962), p. 110.

2. *The Mysterious Stranger*, ed. William Gibson, (Berkley: University of California Press, 1970), pp. 72-73.

3. Actually the Clemens family claimed aristocratic heirs in a line descending from the Earl of Fairfax and they also claimed land wealth in Kentucky. Nevertheless, Judge Clemens can be seen as the democratic replacement for the patriarch, Judge Temple. He roamed from Tennessee to Arkansas to Missouri in ambitious pursuit of a respectable life, not altogether unlike Cooper's squatter Ishmael Bush who acts the role of judge at the end of *The Prairie*.

4. *A Connecticut Yankee in King Arthur's Court*, eds. Bernard L. Stein and Henry Nash Smith, (Berkley: Iowa—University of California Press, 1979), p. 285. Subsequent reference parenthetical.

5. See especially Van Wyck Brooks, *The Ordeal of Mark Twain*, (Cleveland: World Publishing, 1920, revised 1933).

6. Bernard DeVoto, ed. *Mark Twain in Eruption*, (New York: Harper and Brothers, 1940), p. xxvii.

7. This is the thrust of Justin Kaplan's *Mr. Clemens and Mark Twain: A Biography* (New York: Simon and Schuster, 1966). In *Mark Twain: The Fate of Humor* (Princeton: Princeton University Press, 1966), James M. Cox can find "no direct evidence that young Sam Clemens became suddenly a different person upon finding Mark Twain; instead he had discovered a style as well as a structure by means of which he could express as well as explore himself, p. 13. "For Samuel Clemens, Mark Twain became the means of realizing himself." p. 20.

8. Brooks in *The Ordeal*, p. 235.

9. *Mark Twain — Howells Letters*, 2 vols., eds. Henry Nash Smith and William Gibson (Cambridge, Mass: Belknap, Harvard University Press, 1960), I, p. 664.

10. *San Francisco News — Letter* (February 19, 1870). Clemens was a frequenter of John Piper's saloon in Virginia City where the custom was to chalk the credit on the back wall of the bar. Clemens, who loved to drink but not alone, would come in with a companion and call out "mark twain," that is, two chalk marks against his name. This is one explanation for his adoption of the pseudonym as opposed to the more traditional one of taking it from Captain Isaiah Sellers who had signed an article, which Clemens ridiculed, with the name Mark Twain. Ernest E. Leisy examined all the New Orleans newspapers of the time and can find no article signed Mark Twain. Sellers died in 1863 but Clemens had been using the name since 1862. See Paul Fatout, *Mark Twain in Virginia City* (Bloomington: Indiana University Press, 1964), pp. 34-39.

11. Quoted by Henry Nash Smith from a letter to Mrs. Boardman of Hartford, 25 March, 1887, in "Mark Twain's Images of Hannibal: From S. Petersburg to Eseldorf," *Texas Studies in English,* 39 (1958), pp. 3-23.

12. *Life on the Mississippi* (New York: Harper and Bros., 1899), pp. 82-83.

13. *Mark Twain — Howells Letters*, II, p. 841.

14. Brooks in *The Ordeal*, p. 25. According to Brooks, Twain's motive for success was mainly to satisfy his mother and thus succeed according to her values, later transferred to Olivia who revised his manuscripts. But in a comparison of manuscripts, Delancey Ferguson finds that the revisions "are not the excision of scathing passages which Mrs. Clemens or Howells would disapprove of, neither are they the dilution

of grim realism to make it meat for babes. They are the work of a skilled craftsman removing the unessential, adding vividness to dialog and description, and straightening out incongruities. Not more than two or three of the lot are the sort Olivia Clemens is reputed to have insisted on, and these two or three are so trifling that Mark may well have made them himself, without his wife's orders." *Colophon* (Spring 1938), III, pp. 171-8.

15. He had already published a story, "The Dandy Frightening the Squatter," in *The Boston Carpet Bag* (May 1, 1852).

16. *Mark Twain's Autobiography*, 2 vols, ed. Albert Bigelow Paine (New York: Harper and Bros., 1924), I, pp. 146-7.

17. *Autobiography*, II, p. 96.

18. Quoted from Edgar Branch, *The Literary Apprenticeship of Mark Twain* (Urbana: University of Illinois Press, 1950), pp. 224-225.

19. See especially Chapter XIII, pp. 116-18.

20. *Mark Twain's Letters*, 2 vols., ed. A. B. Paine (New York: Harper and Bros., 1917), I, pp. 45-46.

21. Quoted by Branch, *The Literary Apprenticeship of Mark Twain*, p. 49. The letters have been edited by Ernest E. Leisy, *The Letters of Quintus Curtius Snodgrass* (University Press in Dallas, 1946). Twain never claimed authorship but Leisy makes the case for it.

22. In 1884, Twain rewrote the speech as "A Private History of A Campaign that Failed."

23. *Roughing It*, ed. Franklin G. Robers and Paul Baender (Berkley: Iowa—University of California Press, 1972), p. 52. Subsequent references parenthetical.

24. *Letters*, I, p. 64-5.

25. Disgusted with the sleazy reputation he had acquired in the Washoe, Twain began to fancy himself a literary writer, especially after meeting Bret Harte in San Francisco: "I have engaged to write for the new literary paper, the 'Californian,' " he proudly wrote home, "I quit the 'Era' long ago. It wasn't high-toned enough." (*Letters*, I, p. 100.) His buddy, Sam Gillis, interrupted his new career when he was arrested for barroom brawling and when he skipped out on the bail Twain had posted. Twain also took off— to the Sierras, Jackass Hill.

26. Albert Bigelow Paine, *Mark Twain, A Biography*, 3 vols., (New York: Harper and Bros., 1912), I, p. 287.

27. *Letters*, I, p. 122.

28. *Mark Twain's Letters from the Sandwich Islands*, ed. E. Dane (Palo Alto: Stanford University Press, 1938), p. 6.

29. *Mark Twain's Notebooks and Journals*, I, ed. F. Anderson (Berkley: University of California Press, 1975), p. 163.

30. *Letters*, I, p. 90.

31. Franklin Walker and G. Ezra Dane, eds. (New York: Russell & Russell, 1940). These are letters to the *Alta* written on the trip from San Francisco to New York and in New York and St. Louis, 1866-7.

32. *Innocents Abroad*, 2 vols., (New York: Harper and Bros., 1899), I, p. 299.

33. The narrator never directly disparages Louis Napoleon, but praises him since he represents the American genius for progress. Unlike the imitators of his civic improvements in Florence, for example, Napoleon has taken care to provide the necessary foundation—money. Florence, on the contrary is bankrupt. See I, p. 326.

34. *The Gilded Age, A Tale of Today*, ed. Bryant Morley French (Indianapolis and New York: Bobbs-Merrill, 1972), p. 17.

35. *The Adventures of Tom Sawyer*, eds. John C. Gerber, Paul Baender, and Terry Firkins (Berkley: Iowa-University of California Press, 1980), p. 74. Subsequent references parenthetical.

36. *The Adventures of Huckleberry Finn*, eds. Sculley Bradley, Richard Croombeatty, and E. Hudson Long (New York: W.W. Norton, 1961), p. 18. Subsequent references parenthetical.

37. Huck's flight to Jackson's island is of course an easy symbol for popular interpretation as death and rebirth. In *The Innocent Eye: Childhood in Mark Twain's Imagination* (New Haven: Yale University Press, 1960), Albert E. Stone sees the territory also as Twain's unconscious synonym for death. Stone refers to Phillip Young who interprets Huck's journey down river as fulfilling a death wish (he sees thirteen corpses), pp. 153-158.

38. For discussion of Huck's decisions as the manifestation of increasing maturity, see Richard P. Adams, "The Unity and Coherence of Huckleberry Finn," *Tulane Studies in English*, VI (1956), pp. 87-103.

39. *The Complete Humorous Sketches and Tales of Mark Twain*, ed. Charles Neider (New York: Hanover House, 1961), p. 288.

40. *Mark Twain—Howells Letters*, I, pp. 248-249.

41. In *Mark Twain and Southeastern Humor* (Boston: Little, Brown, 1959), Kenneth S. Lynn reviews the opinions of Bernard De Voto and Henry Nash Smith on the reasons Twain quit writing *Huckleberry Finn* after Chapter 16. Basically, the view is that Twain knew little of the North and could not continue unless the journey continued further south, yet to have a slave seek freedom by traveling south was incredible. So Twain abandoned the story for a while. The idea of the Duke

and Dauphin invading the raft and forcing the issue allowed Twain to continue. Lynn rejects this view in favor of his own, that the boy could not return to the slave society but he could not give up "heavenly St. Petersburg" either. Huck can forfeit, however, the down river ugliness of Brickville (Chapter IX). This view is easily challenged by the existence of the "house beautiful"—Grangerford's, Wilks, Phelps'—existing down river as well as in St. Petersburg.

42. The "house beautiful" as Twain had been describing in *Life on the Mississippi* (1883): "Every town and village along the vast stretch of double river frontage had a best dwelling . . . mansion—the home of its wealthiest and most conspicuous citizen . . . the imposing fluted columns and Corinthian capitals were a pathetic sham, being made of white pine, and painted." p. 295. Walter Blair sharply distinguishes Huck's admiring attitude from the author's wry and critical humor (*Mark Twain and Huck Finn* [Berkley: University of California Press, 1960] p. 289). He apparently sees none of the author's nostalgia represented in Huck's admiration, nor any relationship with Twain's own establishment, the mansion in Hartford.

43. p. 160. The term was used by Franklin Delano Roosevelt to name the programs of his administration.

44. Paine's *Biography*, II, p. 889.

45. *Pudd'nhead Wilson and Those Extraordinary Twins* (New York: Harper and Bros., 1899), p. 20. Subsequent references parenthetical.

46. Quoted from a letter to Olivia, in Forward, *The Tragedy of Pudd'nhead Wilson*, ed., Wright Morris (New York: New American Library, 1964), p. xii.

47. Cited by Richard Boyd Hauck, *A Cheerful Nihilism* (Bloomington: Indiana University Press, 1971), p. 159. In *Mark Twain's Fable of Progress* (New Brunswick, N.J.; Rutgers University Press, 1964), Henry Nash Smith remarks that after Huckleberry Finn, "the world is too absurd" for Twain "to be anything but a dream" p. 108. It was not until eight or nine years later, however, that Twain no longer bothered to separate the real and the dream.

48. *Mark Twain's Which Was The Dream?*, ed., John S. Tuckey, (Berkley: University of California Press, 1967), p. 122.

49. *Mark Twain's Notebook*, ed., Albert Bigelow Paine (New York: Harper and Bros., 1935), p. 372.

50. Quoted from *Mark Twain on the Damned Human Race*, p. 114.

51. Daughter Jean had been diagnosed as epileptic and Olivia was bedridden.

52. *Mark Twain on the Damned Human Race*, pp. 200-201.

53. In "Mark Twain's Mask of Satan: The Final Phase" Stanley Brodwin sees "several satans for Mark Twain, each one a mask or persona embodying a different aspect of his thought in a particular work," *American Literature* (May, 1973), pp. 218-227.

54. This is an adulterated version of the "Chronicle of Young Satan" as shown by William M. Gibson in *The Mysterious Stranger*, pp. 2-3. Parts of the last version, "No. 44, The Mysterious Stranger," were grafted onto the "Chronicle" version. The date in Paine's edition, 1590, appears in none of the originals as Gibson presents them. The "Chronicle" is set in 1702 and "No. 44" is set in 1490.

55. *The Mysterious Stranger*, p. 35. Subsequent references parenthetical.

56. Recasting his first 19-page fragment in the more remote setting of Eseldorf, Twain combined Huck and Tom (called George in the fragment but Tom in the notes). Theodore is not easily distinguished from Nicholas (called Huck in the notes) who is killed off early, being superfluous. See John S. Tuckey, *Mark Twain and Little Satan, The Writing of the Mysterious Stranger* (West Lafayette, Indiana: Purdue University Press, 1963). Most of the characters in *The Mysterious Stranger* have been traced to real people in Twain's memory of Hannibal and the John Quarles farm. See Henry Nash Smith, "Mark Twain's Images of Hannibal: From St. Petersburg to Eseldorf," cited, pp. 3-23. "When he wrote fiction," Bernard De Voto writes in the Introduction to *Mark Twain in Eruption*, "the human race was the race he had known in Hannibal," and although there is a "profound difference between Tom Sawyer and Huck Finn . . . one or the other of them is holding the pen in the best, the deepest, and truest of Mark's works."

57. Cited in *Mark Twain's Travels with Mr. Brown*, pp. 252-253.

58. In *Mark Twain: An American Prophet*, Maxwell Geismar also sees Satan as "an older Twain now looking back on the more youthful Twain of life and letters," but associates this insight with the more popular notion of Twain's "double soul." (Boston: Houghton Mifflin, 1970), p. 230. Twain is varying the fictional technique of an older narrator looking back upon the younger self; what is novel here is Twain's use of experience to instruct the inexperienced. The older Twain occasionally signed letters to Harper's Weekly as "Satan."

59. In a letter to Joe Twitchell, dated July 28, 1904, Twain's language is almost identical with Satan's, " . . . there is nothing . . . no God and no universe; . . . only empty spaces, and in it a lost and homeless and wandering and companionless *Thought*. And . . . I am that thought." Cited by William Gibson, *The Mysterious Stranger*, p. 30.

60. p. 404. To find hope in Satan's last instruction is to ignore the context. August is already living in the best dream humanly possible. What bet-

ter dream than the drowsy Eseldorf undisturbed even by the news of the outside world? But that dream is shattered repeatedly from the moment Twain really looked at it in *Huckleberry Finn*. Yet some critics insist on hope here. For Maxwell Geismar, "*The Mysterious Stranger* is the purest bit of divine sunlight to illuminate all the long dark, endless abyss of human history." *Mark Twain: An American Prophet*, p. 230. William M. Gibson finds Satan's instruction to dream better dreams influenced by Twain's reading of *The Tempest* ("We are such stuff as dreams are made on . . .) and therefore the solution is "mold your life nearer to the heart's desire." *Mysterious Stranger*, p. 33. The hopeful feeling August experiences in the final chapter is for death itself, extinction. It is in response to Satan's statement that there is no other life.

61. Twain to Joe Twitchell. Cited in *The Mysterious Stranger*, p. 30.

62. "Books in General," *New Statesman and Nation* (London) XXII, No. 545 (August 2, 1941), p. 113.

63. (New York: Random House, 1929), p. 222.

CHAPTER 8

1. Cited by Kenner, *The Pound Era*, p. 232.

2. *The Marble Faun*, p. 3.

3. "The Author," *Braceridge Hall*, p. 6.

4. *Henry James Letters*, ed. Leon Edel, II (Cambridge, Mass: Belknap, Harvard University Press, 1975), p. 267.

5. *A World Elsewhere: The Place of Style in American Literature* (New York: Oxford University Press, 1966), p. 17.

6. Preface, *The Divided Self* (London: Pelican Books, 1964).

7. *The Fantastic: A Structural Approach to a Literary Genre* (Cleveland: The Press of Case Western University, 1973), p. 33.

8. *Shadow and Act* (New York: Signet New American Library, 1953), p. 114.

INDEX

The Author

Daniel Marder is professor and former head of the English Department at the University of Tulsa. He has taught many years at the Pennsylvania State University and the University of Pittsburgh, and had an earlier career in journalism, reporting for *Time* and *Life* in Spain as well as establishing an American newspaper in Madrid in 1953. He has also served public relations functions for the Bell Telephone Company of Pittsburgh and the Defense Department. At the University of Pittsburgh, he began looking into the papers of Hugh Henry Brackenridge and finished his research with a Ph.D. dissertation and three volumes, *Hugh Henry Brackenridge* (Twayne, 1967), *A Hugh Henry Brackenridge Reader* (University of Pittsburgh Press, 1969), and Brackenridge's *Incidents of the Insurrection* (College and University Press, 1972). He is also the author of *College English* (International Books, 1964) and *Craft of Technical Writing* (Macmillan, 1961). Professor Marder has published numerous professional articles on literature and rhetoric, as well as short stories. Among his unpublished works are several novels.

Typesetting by
Cone-Lewis Printing Co. • 323 E. 3rd • Tulsa, Okla. 74120 • Phone (918) 582-1234